Samoa

John J. Horton is Deputy Librarian of the University of Bradford and was formerly Chairman of its Academic Board of Studies in Social Sciences. He has maintained a longstanding interest in the discipline of area studies and its associated bibliographical problems, with special reference to European Studies. In particular he has published in the field of Icelandic and of Yugoslav studies, including the two relevant volumes in the World Bibliographical Series.

Robert A. Myers is Associate Professor of Anthropology in the Division of Social Sciences and Director of Study Abroad Programs at Alfred University, Alfred, New York. He has studied post-colonial island nations of the Caribbean and has spent two years in Nigeria on a Fulbright Lectureship. His interests include international public health, historical anthropology and developing societies. In addition to *Amerindians of the Lesser Antilles: a bibliography* (1981), *A Resource Guide to Dominica, 1493-1986* (1987) and numerous articles, he has compiled the World Bibliographical Series volumes on *Dominica* (1987), *Nigeria* (1989) and *Ghana* (1991).

Ian Wallace is Professor of German at the University of Bath. A graduate of Oxford in French and German, he also studied in Tübingen, Heidelberg and Lausanne before taking teaching posts at universities in the USA, Scotland and England. He specializes in contemporary German affairs, especially literature and culture, on which he has published numerous articles and books. In 1979 he founded the journal *GDR Monitor*, which he continues to edit under its new title *German Monitor*.

Hans H. Wellisch is Professor emeritus at the College of Library and Information Services, University of Maryland. He was President of the American Society of Indexers and was a member of the International Federation for Documentation. He is the author of numerous articles and several books on indexing and abstracting, and has published *The Conversion of Scripts and Indexing and Abstracting: an International Bibliography*, and *Indexing from A to Z*. He also contributes frequently to *Journal of the American Society for Information Science*, *The Indexer* and other professional journals.

Ralph Lee Woodward, Jr. is Professor of History at Tulane University, New Orleans. He is the author of *Central America, a Nation Divided*, 2nd ed. (1985), as well as several monographs and more than seventy scholarly articles on modern Latin America. He has also compiled volumes in the World Bibliographical Series on *Belize* (1980), *El Salvador* (1988), *Guatemala* (Rev. Ed.) (1992) and *Nicaragua* (Rev. Ed.) (1994). Dr. Woodward edited the Central American section of the *Research Guide to Central America and the Caribbean* (1985) and is currently associate editor of Scribner's *Encyclopedia of Latin American History*.

VOLUME 196

Samoa

(American Samoa, Western Samoa, Samoans Abroad)

H. G. A. Hughes

CLIO PRESS
OXFORD, ENGLAND · SANTA BARBARA, CALIFORNIA
DENVER, COLORADO

British Library Cataloguing in Publication Data

Hughes, H. G. A.
Samoa. – (World bibliographical series; v. 196)
1. Samoan Islands – Bibliography
I. Title
016.9′613

ISBN 1–85109–253–6

ABC-CLIO Ltd.,
Old Clarendon Ironworks,
35A Great Clarendon Street,
Oxford OX2 6AT, England.

ABC-CLIO Inc.,
130 Cremona Drive,
Santa Barbara,
CA 93117, USA.

Designed by Bernard Crossland.
Typeset by Columns Design Ltd., Reading, England.
Printed and bound in Great Britain by Bookcraft (Bath) Ltd., Midsomer Norton.

THE WORLD BIBLIOGRAPHICAL SERIES

This series, which is principally designed for the English speaker, will eventually cover every country (and many of the world's principal regions), each in a separate volume comprising annotated entries on works dealing with its history, geography, economy and politics; and with its people, their culture, customs, religion and social organization. Attention will also be paid to current living conditions – housing, education, newspapers, clothing, etc.– that are all too often ignored in standard bibliographies; and to those particular aspects relevant to individual countries. Each volume seeks to achieve, by use of careful selectivity and critical assessment of the literature, an expression of the country and an appreciation of its nature and national aspirations, to guide the reader towards an understanding of its importance. The keynote of the series is to provide, in a uniform format, an interpretation of each country that will express its culture, its place in the world, and the qualities and background that make it unique. The views expressed in individual volumes, however, are not necessarily those of the publisher.

VOLUMES IN THE SERIES

1 *Yugoslavia*, Rev. Ed., John J. Horton
2 *Lebanon*, Rev. Ed., C. H. Bleaney
3 *Lesotho*, Rev. Ed., Deborah Johnston
4 *Zimbabwe*, Rev. Ed., Deborah Potts
5 *Saudi Arabia*, Rev. Ed., Frank A. Clements
6 *Russia/USSR*, Second Ed., Lesley Pitman
7 *South Africa*, Rev. Ed., Geoffrey V Davis
8 *Malawi*, Rev. Ed., Samuel Decalo
9 *Guatemala*, Rev. Ed., Ralph Lee Woodward, Jr.
10 *Pakistan*, David Taylor
11 *Uganda*, Rev. Ed., Balam Nyeko
12 *Malaysia*, Ian Brown and Rajeswary Ampalavanar
13 *France*, Rev. Ed., Frances Chambers
14 *Panama*, Eleanor DeSelms Langstaff
15 *Hungary*, Thomas Kabdebo
16 *USA*, Sheila R. Herstein and Naomi Robbins
17 *Greece*, Richard Clogg and Mary Jo Clogg
18 *New Zealand*, R. F. Grover
19 *Algeria*, Rev. Ed., Richard I. Lawless
20 *Sri Lanka*, Vijaya Samaraweera
21 *Belize*, Second Ed., Peggy Wright and Brian E. Coutts
23 *Luxembourg*, Carlo Hury and Jul Christophory
24 *Swaziland*, Rev. Ed., Balam Nyeko
25 *Kenya*, Rev. Ed., Dalvan Coger
26 *India*, Rev. Ed., Ian Derbyshire
27 *Turkey*, Merel Güçlü
28 *Cyprus*, Rev. Ed., P. M. Kitromilides and M. L. Evriviades
29 *Oman*, Rev. Ed., Frank A. Clements
30 *Italy*, Lucio Sponza and Diego Zancani
31 *Finland*, J. E. O. Screen
32 *Poland*, Rev. Ed., George Sanford and Adriana Gozdecka-Sanford
33 *Tunisia*, Allan M. Findlay, Anne M. Findlay and Richard I. Lawless
34 *Scotland*, Eric G. Grant
35 *China*, New Ed., Charles W. Hayford
36 *Qatar*, P. T. H. Unwin

37 *Iceland*, Rev. Ed., Francis R. McBride
38 *Nepal*, John Whelpton
39 *Haiti*, Rev. Ed., Frances Chambers
40 *Sudan*, Rev. Ed., M. W. Daly
41 *Vatican City State*, Michael J. Walsh
42 *Iraq*, Second Ed., C. H. Bleaney
43 *United Arab Emirates*, Frank A. Clements
44 *Nicaragua*, Rev. Ed., Ralph Lee Woodward, Jr.
45 *Jamaica*, K. E. Ingram
46 *Australia*, Second Ed., I. Kepars
47 *Morocco*, Rev. Ed., Anne M. Findlay and Allan M. Findlay
48 *Mexico*, Rev. Ed., George Philip
49 *Bahrain*, P. T. H. Unwin
50 *The Yemens*, G. Rex Smith
51 *Zambia*, Anne M. Bliss and J. A. Rigg
52 *Puerto Rico*, Elena E. Cevallos
53 *Namibia*, Stanley Schoeman and Elna Schoeman
54 *Tanzania*, Rev. Ed., Colin Darch
55 *Jordan*, Ian J. Seccombe
56 *Kuwait*, Rev. Ed., Frank A. Clements
57 *Brazil*, Solena V. Bryant
58 *Israel*, Second Ed., C. H. Bleaney
59 *Romania*, Andrea Deletant and Dennis Deletant
60 *Spain*, Second Ed., Graham Shields
61 *Atlantic Ocean*, H. G. R. King
62 *Canada*, Ernest Ingles
63 *Cameroon*, Mark W. DeLancey and Peter J. Schraeder
64 *Malta*, John Richard Thackrah
65 *Thailand*, Michael Watts
66 *Austria*, Denys Salt with the assistance of Arthur Farrand Radley
67 *Norway*, Leland B. Sather
68 *Czechoslovakia*, David Short
69 *Irish Republic*, Michael Owen Shannon
70 *Pacific Basin and Oceania*, Gerald W. Fry and Rufino Mauricio
71 *Portugal*, P. T. H. Unwin
72 *West Germany*, Donald S. Detwiler and Ilse E. Detwiler
73 *Syria*, Ian J. Seccombe
74 *Trinidad and Tobago*, Frances Chambers
75 *Cuba*, Jean Stubbs, Lila Haines and Meic F. Haines
76 *Barbados*, Robert B. Potter and Graham M. S. Dann
77 *East Germany*, Ian Wallace
78 *Mozambique*, Colin Darch
79 *Libya*, Richard I. Lawless
80 *Sweden*, Leland B. Sather and Alan Swanson
81 *Iran*, Reza Navabpour
82 *Dominica*, Robert A. Myers
83 *Denmark*, Kenneth E. Miller
84 *Paraguay*, R. Andrew Nickson
85 *Indian Ocean*, Julia J. Gotthold with the assistance of Donald W Gotthold
86 *Egypt*, Ragai, N. Makar
87 *Gibraltar*, Graham J. Shields
88 *The Netherlands*, Peter King and Michael Wintle
89 *Bolivia*, Gertrude M. Yeager
90 *Papua New Guinea*, Fraiser McConnell
91 *The Gambia*, David P. Gamble
92 *Somalia*, Mark W. DeLancey, Sheila L. Elliott, December Green, Kenneth J. Menkhaus, Mohammad Haji Moqtar, Peter J. Schraeder
93 *Brunei*, Sylvia C. Engelen Krausse and Gerald H. Krausse
94 *Albania*, William B. Bland
95 *Singapore*, Stella R. Quah and Jon S. T. Quah
96 *Guyana*, Frances Chambers
97 *Chile*, Harold Blakemore
98 *El Salvador*, Ralph Lee Woodward, Jr.
99 *The Arctic*, H. G. R. King
100 *Nigeria*, Robert A. Myers
101 *Ecuador*, David Corkhill
102 *Uruguay*, Henry Finch with the assistance of Alicia Casas de Barrán
103 *Japan*, Frank Joseph Shulman
104 *Belgium*, R. C. Riley
105 *Macau*, Richard Louis Edmonds
106 *Philippines*, Jim Richardson
107 *Bulgaria*, Richard J. Crampton
108 *The Bahamas*, Paul G. Boultbee
109 *Peru*, John Robert Fisher
110 *Venezuela*, D. A. G. Waddell

111 *Dominican Republic*, Kai Schoenhals
112 *Colombia*, Robert H. Davis
113 *Taiwan*, Wei-chin Lee
114 *Switzerland*, Heinz K. Meier and Regula A. Meier
115 *Hong Kong*, Ian Scott
116 *Bhutan*, Ramesh C. Dogra
117 *Suriname*, Rosemarijn Hoefte
118 *Djibouti*, Peter J. Schraeder
119 *Grenada*, Kai Schoenhals
120 *Monaco*, Grace L. Hudson
121 *Guinea-Bissau*, Rosemary Galli
122 *Wales*, Gwilym Huws and D. Hywel E. Roberts
123 *Cape Verde*, Caroline S. Shaw
124 *Ghana*, Robert A. Myers
125 *Greenland*, Kenneth E. Miller
126 *Costa Rica*, Charles L. Stansifer
127 *Siberia*, David N. Collins
128 *Tibet*, John Pinfold
129 *Northern Ireland*, Michael Owen Shannon
130 *Argentina*, Alan Biggins
131 *Côte d'Ivoire*, Morna Daniels
132 *Burma*, Patricia M. Herbert
133 *Laos*, Helen Cordell
134 *Montserrat*, Riva Berleant-Schiller
135 *Afghanistan*, Schuyler Jones
136 *Equatorial Guinea*, Randall Fegley
137 *Turks and Caicos Islands*, Paul G. Boultbee
138 *Virgin Islands*, Verna Penn Moll
139 *Honduras*, Pamela F. Howard-Reguindin
140 *Mauritius*, Pramila Ramgulam Bennett
141 *Mauritania*, Simonetta Calderini, Delia Cortese, James L. A. Webb, Jr.
142 *Timor*, Ian Rowland
143 *St. Vincent and the Grenadines*, Robert B. Potter
144 *Texas*, James Marten
145 *Burundi*, Morna Daniels
146 *Hawai'i*, Nancy J. Morris and Love Dean
147 *Vietnam*, David Marr and Kristine Alilunas-Rodgers
148 *Sierra Leone*, Margaret Binns and Tony Binns
149 *Gabon*, David Gardinier
150 *Botswana*, John A. Wiseman
151 *Angola*, Richard Black
152 *Central African Republic*, Pierre Kalck
153 *Seychelles*, George Bennett, with the collaboration of Pramila Ramgulam Bennett
154 *Rwanda*, Randall Fegley
155 *Berlin*, Ian Wallace
156 *Mongolia*, Judith Nordby
157 *Liberia*, D. Elwood Dunn
158 *Maldives*, Christopher H. B. Reynolds
159 *Liechtenstein*, Regula A. Meier
160 *England*, Alan Day
161 *The Baltic States*, Inese A. Smith and Marita V. Grunts
162 *Congo*, Randall Fegley
163 *Armenia*, Vrej Nersessian
164 *Niger*, Lynda F. Zamponi
165 *Madagascar*, Hilary Bradt
166 *Senegal*, Roy Dilley and Jerry Eades
167 *Andorra*, Barry Taylor
168 *Netherlands Antilles and Aruba*, Kai Schoenhals
169 *Burkina Faso*, Samuel Decalo
170 *Indonesia*, Sylvia C. Engelen Krausse and Gerald H. Krausse
171 *The Antarctic*, Janice Meadows, William Mills and H. G. R. King
172 *São Tomé and Príncipe*, Caroline S. Shaw
173 *Fiji*, G. E. Gorman and J. J. Mills
174 *St. Kitts-Nevis*, Verna Penn Moll
175 *Martinique*, Janet Crane
176 *Zaire*, Dawn Bastian Williams, Robert W. Lesh and Andrea L. Stamm
177 *Chad*, George Joffé and Valérie Day-Viaud
178 *Togo*, Samuel Decalo
179 *Ethiopia*, Stuart Munro-Hay and Richard Pankhurst
180 *Punjab*, Darshan Singh Tatla and Ian Talbot
181 *Eritrea*, Randall Fegley
182 *Antigua and Barbuda*, Riva Berleant-Schiller and Susan Lowes with Milton Benjamin
183 *Alaska*, Marvin W. Falk
184 *The Falkland Islands*, Alan Day
185 *St Lucia*, Janet Henshall Momsen

186 *Slovenia*, Cathie Carmichael
187 *Cayman Islands*, Paul G. Boultbee
188 *San Marino*, Adrian Edwards and Chris Michaelides
189 *London*, Heather Creaton
190 *Western Sahara*, Anthony G. Pazzanita
191 *Guinea*, Margaret Binns
192 *Benin*, J. S. Eades and Chris Allen
193 *Madrid*, Graham Shields
194 *Tasmania*, I. Kepars
195 *Prague*, Susie Lunt
196 *Samoa*, H. G. A. Hughes

To Zuzana
in gratitude for her encouragement and support

Contents

Contents

Contents

Introduction

To many readers, mention of Samoa in the South Pacific will conjure up a picture of an island paradise, with sun-drenched beaches and tropical forests, and beautiful, contented people, immune to the cares and problems of the modern world. Indeed, this image has changed little over the last centuries, and has been reinforced by generations of artists, writers and film-makers. However, the truth is that the islands of American Samoa and Western Samoa are very much part of the 20th-century world, and have thus undergone tremendous change since first contact with Europeans in the mid-18th century. Both island groups now find themselves economically dependent on outside financial aid and migrant remittances, facing challenges to their traditional social organization and customs, and experiencing concern over the health of the population and the environment in which they live.

The following sections of this introduction seek to dispel the 'myth' and highlight the 'reality' of the Samoan experience, focusing on Samoa's topography, climate, flora and fauna, society, language, religion, history and current situation.

Land

The Samoan islands extend from about latitude 14° 32′ S, longitude 168° 08′ W to latitude 13° 30′ S, longitude 172° 50′ W. From west to east they are Savai'i, the largest island; Apolima; Manono; 'Upolu, second largest (with its islets of Fanuatapu, Namu'a, Nu'ulua, Nu'usafe and Nu'utele); Tutuila and 'Aunu'u; the Manu'a group, comprising Ofu, Olosega and Ta'ū; and Rose Atoll.

Tutuila and the islands to the east constitute (with Swain's Island, about 350 km NNW of Tutuila) the unincorporated and unorganized United States Territory of American Samoa, with Pago Pago as its capital. The rest of the islands, to the west of Tutuila, make up the independent state of Samoa i Sisifo: Western Samoa, with Āpia as its capital. Western Samoa has a total land area of 2,934 sq. km., while American Samoa has only 197 sq. km.

With the exception of Rose Atoll and Swain's Island, all the islands of the Samoan chain are high islands of volcanic formation. Ranges of hills run east and west in each of the three main islands, with extinct craters along their length at intervals of a few miles, except in Tutuila. In northern Savai'i considerable areas are still covered by lava fields resulting from eruptions by Mauga Afi and Matāvanu. Erosion is widespread in all the high islands, and may be worsened by gradual destruction of the rain forest which covers the hills.

Lakes have formed in some craters, notably at Lanuto'o in 'Upolu and at Pule in Savai'i. Coral reefs, of fringing or barrier form with lagoons, occur round the three largest islands, but are least developed in Savai'i, the youngest in geological formation. There are numerous anchorages, but only one fine harbour, at Pago Pago in Tutuila.

Climate

Samoa's climate is typically oceanic, dominated for eight months, April to November, by south-east trade winds. From December to March, the 'wet season', northerly and westerly winds prevail. Destructive hurricanes can occur from January to March, starting as easterlies and backing through north to south-west.

Temperatures are high but relatively constant, with monthly means ranging from 27°C to 25°C (79°F-77°F). Average annual rainfall is heavy, with 106.8 in. (271.27 cm) at Āpia and 190 in. (482.6 cm) at Pago Pago. Mean annual relative humidity is 83 per cent at Āpia, with a diurnal variation of about 14 per cent. The greatest humidity is in the morning, the lowest in the afternoon.

Vegetation and fauna

All the high islands are covered inland by thick tropical vegetation and tall evergreen rain forest, with tree ferns, except on recent lava flows and eroded areas. Along the shore mangroves occur in swampy areas; the great *Barringtonia asiatica*, pandanus, breadfruit, and coconut trees more widely.

There are remarkably few animals, mainly the Polynesian rat, fruit bats, pigs, horses, and some cattle gone wild in the bush. Only thirty-four species of birds have been observed, sixteen of which are found nowhere else, and some of these are sadly endangered. There are two kinds of snakes, several kinds of lizards (all of them harmless), freshwater shrimps and land crabs.

In very sharp contrast, insects abound. A mosquito (*Stegomyia pseudoscutellaris*) is a vector of filariasis, the cause of elephantiasis. Flies are omnipresent. There are two kinds of centipede and a scorpion, all with painful but not dangerous poisonous sting. The rhinoceros beetle, accidentally introduced from Ceylon in 1911 with rubber plants, was for many years the cause of great damage to crops, but is now reasonably well controlled.

Social organization

Polynesian culture is traditionally based on the interplay of gardening and fishing. Most villages are on the coast, though archaeological research shows that there once were many inland villages. Villages are large and well planned, with canoe or boat houses on the beach, scattered *fale*, a store, the pastor's house, and, dominating all, an imposing church. The village yam gardens, taro fields, coconut and banana plantations are inland, on rising ground. Each village has one or more larger building, usually a round house, in which *fono* meetings and *'ava* ceremonies are held and guests entertained.

Samoa differs from other large Polynesian communities, such as Hawai'i, in that no single dynasty seems ever to have established hegemony and quasi-feudal patterns of organization. Social organization is based rather on an intricate system of graded chiefly titles, essentially of two kinds: *ali'i* (titular chief); and *tulāfale* (orator chief). These chiefs may be of high rank or low rank. *Ali'i* are entitled to courtesies of address and behaviour, and *tulāfale* to privileges. Together, they are essential to the conduct of everyday affairs. The generic term for *ali'i* and *tulāfale*, for all titleholders, is *matai*. Since most titleholders are heads of households the term also refers to them, and to titled men of indeterminate low rank. Essentially, a *matai* is someone who holds a title conferring the right to take part in the deliberations of the local council (*fono*).

> 'In the Samoan system a person receives consideration not as an individual but in virtue of the title which he holds and the privileges which attach to it. Succession to a title is elective within a family, and while heredity is a contributory qualification general ability, popularity and the capacity to make a good speech are the principal considerations borne in mind when a title has to be filled' (*Pacific Islands. Volume two: Eastern Pacific*, London: Naval Intelligence Division, 1943, p. 612-13).

In Western Samoa there has been a trend towards reviving ancient titles and, especially, splitting existing titles. This latter practice has been particularly apparent since the achievement of independence.

One consequence of the proliferation of titles is that the traditional link with the land formerly held by a whole kinship group (*'āiga*) may be weakened. Such land was administered or distributed by the *matai*, but nowadays there is a tendency towards individual ownership of smallholdings or plots of land (especially near urban areas). Land tenure may now be of three types: Government land (much of it sequestrated German-owned plantations); *'āiga* land, with the *pule* (nominal title) vested in a *matai*; and individual ownership (usually on a very small scale).

Social life is characterized by ceremony and formality, with elaborate rules of precedence, oratory (*lāuga*), *'ava* drinking, ceremonial visiting (*malaga*), feasting and dancing. The focus of the *'ava* ceremony and of entertainment was formerly the village hostess (*tāupou*), frequently the daughter of the most prominent chief. All these ceremonial activities have fascinated visitors to Samoa. Indeed, many have seen and described little else but 'exotic' ceremonies. F. J. H. Grattan gives detailed and reasoned explanations of these colourful aspects of Samoa's traditional social life, in his excellent book *An introduction to Samoan custom* (1948).

Samoan society

Several of the missionaries working in 19th-century Samoa have left us detailed accounts of the traditional society which they found, and partly changed. Among the most authoritative of these writers are George Brown, John B. Stair, and George Turner.

Somewhat daunting both in its size and its scholarship is Augustin Krämer's *The Samoan Islands*, now available in a splendid new translation into English by Theodore Verhaaren (1994-95). This is essential reading, for its genealogies and its descriptions of customary usages, but reading it is best delayed until one has a reasonable outline knowledge of Samoan history and tradition. For many years Margaret Mead's *Coming of age in Samoa* (1928) and *The social organization of Manu'a* (1930; 1969) were considered to be 'definitive' works on Samoan society. They have since become the focus of interminable and often ill tempered debate, initiated by Derek Freeman, but are still well worth reading, with a critical mind.

There are many enlightening anthropological studies of Samoan society, but they are often highly theoretical and so not easily accessible by lay readers My personal choice of reliable yet 'reader-friendly' introductions to Samoan traditional institutions and social structures is: Fay C. Ala'ilima, *A Samoan family* (1961); Fay C. Ala'ilima (Fay G. Calkins), *My Samoan chief* (1962); F. J. H. Grattan,

An introduction to Samoan custom (1948); Lowell D. Holmes, Ellen Rhoads Holmes, *Samoan village: then and now* (1992); Tim O'Meara, *Samoan planters* (1990); Bradd Shore, *Sala'ilua: a Samoan mystery* (1982) which is more theoretical than the other books listed here, but is intriguingly focused on an actual murder perpetrated in the Savai'i village of Sala'ilua, highlighting subtleties of how a Samoan village functions; and Albert Wendt, *Leaves of the Banyan Tree* (1979, reprinted 1994), the finest Samoan novel yet written, giving an intimate, utterly realistic picture of how a Samoan *'āiga* 'works'.

The Samoan *fale* is the most visible and ubiquitous sign of a distinctive traditional culture in rural areas. In the urbanized areas of Āpia and Pago Pago, and increasingly in the villages of American Samoa constructions of concrete, timber and corrugated iron are ousting the beautiful, eminently practical 'open-air' houses of traditional design. In Samoa's tropical climate it makes good sense to live in the open yet under a roof, especially in terms of health.

Architects admire the *fale*:

> 'Samoa is the last of the Polynesian countries to make extensive use, even today, of its own traditional architecture in the construction of houses. Nowhere in the Pacific is a more felicitous traditional dwelling to be found. Pleasing to the eye, a standing tribute to its builders, open to the cooling sea breeze, highly resistant to cyclones, able to accommodate large numbers of people for formal meetings, to eat, relax, sleep . . . the *fale* does indeed seem to be without peer in combining so many positive features (F. L. and Peter Higginson, *The Samoan fale*, Bangkok: UNESCO, 1992, p. 1).

Such houses can have relatively little privacy, even with the coconut-frond blinds down. It has been suggested that life in full view of all one's neighbours has been a factor in developing a high degree of social control, communal cohesion, and conformity in social behaviour among Samoans, at least in their homeland.

There may be a grain of truth in this theory and it is certainly true that social control and behavioural conformity have been conspicuously weakened in some areas of the Samoan diaspora, where a trend towards non-traditional, nuclear families is discernible. Carson, a suburb of Los Angeles, California, with a large Samoan population, has had to endure 'obnoxious posses . . . of the violent street gang, SOS – the Sons of Samoa'. In San Francisco, social control is anathema to many young Samoans. In his essay *Mau-mauing the flak catchers* (1989), Tom Wolfe memorably describes a Samoan *razza* on a Social Security office, cornering an official (the Flak Catcher) behind his desk. Samoa and its still mainly conformist youth seem worlds away.

The Samoan language

Samoan is a Polynesian language, closely related to Pukapukan, Tokelauan and Tuvaluan, and more distantly to Maori, Tahitian and Tongan. Counting in Samoans living abroad, in Australia, Hawai'i, mainland USA and New Zealand, Samoan is probably spoken by some 350,000 people. It is used in education at all levels in Western Samoa and American Samoa, together with English. Literacy in Samoan is virtually universal and sustains a flourishing secular and religious press. A modern creative literature in the vernacular is taking shape.

The first book in Samoan, *E tala A.E.F.*, was printed at the London Missionary Press, Huahine, in 1834. The orthography then used was modelled on the transcription systems devised for Tahitian and Rarotongan, with only minor modifications. From 1839 onward, the London Missionary Society had its own printing press at Mālua on 'Upolu, and very considerable editions were produced (even 20,000 copies in the case of some school books). In under ten years, most Samoans became literate in their own language. The translation of the Holy Bible (*'O le Tusi Pa'ia*) gave prestige and authority to one of the two existing varieties of spoken Samoan.

This variety of pronunciation, now known as *tautala lelei* (good speech), is the basis of the written language and is used in education, religion and all formal communication. Professor Even Hovdhaugen of the University of Oslo has it that *tautala lelei* in spoken use 'is mainly restricted to speaking to God, non-Samoans, in school, on the radio, or when singing. It is only obligatory when speaking to God and in singing' (*Samoan reference grammar*, 1992, p. 9). Professor G. B. Milner of the School of Oriental and African Studies, University of London, comments: 'Samoans regard formal pronunciation as the hallmark of a good education and of good breeding and colloquial pronunciation as being uncouth and vulgar' (*Samoan dictionary*, 1966, p. xiv-xv).

The colloquial pronunciation, *tautala leaga* (bad speech), although in general everyday use, does indeed bear a stigma, and is regarded with great disfavour except among young people. More and more often, however, *tautala leaga* is being used by writers of short stories, for dialogue, and by poets. *Tautala lelei* preserves /t/ and /k/, /n/ and /ŋ/ (the velar nasal), /r/ and /l/. These sounds are reduced in *tautala leaga* to /k/, /ŋ/ and /l/ respectively. There are also differences in morphology, syntax and spelling between the Biblical literary language and the modern literary language (influenced by both varieties of spoken language).

Formal pronunciation and colloquial pronunciation share a voiceless glottal stop, a 'break'. This is represented in writing by an inverted apostrophe, though an ordinary comma is sometimes used, incorrectly and ambiguously. All vowels may be phonetically long or short. A long vowel may be distinguished in writing by means of a superior macron. Vowel length can be semantically significant, as in the following words: *matua* – parent (singular); *mātua* – parents (plural); and *matuā* – very, extremely, absolutely, completely. Problems arise (not least in the compilation of this bibliography) from the fact that Samoans largely disregard both inverted apostrophe and macron in writing. If used at all, they are commonly used inconsistently or only sporadically.

Until the publication of G. B. Milner's *Samoan dictionary* in 1966 and of Andrew K. Pawley's linguistic studies in that same year, all earlier descriptions of Samoan, mainly by missionaries, were framed in the classical grammatical categories traditionally used in European philology. However, these are inadequate or misleading when applied to Samoan. Now, gradually, Samoan is being studied anew and is being re-analysed in its own terms. Samoan linguists, such as the pioneering Fana'afi M. Larkin, and others, are beginning to interpret and present the structure and features of their mother tongue in more realistic and original ways.

History

Until the mid-18th century, Samoa had known three millennia of settled existence, in touch only with Tonga and the other Polynesian islands which were accessible by great canoes. Samoans and Tongans intermarried, traded with one another and fought periodic petty wars, interrupted by internal internecine wars.

However, their world began to change, very slowly, from 1722, when Jacob Roggeveen sighted the Samoan group. In 1768 came Louis de Bougainville, who named the group Îles des Navigateurs, the Navigators' Islands. Contacts with Europeans continued, but only infrequently and fleetingly, including La Pérouse in 1787, Edwards in 1791, Otto von Kotzebue in 1824 and John Williams in 1830. From then onwards European contacts, with whalers, seamen and missionaries, became more and more frequent. The missionary paved the way for the trader, both living among the Samoans, usually peaceably.

The coming of Christianity was the greatest catalyst of social change. The new faith was a spontaneous 'people movement' brought in 1828 by Samoans from Tonga to Savai'i. The *Lotu Tonga* spread rapidly, and was already firmly established when John Williams of the London Missionary Society arrived in Savai'i in 1830, with his variant of Christian observance, the *Lotu Tahiti*. The Wesleyan Methodist missionary, the Rev. Peter Turner, writing in 1835, reported forty villages on Savai'i and twenty-five on 'Upolu in which there were persons professing to be of the *Lotu Tonga*. By then Methodist adherents numbered about 4,000. A later writer says:

> 'This was remarkable! Within six years a great spiritual work, self originated, self propagated, and self sustained, had spread from place to place, despite fierce local jealousies. Congregations had been formed, churches built, and societies instituted without a farthing of expense to the Methodist Church; a result unparalleled in the history of modern missions' (Benjamin Danks, 1914, p. 484).

For a while the Wesleyan Church was 'the only Church that could claim to represent the Samoan people'. Though John Williams in 1830 left six teachers on Savai'i and two on 'Upolu, the first Church of the London Missionary Society was not formed until 1837. Methodist withdrawal in 1839, until 1856, left Christian advance to the LMS, which made impressive progress, uncontested until the Society of Mary established the first Roman Catholic mission in 1845. All three denominations became genuinely Samoan in character, motivating and sharing in the ensuing dramatic transformations in the Samoan way of life.

Christianity in its various forms was readily and rapidly accepted by Samoans, and fashioned into a sustaining element in the structure of indigenous society. Sincere belief may have been coupled with calculation and 'enlightened self-interest' on the part of some Samoans, but there can be no doubt that without the strength derived from the new faith Samoans would have fared much worse at the hands of the rapacious breed of traders and planters that sought profit in the islands.

Land alienation began in earnest in the mid-19th century, the pace being set by the Hamburg firm of J. C. Godeffroy und Sohn. Land was traded (sometimes more than once) for European goods or for firearms (which made the continuing local wars more lethal). Vast tracts of land in the coastal plains were lost to the Samoans who had once owned them communally. In addition, Gilbertese and Melanesian indentured labourers were brought in to work the new plantations, the rapid extension of which was driven by the worldwide demand for coconut oil, and later for copra.

Samoa became the focus of interest for the three Great Powers of the age of Victoria, Bismarck and the doctrine of Manifest Destiny. Coaling stations and naval bases became obsessions of statesmen in Berlin, London and Washington, and, less frenetically, in Wellington.

Intrigues, plots, political *démarches*, gunboat diplomacy, and the manipulation of Samoan rivalries combined in an explosive mixture as the 19th century moved towards its close. War between the Great Powers was only averted in 1889 by 'a great wind from Heaven', a hurricane which wrecked German and American warships. In 1899 Samoa was divided, by the tripartite Berlin agreement. Savai'i and 'Upolu and their smaller islands became a German colony in 1900, whereas the United States of America occupied Tutuila and the Manu'a islands to the east. The two parts of dismembered Samoa were to diverge from that tragic year of 1900 onwards.

The colony of German Samoa, though governed by scholarly men, followed the familiar exploitative course of the era in which whole continents were shared out among the more aggressive European states. In American Samoa, laxly and indolently ruled by the United States Navy, nothing of great consequence was to happen for fifty years. In contrast, in German Samoa the collapse of copra prices sparked the first indigenous resistance to German colonial rule, in the *'Oloa* movement. Its leaders were arbitrarily exiled to the German Micronesian colony of Saipan.

The outbreak of the First World War in August 1914 was swiftly followed by the unopposed landing in German Samoa of a New Zealand Expeditionary Force. Military occupation, inept and resented, lasted from 1914 to 1920, when the League of Nations granted a Class C mandate to Britain, to be administered by New Zealand.

New Zealand civil administration was opposed by Samoans from the very outset, largely because of the failure of the earlier military administration to prevent the lethal influenza epidemic of 1918 (which American Samoa escaped, thanks to the prompt and rigorous imposition of quarantine). Insensitive administration, harmful economic measures, neglect of Samoan in schools and racist attitudes on the part of New Zealand officials were among the many factors which provoked Samoan resistance. The *Mau* movement, which took firm shape in 1926, grew rapidly in support and political maturity, despite the exile of some of its leaders. It came to a head in 1929, with the murder of Tamasese, and only the election in 1935 of a Labour government in New Zealand averted insurrection.

The Second World War saw both American Samoa and Western Samoa garrisoned by many thousands of US Marines, whose presence accelerated the social changes already in train. From 1946 New

Zealand continued to administer Western Samoa under a United Nations Trusteeship Agreement. The bitterness of the interwar years was not so much in evidence, and from 1947 to 1961 there was a series of amicably agreed constitutional advances which brought Western Samoa from a dependent status to self-government and independence.

In October 1961, the United Nations General Assembly, at the request of New Zealand and on the claim of Western Samoa to independence, voted unanimously to end the Trusteeship Agreement. Western Samoa became a sovereign state, the first free Polynesian state of modern times.

In American Samoa, administration passed in 1951 from the United States Navy to the US Department of the Interior. The pace of economic and social change quickened as tuna canneries were established, and the educational system underwent wholesale reform, including Instructional Television (soon transformed into commercial TV). Large-scale migration began, to Hawai'i and California, mirroring and far exceeding the migration to New Zealand which was gaining momentum in Western Samoa. In 1956 a Samoan, Peter Tali Coleman, was elected Civil Governor. Western Samoa joined the Commonwealth in 1970, and the United Nations in 1976. ADB, ECAFE, IMF, WHO, the South Pacific Commission and the South Pacific Forum followed.

In American Samoa and in Western Samoa the economies have been dependent on agriculture and on fisheries, both sectors experiencing severe vicissitudes, due to market fluctuations and to repeated devastation by cyclones. New industries in Western Samoa contributed only about 10 per cent to GDP in 1987. Receipts from tourism have assumed greater and greater importance in both territories since the upgrading to international standards of the airports at Faleolo (WS) and Tāfuna (AS).

The mainstay of American Samoa's economy is Federal funding, followed by remittances from Samoans in the USA. Western Samoa depends crucially on financial and technical assistance from New Zealand, Australia, Germany, Britain, France, Japan and other developed countries. Other development partners include the ADB, CFTC, EU, OPEC Fund and the World Bank. Remittances are of very great importance to a MIRAB economy which has been unkindly characterized as 'aid-dependent pauperism'. Huge budget deficits, financial mismanagement and corruption appear to be endemic in both territories. Of Western Samoa Albert Wendt has written, in disgust, that some politicians and members of the country's élite behave worse and more rapaciously than did the colonial exploiters of old.

When Western Samoa achieved independence, its Constitution provided for *matai* suffrage and *matai* candidates for election. In 1991 the Government of Tofilau Eti Alesana introduced universal adult suffrage for all persons over eighteen. It still holds that only *matai* can stand for election. This has generated a sharp debate, as to whether direct democracy or the chiefly system, *fa'amatai*, is the best way forward. Separation of politics and *fa'amatai*, limiting *matai* to family and village concerns, may well kill the *fa'amatai*. In an address to the Pacific Islands Society of the United Kingdom and Ireland in London early in 1995, Fiame Naomi Mata'afa, Western Samoa's Minister of Education and the country's first woman Cabinet Minister, warned of direct challenges to the constitutionally-elected government from the traditional sector. Universal suffrage was challenged (so far unsuccessfully) in the High Court on constitutional grounds. Opposition members claimed that it undermined the country's traditional social structure based on *matai* titleholders.

The other major concern, in both American Samoa and in Western Samoa, is the considerable environmental damage stemming from logging, intensive agriculture, over-population, tourism and ill considered government policies. Particular resentment is directed against government's arbitrary use of sequestrated or untitled land for development projects.

Samoan prospects

In these closing years of the 20th century what are the prospects of Samoan cultural survival? Caroline G. Sinavaiana of American Samoa sees a bleak future: 'Today, threats to the cultural survival of Samoans in both independent Western Samoa and American Samoa, [. . .] derive from interlocking environmental, social, and political forces.

One environmental challenge comes from rapidly intensifying population pressures, fed by both high birth rates and returning émigrés. In American Samoa, where the growth rate is 3.7 percent per year, population increases correlate directly with the depletion of wildlife resources through deforestation, habitat degradation for construction, and the toxicity of aquatic organisms from heavy metals. Since 1986, wildlife resources in American Samoa have fallen 90 percent due to tropical storms and surges in human population. In both Samoas, population pressures have led to the degradation of coral reef biosystems and of the quality and supply of ground water.

A further challenge comes from the inadequate regulation of growth and development. In both Samoas, meaningful community involvement is lacking, and environmental impact studies are applied only erratically.

Environmental problems are exacerbated by the legacies of Western colonialism, characterized in part by a clash between Western ethics, enshrining cash and individual ownership, and indigenous ethics of group relationships and reciprocal exchanges. The resulting loss of Samoan cultural integrity has coupled with insufficient local opportunities for scientific training and employment, fostering a destructive social cycle. Unfulfilled educational and vocational aspirations foster disaffection'. This leads to 'rising rates of substance abuse (especially alcohol) and domestic violence, including youth suicides in Western Samoa and the abuse of women and children in American Samoa' ('Samoa', *Cultural Survival Quarterly*, vol. 17, no. 3 [Fall 1993], p. 37).

Samoa's past can never return as the islands are enmeshed in the global economy, and have yet to discover how they can survive the destructive forces which abound. The problem is clear to many young Samoans, and to know the problem is halfway to solving it. Well tried tradition and progressive modernity can and will be blended, to create a stable, prosperous, sustainable, authentically Samoan society and culture for its fourth millennium. Manuia Samoa!

Current information

Summary information on recent events in Samoa may be found in several annual publications which survey the countries of the world. Key economic and social indicators, the composition of government, and the addresses of major institutions are included in such country profiles.

The Foreign and Commonwealth Office annual *The Commonwealth Yearbook* (London: HMSO) covers Western Samoa and Tokelau. Other annuals also include American Samoa. The Central Intelligence Agency's *The World Fact Book* (Washington, DC, London: Brassey's) presents key data in tabular form, very succinctly. *Whitaker's Almanack* (London: J. Whitaker & Sons) and *Statesman's Year Book* (London: Macmillan; New York: St. Martin's Press) provide a little more information.

The most extensive and detailed profiles of Western Samoa and American Samoa appear in *The Far East and Australasia* (London: Europa Publications). In addition, statistics and regional comparisons may be found in the annual publications of international organizations, such as the United Nations, Food and Agriculture Organization, International Labour Office/Organization, United Nations Educational, Scientific and Cultural Organization and the World Health

Organization. The publications of the Asian Development Bank, Commonwealth Secretariat, International Monetary Fund, South Pacific Commission, South Pacific Forum, World Bank and similar bodies are also excellent sources of information and statistics relating to Samoa.

The bibliography

This bibliography covers the geographical area which today comprises independent *Samoa i Sisifo*/Western Samoa and the dependent Territory of American Samoa. Its historical extent is from prehistory by way of uncolonized Samoa to partitioned German Samoa and American Samoa, the New Zealand mandate of Western Samoa, and its successor state of today.

Books and articles in academic journals provide the great majority of entries. The huge volume of technical reports, by governments, international organizations, voluntary agencies and philanthropic foundations had, perforce, to be set aside. Only a few specially significant examples of such official publications are included. Academic theses and dissertations are very selectively listed in a separate, unindexed section. Anthropology, archaeology, religion, history and linguistics are well represented, reflecting the predominance of those disciplines in the serious, enduring literature on Samoa, and also the lifelong specializations of the compiler.

Academic works provide most of the reliable information on Samoa, and so are given pride of place here. The more ephemeral, 'popular' works which abound are, with some honourable exceptions, of quite staggering banality, even silliness. Many perpetuate illusions, others just mislead. It is a matter for regret that such trivial, 'island-hopping' works still find publishers and readers. A few examples of this meretricious genre are included, as are some works of fiction and books for children. Recently published works, from 1990 to 1996, are intensively represented, with a selection of items published in the period 1975-90. Earlier works of lasting value, special interest and historical relevance, from 1845 onward, are also represented. Most references to articles relate to journals and periodicals currently being published. These and articles in earlier periodicals are all readily obtainable from agencies such as the British Library Document Supply Centre (BLDSC), Boston Spa, Wetherby, West Yorkshire, England LS23 7BQ. Photocopies may be requested through academic or public libraries.

The brief annotations attempt to give an indication of content, character or relevance of the given work. The entries are arranged in broad subject categories, and then ordered alphabetically by title. Each entry is numbered in a continuous series, to facilitate cross-referencing and indexing.

It is imperative to stress that this bibliography is neither comprehensive nor definitive. The unannotated bibliographies and catalogues compiled by Evans Lewin, C. R. H. Taylor, Lowell D. Holmes and Janet A. Pereira list many other works of importance which, in ideal circumstances, might have been included herein. Readers should therefore refer to those bibliographies for further references. The excellent bibliographies published until 1976 in the *Journal de la Société des Océanistes*, and the current bibliographies in *Journal of Pacific History* and *Pacific Studies*, are also prime bibliographical sources.

Samoa has presented many problems in compilation. The most difficult was how to write words and names in Samoan, Hawaiian and other Polynesian languages. Glottal stop and vowel length, though both are meaningful, are only rarely indicated in books and articles, if at all. No attempt has been made to 'improve on' the forms used, in titles or authors' names, in the actual entry. In the annotations, however, glottal stops and macrons at least are inserted, as consistently as possible but not always as accurately as one might wish.

Another problem, not wholly resolved, is created by authors' liking for variety. Some changes of name are legitimate, caused by marriage: for example, Ellen C. Rhoads became Ellen C. Holmes or Ellen R. Holmes, Penelope Schoeffel became Penelope Meleisea, and Fay G. Calkins became Fay C. Ala'ilima. More perplexing were the frequent changes of signature. Te'o Ian John Fairbairn has published as Ian, John, Ian J., T. I., T. I. J. and Te'o. James W. Davidson oscillated from J. to J. W. to Jim and Fata Sano Malifa sometimes appears as Fata Malifa. Such anomalies complicate author entry and indexing but in the main, a policy of non-interference has been followed, relying on the author index to make the necessary connections.

Observant readers will notice that some writers spell Samoan place-names and words in different ways. The capital of American Samoa, for instance, may be found as Pago Pago (the official form) or as Pango Pango. The latter spelling, using the digraph *-ng-*, is meant to show the actual pronunciation of the velar nasal (similar to the final *-ng* in English *sing*). The official Samoan orthography uses *-g-* to represent this sound (e.g. *tuiga* rather than *tuinga*), and this usage is followed in this book, except for titles, where the author's style is retained.

Some audio and video recordings, and some films are included. Information on other available titles may be had from institutions specializing in these media, such as the British Film Institute, London, and the British Library National Sound Archive, London. Similar bodies exist in Australia, Canada, France, Germany, New Zealand and elsewhere. Internet and World Wide Web sites, where information on islands in the Pacific, American Samoa and Western Samoa among them, may be accessed and downloaded electronically, include: The CocoNET Wireless [Contemporary Pacific Islands Press] – http://www.uq.oz.au/jrn/home.html (which includes homepages for American Samoa and Western Samoa); National University of Samoa, Āpia, Western Samoa – nus@pactok.peg.apc.org; and Western Samoa – http://www.interwebinc.com/samoa/.

Because of the historical complexity of Samoa, the general histories by R. P. Gilson and by the Samoan scholar Malama Meleisea should be read before more specialized works. *Amerika Samoa* (1960) by J. A. C. Gray is the best introduction to the history of the eastern islands of Tutuila and Manu'a. To aid readers, I have included a summary chronology, covering events in Western Samoa and American Samoa from the earliest times up to 1996, as well as a glossary of the many Samoan words that readers will certainly encounter.

Every effort has been made to check the accuracy of each entry. Nonetheless, errors will have crept in unnoticed. Readers are asked kindly to send their comments, criticisms and corrections to the compiler, care of ABC-Clio Ltd, Oxford. I hope that this select bibliography will be of interest and service to those who come by it.

'Be to our virtues very kind, and to our faults a little blind'.

H. G. A. Hughes
Afonwen, Clwyd, January 1997

Acknowledgements

An extensive bibliography does not appear by sleight of hand nor by true magic, but is fashioned by slow accretion. It has a long pedigree which must, in all honour, be acknowledged.

My considerable debt is to all those scholarly and indefatigable bibliographers with whom I grew up and grew old, and from whose work I have benefited so greatly. Some are academic or professional colleagues of mine, some close personal friends of many years. They include: Frédéric Angleviel, Dorothy Brown, Floyd M. Cammack, Arthur Capell, Michel Charleux, W. G. Coppell, Helen F. Conover, Diane Dickson, Carol Dossor, Jean-Pierre Doumenge, Irene Fletcher, Bess Flores, Lynette Furuhashi, Nicholas J. Goetzfridt, Renée Heyum, Harold Holdsworth, Felix M. Keesing, H. R. Klieneberger, N. L. H. Krauss, Ida Leeson, Evans Lewin, Phyllis Mander Jones, H. E. Maude, Clive Moore, Patrick O'Reilly, Beverley Carron Payne, Karen Peacock, Janet Aileen Pereira, Édouard Reitman, Shiro Saito, Gillian Scott, Susan Stratigos, C. R. H. Taylor, Jennifer Terrell, Lowell D. Thomas, Margaret Titcomb and Camilla H. Wedgwood.

A successful ascent of the Everest of literature about Samoa is inconceivable unaided – anyone foolhardy enough to try needs a Tenzing. I was fortunate to find many willing helpers, among the illustrious ranks of librarians, information officers and Pacific scholars, in all parts of the world (sadly, only excepting Samoa itself). That this Everest was finally made into a manageable molehill and that a task of such magnitude and complexity was accomplished at all is due to so many kind people. They are responsible for the virtues of this bibliography, I alone for its blemishes. I give my sincere thanks to: K. Haybron Adams (Brigham Young University, Provo, Utah); Anne Alexander (Museum of Mankind, London); Shem Baldeosingh (Commonwealth Parliamentary Association, London); Patrice Belcher (Bernice P. Bishop Museum, Honolulu, Hawai'i); Birgit Brand (Rautenstrauch-Joest-Museum, Cologne); Isabel Byron (International Bureau of Education, Geneva); N. P. Cummins (United Nations Library, Bangkok); Adrian Cunningham (Pacific Manuscripts Bureau, Canberra, ACT); Paul I. Derrick (CJCLDS Family History Library, Salt Lake City, Utah); Taufa V. Domona (University of the South Pacific, Suva); Andrzej Durlik (Food and Agriculture Organization, Rome); Manon Edwards (Denbigh Library, Clwyd); Jutta Engelhard (Rautenstrauch-Joest-Museum, Cologne); Maureen H. Fitzgerald (Faculty of Health Sciences, University of Sydney, Sydney, NSW); Jonathan Guy (Institute of Commonwealth Studies, London); Patricia Hewitt (Sainsbury Research Unit for the Arts of Africa, Oceania & the Americas, University of East Anglia, Norwich); Ingjerd Hoëm (University of Oslo); Richard D.

Hollingsworth (University Microfilms International, Godstone, Surrey); Even Hovdhaugen (University of Oslo); Philip Jane (University of Canterbury, Christchurch, New Zealand); Mark Janse (*Bibliographie Linguistigue*, The Hague); Tove D. Johansen (University of Oslo); Verena Keck (Ethnologisches Seminar der Universität Basel); Paul Machlis (University of California, Santa Cruz, California); Jeannette Marie Mageo (Washington State University); Jayshree Mamtora (Pacific Information Centre, University of the South Pacific, Suva); Marie-Laure Manigand (British Library National Sound Archive, London); Carole Modis (World Health Organization, Geneva); Riley Moffat (Brigham Young University-Hawai'i, La'ie, Hawai'i); N. L. Moore (Bowker-Saur Ltd., East Grinstead, West Sussex); Eileen Murtagh (Commonwealth Secretariat, London); Mark Perkins (Overseas Development Institute, London); Ranjit N. Ratnaike (WHO Regional Office for the Western Pacific, Manila); John D. Ray (Pacific Islands Study Circle of Great Britain); Helen Rehin (Institute of Development Studies, University of Sussex, Brighton); Ken Richardson (University of Queensland, St. Lucia, Queensland); Lori Ritchie (University of California, Santa Barbara, California); Dorothea Scheimann (Die Deutsche Bibliothek, Frankfurt/Main); Darea Sherratt (Alexander Turnbull Library, Wellington); Hanne Gram Simonsen (University of Oslo); Deveni Temu (South Pacific Commission, Nouméa, New Caledonia); John Rees Thomas (Clwyd Library & Information Service, Mold); D. I. Thompson (UNESCO, Paris); Hamish Todd (Oriental and India Office Collections, British Library, London); D. E. Torrijos (UNESCO, Bangkok); S. Michele Walker (Oxford Forestry Institute, Oxford); and Diane Woods (National Library of New Zealand, Wellington).

I greatly appreciate the kind permission given me by ABC-Clio International and by Bowker-Saur Ltd. to make use of their copyright abstracts. Dr Robert G. Neville, of ABC-Clio Ltd. Oxford, has my profound gratitude for his understanding, patience and forbearance when critical personal problems delayed my submission of the finished text. The ABC-Clio editor, Julia Goddard, who gave my clumsy structure both stability and a presentable appearance has my boundless admiration.

Two people especially deserve my thanks and appreciation. Without them, there would be no book. Joyce Wright of Caerwys, who belongs to my own Second World War generation, typed the entire text, indefatigably and with consummate skill. *Per ardua ad astra*! First and foremost, I owe so much to my wife Zuzana, who encouraged and sustained me throughout the seemingly interminable gestation of this book, despite her own cruel and debilitating illness. I dedicate *Samoa* to her, with all my love.

Theses on Samoa and the Samoans

University theses and dissertations, most of them destined to remain unpublished, provide an immense amount of factual information and insights relating to virtually every facet of the history, culture and everyday problems of Samoans, in their partitioned islands and in dispersion.

Doctoral dissertations are commonly listed and abstracted in *Dissertation Abstracts*, and are obtainable in xerox or microfilm formats from University Microfilms International (UMI) of Ann Arbor, Michigan, USA. Alternatively, copies of theses may be purchased from the university which accepted them for a higher degree. Copies of many American and British doctoral dissertations of recent years are also sold or issued on loan by the British Library Document Supply Centre (BLDSC), Boston Spa, Wetherby, West Yorkshire LS23 7BQ, England. Copies of Master and Bachelor theses are usually obtainable by direct application to the respective university, as are Diploma theses.

This list ranges widely, and is representative rather than comprehensive. Many fine theses have had to be omitted. I particularly regret that I could list only a few of the theses submitted to the Pacific Theological College in Fiji. Written by island pastors, these are often the only source of reliable information on aspects of indigenous life and belief. Fortunately, these theses are being made available on microfilm by the Pacific Manuscripts Bureau (PMB) at the Australian National University, Canberra ACT, Australia. PMB publishes lists and catalogues of all materials filmed, and publicizes newly available microfilms in its journal *Pambu*. News of theses may be found in the annual bibliographical supplement to the *Journal of Pacific History*, to which I gratefully acknowledge my debt.

Theses on Samoa and the Samoans

Samoans constitute a global community, with many thousands now at home in California, Fiji, Hawai‘i, New Zealand and Washington. No bibliography focusing on the Samoan people can conceivably overlook their enterprising sons and daughters who have transplanted themselves and their ancestral culture *fa‘a-Sāmoa* to new lands beyond the sea.

Ioane Asalele Afoa. ‘Divorce counselling with Samoan couples’, DMin thesis, Claremont School of Theology, 1980.

R. Ah Wa. ‘The impact of urbanisation on household energy economy of Samoa’, MA thesis, University of Auckland, 1989.

Penelope T. Ala‘ilima-Utu. ‘Feasible study of the Emmanuel Evangelical School in Samoa’, DMin thesis, Fuller Theological Seminary, 1985.

Repeka Ala‘imoana-Nu‘usa. ‘Lost in Samoa: the problems of adjustment of Samoan returnee students’, MEd thesis, University of Hawai‘i, 1993.

Anne Elizabeth Guernsey Allen. ‘Space as social construct: the vernacular architecture of rural Samoa’, PhD thesis, Columbia University, 1993.

Anne Elizabeth Guernsey Allen. ‘The tapa of Tonga and Samoa: a study in continuity and change’, MA thesis, San Diego State University, 1985.

Robert Anae. ‘Economic development, wage labor, and *fa‘a Samoa*’, MA thesis, University of Hawai‘i, 1990.

Joseph Jay Arden. ‘The political development of Western Samoa from mandate to independence’, PhD thesis, University of Oklahoma, 1964.

Rey Lorenzo Baird. ‘A variable recursive mechanism in Samoan’, PhD thesis, Indiana University, 1974.

Richard Berge Baldauf Jr. ‘Relationships between overt and covert acculturation in American Samoa’, PhD thesis, University of Hawai‘i, 1975.

James Patrick Barker. ‘Incentives, income, and institutions: an inquiry into fisheries development in Western Samoa’, PhD thesis, University of California (Riverside), 1982.

Kathleen Graney Baron. ‘Protein nutrition of expectant mothers in American Samoa and its effect on the health of the infant’, MS thesis, Montana State University, 1971.

Ward Judson Barrett. ‘Agriculture of Western Samoa’, PhD thesis, University of California (Berkeley), 1959.

John Michael Barrington. ‘Education and national development in Western Samoa’, PhD thesis, Victoria University of Wellington, 1968.

L. R. Bergin. 'A guide to the Samoan *fagogo* collected by Richard M. Moyle in the Archive of Maori and Pacific Music', MA thesis, University of Auckland, 1975.

James Robert Bindon. 'Genetic and environmental influences on the morphology of Samoan adults', PhD thesis, Pennsylvania State University, 1981.

Mildred Bloombaum. 'The Samoan immigrant: acculturation, enculturation and the child in school', PhD thesis, University of Hawai'i, 1973.

Warren Finlay Boaden. 'The administration of the New Zealand Labour Party in Western Samoa (1936-1948)', MA thesis, University of New Zealand (Auckland), 1949.

Stephen Bradbury. 'The London Missionary Society and Steinberger', MA thesis, University of Auckland, 1972.

John Vincent Broadbent. 'Attempts to form an indigenous clergy in the Vicariates Apostolic of Central Oceania and the Navigators' Islands in the nineteenth century', doctoral thesis, Katholieke Universiteit, Leuven, 1976.

T. P. Brown. 'Children's "voices": a content analysis of Samoan children's stories', MA thesis, University of Auckland, 1986.

Mary Brumber. 'Church and community among Samoan immigrants in San Francisco', MA thesis, University of Chicago, 1970.

Nevin Arthur Bryant. 'Change in the agricultural land use in west Upolu, Western Samoa', MA thesis, University of Hawai'i, 1967.

Richard John Burgess. 'The intercropping of smallholder coconuts in Western Samoa: an analysis using multi-stage linear programming', MADE thesis, Australian National University, 1977.

Horst Cain. '*Aitu*: Untersuchungen zur autochtonen Religion der Samoaner', DPhil thesis, Universität Marburg, 1979.

Rex Solomon Camrass. 'Oral health survey in Western Samoa', DDS thesis, University of Otago, 1971.

Valerie Margaret Carson. 'The Samoan Mission Seminary, 1844-1884: a study of the means of furnishing teachers in Samoa', MA thesis, Victoria University of Wellington, 1983.

Margaret F. Chambers. 'The revivalist movement on Tutuila (Samoa), 1839-1842', MA thesis, University of Melbourne, 1975.

Dorothy Caye Clement. 'Samoan concepts of mental illness and treatment', PhD thesis, University of California (Irvine), 1974.

Wilhelm Clement. 'Die amerikanische Samoapolitik und die Idee des Manifest Destiny', DPhil thesis, Phillipps-Universität Marburg, 1949.

Robin David Connor. 'Rational ecology in the Pacific: the case of Western Samoa', MSc thesis, University of Canterbury, 1990.

Theses on Samoa and the Samoans

Kenneth William Cook. 'A cognitive analysis of grammatical relations, case and transitivity in Samoan', PhD thesis, University of California (San Diego), 1988.

John Cole Cool. 'American administrative policies in Tutuila in relation to the Samoan authority structure', PhD thesis, University of London, 1958.

Charles Wallace Coyner. 'United States colonial policy: a case study of American Samoa', PhD thesis, University of Oklahoma, 1973.

Jeanne Linsdell Crank. 'Samoa tomorrow: developing a system of appropriate and effective public administration in American Samoa: the challenge of finding a workable synthesis between native and Western traditions, concepts and leadership practices', PhD thesis, Golden Gate University, 1981.

Ronald James Crawford. 'The *lotu* and the *fa'a Samoa*: church and society in Samoa, 1830-1880', PhD thesis, University of Otago, 1977.

Douglas Earl Crews. 'Mortality, survivorship and longevity in American Samoa, 1950 to 1981', PhD thesis, Pennsylvania State University, 1985.

Ephrosine Kathleen Daniggelis. 'Cash fishing and subsistence plantations: the impact of a global economy on Samoan children's growth', MA thesis, University of Hawai'i, 1987.

C. Demleitner. 'Das Schul- und Erziehungswesen in West-Samoa', DPhil thesis, Universität München, 1980.

Norman Douglas. 'Latter-Day Saints missions and missionaries in Polynesia, 1844-1960', PhD thesis, Australian National University, 1974.

Barbara Constance Du Bois. 'Hypertension and social support: the medical anthropology of older, urban Samoans', PhD thesis, University of Hawai'i, 1987.

Alessandro Duranti. 'The *fono*: a Samoan speech event', PhD thesis, University of Southern California, 1981.

Thomas Stuart Dye. 'Social and cultural change in the prehistory of the Ancestral Polynesian Homeland (Fiji, Tonga, Samoa)', PhD thesis, Yale University, 1987.

Oscar Raymond Eggers. 'The showplace of the South Seas: United States colonial impression management and the deculturation of American Samoa', PhD thesis, University of Chicago, 1984.

Melvin Lawrence Ember. 'Commercialization and political behavior in American Samoa', PhD thesis, Yale University, 1958.

D. S. Enesa. 'The aging Samoan in Hawaii', MA thesis, University of Hawai'i, 1977.

Foisaga Elisa Eteuati. 'Administrative policies and agriculture in Western Samoa, 1914-1962', MA thesis, University of Canterbury, 1971.

Kilifoti Sisilia Eteuati. '*Evaevaga a Samoa*: assertion of Samoan autonomy, 1920-1936', PhD thesis, Australian National University, 1982.

Te'o Ian John Fairbairn. 'The national income of Western Samoa, 1947-58', PhD thesis, Australian National University, 1963.

Margaret E. Fairburn-Dunlop. 'Samoan parents and the primary school', MA thesis, Victoria University of Wellington, 1981.

Logoleo Tele'a V. Faleali'i. 'A study of the attitudes of public school teachers toward instructional television in American Samoa', EdD thesis, University of the Pacific, 1976.

Justin Peter Fepulea'i. 'From self government to independence: the development of New Zealand's policy towards Western Samoa during the United Nations trusteeship period, 1946-62', MA thesis, University of Auckland, 1994.

Tafatoluomalua T. Filemoni. 'Toward a theory and theology of educational ministry in Samoa', DMin thesis, Claremont School of Theology, 1990.

Niall Anthony Finn. 'The Samoan community in Christchurch: a migration study', MA thesis, University of Canterbury, 1973.

Stewart G. Firth. 'German recruitment and employment of labourers in the Western Pacific before the First World War', DPhil thesis, University of Oxford, 1973.

Maureen H. Fitzgerald. 'Modernization and the menstrual experience among Samoans', PhD thesis, University of Hawai'i, 1989.

Claudia Lalolagi Forsyth. 'Samoan art of healing: a description and classification of the current practice of the *taulasea* and *fofō*', PhD thesis, United States International University, San Diego, 1983.

Robert William Franco. 'The history, role and function of the contemporary Catholic Church in Western Samoa', MA thesis, California State University, 1976.

Robert William Franco. 'Samoan perceptions of work, moving up and moving around', PhD thesis, University of Hawai'i, 1985.

Janet Owens Frost. 'Archaeological investigations on Tutuila Island, American Samoa', PhD thesis, University of Oregon, 1978.

Epi Enari Fua'au. 'Mother, may I stay?', MA thesis, University of Hawai'i, 1989.

Dennis Fitiuta Fuimaono. 'The evolution of jurisprudence in American Samoa', MSc thesis, California State University (Long Beach), 1985.

Seth Peni Galea'i. 'An assessment of the classroom competencies of in-service elementary school teachers in American Samoa', EdD thesis, University of Hawai'i, 1991.

Eleanor Ruth Gerber. 'The cultural patterning of emotions in Samoa', PhD thesis, University of California (San Diego), 1975.

Patrick Gerber. 'Amerikanische und deutsche Kolonialpolitik in Vergleich: das Beispiel Hawaii und Samoa bis 1872-1914', MA thesis, Universität zu Köln, 1982.

Michael Charles Gifford. 'The nature and origins of the Mau movement in Western Samoa, 1926-1936', MA thesis, University of Auckland, 1964.

Jack T. Gill. 'The administration of Major General Sir George Richardson in Western Samoa, 1923-1928', MA thesis, University of New Zealand (Wellington), 1950.

Jerry Gold. 'Modern human migration and the emergence of a class system in American Samoa', PhD thesis, University of Washington, 1988.

Lawrence Paul Greksa. 'Work requirements and work capabilities in a modernizing Samoan population', PhD thesis, Pennsylvania State University, 1980.

Walter Niel Gunson. 'Evangelical missionaries in the South Seas, 1797-1860', PhD thesis, Australian National University, 1959.

Walter Niel Gunson. 'The missionary vocation as conceived by the early missionaries of the London Missionary Society in the South Seas, and the extent to which this conception was modified by their experiences in Polynesia, 1797-1839', MA thesis, University of Melbourne, 1955.

Pisopa Hakai. 'Reconciliation: a Samoan ritual seen in the light of Paul's and Luke's message on reconciliation', MTh thesis, Pacific Theological College, 1990.

Linda G. Hamilton. 'The political integration of the Samoan immigrants in New Zealand', MA thesis, University of Canterbury, 1974.

Volker Harms. 'Der Terminus "Spiel" in der Ethnologie: eine begriffskritische Untersuchung dargestellt anhand von Berichten über die Kultur der Samoaner', DPhil thesis, Universität Hamburg, 1969.

Graham Edgar Harrison. 'Aspects of change in Western Samoa 1962-1974: a statistical analysis', PhD thesis, Australian National University, 1978.

Douglas Raymond Haynes. 'Chinese indentured labour in Western Samoa, 1900-1950', MA thesis, Victoria University of Wellington, 1965.

Timothy Heath. 'The diagnosis and treatment of disease in a rural village in Western Samoa', MA thesis, University of Auckland, 1973.

Peter John Hempenstall. 'Indigenous resistance to German rule in the Pacific colonies of Samoa, Ponape and New Guinea, 1884 to 1914', DPhil thesis, University of Oxford, 1973.

Walther Herkner. 'Drei Systeme kolonialer Herrschaft auf Samoa', Dr jur thesis, Friedrich-Alexander-Universität zu Erlangen-Nürnberg, 1951.

Richard Hertz. 'Das Hamburger Seehandelshaus J. C. Godeffroy und Sohn 1766-1879', DPhil thesis, Universität Hamburg, 1922.

Hermann Joseph Hiery. 'Das Deutsche Reich in der Südsee (1900-1921): eine Annäherung an die Erfahrungen verschiedener Kulturen', Habilitationsschrift, Universität Freiburg im Breisgau, 1993.

Harry Burnette Hill. 'The use of nearshore marine life as a food resource by American Samoans', MA thesis, University of Hawai'i, 1977.

Robert Irwin Hillier. 'The South Seas fiction of Robert Louis Stevenson', PhD thesis, University of New Hampshire, 1985.

Linda M. Holland. 'Migration and the status of women in an urban Samoan community', MA thesis, San Francisco State University, 1989.

Jeannette R. Holmes. 'Aboriginal and modern Samoa: a study of cultural change based upon London Missionary Society journals, 1830-1840', MA thesis, Wichita State University, 1967.

Lowell Don Holmes. 'A restudy of Manu'an culture: a problem in methodology', PhD thesis, Northwestern University, 1957.

Jon David Holstine. 'American diplomacy in Samoa, 1884 to 1889', PhD thesis, Indiana University, 1971.

Tagaloa le Papali'itele Hutchinson. ' *'O aganu'u a Samoa*: a study of chiefly ceremonials in traditional Samoa', MA thesis, University of Auckland, 1992.

David Jackson Inglis. 'Change and continuity in Samoan religion: the role of the Congregational Christian Church', PhD thesis, University of New South Wales, 1991.

Margaret Anne Ingram. 'Louis Becke: a study', MA thesis, University of Hawai'i, 1937.

Ioane. 'House design and construction for solving housing problems in Western Samoa', MPhil thesis, University of Sheffield, 1990.

Fa'afouina Iofi. 'Samoan cultural values and Christian thought: an attempt to relate traditional values to Christian understanding', DMin thesis, Claremont School of Theology, 1980.

Leo A. Jackowski Jr. 'Studies on the factors influencing the epidemiology of filariasis in American Samoa', PhD thesis, Johns Hopkins University, 1952.

Knut Axel Jacobsen. 'Religion and peace in Samoa', MA thesis, University of California (Santa Barbara), 1988.

Gary Douglas James. 'Stress response and lifestyle differences among Western Samoan men', PhD thesis, Pennsylvania State University, 1984.

Craig Robert Janes. 'Migration and hypertension: an ethnography of disease risk in an urban Samoan community', PhD thesis, University of California (San Francisco & Berkeley), 1984.

Richard T. Johnson. 'The growth of creative thinking abilities in Western Samoa', PhD thesis, University of Minnesota, 1963.

L. Kamu. 'Samoan culture and the Christian gospel', PhD thesis, University of Birmingham, 1989.

Dennis T. P. Keene. 'Houses without walls: Samoan social control', PhD thesis, University of Hawai'i, 1978.

Susanna Kelly. 'Art production and the tourist trade in Fiji, Tonga and Samoa, and implications for regional and national identities', PhD thesis, University of London, 1997 [due].

Paul M. Kennedy. 'The partition of the Samoan Islands, 1898-99', DPhil thesis, University of Oxford, 1970.

Keith Thomas Kernan. 'The acquisition of language by Samoan children', PhD thesis, University of California (Berkeley), 1969.

William Kenji Kikuchi. 'Archaeological surface ruins in American Samoa', MA thesis, University of Hawai'i, 1963.

Patricia Jane Kinloch. 'Samoan children in a New Zealand secondary school: a semiological study of social communication', PhD thesis, Victoria University of Wellington, 1976.

Lydia Ruth Dougherty Kotchek. 'Adaptive strategies of an invisible ethnic minority, the Samoan population of Seattle, Washington', PhD thesis, University of Washington, 1975.

Gerda Kröber. 'Das *Matai*-System in Samoa: Rekonstruktion seiner traditionellen Ausprägung und Analyse seiner Resistenz gegenüber dem Akkulturationsdruck', DPhil thesis, Freie Universität Berlin, 1975.

F. T. Lafitaga. 'Wholeness in mission: a discussion of the mission in American Samoa in the light of the theological writings of J. Hoekendijk, J. V. Taylor and D. Niles', MPhil thesis, University of St. Andrew's, 1983.

Ali'ifa'atui Laolagi. 'A descriptive study of Samoan families who have settled in San Francisco', MA thesis, San Francisco State College, 1961.

Netina Matafeo Galo Latu. 'The social determinants of education in Western Samoa', MA thesis, Victoria University of Wellington, 1966.

Tafesilafa'i Lavasi'i. ' "To supply them with knowledge": a history of the Samoan Mission Seminary, 1844-1875', BD thesis, Pacific Theological College, 1984.

Peter R. Leitch. 'The introduction of universal suffrage in Western Samoa: an analysis of the Plebiscite and the 1991 General Election', MA thesis, Victoria University of Wellington, 1992.

Ropeti Fa'afetai Lesa. 'Learning styles of Samoan students', EdD thesis, Brigham Young University, 1981.

Samuel Gary Leung Wai. 'Problems of transition in a dual economy: the case of Western Samoa', MADE thesis, Australian National University, 1975.

David M. Liu. 'A politics of identity in Western Samoa', PhD thesis, University of Hawai'i, 1991.

Brian Albert Lockwood. 'A comparative study of market participation and monetisation in four subsistence-based villages in Western Samoa', PhD thesis, Australian National University, 1968.

Jacob Wainwright Love. 'Sāmoan variations: essays on the nature of traditional oral arts', PhD thesis, Harvard University, 1979.

Jerry King Loveland. 'The establishment of the instruments of modern rule in Western Samoa', PhD thesis, American University, 1967.

I. R. Lowe. 'Some aspects of the teacher's role in development: a comparative study in the two Samoas', MEd thesis, La Trobe University, 1981.

William Stanley Lowe. 'The Samoan mandate (1919-1939)', MA thesis, University of New Zealand (Auckland), 1943.

Christine Loytved. 'Hebammen in Ozeanien zwischen traditioneller und westlicher Medizin: Situation und Weiterbildung traditioneller Hebammen in Samoa and Tonga', DPhil thesis, Universität Göttingen, 1990.

Eudene Luther. 'Development and resistance: rural resistance to economic development practices in Western Samoa', PhD thesis, McMaster University, 1996.

Robin Ray Lyons. 'Emigration from American Samoa: a study of bicultural assimilation and migration', PhD thesis, University of Hawai'i, 1980.

Floyd Warren McCoy Jr. 'The geology of Ofu and Olosega Islands, Manu'a group, American Samoa', MSc thesis, University of Hawai'i, 1965.

Suzanne Cherie MacDonald. 'Educational opportunity and Samoan students in Hawai'i: a case study', EdD thesis, University of Hawai'i, 1987.

Stephen Theodore McGarvey. 'Modernization and cardiovascular disease among Samoans', PhD thesis, Pennsylvania State University, 1980.

George Charles MacGillivray. 'Geography of Western Samoa', MA thesis, Clark University, 1951.

Noël Lawrence McGrevy. ' *'O le tatatau*: an examination of certain aspects of Samoan tattoing to the present', MA thesis, University of Hawai'i, 1973.

Kenneth Starr MacKenzie. 'Robert Louis Stevenson and Samoa, 1889-1894', PhD thesis, Dalhousie University, 1974.

Alastair John Cluny Macpherson. 'Extended kinship among urban Samoan migrants: towards an explanation of its persistence in urban New Zealand', DPhil thesis, University of Waikato, 1975.

Alastair John Cluny Macpherson. 'Intermarriage in the Samoan migrant community in New Zealand', MA thesis, University of Auckland, 1972.

Lisa MacQuoid. 'The women's *mau*: female peace warriors in Western Samoa', MA thesis, University of Hawai'i, 1995.

Mila Maefau. 'The Samoan churches in Southern California: their needs, development and search for identity', DMin thesis, Claremont School of Theology, 1977.

Guenther Mahler. 'Labor importation into colonial Samoa, 1900-1914: a study in geographic mobility', MA thesis, California State University (Hayward), 1975.

Fana'afi Larkin Ma'ia'i. 'Bilingualism in Western Samoa: its problems and implications for education', PhD thesis, University of London, 1960.

Fana'afi Larkin Ma'ia'i. 'A study of the developing pattern of education and the factors influencing that development in New Zealand's Pacific dependencies', MA thesis, University of New Zealand (Wellington), 1957.

Polofeu Viavia Manuma. 'Organizational climate in the elementary schools of American Samoa', PhD thesis, University of Minnesota, 1975.

Marie F. Ma'o. 'The occupational stress of nursing administrators in American Samoa', MSc thesis, University of Hawai'i, 1991.

John Robert Martin. 'Representative institutions in Western Samoa during the mandate, 1919-1946', MA thesis, University of New Zealand (Wellington), 1959.

Robert John Maxwell. 'Samoan temperament', PhD thesis, Cornell University, 1969.

Malama Meleisea. 'Fanua ma suafa', PhD thesis, Macquarie University, 1986.

Malama Meleisea. 'The making of modern Samoa: traditional authority and colonial administration in the history of Western Samoa', PhD thesis, Macquarie University, 1988.

Malama Meleisea. ' '*O tama uli*: Melanesians in Western Samoa, 1905-1975', BA (Hons) thesis, University of Papua New Guinea, 1976.
Penelope Meleisea *see* Penelope Schoeffel.
Ulupago Middleton-Misifoa. ' "Do this in remembrance of me": a consideration of the eucharistic life of the Methodist Church in Samoa', PhD thesis, Pacific Theological College, 1987.
Llevellys Miller. 'Some aspects of the *matai* system in Samoa and New Zealand', MA thesis, University of Auckland, 1980.
George Bertram Milner. 'Problems of the structure of concepts in Samoa: an investigation of vernacular statement and meaning', PhD thesis, University of London, 1968.
Paula Tanaka Mochida. 'Wilhelm Solf: colonialist, educator, humanitarian', MEd thesis, University of Hawai'i, 1984.
S. Moli'oumaseali'i. 'Some aspects of Samoan customary law', ML thesis, University of Auckland, 1974.
Stewart Rutherford Morrison. 'Law and custom in Samoa: a history of native administration in Western Samoa and of the development of its fundamental problems, 1850-1927', MA thesis, University of New Zealand (Dunedin), 1937.
Richard Michael Moyle. 'A preliminary survey of former Samoan music, 1968-1971', MA thesis, University of Auckland, 1967.
Richard Michael Moyle. 'Samoan traditional music', PhD thesis, University of Auckland, 1971. (With tape recordings).
Tafailematagi T. Muasau. 'Samoans in mission in southern Vanuatu: a study of the L.M.S. Samoan missionary enterprise on Aneityum, Tanna and Erromango', MTh thesis, Pacific Theological College, 1991.
Y. M. Mulder. 'Western Samoa and New Zealand: small state - large state relations', MA thesis, University of Canterbury, 1981.
S. Muli'aumaseali'i. 'The quest for sovereignty: Western Samoa, 1800-1962', MA thesis, University of Auckland, 1973.
S. Muli'aumaseali'i. 'Some aspects of Samoan customary law', MA thesis, University of Auckland, 1974.
Muriel E. Myers. 'Cultural borrowing of English words by the Samoan language and the effects of acculturation upon the borrowing', MA thesis, California State University (San Francisco), 1969.
Vijay Naidu. 'State, class and politics in the South Pacific: with case studies of Fiji and Western Samoa', PhD thesis, University of Sussex, 1989.
Katherine Toshiko Nakata. 'Toward a coming of age for Samoa: a structural perspective on Samoa's neo-traditionalist development strategy', PhD thesis, University of Hawai'i, 1981.

James Howard Natland. 'Petrologic studies of linear island chains. Part 1: the Samoan Islands. Part 2: the Line Islands', PhD thesis, University of California (San Diego), 1975.

André Hubert Neu. 'Progress is a comfortable disease: a cross cultural study showing television's effects on an American Samoan family', MS thesis, San José State University, 1990.

Christine Nichol. 'Samoan church music in Wellington', MMus thesis, Victoria University of Wellington, 1979.

U. F. Nokise. 'The role of L.M.S. Samoan missionaries in the evangelisation of the South West Pacific, 1839-1930', PhD thesis, Australian National University, 1992.

Alison Devine Nordström. 'Images of paradise: photographs of Samoa, 1880-1930', MA thesis, University of Oklahoma, 1989.

Charles T. Okino. 'Early Hawai'i and Samoa: a reference unit', MA thesis, University of Hawai'i, 1971.

Frederick Harris Olsen. 'The navy and the white man's burden: naval administration of American Samoa', PhD thesis, University of Washington, 1976.

John Timothy O'Meara. 'Why is village agriculture stagnating?: a test of social and economic explanations in Western Samoa', PhD thesis, University of California (Santa Barbara), 1986.

Neil Stanley Paget. 'Samoa College: its development and role in Samoan education, 1953-1965', MA thesis, Victoria University of Wellington, 1966.

Lanuimoana Mapusaga Palepoi. 'Perceptions of selected functions of Samoan councils of *matai* and American community councils', EdD thesis, Brigham Young University, 1984.

Lindi Temukisa Kaisar Papali'i. 'Samoan associations in New Zealand: success or failure?', MA thesis, University of Auckland, 1977.

Deborah D. Paulson. 'Forest depletion, village agriculture and social changes in rural Western Samoa: a case study', PhD thesis, University of Hawai'i, 1992.

Andrew Kenneth Pawley. 'Samoan phrase structure: the morphology and syntax of a Western Polynesian language', MA thesis, University of Auckland, 1963.

Sam H. Pearsall. 'A geographical-ecological model for landscape conservation in Western Samoa', PhD thesis, University of Hawai'i, 1993.

Jay Dee Pearson. 'Urinary catecholamine excretion, daily activities, and stress in rural Western Samoa, American Samoa, and urban Honolulu', PhD thesis, Pennsylvania State University, 1989.

David Louis Pelletier. 'Diet, activity and cardiovascular disease risk factors in Western Samoan men', PhD thesis, Pennsylvania State University, 1984.

Fiona Petchey. 'The archaeology of Kudon: archaeological analysis of Lapita ceramics from Mulifanua, Samoa and Sigatoka, Fiji', MA thesis, University of Auckland, 1995.

Bernard Francis Pierce: 'Acculturation of Samoans in the Mormon village of Laie, Territory of Hawaii', MA thesis, University of Hawai'i, 1956.

Wilfred J. Pinson. 'The diocese of Polynesia (1868-1910)', BD thesis, Pacific Theological College, 1970.

Peter Nigel Douglas Pirie. 'The geography of population in Western Samoa', PhD thesis, Australian National University, 1963.

David Charles Pitt. 'Aspects of social change in contemporary Samoa', DPhil thesis, University of Oxford, 1966.

Martha Lu Platt. 'Social and semantic dimensions of deictic verbs and particles in Samoan child language', PhD thesis, University of Southern California, 1982.

William Neil Plimmer. 'The military occupation of Western Samoa, 1914-1920', MA thesis, Victoria University of Wellington, 1966.

Umaitua Poloai. 'An investigation of the relationship between self-concept and selected academic variables: Samoan students at Samoa', PhD thesis, Brigham Young University, 1980.

Charles Guy Powles. 'The status of customary law in Western Samoa', LLM thesis, Victoria University of Wellington, 1973.

Erika Fereti Puni. 'Patterns of leadership selection and church growth in the Samoan mission of Seventh-Day Adventists, 1967-1987', MAMiss thesis, Fuller Theological Seminary, 1989.

R. D. D. Quatermass. 'Children of empire: expatriates in Western Samoa, 1946-1961', MA thesis, University of Auckland, 1982.

Shivaji Ramalingam. 'The mosquito fauna of Samoa and Tonga and its relation to subperiodic Bancroftian filariasis', PhD thesis, University of California (Los Angeles), 1965.

Harold Nolan Reed. 'The completion of educational goals and the returnability of Tongan and Western Samoan students at a private American university', EdD thesis, Brigham Young University, 1982.

Barbara V. Reid. 'Gender, culture and morality: a comparative study of Samoans and Pakehas in New Zealand', PhD thesis, University of South Carolina, 1986.

Salu Hunkin Reid. 'Educator's perceptions of teacher education program goals and the educational needs of the Territory of American Samoa', EdD thesis, University of Hawai'i, 1986.

Ellen C. Rhoads. 'Aging and modernization in three Samoan communities', PhD thesis, University of Kansas, 1981.

Helen Annette Riddell. 'New Zealand land and trade interests in Samoa, 1870-1885', MA thesis, University of Otago, 1967.

Elizabeth Marchette Roach. 'From English mission to Samoan congregation: women and the church in rural Western Samoa', PhD thesis, Columbia University, 1984.

Douglas Wilmot Roblin. 'Labor market behavior of disadvantaged migrants: a case study of Samoans in the San Francisco Bay area (California)', PhD thesis, University of Michigan, 1984.

Andrew Eric Robson. 'Public plans and private aspirations: a study of education policies and the outcomes of schooling in Kiribati, Western Samoa and American Samoa', PhD thesis, Australian National University, 1983.

Karla Rolff. '*Fa'asamoa*: tradition in transition', PhD thesis, University of California (Santa Barbara), 1978.

Douglass St. Christian. 'Body/work: aspects of embodiment and culture in Western Samoa', PhD thesis, McMaster University, 1994.

Unisese Elisara Sala. 'A theology of Samoan Christian immigrants in the United States', DMin thesis, Claremont School of Theology, 1980.

Salale Salale. 'Human resources in a South Pacific community: the Western Samoan labour force, 1951-1981', MA thesis, Australian National University, 1978.

William Michael Saleebey. 'Educational problems of Samoan migrants: an exploratory study', PhD thesis, University of California (Los Angeles), 1980.

Pedro Cruz Sánchez. 'Education in American Samoa', PhD thesis, Stanford University, 1956.

Christine Sauer. 'Die "Samoa-Kontroverse" und ihre Auswirkungen auf die Ethnologie', MA thesis, Universität Göttingen, 1991.

Saeu Leau Scanlan. 'A follow-up study of graduates and non-graduates of the Community College of American Samoa for the years 1972, 1973 and 1974', EdD thesis, Brigham Young University, 1975.

Dorothee Schneider-Christians. 'Die alte Religion und das Christentum Samoas', DPhil thesis, Universität Bonn, 1992.

Penelope Schoeffel. 'Daughters of Sina: a study of gender, status and power in Western Samoa', PhD thesis, Australian National University, 1979.

Charles Lorenz Schroth. 'Analysis and prediction of the properties of Western Samoa soils', PhD thesis, University of Hawai'i, 1970.

Terry D. Schwaner. 'Biogeography, community ecology and reproductive biology of the herpetofauna of American Samoa', PhD thesis, University of Kansas, 1979.

T. Senara. 'Samoan religious leadership', MA thesis, University of Otago, 1988.

Samuelu S. Sesega. 'Sustainability and sustainable development: a goal and an approach for development in Western Samoa', MSc thesis, University of Canterbury, 1990.

Fa'atulituli Setu. 'The ministry in the making: a history of the emergence of the ministry of the Church in Samoa, 1830-1900 (Congregational CC)', MTh thesis, Pacific Theological College, 1988.

Fa'auma T. Seui. 'An American philanthropic effort: Barstow Foundation and the development of education in American Samoa', EdD thesis, University of Hawai'i, 1987.

Paul Andrew Shankman. 'Remittances and underdevelopment in Western Samoa', PhD thesis, Harvard University, 1973.

Bradd Shore. 'Adoption, alliance and political mobility in Samoa', MA thesis, University of Chicago, 1972.

Bradd Shore. 'A Samoan theory of action: social control and social order in a Polynesian paradox', PhD thesis, University of Chicago, 1977.

Ramsay Leung-Hay Shu. 'Kinship system and migrant adaptation: the case of the Samoans', PhD thesis, University of Notre Dame, 1980.

Hanne Gram Simonsen. 'Barns fonologi: system og variasjon hos tre norske og et samoisk barn' [Child phonology: system and variation in three Norwegian children and one Samoan child], PhD thesis, University of Oslo, 1990.

Caroline Sinavaiana. 'Traditional comic theater in Samoa: a holographic view', PhD thesis, University of Hawai'i, 1992.

Ruta Sinclair. 'The London Missionary Society (L.M.S.): Samoan missionaries along the Papua coast', MA thesis, University of Papua New Guinea, 1980.

Peter J. Sluyter. 'Frontline Samoa: Western Samoa, a mandated territory's part in World War Two', MA thesis, University of Auckland, 1988.

Ross Sydney Smith. 'The Samoan population of Tokoroa: a study of their mobility and selected demographic, economic and social characteristics', MA thesis, University of Auckland, 1972.

A. P. J. Snell. 'Social problems of Western Samoans in the community', PhD thesis, University of Otago, 1970.

David L. Snow. 'Samoan language and culture', MA thesis, University of Chicago, 1974.

Eneliko F. Sofa'i. 'The history of education in American Samoa', EdD thesis, Brigham Young University, 1984.
Meki Tavita Solomona. 'Characteristics of the public school teachers in American Samoa, 1960-1980', EdD thesis, Brigham Young University, 1983.
Max Edward Stanton. 'Samoan saints: Samoans in the Mormon village of Laie, Hawaii', PhD thesis, University of Oregon, 1973.
Denis J. R. Steley. 'The Seventh-Day Adventist mission in the south central Pacific', PhD thesis, University of Auckland, 1988.
Philippe Stéphan. 'La malnutrition au Samoa occidental et les effets de l'urbanisation sur la nutrition', Thèse de Médecine, Université de Paris VI, 1986.
Theodore J. Stepp Jr. 'Serving Samoan youth in Honolulu: culture, religious education, and social adjustment', MA thesis, University of Hawai'i, 1989.
Gary Dennis Stice. 'The geology and petrology of the Manu'a Islands, American Samoa', PhD thesis, University of Hawai'i, 1966.
Mary Liana Stover. 'The individualization of land in American Samoa', PhD thesis, University of Hawai'i, 1990.
Diane Sulzberger. 'The attitude of Sir Apirana Ngata towards the Cook Islanders and Samoans', MA thesis, University of Auckland, 1972.
Frederic Koehler Sutter. 'Communal versus individual socialization at home and in school in rural and urban Western Samoa', PhD thesis, University of Hawai'i, 1980.
Sharon K. Sutter. 'Health services in Western Samoa', MA thesis, University of Hawai'i, 1967.
Mary Ellen Swanton. 'The visitor perception of the physical and cultural environment of American Samoa', MA thesis, University of Hawai'i, 1969.
Laloulu Elia Tagoilelagi. 'A study of resources for local finance of public education in American Samoa', EdD thesis, Brigham Young University, 1983.
M. L. Tallentire. 'Samoa: the eleven year war', MA thesis, University of Otago, 1979.
Alofa Seuiolo Tanuvasu. 'Western Samoan students of BYU-Hawaii: academic achievements and aspirations for teaching in Western Samoa', EdD thesis, Brigham Young University, 1984.
H. F. Tau'au. 'Environmental ideas as reflected in the *fa'a Samoa*', MA thesis, University of Auckland, 1989.
Philip H. Taylor. 'A history and comparison of dependency administration in Samoa', PhD thesis, Stanford University, 1936.

Jack W. Thacker Jr. 'The partition of Samoa', PhD thesis, University of South Carolina, 1966.

Pamela Thomas. 'Dimensions of diffusion: delivering primary health care and nutritional information in Western Samoa', PhD thesis, Australian National University, 1986.

Walter Warren Tiffany. 'Political structure and change: a corporate analysis of American Samoa', PhD thesis, University of California (Los Angeles), 1971.

Trace V. Tipton. 'Cropping decisions in a semicommercial context in Western Samoa: a multiple criteria approach', MSc thesis, University of Hawai'i, 1991.

I'uogafa Tuagalu. 'Mata'afa Iosefo and the idea of kinship in Samoa', MA thesis, University of Auckland, 1988.

Fagaloa L. S. R. Tufuga. ' "For the time being": Western Samoa's working committee on self-government, 1959-62. Universal suffrage, a constitutional compromise', MA thesis, University of Auckland, 1988.

Tātupu Fa'afetai Matā'afa Tu'i. 'Lāuga: the practice and principles of Samoan oratory', MA thesis, University of Auckland, 1986.

Morgan A. Tuimaleali'ifano. 'The Samoans in Fiji: social and cultural change in a Pacific island migrant community from a historical perspective', MA thesis, University of the South Pacific, 1987.

Eteuati Tuioti. 'Ecclesiastical growth of the Methodist church in Samoa, with special reference to leadership development', BD thesis, Pacific Theological College, 1984.

Lui Talusa Tuitele. 'A study to determine the leadership behavior of American Samoa public school principals', EdD thesis, Brigham Young University, 1983.

Falaniko Chan Tung. 'Monetary developments in independent Western Samoa', MEc thesis, University of New England, 1978.

Leulu Felise Va'a. 'The parables of a Samoan divine: an analysis of Samoan texts of the 1860s', MA thesis, Australian National University, 1987.

Edward N. Vargo. 'A historical study of the educational television system in American Samoa from 1961-1983', EdD thesis, Texas Technical University, 1983.

Bernard E. Vogler. 'Carl Schurz and the German-American conflict, in relation to Samoa, 1887-1889', MA thesis, Catholic University of America, 1941.

Arnfinn M. Vonen. 'The noun phrase in Samoan and Tokelauan', CandPhilol thesis, University of Oslo, 1988.

James Dean Waterhouse. 'Political advancement in Western Samoa: tradition vs progress', MA thesis, University of Auckland, 1974.

Theses on Samoa and the Samoans

A. L. Watkins. 'Samoan speech: some linguistic features of the speech of Samoan adolescents', MA thesis, University of Auckland, 1976.

Raymond Frederick Watters. 'The geography of Samoa about 1840: a study in historical geography', PhD thesis, University of London, 1956.

Alfred Weck. 'Deutschlands Politik in der Samoa-Frage', DPhil thesis, Universität Leipzig, 1934.

Donna Schimeneck Weimer. 'A rhetorical analysis of a scientific controversy: Margaret Mead versus Derek Freeman in cultural anthropology', PhD thesis, Pennsylvania State University, 1990.

M. Weishaar. 'The fertility of Samoan migrants in Hawaii', MA thesis, Pennsylvania State University, 1976.

Ruby Welch. 'Ethnicity amongst Auckland Mormons (Samoans, Tongans)', MA thesis, University of Auckland, 1989.

Albert Wendt. 'Guardians and wards: a study of the origins, causes and first two years of the Mau movement in Western Samoa', MA thesis, Victoria University of Wellington, 1965.

Felix Schulter Wendt. 'A strategy for the development of pre-tertiary level agricultural education in Western Samoa', PhD thesis, Cornell University, 1974.

Ralph Wesseling. 'The effect of being bilingual, in English and Samoan, on reading acquisition', MA thesis, University of Auckland, 1994.

Sharon White Weston. 'Samoan social organization: structural implications of an ambilineal descent system', PhD thesis, University of California (Los Angeles), 1972.

Wayne Arthur Whistler. 'A study of the vegetation of Eastern Samoa', PhD thesis, University of Hawai'i, 1979.

F. A. Wilson. 'Agricultural development, rural change and government policy in small dependent economies: an analysis of post-independence planning in Western Samoa', PhD thesis, University of Bradford, 1992.

Elizabeth Wright. 'Petrology and geochemistry of shield-building and post-erosional lava series of Samoa: implications for mantle heterogeneity and magma genesis', PhD thesis, University of California (San Diego), 1986.

Monica Elizabeth Yost. 'The Samoans of the Nanakuli-Makaha area of Oahu, Hawaii', MA thesis, University of Hawai'i, 1965.

Franklin Arthur Young. 'Stability and change in Samoa', PhD thesis, University of Oregon, 1972.

Chronology

c 1200-1000 BC	Human settlement in Samoa
c 1500 AD	Salamāsina recognized as supreme ruler of Samoa
1722	Jacob Roggeveen sights Ta'ū
1768	Louis-Antoine de Bougainville names the islands *Archipel des Navigateurs* (Navigators' Archipelago)
1787	Seamen of the La Pérouse expedition killed at Ā'asu, Tutuila
1791	HMS *Pandora* (Captain Edward Edwards) visits Tutuila, 'Upolu and Savai'i in search of the mutineers of HMS *Bounty*. Savai'i named Chatham Island
1819	Louis de Freycinet sights Samoa's easternmost atoll, naming it Rose Island, after his wife
1824	Otto von Kotzebue visits Rose Island (naming it Kordinkoff Island), Manu'a, Tutuila, 'Upolu, later warning seaman against venturing among 'these treacherous cannibals'
1828	Spontaneous expansion of Wesleyanism from Tongatabu to Savai'i
1830	John Williams and Charles Barff of the London Missionary Society land from the schooner *Messenger of Peace* at Sapapāli'i, Savai'i Influenza introduced by the *Messenger of Peace*
1832	John Williams lands near Leone, Tutuila, on his second visit to Samoa

1834	First printing in the Samoan language
1835	Rev. P. Turner is the first Wesleyan minister and the first European missionary resident in Samoa, withdrawing in 1839
1836	Whaling vessels begin to call at Āpia
1836-1900	Conversion of the majority of Samoans to Christianity
1837	First major influenza epidemic
1838	Captain Bethune of HMS *Conway* concludes a commercial treaty with the leading Samoan chiefs
	Dumont d'Urville visits 'Upolu
1839	First printing press set up at Falelātai by LMS missionaries
	Charles Wilkes of the United States Exploring Expedition makes a treaty securing the right to enter Pago Pago harbour, to buy stores and refit, for all American vessels
1840	The first European settlers arrive in Samoa
1845	Roman Catholic mission started
	The Samoan Reporter first published
1847	George Pritchard, a former LMS missionary who had been British Consul in Tahiti, appointed as first British Consular Agent in Āpia, to be succeeded in 1856 by his son, William T. Pritchard
	William T. Pritchard establishes the first permanent European store
1848-53	Sporadic warfare in Manono, 'Upolu and Savai'i
1850	European-owned commercial plantations begin to develop
1853	The first United States Commercial Agent to Samoa appointed
1854	Foreign Residents Society formed by non-Samoans, to govern the Āpia waterfront area from Sogi to Matautu
1856	Eli Jennings, an American with a Samoan wife, claims title to Swain's Island
	William T. Pritchard becomes British Consular Agent
	August Unshelm, representative of the Hamburg firm Johann Cäsar Godeffroy und Sohn, opens its first Samoan branch at Matofele

	William Fox, an English trader, murdered by a young Samoan chief on Savai'i
1857	Wesleyan Mission (AWMS) resumes its work in Samoa, using four Tongan teachers
1858	John C. Williams, son of the pioneer LMS missionary, becomes British Consul
1859	HMS *Cordelia* makes a punitive visit to Savai'i, destroying houses and canoes and hanging the alleged murderer of William Fox
1860	Death of Malietoa Moli, humiliated by the British, precipitates wars of confederation
1861	Hamburg appoints a representative in Āpia, later to become German Consular Agent Theodor Weber arrives in Samoa
1863	J. C. Godeffroy und Sohn acquire twelve acres of land at Mulifanua. By 1868 the company owned 2,500 acres
1864	August Unshelm drowned. Theodor Weber takes control of J. C. Godeffroy und Sohn
1868-87	(with interruptions) Malietoa Laupepa is supreme ruler of Samoa
1869-73	Warring Samoans alienate land to Europeans in return for firearms. Sporadic civil wars occur
1870	Franco-Prussian War brings J. C. Godeffroy und Sohn to bankruptcy
1871	Marist Brothers begin work at Āpia USA gains exclusive rights to a coaling station at Pago Pago, first used in 1889
1873	Malietoa Laupepa heads the confederal government set up at Mulinu'u, advised by Colonel A. B. Steinberger
1874	British residents in Samoa press for annexation of Samoa by Britain
1875	Constitution of an independent Samoan state finalized, with Colonel A. B. Steinberger as premier
1876	Colonel A. B. Steinberger deported to Fiji Skirmish in March at Mulinu'u between the Ta'imua and Faipule (who had ousted Malietoa Laupepa in February 1876) and a naval landing party from HMS *Barracouta* (backing Malietoa Laupepa). Three sailors are killed and Samoan casualties are 'numerous'

1878	Godeffroy company in Samoa reconstituted as the DHPG, controlling all Godeffroy assets in the Western Pacific
	Treaty of Friendship with the USA
1878-79	Britain, Germany and USA establish naval stations
1879	Municipality of Āpia established
	Pulefou government established at Mulinu'u, headed by Malietoa Talavou
	Treaty of Friendship between the German Kaiser and the *Ta'imua* government
1882	W. B. Churchward appointed as British Consul, serving until 1885
1885	LDS (Mormon) Mission established
1886	Anglo-German agreement defines respective spheres of influence in the Pacific
1887	Malietoa Laupepa exiled to the German colony of the Marshall Islands
1888	Church of Jesus Christ of Latter-Day Saints formed in Western Samoa
	Tridominium crisis, as Germany tries to re-establish Tamasese by intervention with a naval force
1888-89	Mata'afa rules Samoa, amidst a new outbreak of civil war
1889	Samoa Act of 1889 proclaims Malietoa as 'king', protected by all three foreign powers
	Treaty of Berlin establishes tripartite administration of all Samoa, lasting to 1899 when Britain withdrew
	Eastern Samoa declared neutral territory
	Hurricane wrecks German and American warships in Āpia harbour. Only HMS *Calliope* escaped
1890	Church of Seventh-Day Adventists (SDA) established
1892	R. L. Stevenson publishes *A footnote to history*, 'an honest examination of the plight of the islands'
1899	Villages shelled by British warships
	Samoa partitioned between Germany and the USA, which establishes a naval base at Pago Pago. From January to May Malietoa rules as the last internationally recognized king of all Samoa

1900	Treaty of Berlin of November 1899 ratified by USA. Eastern Samoa placed under the jurisdiction of the Secretary of the US Navy. Tutuila and ʻAunuʻu formally ceded to USA by their *matai*. United States flag raised on 17 April (ʻFlag Day')
	In February, Kaiser Wilhelm II issues an order constituting Western Samoa a German *Schutzgebiet* (protectorate), with Dr Wilhelm Solf as its first governor. The red, white and black flag of the German Empire is hoisted at Mulinuʻu. On 15 August all chiefs of German Samoa are summoned to Mulinuʻu to take the oath of allegiance to the Kaiser
1902-03	Planters' Association in Western Samoa introduces Chinese labour, under contracts, for plantation work
1903-04	Slump in copra prices
1904	Manuʻa islands of Taʻū, Ofu and Olosega, and Rose Atoll formally ceded to USA by Tui Manuʻa and their *matai*
1904-05	*ʻOloa kumpani* movement attempts to set up business ventures for the benefit of Samoans. This was the first overt resistance to German rule
1905	Volcanic eruption of Matāvanu, Savaiʻi, continuing intermittently until 1911.
	Fono a faipule set up at Mulinuʻu, with twenty-seven members appointed by governor Wilhelm Solf
1908	*Mau a Pule* (ʻLauaki *Mau*') movement, based in Savaiʻi, established to resist German rule
1909	*Mau a Pule* head, Lauaki (Lauati) Namulauʻulu Mamoe, leads thousands of armed warriors to Āpia in January 1909, to try to influence government policy
	Wilhelm Solf exiles Lauaki and nine other *Mau a Pule* leaders (with their families) to the German colony of Saipan, for ʻinciting rebellion against the German administration'
1910	O. F. Nelson and S. H. Meredith petition the Reichstag for some form of local council for German Samoa
	Tupua Tamasese visits Germany (1910-11) where he is received by Ludwig of Bavaria and is presented to Kaiser Wilhelm II

1911	Matāvanu, Savai'i, erupts for the last time. Sale'aula, Savai'i buried by molten lava. Its homeless population found the village of Salamumu on 'Upolu's south coast
1914	On 29 August 1914 Dr Erich Schultz-Ewerth, governor of German Samoa, surrenders to the New Zealand Expeditionary Force under Lieutenant-Colonel Robert Logan. Occupation and military administration, using the structures introduced by the Germans, continued to the end of 1920. Samoan leaders establish the Toea'ina Club in Āpia
1915	Lauaki (Lauati) Namulau'ulu Mamoe dies at sea while returning from exile in Saipan, on 14 November 1915
	Hurricane devastates Manu'a, damaging food crops so severely that two-thirds of the population are taken to Tutuila until their houses and gardens can be restored
1918	Dr Mabel Christie and a New Zealand medical team begin to set up village women's committees (*komiti tumamā*) to improve public health
	In November, the New Zealand passenger and cargo vessel S. S. *Talune*, from Auckland via Fiji, introduces pneumonic ('Spanish') influenza. This spreads through 'Upolu and Savai'i, killing many thousands of people, estimated at at least twenty-two per cent of the total population. Logan is blamed for failing to quarantine Western Samoa. American Samoa escaped the influenza epidemic, thanks to the Governor's timely imposition of a strict quarantine on all vessels entering the port of Pago Pago
1919	New Zealand resumes recruitment of Chinese indentured labourers for Western Samoa (where 838 of previous intake still worked on the plantations of 'Upolu and Savai'i). At a *fono* to welcome the incoming Resident Administrator of Western Samoa, Colonel R. W. Tate, Samoan leaders plead to be handed over to the American administration at Pago Pago or to be administered by the British Colonial Office - but on no account by New Zealand

	American naval personnel are forbidden to marry Samoan women without the personal consent of the Governor of American Samoa
1920	On 17 December Western Samoa becomes a League of Nations Class C mandate, to be administered by New Zealand
	Military administration ends, *Fono a faipule* asks that two Samoan members should be allowed to sit in the New Zealand Parliament. The Samoa Act, 1920, is challenged by the Citizens' Committee and by *Fono a faipule*
1921	Samoa Act, 1921, formalizes New Zealand's obligations under the Class C mandate for Western Samoa
	In June, Samoan *matai* petition King George V (*Tupu sili*), in whom the mandate was ultimately vested, expressing their dissatisfaction with New Zealand rule
1923	Western Samoa Amendment Act, 1923 gives statutory recognition to *Fono a faipule* and allows local Europeans to elect their representatives on Legislative Council. O. F. Nelson, A. Williams and G. E. L. Westbrook elected
1925	American Samoa assumes administrative responsibility for Olohega (Swain's Island)
1926	*Samoa Guardian* published by O. F. Nelson. Coalition formed between Samoans and local Europeans
1926-36	*'O le Mau* (Samoan League) resistance movement in Western Samoa, led by O. F. Nelson, rejects external control and asserts 'Samoan capacity for autonomy within the sphere of traditional authority'. Forcefully suppressed in 1930
1927	New Zealand government sets up a Royal Commission, under the Chief Justice, to inquire into the failure of the administration of Western Samoa
1928	O. F. Nelson banished
1929	USA formally assumes sovereignty over Eastern Samoa
	On 'Black Saturday', 28 December, New Zealand police open machine-gun fire on a peaceful *Mau* procession in Āpia, killing Tupua Tamasese Lealofi III and ten other Samoans

1930	Warship sent to arrest *Mau* leaders. *'O le Mau* suppressed
1932	*Fono* of American Samoa forbids the holding of *matai* titles by anyone of less than three-quarter Samoan ancestry
1933	*Mau* leader O. F. Nelson returns to Āpia on 20 May 1933 after exile since 1928
1934	Persons of mixed race (*'afakasi*) in Western Samoa legally forbidden to hold *matai* titles
1935	Legislation declaring *Mau* to be a 'seditious organization' repealed
1936	September *Fono a faipule* elections result in election (out of 39) of 33 *Mau* supporters, two *Mau* officials, and only four supporters of the Western Samoan administration
1939	Death of Malietoa Tanumafili I
1941-45	Pago Pago a major naval base in the war with Japan
1942	On 11 January, a Japanese submarine shells Pago Pago from behind the mountains to the north
	About 40,000 US Marines occupy Western Samoa, as a protective garrison
1946	United Nations Trust Territory of Western Samoa, administered by New Zealand (the League of Nations mandatory authority since 1920)
1947	Legislative Assembly (*Fono*) created in Western Samoa, with forty-five members chosen by *matai* suffrage, two by universal suffrage. Western Samoa Council of State set up, consisting of the New Zealand High Commissioner (formerly Administrator) as president and the two leading Samoan chiefs holding office as *fautua* (adviser)
	First United Nations Mission to Western Samoa
1951	Pago Pago naval base dismantled. Thirteen hundred American Samoans emigrate to Hawai'i. US Department of the Interior takes over administration of American Samoa from US Navy
1954	Western Samoan constitutional convention adopts plan for internal self-government
	Van Camp Seafood Company opens a tuna cannery at Pago Pago, supplied by Japanese fishermen
	Local government established on Swain's Island

1954-60	Measures of internal self-government gradually introduced in Western Samoa, culminating in adoption of an independence constitution by a constitutional assembly held in October 1960
1955	Inter-Samoan Consultative Committee established
	American Samoa exempted from Fair Labor Standards Act, to promote economic development
1956	Executive committee established in Western Samoa, to govern with the High Commissioner
	Peter Tali Coleman appointed governor of American Samoa on 15 October
1957	Parliament of elected district representatives established in Western Samoa
	New Zealand returns to the people of Western Samoa all the land and assets of the reparation estates, once German-owned
1959	Bank of Western Samoa formed, of which seventy-five per cent owned by the ANZ Banking Group and twenty-five per cent by the Government of Western Samoa
	Polynesian Airlines (Holdings) Ltd. incorporated, owned by the Government of Western Samoa
	In October, Fiame Mata'afa becomes Western Samoa's first prime minister, in its first cabinet government
1960	American Samoa becomes an 'unincorporated and unorganized territory' of the USA. Constitution promulgated (revised six years later)
	In October, a constitutional assembly adopts an Independence Constitution for Western Samoa
1961	Plebiscite in May, supervised by the United Nations, approves the Western Samoa Independence Constitution of October 1960
1962	On 1 January Western Samoa achieves full political sovereignty, the first independent Polynesian state. On 1 August Western Samoa and New Zealand sign a Treaty of Friendship
	American Samoa's education system completely reorganized

	American Samoa Development Corporation formed by private Samoan interests
	Pago Pago International Airport opened at Tafuna, Tutuila
1963	Tupua Tamasese dies on 5 April 1963
	Malietoa Tanumafili II becomes sole Head of State of Western Samoa for life
	Star Kist tuna cannery and a can-manufacturing plant opened in Pago Pago
1964	Instructional television (ITV), initially serving elementary schools, begins on 4 October 1964 in American Samoa, from KVZK-TV Utulei, the non-commercial station owned by the Government of American Samoa
1965	Mount ʻAlava cable car built across Pago Pago Harbour
1966	Most cash and food crops in Western Samoa damaged by hurricane on 29 January
	Instructional television extended to all secondary schools in American Samoa
1967	*Fono a Ekalesia i Samoa* (Samoa Council of Churches) formed in Western Samoa
1969	American-based logging company, Potlatch Forests Inc., leases 28,000 acres in Western Samoa
	Future Political Status Study Commission set up in American Samoa
	Government-owned, not-for-profit Development Bank of American Samoa founded
	Airport terminal built and landing facilities upgraded at Faleolo, eighteen miles from Āpia
1970	Western Samoa joins the Commonwealth
	National Spiritual Assembly of Samoa (Bahá'i) formed
1971	American Samoa Community College founded and educational system reorganized
	Commercial television introduced in American Samoa
1972	*Fale Fono*, Western Samoa's new Parliament House, opened at Mulinuʻu
1973	American Samoa's *Maota Fono* completed in Fagatogo, at cost of US $1 million

1974	Development Bank of Western Samoa established by government, to promote economic and social development Territorial Administration on Aging (TAOA) established in American Samoa, administering federal and local government funds for programmes for the aged, including one to encourage retention of traditional craft skills in weaving and carving A Samoan is appointed as director of the American Samoan public school system
1975	University of the South Pacific School of Agriculture established at Alafua, ‘Upolu Car ferry links ‘Upolu and Savai‘i. A larger ferry is donated by Australian government in 1977
1976	Western Samoa joins the United Nations
1977	On 8 November American Samoans elect their own governor for the first time, after years of declining to do so Western Samoa's first independent bank, Pacific Commercial Bank Ltd., established, jointly owned by Westpac Banking Corporation (Australia), Bank of Hawaìi International Inc. (USA) and private Western Samoan interests (14.6%)
1978	Peter Tali Coleman inaugurated in January as American Samoa's first elected governor *‘O le Pupu-Pu‘e* National Park created in Western Samoa
1979	Human Rights Protection Party (HRPP) formed, as Western Samoa's first formal political party. Amerika Samoa Bank (commercial) founded Palolo Deep, north of Āpia, declared a protected Marine Reserve
1980	Treaty of Tokehega signed in December, delimiting the sea boundary between New Zealand and USA in the waters around Tokelau
1981	Formation of Western Samoa Public Services Association (WSPSA), affiliated to the International Confederation of Free Trade Unions (ICFTU) WSPSA calls Western Samoa's first strike (for higher wages) lasting three months and precipitating severe government crisis

1982	Constitutional crisis in Western Samoa, with three prime ministers within one year
	Opposition Human Rights Protection Party (HRPP) wins 24 of 47 seats in Western Samoa's *Fono* elections in February 1982
	Citizenship (Western Samoa) Act, 1982
1982-85	Crown of thorns starfish (*alamea*) causes serious damage to coral reefs (previous outbreaks in 1967-70, 1977-80)
1983	Treaty of Tokehega of December 1980 ratified by New Zealand and USA despite dissent in Tokelau
	Economic adjustment programme adopted in Western Samoa, limiting government spending, restricting imports, and devaluing the *tala*
1984	National University of Western Samoa established
	Constitutional Convention in American Samoa
	Central Bank of Samoa established in Āpia
1985	South Pacific Nuclear-Free Zone Treaty (Treaty of Rarotonga) signed by Western Samoa
	Human Rights Protection Party (HRPP) wins 31 of 47 seats in Western Samoa's *Fono* elections in February 1985, increasing its majority from one to fifteen
1986	Constitution of American Samoa comprehensively revised by Constitutional Convention
	Western Samoa and American Samoa sign memorandum of understanding, establishing a permanent committee to ensure mutual economic development
1987	Manu'a group declared a disaster area on 18 January, after Hurricane Tusi leaves 2,000 people homeless
1988	Samoan National Development Party (SNDP) founded in Western Samoa as a coalition comprising the Christian Democratic Party (CDP) and several independents
	American Samoa National Park designated, including much of Ta'ū, part of Ofu, and a large area of the northern slopes of Tutuila
	Agricultural Development in the American Pacific (ADAP) Program instituted

1989 Severe financial crisis in American Samoa
In May, New Zealand agrees to continue quota of 1,100 migrants a year from Western Samoa
Tourism brings 55,000 visitors to Western Samoa, 47,188 to American Samoa
In October, Western Samoa sets up its first Environment Department

1990 Western Samoa embassy opened in Washington, DC. (Closed in 1993 due to financial mismanagement)
Pay cuts for 3,800 government employees and price freeze in American Samoa. Budgetary deficit estimated at US $17.7 million
In February, Cyclone Ofa makes an estimated 10,000 people homeless in Western Samoa
'O le Si'osi'omaga Society formed in Āpia in July, dedicated to conservation and environmental protection
Western Samoa referendum in October votes for universal suffrage by all citizens of 21 years of age or over. Only *matai* to stand for election
American Samoa referendum in November rejects a proposal to restrict the Governor's power of veto in legislative matters, by a 75 per cent majority. Peter Tali Coleman proposes autonomy for American Samoa
In December 1990 Western Samoa's *Fono* approves a bill to implement universal suffrage, despite strong opposition by the Samoan National Development Party (SNDP)
Samoa Land Corporation formed in Āpia

1991 Tourism Council of the South Pacific proposes ten-year development plan for tourism in Western Samoa, current earnings from which were estimated at double those from exports
Yazaki multinational company sets up a factory in Western Samoa to produce electrical equipment for cars
Āpia port facilities improved, funded by aid from Japan
Following dissolution of *Fono* in February, Western Samoa's first election based on universal suffrage held on 5 April, with an estimated

80,000 newly enfranchised voters. HRPP wins 30 seats, SNDP 16, independents 3

In May 1991 Fiame Naomi appointed as Western Samoa's first woman cabinet member

Western Samoa's ruling HRPP initiates constitutional changes, increasing the parliamentary term from three to five years, creating two additional seats, and adding four new ministers with seats in cabinet

Western Samoa census on 3 November records a total population of 159,862

In December Cyclone Val devastates infrastructure, buildings and crops in American Samoa and Western Samoa, killing thirteen people and large numbers of animals. Almost all official buildings and 90 per cent of dwellings damaged, along with fields and plantations. Damage in Western Samoa estimated at 662 million *tala*

1992 HRPP wins two newly established seats in Western Samoa's *Fono*

Concern expressed in Western Samoa at decline in inshore fishing catch, from an estimated 1,890 metric tons in 1989 to 565 metric tons in 1991

Western Samoa introduces a programme to attract foreign investment, in export-led manufacturing and in tourism. Wire factory opened by a Japanese company, garment factory by an American company

Two of Western Samoa's three plants processing coconut cream closed, as a consequence of lower coconut production caused by cyclone devastation

In June 1992 population of American Samoa estimated at 39,000, with about 85,000 American Samoans resident in USA

Delegate of American Samoa to US House of Representatives elected in November 1992

On 3 November A. P. Lutali elected as Governor of American Samoa. Severe cuts in number of government employees, to reduce budgetary expenditure

1993 In March, Samoa Democratic Party (SDP) formed in Western Samoa by the independent *Fono* member Sir Tagiloa Peter

Television Western Samoa launched on 29 May 1993, owned by the Western Samoa Government and operated with commercial sponsorship by Television New Zealand. By 1996 Television Samoa had six transmitters in use

Three HRPP members of Western Samoa's *Fono* expelled from their party for recommending reduction in government expenditure, and for advocating a change of government

Virulent fungal taro-leaf blight (*Phytophthora colocasiae*) spreads through Western Samoa and American Samoa, and emergency spraying programme begun. State of disaster declared in Tutuila

1994 Australian and Samoan interests plan development of 'eco-tourism', based on appreciation and conservation of Western Samoa's natural environment

Intention announced to establish a trade union for private sector workers in Western Samoa

In January, imposition of Value Added Tax (VAT) on goods and services in Western Samoa greatly increases cost of food and fuel, provoking protest rallies and demonstrations. In March Government agrees to amend VAT rules

In March, four members of Western Samoa's *Fono*, including three expelled from the HRPP, establish the Samoa Liberal Party (SLP), led by the former Speaker, Nonumalo Leulumoega Sofara

Western Samoa's national airline in financial crisis in May, with services disrupted and with debts estimated at over 45 million *tala*. In July Western Samoa's Chief Auditor accuses Government of serious financial mismanagement of Polynesian Airlines. Several cabinet ministers charged with fraud and financial negligence, and Commission of Enquiry formed to investigate

1995 Western Samoa's Central Bank eases restrictions on foreign exchange transactions, following strong recovery in agriculture and manufacturing and continued growth in tourism

Western Samoa reportedly losing the fight against the Giant African Snail, which defoliates crops. The snail is thought to have been introduced from American Samoa in 1990

Australia gives Western Samoa A$600,000 'for policy and management reform', to encourage good resource management

US House of Representatives passes bill allowing the Government of American Samoa (rather than the US State Department) to collect fees from foreign vessels fishing within the Territory's exclusive economic zone (EEZ)

1996

Western Samoa's Agriculture Department bans imports of taro in March, to assist local efforts to grow the plant

Samoa All People's Party is set up in March, led by Matatumua Maimoaga, one of the two women in Western Samoa's *Fono*

Western Samoa Art and Crafts Fair is held in March, dedicated to reviving ancient designs and traditions

In April, Governor A. P. Lutali of American Samoa questions the high air fares charged by Hawaiian Airlines between American Samoa and the United States

Greenpeace Pacific releases in April a study of Western Samoa's electricity needs which recommends a radical change in power-generation methods

Western Samoa's Prime Minister Tofilau Eti Alesana wins another five-year term in office in May, to become the longest-serving prime minister in the South Pacific

Governor A. P. Lutali proposes legislation in June for a government-run lottery to raise money for sports, education and public health

In June, Western Samoa's Supreme Court find former *Fono* Speaker Afamasaga Fanu and Toalepa'iali'i Toeosulululu, the leader of the Samoa Labour Party and Fanu's political rival, both guilty of corrupt electoral practices

Western Samoa's Prime Minister Tofilau Eti Alesana receives medical attention in New Zealand in July following surgery in Australia to remove a liver tumour

Tavui Lene, a member of Western Samoa's *Fono*, loses her seat in July after the Supreme Court found that she illegally retained voter identification cards

In July, an agreement signed by Western Samoa and China, coming into force on 1 July 1997. Western Samoa citizens and holders of Hong Kong passports issued by China may visit each other's countries without visas, for up to thirty days

Administrators of Samoa, 1900-97

German Samoa 1900-14

Western Samoa became a German protectorate in 1900.

Governors:
Dr Wilhelm Heinrich Solf (1900-11)
Dr Erich Schultz (1911-14)

Western Samoa 1914-97

Western Samoa was occupied by New Zealand forces 1914-18. From 1919 it was administered by New Zealand under a League of Nations (later United Nations) mandate. In 1959 self-government was attained, followed by independence on 1 January 1962, as Samoa i Sisifo/Western Samoa.

Administrators and High Commissioners 1914-62:
Colonel Robert Logan (1914-19)
Colonel R. W. Tate (1920-23)
Major General G. S. Richardson (1923-28)
Colonel Stephen Allen (1928-31)
Brigadier General Herbert E. Hart (1931-35)
Alfred Turnbull (Acting 1934-43, Administrator 1943-46)
Lieutenant Colonel F. W. Voelcker (1946-49)
Guy R. Powles (1949-62)

Heads of State 1962-97:
The Independence Constitution provided for two traditional rulers to act as joint Heads of State.

Tupua Tamasese Mea'ole (January 1962-April 1963)
Malietoa Tanumafili II (January 1962-April 1963)

In 1963 Malietoa Tanumafili II became Head of State for life, performing duties akin to those of a constitutional monarch.

Malietoa Tanumafili II (April 1963-)

Deputy Head of State (1995):
Mata'afa Fa'asuamaleaui Puela

Prime Ministers 1959-97:
Fiame Mata'afa Mulinu'u II (October 1959-March 1970)
Tupua Tamasese Leolofi IV (March 1970-March 1973)
Fiame Mata'afa Mulinu'u II (March 1973-May 1975)
Tupua Tamasese Leolofi IV (May 1975-March 1976)
Tupuola Taisi Efi (March 1976-February 1982)
Va'ai Kolone (February 1982-September 1982)
Tupuola Taisi Efi (September 1982-December 1982)
Tofilau Eti Alesana (December 1982-December 1985)
Va'ai Kolone (January 1986-February 1988)
Tofilau Eti Alesana (April 1988-February 1991)
Tofilau Eti Alesana (May 1991-)

American Samoa 1900-97

Tutuila and 'Aunu'u were formally ceded to the United States of America in 1900, by their *matai*. Cession of Ta'ū, Olosega, Ofu and Rose Atoll (Manu'a District) followed in 1904. Swain's Island came under United States administration as part of American Samoa in 1925. Administration by the US Department of the Navy was replaced by that of the US Department of the Interior in 1951.

US Naval Governors 1900-51:
Commander B. R. Tilley (1900-01)
Captain U. Sebree (1901-02)
Lieutenant Commander H. Minett (Acting 1902-04)
Commander E. B. Underwood (1904-05)
Commander C. B. T. Moors (1905-08)
Captain John F. Parker (1908-10)
Commander W. M. Gross (1910-13)
Lieutenant N. W. Post (1913-14)
Commander C. V. Stearns (1914)
Lieutenant N. W. Post (Acting 1914)
Lieutenant C. A. Woodruff (Acting 1914-15)
Commander John M. Poyer (1915-19)

Commander Warren J. Terhune (1919-20)
Captain Waldo Evans (1920-22)
Captain Edwin T. Pollock (1922-23)
Captain Edward S. Kellogg (1923-25)
Captain Henry F. Bryan (1925-27)
Captain Stephen V. Graham (1927-29)
Captain Gatewood S. Lincoln (1929-31)
Commander James S. Spore (1931)
Lieutenant Commander Arthur Emerson (Acting 1931)
Captain Gatewood S. Lincoln (1931-32)
Captain George B. Landergerber (1932-34)
Lieutenant Commander T. C. Latimore (Acting 1934)
Captain Otto Dowling (1934-36)
Lieutenant Commander T. B. Fitzpatrick (Acting 1936)
Captain MacGillvray Milne (1936-38)
Captain Edward Hanson (1938-40)
Lieutenant Commander J. R. Wallace (Acting 1940)
Captain Lawrence Wild (1940-42)
Captain John G. Moyer (1942-44)
Captain Allen Hobbs (1944-45)
Captain Ralph W. Hungerford (1945)
Commander Samuel W. Cana (Acting 1945)
Captain Harold A. Houser (1945-47)
Captain Vernon Huber (1947-49)
Captain Thomas F. Darden (1949-51)

Civil Governors 1951-78:
Phelps Phelps (1951-52)
John C. Elliott (1952)
James Arthur Ewing (1952-53)
Lawrence M. Judd (1953)
Richard B. Lowe (1953-56)
Peter Tali Coleman (1956-61)
H. Rex Lee (1961-67)
Owen S. Aspinall (1967-69)
John M. Haydon (1969-74)
Frank C. Mockler (Acting 1974-75)
Earl B. Ruth (1975-76)
Frank Barnett (Acting 1977-78)

Elected Governors 1978-97:
Peter Tali Coleman (1978-84)
A. P. Lutali (1985-89)
Peter Tali Coleman (1989-93)
A. P. Lutali (1993-)

Elected Lieutenant-Governors 1978-97:
- Tufele Li'a (1978-84)
- Faleomavaega Eni Hunkin Jr. (1984-88)
- Galea'i Poumele (1988-93)
- Tauese P. Sunia (1993-)

Glossary of Samoan Terms

With acknowledgement to G. B. Milner's *Samoan dictionary*, 1966.

'Afakasi — Part-European, person of mixed race (also *totolua*).

Aga — Conduct, behaviour, social norm, social agreement (linked to social roles and appropriate contexts). *cf. āmio*.

Agānu'u — Custom(s), local customary usage.

'Āiga — Nuclear family, extended family, kin, lineage, descent group.

'Āiga potopoto — Collective term for all the members of a lineage who have the right to be present at, and to take part in, the election of a new *matai*.

Aitu — Spirit, ghost, demon.

Ali'i — Chief, lord, *matai* with an *ali'i* title. *Ali'i sili o Samoa*: supreme chief of Samoa.

Alofa — Love, affection (stressing social bonding and obligation); empathy, sympathy.

Āmio — Conduct, behaviour, habits, manners, ways; personal impulse; the actual behaviour of individuals as it emerges from personal drives and urges. *cf. aga*.

Atua — God (as revealed in Christ); god (heathen).

Aualuma — Semi-formal association of unmarried women in each village, concerned with reception of visitors, ministering to the *tāupou*, *'ava* ceremony, dances and other duties.

'Aumāga	*'Ava* attendants (chewers): society comprising all young, untitled men in a village, who carry out *matai* orders in large-scale projects such as planting, building and maintenance.
'Ava	Shrub (*Piper methysticum*); *kava*: a beverage made with the dried and pulverized root of the shrub mixed with water.
Fa'afāfine	Effeminate man or youth; transvestite, with female behavioural style. *NB*. not a homosexual.
Fa'alavelave	Anything which interferes with normal life and calls for special activity (from an accident to a celebration); important occasion or traditional ceremony; occasion for giving and receiving gifts; social occasion or entertainment.
Fa'alupega	Formal greeting; ceremonial style and address of a person or social group traditionally associated with a certain area. Usually refers to a village's most important titles and descent groups in strict order of precedence.
Fa'apālagi	European ways, culture, language (i.e. English) (*fa'apapālagi*).
Fa'a-Sāmoa	Samoan custom, ways and traditions. *'O le āmioga fa'a-Sāmoa*: Samoan custom, Samoan way of life.
Fa'asausauga	Night assembly, when old men discuss Samoan customs, legends and myths, primarily for the benefit of the young men of the village.
Fāgogo	Tale; fictional story incorporating a song (*tagi*); legendary or fabulous tale.
Faife'au	Pastor, clergyman or minister (usually Samoan).
Failāuga	Orator.
Faipule	Man or group of people exercising authority in a village; representative of all the *matai* of a political district; member of legislature.
Fale	House. *Fale'afa*: house built with sennit (i.e. in Samoan style); *fale fa'aāfolau*: long house; *falelalaga*: house where fine mats (*tōga*) are woven; *fale'oloa*: shop, store; *falesā* (*fale tāpua'i*): church or chapel building; *fale talimālō*: guest-house (traditional); *faletele*: round house (suitable for entertaining visitors and holding meetings).
Faleaitu	'House of spirits': Samoan comic sketch, skit, comic turn or play, clownery.

Fautasi — Large whale-boat with up to twenty-one pairs of oars.

Fautua — Intercessor, adviser, advocate (title given to the two Samoan leaders of highest rank).

Feagaiga — Agreement, contract, treaty, bond; special relationship (a kind of perpetual kinship) between two kin-groups.

Fono — Meeting, council, conference; *Fono a ʻEkālēsia i Sāmoa*: Samoa Council of Churches.

Gafa — Lineage, descent line, pedigree, genealogy.

ʻIe — Kind of pandanus, the leaf (*lauʻie*) of which is used for weaving fine mats; general name given to finely plaited mats and matting.

ʻIe tōga — Fine mat (the most valuable and significant object in Samoan custom).

Ifoga — Ceremonial request for forgiveness made by an offender and his kinsmen to those injured; ceremonial abasement; ceremonial reparation (e.g. for discovered adultery).

Komiti tumamā (komiti fafine) — Village women's committee (comprising all female residents), set up from 1918 onward to improve nutrition, public health, hygiene and sanitation.

Lāuga — Formal speech; oratory; ceremonial oration at the beginning of a *fono*.

Laulautasi — Customary presentation of food to distinguished travellers, *malaga* party, or housebuilders and carpenters. (Also known as *umufono*).

Lāvalava — Skirt-like, wrap-around garment.

Loto — Heart, feeling, emotion (as opposed to mind, intellect, reason).

Lotu — Act of worship (including prayer); church service; religious denomination's religious ceremony.

Maʻiaitu — Spirit possession; illness or condition said to be caused by temporary possession of a person by a ghost or a devil.

Malae — Open space in the middle of a village, 'village-green' (the political focus of a village).

Malaga — Ceremonial visit paid according to Samoan custom; inter-village visiting; party of travellers or visitors.

Mālamalama — Light, enlightenment; 'time of enlightenment', after the coming of Christianity to Samoa.

Mālō	Prevailing or dominant party (as opposed to *vāivai*, losing party); power in authority; government; Legislative Assembly; state. *'O le mālō 'o Sāmoa i Sisifo*: the state of Western Samoa.
Mana	Supernatural or sacred power (*c.f. pule*).
Mānaia	Son of an *ali'i* (chief); a special position which is institutionalized and endowed with certain ceremonial duties and privileges (*c.f. tāupou*); head of the group of young, untitled men (*'aumāga*).
Maota	House or residence of a titled *matai* (chief).
Matai	*Matai*, titled head of a Samoan extended family (*'āiga*), formally elected and honoured as such.
Mau o Pule	Samoan resistance movement, led by Lauaki (Lauati) Namulau'ulu Mamoe (d. 1915). A later movement (1926-36) was *'O le Mau*.
Nu'u	Village, settlement; village community (the basic political entity).
'Oloa	Goods (especially trade-goods); gifts by a bridegroom's family; men's gifts, traditionally consisting of food and implements of practical value, now often replaced by payments of money.
Papālagi, pālagi	European, white person.
Pe'a	Tattoo, tattooing (also *tatau*).
Pese	Song. *'O pese mai anamua*: song from Samoan antiquity; *'o pese fa'a-Sāmoa*: traditional Samoan song or music; *'o pese Sāmoa*: Samoan songs, both traditional songs and compositions in European styles.
Pisupo	Corned beef, salt beef, any kind of meat in tins (from English 'pea soup').
Pōula	Traditional night dance, largely (but not entirely) discontinued under missionary pressure, because of its explicitly erotic features.
Pōuliuli	Darkness; 'time of darkness', before the coming of Christianity to Samoa.
Pule	Authority, power; corporate body in authority; council of chiefs and orators; power associated largely with utilitarian activities; title given to six villages in Savai'i which have traditional privileges. *Pulenu'u*: *matai* appointed (with a small salary) to represent Government in a village; village mayor.

Sā Collective name of a kin-group or extended family: *Sā Nāfanua*, *Sā Soliā*, *Sā Tagaloa* (skilled housebuilders and canoe builders).

Sa'otama'ita'i Woman holding a title in her own right; wife of a chief; village maiden (*tāupou*).

Siapo Bark-cloth or clothing (made from bast of paper mulberry); tapa cloth.

Siva Samoan dance; formal dance at the centre of the dance floor.

Soifua Ceremonial greeting or farewell. *Tōfā, soifua*: good-bye.

Suafa (suafa matai) Name, title (a very important part of *'āiga* property. Every *'āiga* has a *matai* title and some have many).

Tafa'ifā Single person holding all four titles which together give full royal status. *Sā tafa'ifā Salamāsina* (Queen Salamāsina held the four titles).

Talanoaga Discussion, conversation; a relatively informal Samoan speech genre, following *lāuga* in a *fono*.

Taligā Ceremonial presentation of fine mats (*'O le taligā o tōga*).

Tālofa Form of general greeting. *Tālofa lava*.

Tama'āiga Term used since the 19th century to refer to the four titles now regarded in Western Samoa as paramount: Mālietoa, Matā'afa, Tuimaleali'ifano, Tupua Tamasese.

Tānoa Wooden bowl of distinctive shape, reserved for *'ava*.

Tapu Interdiction, taboo.

Tatau Man's tattoo, extending from the knees to the waist (*c.f. pe'a*).

Taulāitu (taula aitu) Spirit medium, diviner by supernatural possession; shaman.

Taulāsea Person skilled in the use of native medicines, traditional healer, 'bush-doctor'; doctor, medical practitioner.

Taule'ale'a Young man, youth; untitled man (as opposed to *matai*). (plural: taulele'a)

Tāupou Title of village maiden (ostensibly a virgin), usually the daughter of the highest-ranking chief in the village (not all villages have the right to appoint a *tāupou*). She mixes the *'ava*, straining it with *fau*, leads the dancing, and heads the

	aualuma (association of unmarried women). Female counterpart of *mānaia*.
Tautai	Master fisherman; captain of a boat or ship.
Tautala leaga	Intimate or informal way of speaking (associated with *āmio*), characterized by use of *k* rather than *t*, etc.
Tautala lelei	Formal way of speaking, associated with dignified and controlled occasions in which personal impulses (*āmio*) are subordinate to social needs and conventions (*aga*). It follows the style of the Samoan Bible, using *t* rather than *k*.
Tautua	Service and duties owed by untitled men and other dependents to a *matai*.
Tōfā	Goodbye, farewell.
Totolua	Person of mixed descent (*c.f.* *'afakasi*).
Tufuga	Craftsman, expert, specialist. *Tufuga faifale*: master housebuilder; *tufuga fauva'a*: skilled boat-builder; *tufuga tātatau*: tattooing specialist.
Tui	Ceremonial title of paramount chief of a whole district. *'O le Tui Manu'a*; *'o le Tui Ā'ana*.
Tuiga	Ceremonial head-dress made of tufts of hair, and bark-cloth, with an upper structure of sticks; decorated with mother-of-pearl (*tifa*) or mirrors.
Tulāfale	Orator, talking chief, *matai* who holds an orator's title; spokesman.
Tulāfono	Law, legislation; rule, regulation. *'O le fono faitulāfono*, Legislative Assembly.
Tupu	*Ali'i* recognized as paramount in a region or over all the islands of Samoa: sovereign, monarch.
Tupua	Family god or totem, embodied in a bird, fish, or animal.
Tusi Pa'ia	*'O le Tusi Pa'ia*: Holy Bible.
Umufono	Customary presentation of food; food provided by a *matai* to housebuilders and carpenters (also *laulautasi*).

Abbreviations and Acronyms

ACP	African, Caribbean, Pacific [states]
ACWMC	Australasian Conference of the Wesleyan Methodist Church
ADAB	Australian Development Assistance Bureau
ADB	Asian Development Bank
AIDAB	Australian International Development Assistance Board
ANL	Australian National Library
ANU	Australian National University
ANZCERTA	Australia New Zealand Closer Economic Relations Trade Agreement
APECO	Asia-Pacific Economic Cooperation Organisation
APNET	Asia Pacific Network of the International Forum for Social Sciences in Health
ASCC	American Samoa Community College
ASDC	American Samoa Development Corporation
ASPEI	Association of South Pacific Environmental Institutions
ATL	Alexander Turnbull Library
AWMS	Australian Wesleyan Missionary Society
BM	Bishop Museum
BPBM	Bernice P. Bishop Museum
BYU-H	Brigham Young University-Hawai'i
CBS	Central Bank of Samoa
CCCAS	Congregational Christian Church in American Samoa
CCCS	Congregational Christian Church in Samoa

CCH	Church College of Hawai'i
CCJS	Congregational Church of Jesus in Samoa
CCOP/SOPAC	Committee for Coordination of Joint Prospecting for Mineral Rights in South Pacific Offshore Areas
CDP	Christian Democratic Party
CER	closer economic relations(hip)
CFTC	Commonwealth Fund for Technical Cooperation
CMS	Central Medical School
CNPPA	World Conservation Union Commission for National Parks and Protected Areas
CO	Colonial Office
CPI	consumer price index
CPLPC	Central Polynesian Land and Plantation Company
CSIRO	Commonwealth Scientific and Industrial Research Organization
CSPS	Centre for South Pacific Studies
DAFF	Department of Agriculture, Forests and Fisheries
DBWS	Development Bank of Western Samoa
DHPG	Deutsche Handels- und Plantagen Gesellschaft der Südsee-Inseln
DSG	Deutsche Samoa-Gesellschaft
DVGB	District and Village Government Board
EA	Department of External Affairs
ECE	early childhood education
EEZ	exclusive economic zone; economic exclusion zone
EFKS	'Ekalesia Fa'apotopotoga Kerisiano i Samoa; Congregational Christian Church in Samoa (CCCS)
EIA	environmental impact assessment
EMS	'Ekalesia Metotisi i Samoa; Methodist Church in Samoa
ESCAP	Economic and Social Commission for Asia and the Pacific (ECAFE to 1974)
FCO	Foreign and Commonwealth Office
FFA	Forum Fisheries Agency
FPIN	Foundation of Pacific Island Nations
FRS	Foreign Residents' Society
HMAS	His Majesty's Australian Ship
HMNZS	His Majesty's New Zealand Ship
HRPP	Human Rights Protection Party

IPS	Institute of Pacific Studies
ISNAR	International Service for National Agricultural Research
IT	island territories
ITV	instructional television
JAWS	Journalists Association of Western Samoa
JCC	Joint Commercial Commission
JCG & S	J. C. Godeffroy und Sohn
JPH	*Journal of Pacific History*
JPS	*Journal of the Polynesian Society*
JSO	*Journal de la Société des Océanistes*
LDC	less-developed country
LDS	Church of Jesus Christ of Latter-day Saints
LMS	London Missionary Society
LTC	Land and Titles Court
MB	Marist Brothers
MC	Permanent Mandates Commission of the League of Nations
MIRAB	Migration, Remittances, Aid, and Bureaucracy
ML	Mitchell Library
MLA	Member of Legislative Assembly
MLC	Member of Legislative Council
MTC	Mālua Theological College
NDC	National Disaster Council
NIC	newly-industrializing country
NIE	newly-industrializing economy
NLNZ	National Library of New Zealand
NML	Nelson Memorial Library
NOSA	National Office of Samoan Affairs
NSA	National Spiritual Assembly (Bahá'i)
NUS	National University of Samoa
NZEF	New Zealand Expeditionary Force
NZLP	New Zealand Labour Party
NZPD	*New Zealand Parliamentary Debates*
NZSDL	New Zealand Samoan Defence League
NZSG	*New Zealand Samoa Guardian*
NZSU	New Zealand Seafarers' Union; New Zealand Seamen's Union
OCA/PAC	Oceans and Coastal Areas Programme Activity Centre
OTA	Office of Tokelau Affairs
OTIA	Office of Territorial and International Affairs, US Department of the Interior

PA	Planters' Association
PAA	Pacific Arts Association
Pacnews	Pacific News Service
PACON	Pacific Congress on Marine Science and Technology
Pambu	Pacific Manuscripts Bureau
Pawornet	Pacific Women's Communication/Information Network (PWICN)
PCC	Pacific Council of Churches
PCC	Polynesian Cultural Center
PCL	Progressive Citizens' League
PEACESAT	Pan-Pacific Education and Communications Experiments Using Satellites
PFL	Pacific Forum Line
PIALA	Pacific Islands Association of Libraries and Archives
PIBA	Pacific Islands Broadcasting Association
PIM	*Pacific Islands Monthly*
PIMA	Pacific Island Museum Association
PINA	Pacific Islands News Association
PIPC	Pacific Islands Presbyterian Church
PISC	Pacific Islands Study Circle of Great Britain
PISUKI	Pacific Islands Society of the United Kingdom and Ireland
PJA	Pacific Journalists Association
PJT	*Pacific Journal of Theology*
PMB	Pacific Manuscripts Bureau
PMC	Permanent Mandates Commission of the League of Nations
PNG	Papua New Guinea
PREMO	Prévention dans les Musées d'Océanie
PSA	Public Service Association
PTC	Pacific Theological College
PWICN	Pacific Women's Communication/Information Network (*Pawornet*)
RAN	Royal Australian Navy
RKolA	Reichskolonialamt
RLS	Robert Louis Stevenson
RMA	Reichsmarineamt
RMTCP	Regional Marine Turtle Conservation Programme
RNZN	Royal New Zealand Navy
RSPS	Research School of Pacific Studies
SCC	Samoa Council of Churches

SCE	single crop equivalent area
SDA	Seventh Day Adventist Church
SDC	Samoan District Committee of the London Missionary Society
SDL	Samoa Defence League
SDP	Samoan Democratic Party
SDR	special drawing rights
SEF	Samoa Expeditionary Force
SL	Samoan League
SMS	Samoan Mission Seminary
SMS	Seine Majestäts Schiff
SNDP	Samoa National Development Party
SOE	state-owned enterprise
SOPAC	South Pacific Applied Geosciences Commission
SOPACNEWS	South Pacific News Service Ltd.
SPACLALS	South Pacific Association for Commonwealth Literature & Language Studies
SPAFH	South Pacific Alliance for Family Health
SPARTECA	South Pacific Regional Trade and Economic Co-operation Agreement
SPATS	South Pacific Association of Theological Schools
SPC	South Pacific Commission
SPC	South Pacific Conference (1950-70)
SPCenCIID	South Pacific Centre for Communication and Information in Development
SPEC	South Pacific Bureau for Economic Co-operation
SPF	South Pacific Forum
SPFFA	South Pacific Forum Fisheries Agency
SPNFZT	South Pacific Nuclear-Free Zone Treaty
SPOCC	South Pacific Organisations Coordinating Committee
SPREP	South Pacific Regional Environment Programme
SRF	Samoa Reserve Force; Samoan Relief Fund
STABEX	stabilization of export earnings
SWL	Samoa Welfare League
TCSP	Tourism Council of the South Pacific
TIMS	Tokelau Island Migrant Study
TPS	Tokelau Public Service
UCP	United Citizens' Party
UCSB	University of California, Santa Barbara, California
UCSC	University of California, Santa Cruz, California
UH	University of Hawai'i

UNCED	United Nations Conference on the Environment and Development
UNCLDC	United Nations Conference on the Least Developed Countries
UNCTAD	United Nations Conference on Trade and Development
UNDP	United Nations Development Programme
UNEP	United Nations Environment Programme
UNEPRSP	United Nations Environment Programme Regional Seas Programme
UNFPA	United Nations Fund for Population Activities
UNSW	University of New South Wales
UNTTWS	United Nations Trust Territory of Western Samoa
UPNG	University of Papua New Guinea
USAID	United States Agency for International Development
USEE	United States Exploring Expedition
USMC	United States Marine Corps
USN	United States Navy
USP	University of the South Pacific
USP/SOA	University of the South Pacific School of Agriculture
USS	United States Ship
USSC	Union Steam Ship Company
VPB	Report of the Commission of Inquiry into the state of Samoa's public service, December 1928-January 1929 (Paul Verschaffelt, Alexander Park, Carl Berendsen)
VSA	Voluntary Service Abroad
WCC	World Council of Churches
WMMS	Wesleyan Methodist Missionary Society
WMO	World Meteorological Organization
WMS	Wesleyan Missionary Society
WPHC	Western Pacific High Commission
WSBS	Western Samoa Broadcasting Service
WSPSA	Western Samoan Public Service Association
WSRNA	Western Samoan Registered Nurses Association
WST	Western Samoan *tala* ($WS)
WSTEC	Western Samoa Trust Estates Corporation

More abbreviations and acronyms commonly used in the South Pacific region (with some older usages) may be found in the two following works: *The Australian dictionary of acronyms &*

abbreviations, by David J. Jones (Leura, New South Wales: Second Back Row Press, 1981. 2nd revised edition. 220p.); and *Pacific Index of abbreviations and acronyms in common use in the Pacific Basin area*, by Arthur E. E. Ivory (Christchurch, New Zealand: Whitcoulls Publishers, 1982. 370p.).

Samoa and the Samoans

Samoa

1 **General review of the Samoa group.**
In: *Pacific islands. vol. 2: Eastern Pacific.* [London]: Naval Intelligence Division, 1943, p. 582-677. maps. bibliog. (Geographical Handbook Series, B.R. 519 A).

This is a first-rate, well informed summary account of Samoa. It covers: the physical geography; history; growth and distribution of population; the Samoan people; administration; social services; economics; and communications and ports of the Samoan group. Savai'i, 'Upolu, Tutuila, Manu'a and Rose Atoll have specific sections of their own. The work is profusely illustrated with useful maps, photographs and striking drawings by Aletta Lewis, taken from her *They call them savages* (q.v.). Lewis was (with Adrian Digby, Raymond Firth and T. G. Tutin, authors of volume two) a collaborator in the preparation of the Geographical Handbook series.

2 **Imperialism and Samoan national identity.**
Sereisa Milford. *Amerasia Journal*, vol. 12, no. 1 (1985-86), p. 49-56. bibliog.

Immemorially, the people of Samoa shared a common culture. However, the partition of the islands by Germany and the USA at the turn of the century began a process of separate cultural development in the two zones. This division has caused some identity problems among older Samoans. Milford believes that young people now seem to be returning to pre-contact values, to *fa'a-Sāmoa*.

3 **Into all the world: *tala Samoa*.**
Donald Hemingway. Hamilton, New Zealand: Published by the author, 1993. 120p. ISBN 0473021366.

A privately published introduction to Samoan history and everyday life, and to the growth of the global community of Samoans. See also *A dollar's worth of love in Samoa* by John W. Harold (Philadelphia: Dorrance, 1966. 78p.). Despite its catchpenny title, this brief book contains some interesting accounts of education in Samoa and of social life and customs.

4 **Modern Samoa: its government and changing life.**
Felix M. Keesing. London: George Allen & Unwin; New York: Institute of Pacific Relations, 1934. 506p. map. bibliog.

This still essential book provides the result of some eight months of fieldwork in the Mandated Territory of Western Samoa and in American Samoa, as part of a general research project on 'dependencies and native peoples of the Pacific' initiated at the third biennial conference of the Institute of Pacific Relations held in 1929. A lively summary of 19th-century history sets the frame for critical studies of native government, justice and public order, land ownership and custom, economic life, contract labour in Western Samoa, health and medical work, religion, educational influences and people of mixed parentage.

5 **The Pacific islands: politics, economics, and international relations.**
Te'o I. J. Fairbairn, Charles E. Morrison, Richard W. Baker, Sheree A. Groves. Honolulu: East-West Center International Relations Program, 1991. 171p. maps. bibliog.

A succinct and up-to-date introduction to the contemporary Pacific islands, identifying trends, issues and recent developments in politics, economics and international relations. The individual maps and brief profiles include American Samoa (p. 112-13) and Western Samoa (p. 152-53).

6 **Pirating the Pacific: images of travel, trade & tourism.**
Edited by Ann Stephen. Haymarket, New South Wales: Powerhouse Publishing, 1993. 79p. map. bibliog.

Published to coincide with the exhibition, *South Pacific stories*, at the Powerhouse Museum, Sydney, this illustrated symposium explores how Australians have come to understand and 'see' the islands (including Samoa) through images. Visual culture and colonial history are the themes uniting the introduction by Ann Stephen, and three stimulating essays. These are: 'I could not see as much as I desired' (Ross Gibson); 'The beautiful and the damned' (Nicholas Thomas); and 'Familiarising the South Pacific' (Ann Stephen). Illustrations include 'Samoan trading station, 1870-1900', 'Tales of Louis Becke', 'Portrait of Louis Becke', and 'A Samoan family, 1895'.

7 **Samoa.**
Graeme Lay, photographs by Evotia Tamua. Auckland, New Zealand: Pasifika Press, 1997. 80p. (Pacific Pride).

An introduction to Western Samoa and American Samoa, which provides a detailed history and essential information on geography, politics, migration and traditions. Lay's text is splendidly illustrated, in colour, by Samoan photographer Evotia Tamua. See also 'The two Samoas still coming of age', by Robert Booth, photographs by Melinda Berge (*National Geographic Magazine*, vol. 168, no. 4 [Oct. 1985], p. 452-72. 2 maps), a colourful photographic essay which sharply contrasts economically poorer, more traditional Western Samoa with American Samoa; and *Western Samoa: a pictorial journey through perhaps the most beautiful and untouched islands of the South Pacific*, colour photographs by Brian Hughes, L. Pearce, Campbell Hope (Apia:

Commercial Printers, 1983. [32p.]), a charming collection of colour photographs of Āpia and of coastal villages in ‘Upolu and Savai‘i, captioned in English, German and Japanese.

8 **Samoa in colour.**
James Siers. Wellington: A.H. & A.W. Reed, 1970. 128p.

Siers' beautiful colour plates (p. 25-120) are of verdant Samoan landscapes, *fale* and churches, people (including the celebrated Aggie Grey), parades, horse-races and *siva*. The introduction provides a brief but informed history of the islands, supplemented by two essays comprising Siers' personal impressions of Western Samoa (p. 15-24) and of American Samoa (p. 121-25). See also *Hawaii & Polynesia* by James Siers (New York: Doubleday, 1973. 131p.), in which over seventy-five magnificent colour photographs enhance a photo-essay covering Samoa, Tahiti, Hawai‘i, New Zealand and Fiji.

9 **Samoa ma le fa‘aSamoa.** (Samoa and the Samoan way.)
Photographed by Gregory Riethmaier, text by Richard A. Goodman. Auckland, New Zealand; London: Collins, 1973. 111p. 4 maps.

Riethmaier's colour and monochrome photographs focus on village life in Tutuila, ‘Upolu and Savai‘i, from Independence Day parades in June to *fautasi* regattas, and rhinoceros beetles devastating coconut plantations. Richard A. Goodman's ‘Journey into Samoa' (p. 97-111) offers an informed essay on the Samoan way of life, illuminated by his anthropological research. See also: *American Samoa in the South Seas* by Chris Christensen (Honolulu: Robert Bloom, 1973. [28p.]), a brief history and photo-essay, with over twenty-five colour photographs; and *Isles of the South Pacific* by Maurice Shadbolt, Olaf Ruhen (Washington, DC: National Geographic Society, 1968. 211p. maps), outstanding for its colour photographs. It includes ‘Samoa: the changed and the changeless' (p. 50-69), covering both American Samoa and Western Samoa. One of the authors earlier produced a notable photo-essay on Western Samoa's achievement of political independence: ‘Western Samoa: the Pacific's newest nation', by Maurice Shadbolt (*National Geographic Magazine*, vol. 122 [Oct. 1962], p. 572-602).

10 **Samoa: a photographic essay.**
Frederic Koehler Sutter, introduction by Peter Pirie. Honolulu: University of Hawai‘i Press, 1971. 92p. 4th printing 1982.

In this collection of technically splendid colour photographs, Sutter tries to present the people of Samoa, their culture and their islands as he has seen and experienced them. ‘The photo essay was conceived of as a day in Samoa – in actuality a composite of many places and days – as it is lived by the chiefs, pastors, men, women, and children'. Several themes are interwoven: the village day; the cycle of life; work and responsibility; and ceremonies, celebrations and religious life. The photographs are accompanied by Samoan proverbs and sayings, and by ‘fairly literal' English translations. The proverbs come from collections made by Dr Erich Schultz, Brother Herman, the Reverend George Brown and the Reverend George Pratt. All who know rural Samoa will recognize in this volume a faithful depiction of everyday life.

11 **Samoa: the Polynesian paradise: an introduction to ancient and modern Samoa and the Polynesian triangle.**
Kipeni Su'apa'ia. New York: Exposition Press, 1962. 127p. 2 maps.

Provides a Samoan view of aspects of Samoan society and culture which are held to be of particular significance, and of Samoa's place in Polynesia.

12 **The Samoans: a global family.**
Frederic Koehler Sutter, forewords by A. P. Lutali, Peter Tali Coleman. Honolulu: University of Hawai'i Press, 1989. 221p. map. bibliog.

The final volume in Sutter's photographic trilogy, this sumptuous work exalts the personal achievements of Samoans, both in Samoa and throughout the world. Magnificent colour photographs, of scenes in the expatriate's adopted country, are matched with personal photographs and apposite proverbs. Compact autobiographies are also appended (p. 158-216), including those of Malietoa Tanumafili II, Tofilau Eti Alesana, Aggie Grey, David Toganivalu, Albert Wendt, Peter Tali Coleman, Mary Pritchard, John Kneubuhl, A. P. Lutali and many, many more.

13 **The two Samoas and the New Zealand dependencies.**
Harry Luke. In: *Islands of the South Pacific*. Harry Luke. London: George G. Harrap, 1962, p. 194-222. map.

This scholarly synopsis was written in 1957-58 at Vailima, then the official residence of the Governor of Western Samoa, by Sir Harry Luke, Governor of Fiji and High Commissioner for the Western Pacific, 1938-42. He contrasts Tokelau's limited economy and simple society with the formalized *matai* system of 'sophisticated' Samoa. The building housing the Western Samoan parliament, and the legislature's ceremonial mace are illustrated opposite p. 240.

American Samoa

General

14 **American Samoa.**
Richard Barrett Lowe. In: *Problems in paradise: the view from Government House*. Richard Barrett Lowe, with a foreword by Wayne N. Aspinall. New York: Pageant Press, 1967, p. xix-248. maps.

Lowe was the fifth civil governor of American Samoa, 1953-56. He was responsible for setting up the Constitutional Committee; for leasing the defunct tuna packing plant on Pago Pago harbour to the Van Camp Seafood Company; and for initiating the rebuilding of the abandoned and inadequate military airport at Tāfuna. He describes his years in office in great detail and with great gusto, shedding light on the state of Samoan society, on Department of the Interior policies, and on events such as the wreck of the *Joyita* in 1955. He refutes claims that the islands were 'an American slum'. There is also an important chapter on labour disputes on Swain's Island, and a chronology of major events, covering the period 1951-56.

15 **Amerika Sāmoa: an anthropological photo essay.**
Frederic Koehler Sutter, foreword by Peter Tali Coleman. Honolulu: University of Hawai'i Press, 1984. 128p. bibliog.

This is the second of Sutter's brilliant studies of Samoan life, portrayed in colour photographs and proverbs. Sutter recognizes that seemingly brash American Samoa's 'most precious resource' is not new technology or an industrial product, but rather its culture. He explains his purpose: 'This anthropological photo essay is an attempt to record traditional practices by documenting the rich and varied celebration of the human spirit that is every Samoan's heritage'. As in *Samoa: a photographic essay* (q.v.), the photographs are extensively annotated, and their significance explained.

16 **The Pacific dependencies of the United States.**
John Wesley Coulter. New York: Macmillan, 1957. 388p. maps.

A systematic, well documented survey of American territories in the Pacific, which embraces economy, politics, social structure, culture and education. Coulter writes with particular authority on American Samoa, especially of its agriculture. This volume is still of considerable value for its shrewd assessments and comparisons.

17 **Samoa: yesterday, today and tomorrow.**
Napoleone A. Tuiteleleapaga. Great Neck, New York: Todd & Honeywell, 1980. 165p.

Chief Tuiteleleapaga of Tutuila, American Samoa, a Roman Catholic, lawyer and composer of the song *Amerika Samoa*, worked for the United States Navy administration for almost fifty years. He also acted as interpreter and informant for Dr Margaret Mead, in connection with her *Coming of age in Samoa* (q.v.). His pioneering 'treasury of astute comments' on history, customs and culture, seen from within Samoan society, is especially enlightening on chiefs and 'semi-chiefs', family life, the role of women, social offences, juvenile delinquency, tattooing and the legal system of Samoa. However, the authenticity of the introduction by Margaret Mead has been questioned.

18 **Samoan interlude.**
Marie Tisdale Martin. London: Peter Davies, 1961. 221p.

Entertainingly written by the wife of an American specialist in tropical medicine serving a two-year contract in Pago Pago, this is a perceptive account of life in that 'somewhat shabby paradise'. *Fa'a-Sāmoa*, Samoan village life, *'ava* ceremonies, and health care are among the main themes. There are also accounts of visits to Āpia in Western Samoa, to the three Manu'a islands of Ta'ū, Ofu and Olosega, and to Swain's Island, 'a mere bracelet of coconuts encircling a large fresh-water lagoon'. Ethnically and culturally Tokelauan, Swain's Island (known as Olohega to the Tokelauan plantation workers) was acquired in 1856 by the American Eli Jennings. It was transferred from the Gilbert and Ellice Islands Colony to New Zealand administration in 1925, but in 1980 sovereignty over the island passed by treaty to the USA.

19 **The Samoan Islands.**

George H. Dodenhoff, William D. Munsey. In: *National security and international trusteeship in the Pacific*. Edited by William Roger Louis. Annapolis, Maryland: Naval Institute Press, 1972, p. 35-51, 152-53. maps. bibliog.

A colonel, US Marine Corps, and a commander, US Navy, join forces in a retrospect of the American presence in Samoa and in a critical assessment of the likely direction of political change in American Samoa under the tutelage of the US Department of the Interior. Of the period of Naval administration, the authors write: 'Deciding that a "Samoa for Samoans" policy was best, the Navy for 51 years did little more than supply minimal education and health services'. The departure of the Navy in 1951 left the island economy stripped. 'A man of steely determination', governor H. Rex Lee, is credited with change for the better, and with attempting to accelerate social change. The authors remark: 'The people find it more or less acceptable to be a part of the United States'.

20 **Samoan village: then and now.**

Lowell D. Holmes, Ellen Rhoads Holmes. Forth Worth, Texas: Harcourt Brace Jovanovich College Publishers, 1992. 162p. map. bibliog.

Although stated to be the second edition of Lowell D. Holmes' *Samoan village* (New York; London: Holt, Rinehart & Winston, 1974. 111p. maps. bibliog. [Case Studies in Cultural Anthropology]), this excellent, joint-authored study contains so much new material as to be virtually a distinct work. It is a distillation of study and fieldwork from 1954 to 1988, a period of thirty-seven years, and focuses on Fitiuta and Ta'ū in Manu'a, American Samoa. The many changes are highlighted. A postscript, 'Samoan character and the academic world – the Mead/Freeman controversy' (p. 139-52), evalutes Margaret Mead's Manu'a data and Derek Freeman's refutation, and adds a psychometric analysis of Samoan character, and a survey of professional reactions.

21 **Study mission to Eastern (American) Samoa: report of Senators Oren E. Long, of Hawaii, and Ernest Gruening, of Alaska, to the Committee on Interior and Insular Affairs, United States Senate, pursuant to Senate Resolution 300, 86th Congress.**

United States Congress. Senate. Committee on Interior and Insular Affairs. Washington, DC: Government Printing Office, 1961. 184p. maps. (87th Congress, 1st Session. Senate. Document no. 38).

This searching investigation of economic conditions in American Samoa under civil administration provoked urgent remedial action by the US Department of the Interior. The report presages the problems of subsequent decades, with loss of manpower through migration, and intractable budgetary deficits.

22 **They call them savages.**

Aletta Lewis. London: Methuen, 1938. 262p.

When Aletta Lewis, a young British artist then teaching at Sydney Art School, expressed the wish to paint 'brown people', anthropologist A. R. Radcliffe Brown recommended that she go to Samoa. Margaret Mead, fresh from fieldwork in Manu'a, urged: 'Stick to American Samoa. Don't go to the British group. There's not the good feeling there between the natives and the whites that there is in the American islands. Besides, there are too many white people there and the Samoans are not so primitive' (p. xi). Lewis spent six months in Samoa in 1929, living in Samoan homes in Pago Pago, Ālao and Āmouli on Tutuila, and in Ta'ū, Ofu and Olosega in Manu'a. She recalls her experiences (including that of *tāupou*) simply and with evident affection for her Samoan hosts, and portrays the islands she knew by striking engravings. US Naval Governor Captain Stephen V. Graham and Mrs Graham figure prominently in this recollection of life under US Naval administration.

Rose Atoll

23 **Rose Atoll: an annotated bibliography.**
Edited by K. A. Rodgers. Sydney South, New South Wales: Australian Museum, 1993. 37p. (Technical Reports of the Australian Museum, no. 9).

This collective bibliography extends to 1992, and is especially useful for its informative annotations. See also 'Bibliography of Rose Atoll, American Samoa' by N. L. H. Krauss (*Pacific Islands Studies and Notes* [Honolulu], no. 5 [May 1972], p. 1-6).

24 **A summary of information on Rose Atoll.**
Marie-Hélène Sachet. *Atoll Research Bulletin*, no. 29 (1954), p. 1-25. bibliog.

'Rose Atoll, the easternmost of the Samoan Islands, is one of the smallest atolls known and is of special interest, because it has hardly been influenced by man'. This paper summarizes all available information on land aspects of the uninhabited atoll, now a nature conservancy area.

Swain's Island (Olohega)

25 **Bibliography of Swain's Island, American Samoa.**
N. L. H. Krauss. Honolulu: Published by the author, 1970. 7p.

An unannotated list of eighty-seven items, arranged alphabetically by author and indexed by subjects. See also *Bibliographies of the Kermadec Islands, Niue, Swain's Island and the Tokelau Islands* by William George Coppell (Honolulu: University of Hawai'i, 1975. 99p. [Pacific Islands Studies Program, Miscellaneous Work Papers 1975, no. 2]), which provides unannotated bibliographies, and includes many elusive items.

26 **The Swains adventure.**

E. H. Bryan, Jr. In: *Panala'au memoirs.* E. H. Bryan, Jr. Honolulu: Pacific Scientific Information Center, Bernice P. Bishop Museum, 1974, p. 136-65. map.

A highly informative account of a visit in 1935 to Swain's Island, variously known as Olosega/Olohega, Jennings' Island, and Quiros Island. Eli Jennings, a US citizen, and his Samoan wife, acquired ownership of Swain's Island as a plantation, and the island is still owned by the family descendants. The history of the Jennings family is outlined and one of the eight black-and-white photographs is of Mr and Mrs Alexander Eli Jennings and their daughter at Etena. A detailed map is also provided (p. 136).

27 **A Tokelau account of Olosega.**

Antony Hooper. *Journal of Pacific History*, vol. 10, no. 4 (1975), p. 89-93. bibliog.

The island concerned here is not Olosega in the Manu'a district of American Samoa, but Olohega (Swain's Island). The Samoan text (with English translation) of a letter transcribed by Hooper in Fakaofo (one of Tokelau's three atolls) refers to the attempt by planter Sula (Jules Tirel) to achieve hegemony over the Fakaofo settlers. Tokelauans regard Olohega as historically part of Tokelau.

Western Samoa

28 **My Samoan chief.**

Fay G. Calkins. London: Frederick Muller, 1963. 224p. maps.

A chance encounter in the Library of Congress led young American student Fay Calkins to marry into an hospitable and very extensive Samoan family. Here she retells the problems and pleasures of her adjustment to life *fa'a-Sāmoa* and to the creation of a banana plantation at Lafulemu affectionately, humorously and with true insight. Despite the wide divergence between the Samoan and American outlook on life, her experiences convinced her of 'the human satisfaction and security of close communal relationships'. She later co-authored articles on Samoan society, economic development and election campaigns, writing as F. C. Ala'ilima (q.v.).

29 **Samoan medley.**

C. C. Marsack. London: Robert Hale, 1961. 192p.

The author, for fifteen years Chief Justice of Western Samoa, was constrained to write these authoritative 'glimpses of Samoan life' because so much that has been written, by itinerant journalists and novelists in a hurry, seemed to him 'utter nonsense'. Twenty vignettes, enlivened by anecdotes and humour, accurately and informatively portray Samoa in the two decades before independence, shedding light on aspects as diverse as the *matai* system, Samoan pastors (*faife'au*), personal names, fine mats, missions, the quirks of liquor law, Samoan house-girls, elections, and, especially, Samoan reactions to alien laws.

30 **Samoana: a personal story of the Samoan Islands.**
C. G. R. McKay. Wellington: A.H. & A.W. Reed, 1968. 177p. bibliog.

This discursive, engaging personal account of service as Secretary of Samoan Affairs in Āpia covers the period of New Zealand administration, 1914-62. McKay displays profound respect for and knowledge of Samoan language and culture, and is especially interesting with regard to the role and importance of oratory. He maintains that there was almost no cultural conflict despite the deep-seated political tensions, which were only resolved by independence in 1962.

31 **Some recollections of early Samoa.**
Harry J. Moors. Apia: Western Samoa Historical and Cultural Trust, 1986. 174p. maps.

Moors' interesting recollections relate mainly to the 19th century, before the partition of the Samoan Islands. Written originally as a series for the *Samoa Times*, 13 June 1924-2 April 1926, they illuminate some of the changes brought about in Samoan society by the advent of missionaries, traders and planters, and provide details which supplement Moors' earlier *With Stevenson in Samoa* (q.v.).

32 **Western Samoa.**
Linden A. Mander. In: *Some dependent peoples of the South Pacific.* Linden A. Mander. Leiden, Netherlands: E. J. Brill, 1954, p. 81-138. bibliog.

Informed by the three disciplines of anthropology, history and colonial administration, this thoughtful essay evaluates the quality of New Zealand rule in Western Samoa, and discusses future options. Mander stresses that colonial policy must be conceived as 'a two-way process'. 'The West will commit a grave error if it assumes that its only role is to teach, and that it has nothing to learn from, the dependent peoples'. He quotes, with evident approval, F. J. H. Grattan's view that the Samoan system 'is, with all its faults, something that is rare and rather wonderful'.

33 **Western Samoa.**
The Courier, no. 128 (1991), p. 29-44.

A thorough country report, which touches on all salient aspects of agriculture, economic activity, health, education, political and social development, tourism and migration. A similar, earlier country report is: 'Western Samoa' (*The Courier*, no. 93 [1985], p. 27-37).

34 **Western Samoa: land, life and agriculture in tropical Polynesia.**
Edited by James W. Fox, Kenneth B. Cumberland. Christchurch, New Zealand: Whitcombe & Tombs, 1962. 337p. maps. bibliog.

A highly factual report of a University of Auckland survey carried out on the eve of Western Samoa's independence. With its special emphasis on the implications of the Samoan traditional land tenure system and the growing pressure on natural resources, it provided essential data for subsequent policy decisions. It forecast 'an increase in the difficulties and an intensification of the country's problems', at least in the first decade of Samoan autonomy.

35 **Western Samoa 25 years after: celebrating what?**
Albert Wendt. *Pacific Islands Monthly* (June 1987), p. 14-15.

Wendt paints a bleak picture of Western Samoa after a quarter-century of political independence, with a precarious, vulnerable economy, endemic corruption in official circles, and reliance on foreign aid and on remittances from Samoan expatriates. Was independence no more than a mirage?

Geography

General

36 **The physical geography of Western Samoa.**
Leslie Curry. *New Zealand Geographer*, vol. 11, no. 1 (April 1955), p. 28-52. 12 maps. bibliog.

Based on a reconnaissance survey, this comprehensive report 'sums up present knowledge and provides a basis for future work'. The physical facts are evaluated where possible from the point of view of potential human use. Curry includes a discussion of vegetation, with altitudinal zonation of forest, and maps of slope, rainfall and parent material. See also 'Wasserfälle auf Samoa' (Waterfalls in Samoa) by K. Johannes (*Der Erdball*, vol. 4 [1930], p. 27-29); and 'Die deutsche Samoainsel Apolima' (Apolima in German Samoa) by K. Wegener (*Petermanns Mitteilungen*, vol. 57 [1911], p. 322-24), a first-hand geographical account of the island of Apolima as it was under German rule.

37 **Les Samoa: esquisse d'une géographie politique.** (Samoa: sketch of a political geography.)
P. J. Perry. *Les Cahiers d'Outre-Mer: Revue de Géographie de Bordeaux*, no. 170 (1990), p. 189-204. map. bibliog.

An excellent outline of the current political geography of Western Samoa and American Samoa. Earlier studies include: *Polynésie: les Samoa* (Polynesia: Samoa) by Pierre Métais (Lausanne, Switzerland: Payot, 1956. 88p. maps. bibliog. [Le Monde et ses Habitants, vol. 3]), an introductory human geography and description of American Samoa and Western Samoa, with mounted illustrations; and *Elementary geography of the Samoan Islands and Tokelau* by Fred Henry ([Pago Pago]: Department of Education, Government of American Samoa, 1946. 2nd ed. 40p. maps), an interesting textbook, based on local knowledge, of all the Samoan islands and of the three atolls of Tokelau.

Geology, petrography and vulcanology

38 **Age progression and petrological development of Samoan shield volcanoes: evidence from K-Ar ages, lava compositions, and mineral studies.**

J. H. Natland, D. L. Turner. In: *Investigations of the northern Melanesian borderland.* Edited by T. M. Brocher. Houston, Texas: Circum-Pacific Council for Energy and Mineral Resources, 1985, p. 139-71. (Earth Science Series, vol. 3).

Using petrological and mineralogical evidence, the authors attempt to trace the history of volcanism in the Samoan archipelago. See also: 'The geology of Samoa, and the eruptions in Savaii' by I. Jensen (*Proceedings of the Linnean Society of New South Wales*, vol. 31 [1907], p. 641-72. bibliog.), a general view of the geology of the Samoan archipelago, and a detailed, illustrated account of the recent volcanic eruptions and lava flows in Savai'i; and 'The volcano of Matavanu in Savaii' by Tempest Anderson (*Quarterly Journal of the Geological Society*, vol. 66 [1910], p. 621-39. map), a vivid account of the volcanic eruption that began in 1905 in Savai'i, burying wide tracts of the island in molten lava. Some of the displaced villagers were resettled in western 'Upolu.

39 **Coral soil problems with particular reference to Western Samoa and Tokelau Islands.**

S. G. Reynolds. *New Zealand Soil News*, vol. 20, no. 3 (1972), p. 65-74.

A prolific writer on soils and fertility summarizes the problems associated with coral soil, such as crusting, and proposes methods of enhancing its nutritive qualities. See also: 'The soils and agriculture of Western Samoa' by W. M. Hamilton, L. I. Grange (*New Zealand Journal of Science and Technology*, vol. 19 [1938], p. 593-624), a succinct review of the many types of soil found in Western Samoa and of their use in agriculture and food production; *The soils of Western Samoa*, by W. M. Hamilton, L. I. Grange (Wellington: Department of Scientific and Industrial Research, 1938. [DSIR Bulletin, no. 61]); and *Soils and land use in Western Samoa* by A. C. S. Wright (Wellington: DSIR, 1963. [New Zealand Soil Bureau Bulletin, no. 22]).

40 **Geological notes on Western Samoa.**

D. Kear. *New Zealand Archaeological Association Newsletter*, vol. 14 (1967), p. 142-56. bibliog.

An outline of geological facts of importance to archaeologists. For greater detail, see *The geology and hydrology of Western Samoa* by D. Kear, B. L. Wood (Wellington: New Zealand Geological Survey, 1959. 92p. [Bulletin, no. 93]).

41 **Geology of the Samoan islands.**

Harold T. Stearns. *Bulletin of the Geological Society of America*, vol. 55, no. 11 (Nov. 1944), p. 1,279-332. maps. bibliog.

The geology of the whole Samoan archipelago is described, especially Tutuila where detailed work was done, and the geological literature is reviewed. Tutuila was formed by five volcanoes. 'Upolu is a deeply eroded mass of Pliocene lavas surrounded by a drowned barrier reef and partly buried by late Pleistocene and Recent lavas. There has been continued volcanism in historic time with a submarine eruption between Ta'ū and Olosega in 1866 and several eruptions on Savai'i, the last ending in 1911. A detailed, fold-out, geological map of Tutuila is provided, at the scale of two statute miles to the inch. See also: *The geology of American Samoa* by R. A. Daly (Washington, DC: Carnegie Institution of Washington, 1924, p. 95-145 [Publication no. 340]); 'The geology of Western Samoa' by J. A. Thomson (*New Zealand Journal of Science and Technology*, vol. 4, no. 2 [1921], p. 49-66); and 'Petrography of the Samoan Islands' by Gordon A. Macdonald (*Bulletin of the Geographical Society of America*, vol. 55, no. 11 [Nov. 1944], p. 1,333-62. bibliog.), which is based largely on specimens collected during 1941 and 1943.

Climate

42 **Assessment of coastal vulnerability and resilience to sea-level rise and climate change: case study: Upolu Island, Western Samoa: phase 1: concepts and approach.**
R. C. Kay and others. Apia: South Pacific Regional Environment Programme (SPREP), 1993. 101p. maps.

This SPREP study of areas of 'Upolu which are likely to be adversely affected by sea-level rise (and they include much of the Āpia urban area) is concerned with establishing the basic ideas required for monitoring the potential threat posed by climate change. See also *Assessment of coastal vulnerability and resilience to sea-level rise and climate change: case study: Savai'i Island, Western Samoa: phase 2: development of methodology* by N. Mimura and others (Apia: South Pacific Regional Environment Programme [SPREP], 1994. 109p. maps), a study of Savai'i which tests the analytical methodology applicable, stemming from the concepts and approach presented in the 'Upolu study above.

43 **Implications of expected climate changes in the South Pacific region: an overview.**
UNEP. Edited by J. C. Pernetta, P. J. Hughes. Nairobi: Oceans and Coastal Areas Programme Activity Centre, United Nations Environment Programme, 1990. 279p. maps. bibliogs. (UNEP Regional Seas Reports and Studies, no. 128).

This sombre symposium reviews the likely consequences of global warming and sea level rise for Pacific island territories, including American Samoa, Western Samoa and Tokelau. Tokelau, with the highest impact level of 18.7, may cease to exist. American Samoa (10.69) may have locally devastating impacts. Western Samoa (7.62) may have locally severe to catastrophic impacts. Specific discussion of Tokelau (p. 88-115) highlights the likely need for continued migration and for resettlement. Two papers by Patrick D. Nunn (p. 127-60) forecast the possible flooding of most of the commercial centre of Āpia, including the Mulinu'u peninsula. See also *Climate change: report by a Commonwealth Group of Experts* (London: Commonwealth Secretariat, 1989. 131p. bibliog.) in which world climatic changes, likely to have serious consequences for small countries, are reviewed, and proposals made for Commonwealth action.

44 **Weather and climate.**

Leslie Curry. In: *Western Samoa: land, life, and agriculture in tropical Polynesia.* Edited by J. W Fox, K. B. Cumberland. Christchurch, New Zealand: Whitcombe & Tombs, 1962, p. 48-62. maps. bibliog.

A succinct outline of the climatological data for the Samoan archipelago as a whole, with detailed treatment of precipitation, temperatures, humidity, sunshine, winds, etc. for 'Upolu and Savai'i. See also: *Observations of upper air-currents at Apia, Western Samoa. Lat. 13° 48.4′ S.; long. 171° 46.5′ W* by Andrew Thomson (Wellington: Government Printer, 1929. 79p. [New Zealand. Department of Scientific and Industrial Research. Second Series]); 'The British army visits Western Samoa' by R. P. Wolstenholme (*Army Quarterly and Defence Journal* [Great Britain], vol. 120, no. 4 [1990], p. 429-32), a vivid personal account, by an officer sent to help repair storm damage caused by hurricanes, of what needed urgently to be done and how it was done, with foreign aid; and *The climate and weather of Western Samoa* by Stuart M. Burgess (Wellington: New Zealand Meteorological Service, 1987).

Effects of climate on certain cultural practices.
See item no. 424.

Maps and atlases

Pacific

45 **Atlas des îles et états du Pacifique Sud.** (Atlas of the islands and states of the South Pacific.)

Benoît Antheaume, Joël Bonnemaison. Montpellier, France: GIP Reclus; Paris: Publisud, 1988. 126p. bibliog.

This is much more than an attractive assembly of modern coloured maps. Section one, 'Le Pacifique, les Pacifiques?', contains fourteen thematic chapters on the region as a whole. Section two, 'Le Pacifique Sud d'île en île', devotes a map, statistical tables, and a bibliography to each of twenty island territories including American Samoa and Western Samoa. This useful compilation is, however, blemished by lack of an index.

46 **Inventory of world topographic mapping. Volume 3: Eastern Europe, Asia, Oceania and Antarctica.**

Compiled by Rolf Böhme, English language editor Roger Anson. London; New York: Elsevier Applied Science Publishers, on behalf of the International Cartographic Association, 1993. 466p. maps. bibliogs. (ICA Series).

This final volume of the ICA's trilogy includes American Samoa (p. 321) and Western Samoa (p. 364-65). The information given for each territory consists of: a brief history of its topographic mapping; geodetic data; map scales and series; extracts of maps and index sheets illustrating the present status of map coverage; and a bibliography. Both territories are fully mapped.

47 **Pacific island names: a map and name guide to the New Pacific.**

Lee S. Motteler. Honolulu: Bernice P. Bishop Museum, 1986. 100p. maps. bibliog. (Miscellaneous Publications, no. 34).

A complete revision of *Guide to islands in the tropical Pacific* by E. H. Bryan Jr. (Honolulu: Bernice P. Bishop Museum, 1972). It contains maps and a comprehensive gazetteer listing officially accepted island names, cross-referenced to all known variant names and spellings (including those for islands in American Samoa and Western Samoa). Island groups are arranged according to their political status in 1986.

48 **Reference map of Oceania: the Pacific islands of Micronesia, Polynesia, Melanesia.**

Cartography by James A. Bier. Honolulu: University of Hawai'i Press, 1995. 36 × 23 in. flat, double-sided.

This full-colour, fully indexed map is accurate, detailed and up-to-date. It contains fifty-two inset maps of the principal islands and island groups, at larger scales. These insets include Western Samoa, Āpia, Tutuila, Manu'a, Pago Pago Harbor, Tokelau, Fakaofo and Auckland. The index gives approximate, undated population data: American Samoa (46,800), Pago Pago (3,525), Western Samoa (162,350), Āpia (34,095). See also *Islands of the South Pacific [map]* (Wellington: Department of Survey and Land Information, 1995. reprint of 3rd edition of 1989. Scale 1:10,000,000. colour. [Infomap, no. 275]), which is based on information obtained from official sources in 1988, and which represents a good general-purpose map to be recommended without hesitation. Land relief, bathymetry, international boundaries, altitudes and principal towns are clearly shown.

49 **Uncharted and dangerous waters: French atlases of the Pacific.**

Wellington: National Library of New Zealand, 1991. [12p.]. bibliog.

The catalogue of an exhibition of French atlases from the Alexander Turnbull Library. The atlases were produced by participants in seven French voyages of exploration to the Pacific in the 18th and 19th centuries. Bougainville's chart of *Archipel des Navigateurs* (1768) is illustrated.

Samoa

50 **Islands of Sāmoa: Tutuila, Manu'a, 'Upolu, Savai'i [map].**
Cartography by James A. Bier. Honolulu: University of Hawai'i Press, 1990. 2nd ed. colour. 35 × 18 in. flat.

First published in 1980, these are the best available maps of all islands in American Samoa and Western Samoa, in various scales. There are inset maps of Āpia, Āpia and vicinity, Pago Pago Harbor and vicinity, Pago Pago-Utulei, Swain's Island and Rose Atoll (*Nu'u o Manu*). Gazetteers of all placenames are also provided, referring to the map grids. See also *Sāmoa Islands [map]* (New Zealand. Department of Survey and Land Information. Wellington: Department of Survey and Land Information, 1992. Scale 1:250,000. Transverse Mercator projection, colour. 83 × 60 cm. [Infomap, no. 341]), which covers both American Samoa and Western Samoa, including an inset map of Āpia at a scale of 1:25,000.

American Samoa

51 **American Samoa [map].**
Honolulu: Pacific Islands Development Program, East-West Center, 1990. colour.

An excellent, up-to-date map of all of the Territory of American Samoa, suitable for school or tourist use. See also *Coastal zone management atlas of American Samoa* ([Honolulu]: Cartographic Laboratory, 1981. 56 maps), an atlas of coloured maps of the inshore territorial waters and coastlines of American Samoa, at scales of 1:24,000 and 1:120,000.

Western Samoa

52 **Western Samoa [map].**
Springwood, Queensland: Hema Maps, for South Pacific Maps, 1992. colour.

Provides good tourist maps of Savai'i and 'Upolu, at a scale of 1:235,000, and of Āpia Town at 1:15,000. Āpia is indexed by features of interest to visitors, and the two main maps indicate places of interest to tourists. The extensive background information is provided by the Western Samoa Visitors Bureau, Āpia. See also: *Western Samoa [map]* (Honolulu: Pacific Islands Development Program, East-West Center, 1990. colour), a clear, up-to-date map of 'Upolu, Savai'i, Apolima, Manono and the smaller islands of Western Samoa; and *Western Samoa topographical map: scale 1:20,000* (Apia: Department of Lands and Survey, 1980. 28 coloured maps), an exceptionally useful presentation of the physical geography of Western Samoa, with all major peaks, rivers, bays, capes and islets named.

Travellers' Accounts and Reminiscences

Pre-19th century

53 **The journal of Jacob Roggeveen.**

Jacob Roggeveen, edited by Andrew Sharp. Oxford: Clarendon Press, 1970. 181p. 2 maps. bibliog.

A full-length translation from the Dutch of the journal kept by Jacob Roggeveen (1659-1729) of his voyage from the Netherlands round Cape Horn and across the Pacific to New Ireland in 1721-22. Roggeveen's three ships, *Den Arend*, *Thienhoven* and *De Africaansche Galey* discovered most of the islands of eastern Samoa and 'Upolu in 1722. On 13 June 1722 Cornelis Bouman of *Thienhoven* sighted and named Vuyle Island (Rose). The four islands of Manu'a were named Bouman's Islands. Tutuila was named Thienhoven, and 'Upolu Groeningen.

54 **The journal of Jean-François de Galaup de La Pérouse, 1785-1788.**

Jean-François de Galaup de La Pérouse, translated and edited by John Dunmore. London: Hakluyt Society, 1995. 613p. maps. bibliog.

The first volume (of two) of this scholarly new edition of La Pérouse's journal is notable for Dunmore's introduction, which is rich in details of the Comte's early life and career. It also provides the maritime and scientific context of the three-year expedition by the *Boussole* and the *Astrolabe*. See also *A voyage round the world, performed in the year 1785, 1786, 1787, and 1788 by the Boussole and Astrolabe* by Jean de La Pérouse (Amsterdam: N. Israel; New York: Da Capo Press, 1968. 3 vols. [Bibliotheca Australiana, vols. 27-29]). This is a facsimile reprint of the London edition of 1799, with some 1,156 pages and seventy-one plates and maps. Included are the observations made of the Samoan islands and the record of the bloody clash with Samoans in Tutuila, at the place which came to be known as Massacre Bay.

19th century

55 **An American artist in the South Seas.**

John La Farge, with an introduction by Kaori O'Connor. London; New York: KPI, 1987. 480p. bibliog. (Pacific Basin Books).

In this work, first published in 1914, there is an extensive section on Samoa (p. 68-287). John La Farge (1835-1910) first encountered Samoans on Tutuila in 1890; they represented to him 'the poetry of form and color' of a rustic Greece. La Farge and his travelling companion, Henry Brooks Adams (1838-1918), settled at Vāiala near Āpia, where they often visited Robert Louis Stevenson (viewed with some reserve and disapproval). La Farge's impressions of Mata'afa ('a gentleman among gentlemen') and Malietoa Laupepa, and his analysis of the Samoan situation differ from those given by Stevenson in his *A footnote to history: eight years of trouble in Samoa* (q.v.).

56 **Brown men and women: or the South Sea islands in 1895 and 1896.**

Edward Reeves. London: Swan Sonnenschein, 1898. 294p. map.

The New Zealand author claims absolute authenticity for his racy but useful account of life in Tonga, Fiji, Tahiti, the Cook Islands, and Samoa (27p.). He writes: 'I have no imagination, and can invent nothing. I simply record plain facts'. He succeeds in conveying something of the frenetic, conspiratorial atmosphere of 'Upolu as internecine Samoan conflicts moved towards their climax while Germany and the United States stood poised and ready to pounce.

57 **Girlhood in the Pacific: Samoa – Philippines – Spain.**

Marjorie Leslie (Mrs Shane Leslie). London: Macdonald, 1943. 3rd impression. 110p.

Born in Vermont, the author is the youngest daughter of Henry Clay Ide, American Commissioner and later Chief Justice in Samoa at the turn of the 19th century. Marjorie Leslie's recollections of her four 'idyllic' years in Āpia are vivid and neatly presented, with a dash of hindsight. The main reminiscences are 'Samoa' (p. 14-20), 'Robert Louis Stevenson' (p. 29-42) and 'German naval officers' (p. 43-45). Plates include: a bust of Henry Clay Ide by J. Massey-Rhind; Āpia; and Samoan chiefs and *tāupou* on a ceremonial visit.

58 **Îles Samoa: notes pour servir à une monographie de cet archipel.**

(The Samoan Islands: notes towards a monography on that archipelago.)

A. Marques. Lisbon: Imprimerie Nationale, 1889. 158p. maps.

An important early source of scientific information on Samoa, the author having visited the islands. It includes accounts of topography, geology, volcanoes, soils, climate, vegetation and economic plants. The work was also published as 'Notes pour servir à une monographie des Îles Samoa' (*Boletim da Sociedade de Geographia de Lisboa*, vol. 8 [1889], p. 5-158. maps).

59 **In Stevenson's Samoa.**

Marie Fraser. London: Smith, Elder, 1895. 190p.

Marie Fraser, an actress and a keen observer of events and people, provides a highly personal, rather naive account of Āpia life. A chance meeting with Robert Louis

Stevenson, 'a most picturesque figure, riding a slim, dun-coloured horse', led to closer acquaintance with the Vailima family, all 'inveterate smokers'. Though slight, a more attractive portrait of 'a man of genius' has seldom been presented. Fraser is interesting on Samoan customs, impatient of the 'tiresome old talking-men', and approving of tattooing, which made the men look 'thoroughly clothed and trim', as though wearing 'decorous knee-breeches'. She reveals that Mr Stevenson had 'the greatest horror of the native men wearing European dress', and preferred to bury his old clothes rather than to give them away.

60 **The lotus land of the Pacific.**

John Harrison Wagner. *Harper's New Monthly Magazine*, vol. 95, no. 568 (1897), p. 620-29.

In her essay 'Photography of Samoa: production, dissemination, and use', Alison Devine Nordström (q.v.) describes this article as 'a leering travelogue', and tells how a widely distributed photograph of a smiling young girl was 'corrected' in it, to reinforce the stereotype of the available and compliant Polynesian woman of 'the exotic and erotic South Seas', with bare breasts and garlands of flowers. This image reappeared in an advertisement for the Union Steamship Line and was the basis for G. Pieri Nerli's painting, now in Scotland, entitled 'A friend of the Stevenson household'!

61 **The navigators.**

B. F. S. Baden-Powell. In: *In savage isles and settled lands: Malaysia, Australasia, and Polynesia 1888-1891.* B. F. S. Baden-Powell. London: Richard Bentley & Son, 1892, p. 345-77.

Baden-Powell found Āpia both absurd and unsettling, with white residents giving Christy Minstrel performances while Tamasese and Mata'afa challenged the precarious authority of Malietoa, ruling in the shadow of the three consuls, Cusack Smith, Sewall and Stuebel. 'Malietoa did not impress me favourably', he writes. Of Robert Louis Stevenson: 'At first ... I mistook him for a postman, and a very peculiar-looking one too'. There are vivid descriptions of the 'awful solemnity' of the reception for Baron Cedercrantz, the chief justice nominated by the King of Sweden; the 'nasty old men' chewing 'cava' (*'ava*); and the marriage of Mr Girr and Fanua, *tāupou* of Āpia and daughter of Suamana, chief of Āpia. He also notes the widespread elephantiasis and leprosy; the numerous hunchbacks; the 'dirty and uninviting' 'so-called' hotels and restaurants of Āpia; prayers for Malietoa in the Protestant church; and the Samoan flag (red, with a white St. George's cross, and a five-pointed star in the inner top corner). Some of his sketches are unkind to women, of whom he writes: '... *I* certainly never saw a single woman in Samoa, that, in my opinion, had the slightest pretensions to good looks'.

62 **A new voyage round the world in the years 1823-26.**

Otto von Kotzebue. London: Colburn & Bentley, 1830. 2 vols.

Kotzebue's contacts with Samoans (described herein) disposed him to regard them as savage and treacherous. He warned other seamen to avoid the archipelago, and for forty years his advice was often followed, even by Peruvian slave raiders. The stereotype of the savage (even 'cannibalistic') Samoan gradually improved as Christian missions gained ground and laid the basis for a new image, that of handsome, gentle and devout 'tropical peasants'.

63 **Pearls of the Pacific.**

J. W. Boddam-Whetham. London: Hurst & Blackett, 1876. 362p.

This is an extensive account (p. 138-242), by a perceptive early traveller, of Samoa in 1874, when it was under the heptarchy of *Ta'imua* and when trade and commerce were almost entirely in the hands of the Germans. Boddam-Whetham visited Pago Pago (not yet a coaling station), 'Upolu, Manono, Apolima and Savai'i (where he describes a Tongan raid). In Āpia he saw a Samoan girl taking the veil as a nun, suffered from the ubiquitous flies and mosquitoes, and noted the prevalence of elephantiasis, tuberculosis, fever and old Enfield rifles. A nearby, German-owned cotton plantation was worked by indentured labourers from Tanna and the Line Islands. He remarks that the Samoan *t* was pronounced almost like *k*, and lists the Samoan and Latin names of birds seen (p. 198-99). Some of his comments are startling, e.g. 'Paying taxes in Samoa is a matter of great rejoicing and festivity ...', and '... the natives who speak the best English are invariably the greatest scoundrels'.

64 **Realms and islands: the world voyage of Rose de Freycinet in the corvette *Uranie*: from her journal and letters and the reports of Louis de Saulces de Freycinet, capitaine de corvette.**

Marnie Bassett. London: Oxford University Press, 1962. 275p. maps. bibliog.

On 21 October 1819, the *Uranie* sighted an apparently undiscovered island which its captain named Île Rose, after his wife, Rose-Marie de Freycinet, who was sailing with him illegally. In fact, Rose Island had been discovered on 13 January 1722 by Jacob Roggeveen, who named it Vuyle Eyland. Plate 39 (opposite p. 164) has a view and chart of the island by L. J. Duperrey, chief hydrographer in the *Uranie*. Louis de Freycinet (1779-1842) was predeceased by his 'extremely dear' wife, who died of cholera in 1832 at the age of thirty-seven.

65 **Samoa.**

The Earl and the Doctor. In: *South Sea bubbles*. The Earl and the Doctor. Leipzig: Bernhard Tauchnitz, 1902, p. 199-236. (Collection of British Authors, vol. 1426). First published in London: Bentley, 1872. 312p.

The Earl is George Robert Charles Herbert, Earl of Pembroke, and the Doctor George Henry Kingsley, who visited 'lovely Samoa' in 1870. They were fascinated by the ritual *'ava* ceremony, *palolo* fishing, wooded hills 'marked with beautiful curves and long graceful sweeps of vivid green', the fine stands of timber, 'breathless' ravines, the rare didunculus bird, and '*the* princess, the greatest beauty and richest match in all Samoa' who turned out to be a 'naughty, naughty girl!'. In the Earl's view, the only blight on a delectable land was the 'ruthless missionary'.

66 **Samoa: die Perle der Südsee à jour gefaßt [Samoa: the pearl of the South Seas].**

Otto E. Ehlers. Berlin: Verlag von Hermann Paetel, 1895. 199p.

First published as a series of letters, 'Briefe aus dem fünften Weltteil', in *Tägliche Rundschau*, this is one of the most engaging early accounts of travel in Samoa, prepared for publication by Consul Franz Hernsheim in Hamburg. Ehlers was entranced by what he saw of Samoan life in 'Upolu, Manono and Tutuila, and decided that Samoa must without fail become a German colony. He shrewdly assesses the economic power of the DH & PG plantation (die 'Firma'), and the Samoan contenders for hegemony. At Massacre Bay in Tutuila he paid homage to the dead of 11 December 1787: Vicomte de Langle, *commandant* of the *Astrolabe* (and six seamen) and M. de Lamanon, *docteur* of the *Boussole* (and three seamen). The frontispiece is a montage by A. Metz (1895), including a view of Āpia bay, portraits of Malietoa, Tamasese and Mata'afa, and a facsimile of Malietoa's signature.

20th century

Samoa

67 **Adventures in paradise: Tahiti, Samoa, Fiji.**
Willard Price. London; Melbourne; Toronto: William Heinemann, 1956. 245p. maps.

In 'This is Samoa's Golden Age' (p. 157-220), Price, author of numerous books on the Pacific Basin, contrasts 'Upolu, 'an island made for man', with American Samoa, 'too mountainous to be of much practical use'. He outlines the 'pretty mess' left by the abandonment of the Pago Pago naval base in 1951, and the difficulties later experienced by the Japanese in establishing a fish cannery. A notably intelligent observer, Price comments shrewdly on problems which still exist: population pressure and urbanization; the nature of Samoan education; mixed marriages; and sexual mores and practices (including the piratical *moetotolo*, or sleep crawling, defined as a verb by G. B. Milner as 'possess [or attempt to possess] a woman while she is sleeping at night').

68 ***Aloha*: en Sydhavsfaerd.** (*Aloha*: a South Sea journey.)
Aage Krarup Nielsen. Copenhagen: Gyldendal, 1939. 200p.

Illustrated by forty-eight pages of black-and-white photographs, this Danish-language account of visits to Fiji, French Polynesia, Hawai'i and Samoa records a way of life which was soon to be drastically affected by the war with Japan. This was especially so in Samoa as the placidity of Samoan life so pleasantly depicted in this book was soon to be shaken by the arrival of thousands of American troops.

69 **The happy lagoons: the world of Queen Salote.**
Jørgen Rosendal, translated from the Danish by Eiler Hansen, J. F. Burke. London: Jarrolds, 1961. 224p.

First published in Denmark by Det Schønbergske Forlag in 1957, this breezy travelogue belies its title by devoting two chapters (p. 101-65) to Western Samoa and American Samoa. There is an extensive, speculative account of the *Joyita* mystery. The *Joyita*, built in Los Angeles in 1931 as a pleasure yacht for Mary Pickford, was bought in 1952 by Dr Katherine Luomala, anthropologist and authority on both Polynesia and Micronesia. Captained by 'Dusty' Miller, *Joyita* was chartered by the Āpia firm of E. A. Coxon & Company to carry copra from the Tokelau Islands to

Samoa. She vanished, with all twenty-five crew and passengers, in 1955. The motorship *Tuvalu* later found the heavily listing *Joyita*, drifting about ninety miles off Udu Point on Vanua Levu. Rosendal holds Samoa to be 'an unsurpassed tourist paradise, but this globe-trotter's paradise would sooner be free of tourists'.

70 **In search of Tusitala: travels in the Pacific after Robert Louis Stevenson.**

Gavin Bell. London: Picador, 1994. 333p. map.

Bell, a veteran journalist and foreign correspondent, visited the ports-of-call of Stevenson's voyages of 1888-89 in the yacht *Casco* and the schooner *Equator*, ending in Āpia, 'a colourful little town'. He deplores the Central Bank's 'monstrous cage of glass and lime-green concrete' and the Chinese-built, seven-storey government building 'in the post-Mao repressionist style'. Mormon businessmen, led by Rex Maugham, were rebuilding Vailima as a literary Museum, set in the seventeen acres left from the 400 acres bought by Robert Louis Stevenson. Bell vividly describes a visit to Āmaile village, the Vāiala rugby team, *kirikiti* (the Samoan version of cricket), hurricane Lin, and the high rate of suicide among young men, often by drinking Paraquat. Pago Pago, 'bustling with life and industry', suffers from 'contaminants, sewage, and garbage' in the harbour, and from the 'incredibly foul stench' of its tuna canning factories, supplied by Korean long-liners and by Croatian purse-seiners based in Guam. Bell sensitively describes the village of 'Aoa, at the eastern end of Tutuila, and the island of 'Aunu'u, both visited by Stevenson.

71 **The islands of Samoa.**

Husein Rofé. *Eastern Horizon*, vol. 18, no. 3 (1979), p. 22-31.

Provides impressions and sensible opinions regarding the state and attractions of each of Samoa's main islands. Rofé records an interesting interview with Āpia's leading hotelier, Aggie Grey. Earlier travellers' accounts include: *Stevenson's isles of paradise: a true story of adventures in the Samoan South Sea islands* by Alva Carothers (Santa Barbara, California: Carothers, 1931. 2nd ed. 294p.), a description of things seen and people encountered; *Adrift in the South Seas: including adventures with Robert Louis Stevenson* by Thomson Murray MacCallum (Los Angeles: Wetzel Publishing Co., 1934. 324p.), which is typical of books on travel in Samoa of its period, making much of relatively minor occurrences, especially the 'adventures' with Stevenson; *In a junk across the Pacific* by E. Allen Petersen (London; New York: Elek, 1954. 224p.), a pleasant narrative of a long Pacific voyage by Allen and Tani Petersen in their Chinese junk, the *Hummel Hummel*, which briefly describes the closed port of Pago Pago, and an unwelcoming Āpia, shortly before the bombing of Pearl Harbor in 1941; and *South seas magic* by Ronald Rose (London: Robert Hale, 1959. 192p.), which includes starry-eyed impressions of Samoa, and is illustrated by the author's own photographs.

72 **The Navigators' Islands.**

Alain Gerbault. In: *In quest of the sun: the journal of the Firecrest*. Alain Gerbault. London: Rupert Hart-Davis, 1955, p. 102-12. (The Mariners Library).

Originally published in 1929, Gerbault's account of his voyage in the yacht *Firecrest* from New York to Le Havre, by way of Panama, Mangareva, Tahiti, Fiji and Cape Town, is now a classic of its genre. In the summer of 1926 he arrived at Pago Pago.

This chapter includes his favourable impressions of 'the able administration of the United States Navy', and its 'rigid barrier between whites and natives'. He found Āpia of 'little interest to the traveller', apart from a rugby football match between two 'picturesque' native teams from Samoa and Tonga.

73 **On copra ships and coral isles.**

Rosaline Redwood. London: Robert Hale, 1966. 192p. maps. Large print edition, Leicester, England: Ulverscroft, 1992. 346p. maps.

Rosaline Redwood travelled alone through what she calls the 'remote regions of the Pacific'; these include 'Upolu, Savai'i and Tutuila (p. 107-50). Her light-hearted impressions of Samoans, as grave, courteous, amusing and (in Pago Pago) light-fingered, are based on shrewd observation. From the Casino Hotel to the Virgin's Grave, Redwood *liked* Samoa. Only the fish caught inside the reef worried her: 'I hadn't thought about the frightening combination of worms and lavatories and fish before'.

74 **Pacific prelude: a journey to Samoa and Australasia, 1929.**

Margery Perham, edited and with an introduction by A. H. M. Kirk-Greene. London: Peter Owen, 1988. 272p. map. bibliog.

Margery Perham (1895-1982) was among the outstanding women of her age, an Oxford academic from 1924 to 1963 and a leading authority on comparative colonial administration. This is the edited diary of her visit to the Pacific in 1929 on a Rhodes Trust Travelling Fellowship, visiting Pago Pago, 'the nearest place to Paradise on earth', and Āpia. The administration of mandated Western Samoa by New Zealand is compared unfavourably with that of German Samoa under Dr Wilhelm Solf and Dr Erich Schultz-Ewerth, both scholars. The New Zealand administrators are described as 'men with little general culture, little powers of generalization, many with the outlook of a clerical grade, and with no inkling of their own ignorance about native administration'. Perham deplores New Zealand's handling of the endemic *Mau* unrest. In Auckland, she interviewed the movement's leader, O. F. Nelson (p. 125-27), 'a strange mixture of sharpness and simplicity', and the ex-governor of Samoa, General Sir George Richardson, who deported Nelson. Kirk-Greene's copious, scholarly notes contribute many valuable facts and insights relating to Samoa, both east and west.

75 **Samoa: the last paradise.**

Bernd Lohse. In: *Australia and the South Seas*. Bernd Lohse, translated by Kenneth S. Whitton. Edinburgh, London: Oliver & Boyd, 1959, p. 98-114.

During his visit to Samoa in the mid-1950s, Lohse became instantly enamoured of 'spotless Apia', well-ordered cocoa and coffee plantations, and 'happy aristocracy'. He described speaking pidgin English to an exquisite Samoan girl, who replied: 'My name is Margarete von Dinklage'. The photographs include one of an open ward in Āpia's infirmary, with a patient's family doing their housework by the sick-bed. The work was originally entitled *Australien und Südsee heute* (Frankfurt am Main, West Germany: Umschau Verlag, 1958).

76 **Samoa sketchbook.**

Text by Nelson Eustis, drawings by A. J. Peake. Adelaide, South Australia: Hobby Investments, 1979. 64p. map.

An engaging book of impressions, mainly but not exclusively of Western Samoa, by two South Australians, author and artist respectively. Anecdotal in style, the text briskly presents the highlights of Samoan history and way of life. The thirty-four drawings are charming representations of scenes and buildings, typical (churches, *fale fono*, or *fale la'itiiti*) or significant (the tiered monument of the Tuimaleali'ifano family, the graves of the Malietoa, and the mausoleums [*loa*] of the Tamasese and the Mata'afa, all on the Mulinu'u peninsula). Perhaps of greatest symbolic significance is the *Mau* 'bandstand' office which acted as the headquarters of the movement in the 1920s (p. 55). There is also a schematic map of Āpia and 'environments' [sic]. Four of Peake's drawings of churches appeared on the 1979 Western Samoa Christmas stamps.

77 **Slow boats home.**

Gavin Young, illustrated by Salim. London: Hutchinson, 1985. 442p. 8 maps.

This is the vividly related story of a leisurely peregrination of the Pacific in a series of ships. Among the ports visited are Āpia and Pago Pago, described both as they now are and as portrayed in well known literary works by Robert Louis Stevenson and others. Young considers that the romantic and laudatory literary portrayal of Samoans is in no way exaggerated.

78 **South Sea foam: the romantic adventures of a modern Don Quixote in the southern seas.**

A. Safroni-Middleton. New York: George H. Doran, 1920. 350p.

These 'purple impressions' of 'the amorous violinist' include a vignette of Robert Louis Stevenson's life in Samoa. Memories of Samoa also feature in Safroni-Middleton's *Tropic shadows* (London: Richards Press, 1927. 302p.), which includes a meeting with Joseph Conrad, and in *Wine-dark seas and tropic skies* (London: Grant Richards, 1918. 304p.). *Tides of sunrise and sunset: the fourth dimension of romance* (London: Heath Cranton, 1932. 219p.) covers much the same ground in a similar vein.

79 **South Sea islands.**

Charles A. Borden. London: Robert Hale, 1963. 192p. map.

Packed with facts culled from encyclopaedias and specialist works, this busy travelogue includes sober (and accurate) summaries of history and modern life in Western Samoa, Tokelau and American Samoa (p. 141-70). There are no personal impressions or anecdotes, and some ill considered statements, as in the caption to plate 21: 'Samoan craftsmen no longer use stone tools to carve the many-legged *ava* ceremonial bowls'.

80 **The South Seas dream: an adventure in paradise.**

John Dyson. London: Heinemann, 1982. 243p. map.

Professional writer John Dyson sets out to explore all aspects of the dream of a romantic South Sea paradise, and does so with verve and imagination. He shows how the Western conception of idyllic islands has altered native culture, and examines the hard decisions that the new generation of educated islanders must make. Western Samoa is described (p. 140-56) with a keen journalistic eye for the colourful and the potentially newsworthy story. 'Over-education' is a problem. Tupuola Efi, the prime minister, is 'deeply troubled' about the desire for Western goods, especially tinned food. Dyson considers the Western Samoans to be 'a stylish people'. American Samoa (p. 157-68) 'mildewed' Dysons's spirits with its 'solid dementing rain', and depressed him with its smugness and sloth and its garbage-littered streets.

81 **Summer isles of Eden.**
Frank Burnett. London: Sifton, Praed, 1923. 213p. map.

The author of *Through tropic seas* (London: Griffiths, 1910. 173p.) and *Through Polynesia and Papua* (London: Dell, 1911. 197p.) revisits Samoa after some eighteen years, to find that Āpia has grown from 'a characteristic South Sea Island beach settlement' into 'quite a respectable modern town'. He travelled extensively in Savai'i, staying with Nelson Stores traders. The fourteen photographs include 'Large double war canoe', and 'Church overwhelmed with lava' (Savai'i). The words of the Samoan farewell song, *Tofā ma feleni*, are given in Samoan and English.

82 ***Talofa Samoa!*: gjensyn med sydhavsøya som forandret vår tilvaerelse.** (Hello Samoa!: re-encounter with the South Sea island that changed our life.)
Erik Damman. Oslo: Gyldendal, 1981. 261p.

An affectionate account, in Norwegian, of a happy return to Samoa, to find old friends and to see what remains of a cherished way of life. There is a translation into Swedish: *Talofa Samoa!: tillbaka till den söderhavsö som förandräde vår tillvaro; översättning av Bo och Ethel Kärnekull* (Stockholm: Askild & Kärnekull, 1983. 243p.).

83 **The teller of tales: in search of Robert Louis Stevenson.**
Hunter Davies. London: Sinclair-Stevenson, 1994. 290p. bibliog.

Written to celebrate the centenary of Stevenson's death in 1894, this hybrid work juxtaposes Davies' own retracing of the writer's travels with an entertaining though sketchy account of his life and work. Chapters seventeen to twenty-two (p. 175-251) are devoted, fleetingly, to the Pacific voyages and, more extensively, to Samoa, then and now. The story of Stevenson's life at Vailima is a bare summary of common knowledge, and the description of Āpia today is trivial and banal.

84 **Unconducted wanderers.**
Rosita Forbes. London; New York: John Lane, 1919. 198p.

Joan Rosita Forbes (1893-1967) gave up driving Ministers of the Crown to Dulwich and embarked on a round-the-world journey while the First World War still raged. She became a tireless traveller and an extremely popular travel writer. In this first book, she visits Pago Pago, witnessing the arrival of the seamen marooned on Mopelia by a German raider. She describes Āpia harbour as 'a tragic sight', with the iron skeletons of the seven German and American men-of-war which were wrecked there twenty years previously still clearly visible on the cruel barrier reefs. 'A horde of particularly vicious and vigorous mosquitoes with striped legs' drove her to visit Savai'i, 'a delightful spot outside the realms of civilization', where she crossed the dead lava field, fifteen miles wide and cutting the island in two, to climb to the volcano's crater.

German Samoa

85 **In the tracks of the trades: the account of a fourteen thousand mile yachting cruise to the Hawaiis, Marquesas, Societies, Samoas and Fijis.**

Lewis R. Freeman. London: William Heinemann, 1921. 380p.

First published in New York in 1920 by Dodd, Mead and Company, this includes the story (p. 209-85) of a visit before the First World War to Pago Pago and Āpia, when Dr Solf ruled in German Samoa and Captain E. B. Underwood, USN in American Samoa. Tutuila, to Freeman, 'is deserving of being called a model tropical colony'. German rule, in contrast, was repressive. Freeman describes Samoan cricket (illustrated) on Tutuila; pleasant meetings with Dr Solf, distinguished statesman and scholar; and the *'ava* ceremony and *siva*, all accompanied by nineteen photographs by the author, including the naval station at Pago Pago, a *fita-fita* sergeant, the *John Williams*, a seated *siva*, and four examples of splendid *tuiga* head-dresses.

86 **Rupert Brooke: a biography.**

Christopher Hassall. London: Faber & Faber, 1965. 557p.

Chapter eleven, 'A deep sleep' (p. 396-447), recounts the Grantchester Old Vicarage poet's travels in America and in Hawai'i, Samoa, Fiji and Tahiti from May 1913 to June 1914. Brooke landed from the S.S. *Ventura* at Pago Pago on 2 November 1913, sailing in a schooner for Āpia, eighty miles to the west, the same night. Returning to Pago Pago, on about 13 November he boarded the S.S. *Tofua* for Fiji, en route to Tahiti where he remained for three months. An article in the *New Statesman*, descriptions of R. L. Stevenson's house and grave and of a *siva-siva* at Pago Pago, letters to friends, and approving comments on the colonial régime in German Samoa are the only records of his brief visit to the partitioned Samoan islands. Of Stevenson he wrote: 'His memory is sweet there, in Samoa; especially among the natives'. See also *The letters of Rupert Brooke*, chosen and edited by Geoffrey Keynes (London: Faber & Faber, 1968. 710p.), which reproduces Brooke's letters from the Pacific in 1913-14 (p. 515-74), include some relating to Samoa (p. 527-34). Most fail to transcend the banality of tourist reactions to a supposed 'paradise'.

87 **Samoa.**

Stanley Unwin, Severn Storr. In: *Two young men see the world.*
Stanley Unwin, Severn Storr. London: George Allen & Unwin, 1934, p. 389-407.

Edited from letters sent to friends, this account of a visit to Āpia in German Samoa in 1913 describes Vailima; Miss Schultze's school for Samoan girls; meetings with H. J. Moors ('*the* agitation in Apia'); the Rev. Will Sibree of the LMS; and Chief Asi (slightingly mentioned in Stevenson's *Vailima letters*). Of particular interest is the summary of an interview with Herr Helg, Swiss manager of the DH & PG plantation at Mulifanua, with an output of some 12,000 tons of copra a year from about 4,000 acres worked by around 400 *kanakas* and ten white overseers. The black labourers 'were satisfied' with a payment of about £3.10s. per annum, together with their food.

American Samoa

88 **American Samoa: the littered lagoon.**
Paul Theroux. In: *The happy isles of Oceania: paddling the Pacific.* Paul Theroux. London: Penguin Books, 1992, p. 472-90.

Theroux has few kind words for the Samoans he met in Pago Pago, Leone and the small island of 'Aunu'u, and deplores the seventy-five million dollars or so provided annually to American Samoans by the United States government. He asserts that the average per capita income in American Samoa is almost ten times greater than Western Samoa's $580 a year, but is 'all funny money', most of it foreign aid. He claims that America has removed the Samoans' 'cultural props', by creating a cash economy: 'The worse effect of this has been a kind of competitive selfishness which has fragmented the family'. An encounter in the hamlet of 'Au'asi, with seven 'tedious little bastards', stirs Theroux to characterize Samoans as 'the most pathetic conformists, and so the greatest bullies, in the Pacific'.

89 **Pango Pango (American Samoa).**
Charlotte Cameron. In: *Wanderings in south-eastern seas.* Charlotte Cameron. London: T. Fisher Unwin, 1924, p. 223-34. map.

'In American Samoa life is protected by cleanliness', is Cameron's immediate conclusion when informed that the Pago Pago birth-rate had increased by forty-one per cent. These briskly told impressions of a brief visit in 1922 include a description of Government House, then occupied by Governor Waldo Evans and Mrs Evans. The illustrations include 'Tapping rubber trees, Samoa' and 'Native war canoe, Samoa'. The latter shows an eighteen-oared *fautasi* of modern construction, crowded with passengers, eight of them with black umbrellas! (Pago Pago is known for its high rainfall.)

90 **Polynesian paradise: an elaborated travel journal based on ethnological facts.**
Donald Sloan. London: Robert Hale, 1941. 288p.

Sloan vividly describes a hurricane which devastated the fifty villages of Tutuila. Later, seeking 'the old native life', he is advised to go out to the islands of Manu'a, where 'they still speak the old language and honour the customs of old. ... There the people are happy, for the white man's curse has not yet found them out'. Sloan provides a racy yet informed account of everyday life, ceremonies, and shark fishing among the 'very, very conservative' islanders of Manu'a, on Ta'ū and Olosega (Sloan's Olosenga) and in the villages of Ofu and Sili. He identifies the Tutuila village torn down to make room for the US Navy's wharves and barracks as Fagatogo. The work was first published as *The shadow catcher* (New York: Book League of America, 1940. 296p.).

91 **Samoa.**
Dwight Long. In: *Sailing all seas in the 'Idle Hour'.* Dwight Long. London: Hodder & Stoughton, 1938, p. 132-55.

A simple account of visits to Ta'ū and Tutuila, by the skipper of the Seattle ketch *Idle Hour*. He was impressed by the cockroaches infesting the Pago Pago naval base, by the great rainfall precipitated from every passing cloud by Mount Pīoa, the

'Rainmaker', and the 'most useless' ground of Tutuila. He comments caustically on the London Missionary Society's yearly 'begging' schooner: 'During the last ten years, over 15,000 dollars had been collected annually by the mission boat in this way – the ostensible object being to help the poor people in England!'

Western Samoa

92 **In the backwaters of Western Samoa.**

Paul Theroux. In: *The happy isles of Oceania: paddling the Pacific.* Paul Theroux. London: Penguin Books, 1992, p. 435-71.

Theroux considers Āpia to be a 'squalid harbor town', 'mournfully rundown'. Samoans, more especially the young, 'rather gloatingly rude and light-fingered, quoting the Bible as they picked your pocket', react to outsiders with 'gratuitous hostility'. His fleeting impressions of 'Upolu and Savai'i lack depth and sympathy. To him, 'it was all backwaters'. Another example of the author's idiosyncratic views is his belief that Robert Louis Stevenson chose to end his days in 'Upolu only because of the regular, monthly postal service.

93 **Over the reefs.**

Robert Gibbings, with engravings by the author. London: J. M. Dent & Sons, 1948. 240p.

Robert John Gibbings (1889-1958), a wood-engraver of note, sketches an artist's impression of life in Tonga, Samoa, Tokelau, Rarotonga, Mangaia, Manihiki, Penrhyn and Tahiti. Chapters five to twenty (p. 27-137) describe villages on 'Upolu, Savai'i, Tokelau (p. 84-89) and Manono, vividly, realistically and sympathetically. On Manono, Gibbings enjoyed a village play rehearsal, and was accorded the title *Tamafaiga*. Elsewhere, he saw the *palolo* rising and tumultuous games of *kirikiti*, introduced into Samoa in 1885 by the officers and crew of HMS *Diamond*. The black-and-white engravings greatly enhance the charm of the recollections of an accomplished man, wholly at ease with his Samoan neighbours.

94 **Pacific hitch-hike – to Jambolana.**

Jack F. Rolley. New York; Los Angeles; Chicago: Vantage Press, 1989. 373p.

This lively, highly subjective diary of travel in the islands includes impressions (p. 287-343) of 'Upolu and Savai'i in 1950, when Rolley, an Englishman, was en route to Tahiti, where he married and settled down. He stayed for a time at Aggie Grey's boarding house in Āpia, then full of 'yes men' from the administration and large trading firms. 'Each was a little jack-in-office, very conscious of being a white person, and thinking himself way superior to the Samoans'. Of *fa'a-Sāmoa*, he writes: '... it's terrific. It controls every Samoan's life. It's as pervasive as air, as rigid as a ramrod, and Procrustean in nature'. 'Conformity' is the Samoan watchword. Only the Mormons and Seventh Day Adventists stood out for their own, distinctive codes of conduct.

95 ***Samoa 'uma*: where life is different.**
Llewella Pierce Churchill. London: Sampson Low, Marston; New York: *Forest and Stream*, [1902]. 295p.

Wife of William Churchill, United States consul-general in Āpia, the author seeks to present 'characteristic views of the real way of life of the islanders themselves and of the small colony of white people set down among a savage, though Christianized, community'. Her observation is keen and her style lively, making this perhaps the most informative and certainly the most readable of all books by residents of Āpia. It is packed with curious facts on: the weed that catches fish; how to count drinking nuts; *palusami*; fish; 'fine and tasty' fried rat for breakfast; and King Malietoa Laupepa's monthly wages of $48.60. Among the twenty-four excellent photographs by T. Andrew and J. Davis of Āpia is 'The wharf of the German firm, Apia'. *Samoa 'uma* is dedicated to Dr Bernard Funk whose 'great skill and unceasing care' saved the life of the author's son. See also 'Sports of the Samoans', by Llewella P. Churchill (*Outing* [March 1899], p. 562-68).

Tourism

Guides and information

96 **Landfalls of paradise: cruising guide to the Pacific islands.**
Earl R. Hinz. Honolulu: University of Hawai'i Press, 1993. 3rd ed. 384p. maps.

Authoritative and indispensable, this profusely illustrated guide covers ports of entry, harbours and anchorages in thirty-two island groups, including American Samoa and Western Samoa. Interesting features are highlighted. There are photographs of local waters and landing sites, and abundant data on oceanographic and meteorological phenomena. Appendices include a trilingual dictionary for port entry, a glossary of cruising terms, and Pacific race schedules.

97 **Samoa: Western & American Samoa: a Lonely Planet travel survival kit.**
Deanna Swaney. Hawthorn, Victoria: Lonely Planet Publications, 1994. 2nd ed. 202p. maps. bibliog.

Packed with up-to-date facts and sensible advice, illustrated by many clear maps and by attractive colour photographs, this is the best guidebook to Samoa (including Swain's Island and Rose Island) available in English. The three sections are Samoa generally, Western Samoa and American Samoa. The subdivisions are: facts; facts for the visitor; getting there and away; getting around; followed by specific information on each island in turn. There are indexes to maps and text.

98 **South Pacific handbook.**
David Stanley. Chico, California: Moon Publications, 1993. 5th ed. 780p. 139 maps. bibliog.

First published in July 1979 and a companion volume to the author's *Micronesia handbook*, this is a detailed tour guide to all major islands in Polynesia and Melanesia. Extensive outlines of Pacific history, culture and wildlife, practical travel information, a booklist, and glossaries of island languages make this the most useful guidebook available. The highly informative sections on American Samoa (p. 349-70), and Western Samoa (p. 371-407) provide maps for each individual island, and plans for Āpia and Pago Pago. The guide is revised regularly, at intervals of three to four years. A German translation, *Südsee Handbuch*, is published by Verlag Gisela E. Walther, Bremen, Germany.

99 **Die Südsee: Inselwelten im Südpazifik.** (The South Seas: island worlds in the South Pacific.)
Sabine Ehrhart. Cologne, Germany: DuMont Buchverlag, 1993. 378p. maps. bibliog. (DuMont-Dokumente: DuMont Kultur- und Landschaftsführer).

Splendidly illustrated, this is an intelligent, brisk guidebook which is strong on history and culture. Each country section is supplemented by an A-Z of essential tourist information. Western Samoa and American Samoa are described together (p. 132-64, 336-42), and the maps and plans are up-to-date. Photographs include villages in the 1920s, a warrior (from the *Godeffroy-Album*), and Governor Wilhelm Solf and Tamasese in Berlin in 1911.

100 **Tourism News of Samoa.**
Apia: *Tourism News of Samoa*, 1991- . monthly.

Presents travel and tourism news about Samoa, in English and Japanese. Well illustrated, this colourful journal has a circulation of about 5,000 copies. It is distributed in Western Samoa and American Samoa, and is available from Western Samoan government tourist offices in Australia, Germany, Japan, New Zealand and USA. See also *Tourism Topics* (Suva: Tourism Council of the South Pacific, 1988- . monthly), a newsletter devoted to island travel and tourism. Issued free of charge, it has a circulation of about 3,500 copies.

101 **West- und Amerikanisch-Samoa.**
Angelika Regel, Rosemarie Schyma. In: *Südsee: Tonga, Samoa, Cook-Inseln, Französisch-Polynesien, Fidschi, Vanuatu, Salomonen.* Angelika Regel, Rosemarie Schyma. Cologne, Germany: DuMont Buchverlag, 1994, p. 80-111, 283-98. 6 maps. bibliog. (p. 359). (Richtig Reisen).

This beautifully illustrated guide to the main attractions of ‘Upolu, Savai‘i and Tutuila highlights associations with the German colonial period. The addresses and telephone numbers (including Manu‘a) and the A-Z of essential information for visitors are notably up-to-date and practical.

Social and economic impact

102 **'The best kept secret': tourism in Western Samoa.**
Malama Meleisea, Penelope Meleisea. In: *Pacific tourism as islanders see it.* Edited by Freda Rajotte, Ron Crocombe. Suva: Institute of Pacific Studies, University of the South Pacific, in association with the South Pacific Social Sciences Association, 1980, p. 35-46. map. bibliog. (p. 168-71).

The development of transport and of hotel accommodation is summarized in respect of 'Upolu and Savai'i. Tourist facilities are largely contained within the Āpia area, with a high degree of local ownership and control. According to the authors, 'Most Samoans, with the possible exclusion of members of the Chamber of Commerce, are ambivalent about tourism'. Many dislike the prospect of further resort development in the rural areas with environmental damage, water and electricity supply being matters of concern. Modest expansion of the tourist industry should 'emphasise high quality, small scale hotel facilities that offer visitors the best in Samoan hospitality and culture'. The authors stress: 'A tourist industry should be the icing on the economic cake, with the emphasis on quality rather than quantity'. See also *A new kind of sugar: tourism in the Pacific,* edited by B. R. Finney, K. A. Watson (Honolulu: East-West Center; Santa Cruz, California: Center for South Pacific Studies, University of California-Santa Cruz, 1977. 2nd ed. 262p.). These still relevant papers, from a workshop held in 1974, discuss: the economic and cultural impact of tourism in the Pacific islands; alternative approaches to economic diversification; the creation of employment; foreign control of tourism; and other problems which remain unsolved.

103 **Gender, culture and tourism development in Western Samoa.**
Peggy Fairbairn-Dunlop. In: *Tourism: a gender analysis.* Edited by Vivian Kinnaird, D. Hall. London; New York: Routledge, 1994, p. 121-41. bibliog.

The author, on the staff of the USP School of Agriculture at Alafua, surveys the respective roles played by men and women in the provision of tourist facilities in the 1990s, and puts forward suggestions as to how greater involvement of women might be achieved.

104 **Tourism sector report: Western Samoa: evaluation and development needs.**
Jan-B. Bjarnason. Suva: Tourism Council of the South Pacific, 1990. 22p.

Bjarnason critically assesses factors inhibiting growth of tourism, especially problems of water supply, sewerage, pollution and transport.

105 **Warum Samoa?: Touristen und Tourismus in der Südsee.** (Why Samoa?: tourists and tourism in the South Seas.)
Hans Fischer. Berlin: Dietrich Reimer Verlag, 1984. 360p. 3 maps. bibliog.

An exceptionally thorough and revealing investigation of why tourists visit Samoa, of what they think of Samoans (and vice versa), and of the effects of tourism on the islands. The author, an anthropologist, acknowledges and includes research by his wife, Dr C. B. Wilpert, especially with regard to the trade in souvenirs and craft items. There are extensive extracts from the many interviews, with Samoans and visitors, on which the study is based. Fischer explores the history of tourism in Samoa, and the way in which an 'image' of the islands has been created (p. 218-34). The bibliography covers Pacific tourism generally, and includes many references to German periodicals such as *Globus*, *Zeitschrift für Ethnologie* and *Journal des Museum Godeffroy*. For an analysis of the ways in which the very meaning of ethnicity and culture is being contested and reworked in the wake of tourism's impact, see *Tourism, ethnicity, and the state in Asian and Pacific societies*, edited by Michel Picard, Robert E. Wood (Honolulu: University of Hawai'i Press, 1997. 280p. 4 maps. bibliogs.).

106 **Western Samoa tourism development plan, 1992-2001.**
Tourism Council of the South Pacific. [Suva]: Tourism Council of the South Pacific, for the Government of Western Samoa, 1992. 341p. maps.

Presents a comprehensive ten-year plan for improving tourist facilities and infrastructure. The emphasis is on encouraging eco-tourism and environmentally friendly activities.

107 **Western Samoa visitor survey 1994.**
Suva: Tourism Council of the South Pacific, 1994. 80p. (TCSP Survey Report, no. 16).

An analysis of officially recorded data relating to visitors to Western Samoa, including origin, mode of transport, local destinations, purpose of visit, together with notes on problems encountered. New Zealand heads the list of countries of origin, both in terms of tourism and of migrants returning permanently or temporarily.

Fauna and Flora

Fauna

Samoa

108 **The cicadas of the Fiji, Samoa and Tonga Islands: their taxonomy and biogeography (*Homoptera, Cicadidae*): with a chapter on the geological history of the area by A. Ewart.**
J. P. Duffels, A. Ewart. Leiden, Netherlands; New York: E. J. Brill/ Scandinavian Science Press, 1988. 108p. maps. bibliog. (Entomonograph, vol. 10).

An entomological treatise on cicadas, a family of insects with a stout body, wide blunt head and large transparent wings. Male cicadas produce a shrill singing noise by means of a pair of drumlike organs at the base of the abdomen. This noise is characteristic of night in tropical areas.

109 ***Cyclophoridae* and *pupinidae* of Caroline, Fijian and Samoan Islands.**
William J. Clench. Honolulu: Bernice P. Bishop Museum, 1949. 52p. bibliog. (Bulletin, no. 196).

A comparative study of two kinds of gastropods found in Samoa.

110 **Land snails from Hawaii, Christmas Island and Samoa.**
Henry A. Pilsbry, C. Montague Cooke Jr., Marie C. Neal. Honolulu: Bernice P. Bishop Museum, 1928. 49p. bibliog. (Bulletin, no. 47).

A comparative malacological study, covering land snails from both American Samoa and Western Samoa.

111 **'Palolo': notes on the periodic appearance of the annelid worm *Eunice viridis* (Gray) in the South-west Pacific islands.**
William Burrows. *Journal of the Polynesian Society*, vol. 64, no. 1 (March 1955), p. 137-54.

Burrows provides an extensive discussion of the geographical distribution (including notably American Samoa and Western Samoa) of *palolo*, with a table of its appearance dates. This article is based on published accounts and on reports from local residents.

112 **Report on a collection of Samoan *coleoptera.***
Elwood Curtis Zimmerman. Honolulu: Bernice P. Bishop Museum, 1941. (Occasional Papers, vol. 16, no. 7, p. 159-76. bibliog.).

These are detailed entomological studies of various kinds of winged beetles found in Samoa.

113 **Samoan *foraminifera.***
Joseph A. Cushman. Washington, DC: Carnegie Institution of Washington, 1924. 75p. bibliog. (Publications, no. 342).

Includes studies of an order of chiefly marine single-celled animals (protozoans) similar to but larger than the related amoebas. *Foraminifera* usually have chalky shells perforated with minute holes through which slender pseudopodia protrude.

American Samoa

114 **The introduction of mosquitoes of the genus *Toxorhynchites* into American Samoa.**
G. D. Peterson. *Journal of Economic Entomology*, vol. 49 (1956), p. 786-89. bibliog.

Peterson describes American Samoan experiments in using a biological control agent and mosquito predator to eradicate the mosquito vectors of endemic diseases such as filariasis. See also 'The occurrence of *Toxorhynchites amboinensis* in Western Samoa' by B. Engber, P. F. Sone, J. S. Pillai (*Mosquito News*, vol. 38 [1978], p. 295-96); and *Fourth joint seminar on filariasis and vector control. Apia, Western Samoa, 1-10 July, 1974* (Geneva: WHO; Nouméa, New Caledonia: SPC, 1974. 46p.).

115 ***Lepidoptera* of American Samoa: with particular reference to biology and ecology.**
W. P. Comstock. Honolulu: Bernice P. Bishop Museum, 1966. 74p. bibliog. (Pacific Insects Monographs, no. 11).

A detailed scientific study of the butterflies, moths, skippers, larvae and caterpillars found in American Samoa.

116 **Wildlife and wildlife habitat of American Samoa.**
A. B. Amerson, Jr., W. A. Whistler, T. D. Schwaner. Washington, DC: Fish and Wildlife Service, US Department of the Interior, 1982. 2 vols. maps. bibliog.

An exceptionally thorough, illustrated survey of all aspects of ecology and wildlife in American Samoa. Volume one is entitled *Environment and ecology* and volume two *Accounts of flora and fauna.* See also *A 1986 survey of the forest birds of American Samoa* by J. Engbring, F. L. Ramsey (Washington, DC: Fish and Wildlife Service, US Department of the Interior, 1989).

Western Samoa

117 ***Rattus exulans* in Western Samoa.**
R. R. Marples. *Pacific Science*, vol. 9 (1955), p. 171-76. bibliog.

A scientific study of one species of Pacific rat commonly found in Western Samoa.

118 **The rhinoceros beetle in Western Samoa.**
R. A. Cumber. Nouméa, New Caledonia: South Pacific Commission, 1957. 32p. map. (Technical Paper, no. 107).

This profusely illustrated paper provides basic information on the major pest of Samoan coconut plantations, a very large horned scarabaeid beetle of the subfamily Dynastinae (Dynastes). It includes maps of infested areas and of the distribution of coconut groves on 'Upolu. See also 'Rhinoceros beetle control in Western Samoa' by U. Beichle (*Alafua Agricultural Bulletin*, vol. 5, no. 3 [1980], p. 52-54), a status report on the struggle to eradicate the pest.

119 **Spiders from Western Samoa.**
B. J. Marples. *Journal of the Linnean Society of London: Zoology*, vol. 42, no. 287 (1955), p. 453-504. bibliog.

Provides scientific descriptions of spiders (especially *Filistata bakeri*) found in Western Samoa.

Teachers' handbook to fauna of Western Samoa: a vernacular listing.
See item no. 336.

Birds

120 **The birds and birdlore of Samoa: 'O manu ma tala'aga o manu o Samoa.**
Corey Muse, Shirley Muse. Walla Walla, Washington: Pioneer Press, 1982. 156p. 4 maps. bibliog.

Sponsored by the National Audubon Society and based on six months' fieldwork in Western Samoa and American Samoa, this attractive guide lists and discusses seventy-two kinds of birds, illustrating them with first-rate colour photographs and drawings by Norman Adams. Of special interest is the discussion of birds in Samoan tradition and culture, on the basis of proverbs containing ornithological imagery. The Samoan texts are accompanied by English translations and by interpretations of their meaning and significance.

121 **Birds of Fiji, Tonga and Samoa.**
D. Watling, illustrated by C. Talbot-Kelly. Wellington: Millwood Press, 1982. 176p. bibliog.

The first section of this useful guide considers the ornithological history of the islands, the composition of their avifauna, and the geographical and climatic conditions. Colour plates illustrate all birds found, then grouping them as land birds and sea birds. In the latter two sections birds are described according to: identification; flight; song; food; breeding; habitat and range; and allied species. The fifth section's extensive appendices include a glossary, a bibliography, a checklist of birds recorded in Samoa, and indexes of scientific, English and local names.

122 **The birds of Swain's Island, South-central Pacific.**
Roger B. Clapp. *Notornis*, vol. 15, no. 3 (1968), p. 198-206. map. bibliog.

A record of the species observed on six visits in 1966-67 by field parties of the Smithsonian Institution's Pacific Ocean Biological Survey Program.

123 **A field guide to the birds of Hawaii and the tropical Pacific.**
H. Douglas Pratt, Phillip L. Bruner, Delwyn G. Berrett. Princeton, New Jersey: Princeton University Press, 1987. 409p. maps. bibliog.

Species are illustrated by area, with birds of wide distribution, such as seabirds, shorebirds and ducks, illustrated together. Plumage variations are shown, and descriptions include occurrence, appearance, habits, voice and names. Photographs illustrate plants on which birds rely for survival, and the history and future of conservation in the islands are outlined. Regional maps and six area checklists are also provided.

124 **Guide to the birds of Samoa.**
Myrtle J. Ashmole. Honolulu: Bernice P. Bishop Museum, 1963. 21p. bibliog. (PSIC 2).

A publication of the Bishop Museum Library's Geography and Map Division, consisting of a preliminary list of avian species in both American Samoa and Western Samoa. See also *Hand-list to the birds of Samoa* by John S. Armstrong (London: Bale, Sons & Danielsson, 1932. 91p. bibliog.), a handy guide to the species of birds encountered in the Samoan Islands, with their scientific and English names (and some vernacular names). Each bird is carefully described, together with its habitat and foods.

Fishes

125 **An annotated checklist of the fishes of Samoa.**
R. C. Wass. Seattle, Washington: National Marine Fisheries Series, 1984. 43p. (NOAA Technical Report, SSRF 781).

Scientific names of species are given in all cases, with Samoan names where ascertained. The brief annotations include details of habitat, feeding and uses. See also *The fishes of Samoa: description of the species found in the Archipelago, with a provisional checklist of the fishes of Oceania* by David S. Jordan, Alvin Seale (Washington, DC: Government Printing Office, 1906. 455p. [US Bureau of Fisheries. Bulletin, no. 25; Document 605]), which includes a 'Glossary of principal words composing native names of Samoan fishes' by W. E. Safford (p. 446-55).

126 **Fishes obtained at Samoa in 1929.**
Henry W. Fowler. Honolulu: Bernice P. Bishop Museum, 1932. 16p. (Occasional Papers, vol. 9, no. 18).

A detailed, scientific study of fish specimens from the Samoan archipelago preserved at the Bishop Museum. See also: 'A collection of fishes from Samoa' by Henry W. Fowler, Charles F. Silvester (Washington, DC: Department of Marine Biology, Carnegie Institution of Washington, 1922 [Publications, no. 312. Papers, vol. 18, p. 109-26]); and *Fishes of Guam, Samoa, and Tahiti* by Henry W. Fowler (Honolulu: Bernice P. Bishop Museum, 1925. 38p. bibliog. [Bulletin, no. 22]).

Fish names of Western Polynesia: Niue, Samoa, Tokelau, Tonga, Tuvalu, Wallis and Futuna, Outliers.
See item no. 332.

Flora

Botanical bibliographies

127 **A botanical bibliography of the islands of the Pacific.**
Elmer Drew Merrill, with a subject index by E. H. Walker. Washington, DC: Government Printing Office, 1947. 404p. (Smithsonian Institution. Contributions from the United States National Herbarium, vol. 30, part 1).

The first section of this bibliography of some 3,800 entries consists of a revision, 'with the addition of numerous titles', of: *Bibliography of Polynesian botany* by Elmer Drew Merrill (Honolulu: Bernice P. Bishop Museum, 1924. 68p. [Bulletin, no. 13]); and *Polynesian botanical bibliography, 1773-1935* by Elmer Drew Merrill (Honolulu: Bernice P. Bishop Museum, 1937. 194p. [Bulletin, no. 144]). A still valuable introduction to Pacific botany is *Plant life of the Pacific world*, also by Elmer Drew Merrill (New York: Macmillan, 1945. 295p. map. bibliog.).

128 **Island bibliographies: Micronesian botany; Land environment and ecology of coral atolls; Vegetation of tropical Pacific islands.**
Marie-Hélène Sachet, F. Raymond Fosberg. [Washington, DC]: National Research Council, National Academy of Sciences, 1955. 577p.

Compiled under the auspices of the Pacific Science Board, this work consists of three major bibliographies and 'a List of serial abbreviations'. All four sections have lists of addenda. References to Rose Atoll and Swain's Island (Olohega), including several from the Tutuila official periodical *'O le Fa'atonu*, appear mainly in the second bibliography, and those to Samoa in the third. Coverage extends to 1954. The volume is dedicated to Elmer Drew Merrill (q.v.) of Harvard University, 'whose bibliographies of the botany of the Pacific area form the foundation for all subsequent work in this field'. Each bibliography is thoroughly cross-referenced by island, author, systematic name and broad subject. See also *Island bibliographies supplement* ... by Marie-Hélène Sachet, F. Raymond Fosberg (Washington, DC: National Academy of Sciences, 1971. 427p.).

129 **Papuasia and Oceania.**
D. G. Frodin. In: *Guide to the standard floras of the world: an annotated, geographically arranged systematic bibliography of the principal floras, enumerations, checklists, and chronological atlases of different areas.* Cambridge, England: Cambridge University Press, 1984, p. 495-533.

With informative annotations and thorough coverage, even of small islands, this is an essential complement to E. D. Merrill's *A botanical bibliography of the islands of the Pacific* (q.v.). Samoa figures prominently among the references.

Samoa

130 **Checklist of the weed flora of Western Polynesia: an annotated list of the weed species of Samoa, Tonga, Niue, and Wallis and Futuna, along with the earliest dates of collection and the local names.**
W. Arthur Whistler. Nouméa, New Caledonia: South Pacific Commission, 1988. 69p. (SPC Technical Paper, no. 194).

The 'weeds' listed here by their botanical and vernacular names are those plants for which no nutritional, medicinal or economic uses were known to Whistler. This represents a useful contribution to botany and also to lexicography, as many of the Samoan names are not to be found in the Pratt and Milner dictionaries. See also 'On various Samoan plants and their vernacular names' by Thomas Powell (*Journal of Botany*, vol. 6 [1868], p. 278-85, 342-47, 355-70), compiled by a LMS missionary. Powell's careful botanical and linguistic notes include some plant species and Samoan names which are no longer common, if found at all.

131 **Flowering plants of Samoa.**

Erling Christopherson. Honolulu: Bernice P. Bishop Museum, 1935-38. 2 vols. (Bulletin, no. 128; no. 154).

A detailed botanical description and taxonomy of flowering plants in the Samoan archipelago, with their Latin and Samoan names. Other publications by the Bernice P. Bishop Museum are: *A revision of the pteridophyta of Samoa* by Carl Christensen (Honolulu: Bernice P. Bishop Museum, 1943. 138p. bibliog. [Bulletin, no. 177]); and *Samoan pandanaceae* by Ugolino Martelli (Honolulu: Bernice P. Bishop Museum, 1934. 24p. [Occasional Papers, vol. 10, no. 13]). See also: *Plants of Samoa* by B. E. V. Parham (Wellington: Government Printer, 1972 [Department of Scientific and Industrial Research, Information Series, no. 85]); and *Flora of Samoa* by Curtis G. Lloyd, Walter H. Aiken (New York: Lloyd Library, 1934. 113p. [Bulletin, no. 33: Botanical Series, no. 4]).

132 **Flowers of the Pacific island seashore: a guide to the littoral plants of Hawai‘i, Tahiti, Samoa, Tonga, Cook Islands, Fiji and Micronesia.**

W. Arthur Whistler. Honolulu: Isle Botanica, 1992. 154p. bibliog.

This colourful guide covers littoral species and littoral vegetation of all types, with botanical names followed by species, one page to each. Each has a colour photograph, description and note of distribution. A glossary of botanical terms, and indexes of scientific and vernacular names are also provided. See also *Coastal flowers of the tropical Pacific* by W. Arthur Whistler (Lawai, Hawai‘i: Pacific Tropical Botanical Garden, 1980. 83p. bibliog.).

133 **Kava: the Pacific drug.**

Vincent Lebot, Mark Merlin, Lamont Lindstrom. New Haven, Connecticut: Yale University Press, 1992. 255p. maps. bibliog.

A comprehensive, academic study, in the series Psychoactive Plants of the World, of *kava* (*Piper methysticum.* Forst.f.), which is consumed in a wide range of Pacific Ocean societies, from New Guinea to Hawai‘i. The botany, chemistry, ethnobotany, anthropology and economics of *kava* varieties are discussed in considerable detail, including its cultivars, origin myths, and traditional medicinal uses in Samoa. The authors suggest that use of *kava*, known in Samoa as *‘ava*, may spread beyond its regional base: ‘As *kava* is internationalized, the Pacific drug is becoming a world drug’. See also *Kava: a bibliography* by Y. N. Singh (Suva: Pacific Information Centre, University of the South Pacific, 1986. 111p.), a comprehensive bibliography of *kava* with 793 references to the plant’s botany, chemistry, ethnology and medicinal uses. The work is indexed only by author and title.

134 **Plants of Hawaii National Park illustrative of plants and customs of the South Seas.**

Otto Degener. Ann Arbor, Michigan: Braun-Brumfield, 1973. 312p.

This profusely illustrated guide to the plants of Hawai‘i National Park highlights the ethno-botanical links with other areas of Polynesia, and the varied uses made of plants such as pandanus and candlenut. See also: *Flowers of the South Pacific* by H. R. Hughes, photography by C. Cheng (Milton, Queensland: Jacaranda Press, 1972. 105p. bibliog.), a well illustrated, brief guide to the flowering trees and shrubs of the South

Pacific region, indicating for each item family, origin, habitat, description and general notes; and *Tropical blossoms of the Pacific* by D. Hargreaves, B. Hargreaves (Lahaina, Hawai'i: Ross-Hargreaves, 1970. 64p.), in which each flowering plant commonly found in the islands is described, and illustrated by a colour plate.

135 **Wayside plants of the islands: a guide to the lowland flora of the Pacific islands: Hawai'i, Samoa, Tonga, Tahiti, Fiji, Guam, Belau.**
W. Arthur Whistler. Honolulu: Isle Botanica, 1995. 202p. map. bibliog.

Designed as a guide to identification of the most common plant species found in the islands, and splendidly illustrated by 170 colour photographs, this is an essential companion to Whistler's *Flowers of the Pacific island seashore* (q.v.), and is based on *Weed handbook of western Polynesia* by W. Arthur Whistler (Eschborn, West Germany: Deutsche Gesellschaft für Technische Zusammenarbeit, 1983. 151p.). Samoa is represented by 120 species, all with scientific, common and vernacular name indicated.

Folk plant nomenclature in Polynesia.
See item no. 333.

American Samoa

136 **American Samoa: vegetation of Tutuila Island; ethnobotany of the Samoans; vegetation of Rose Atoll.**
William Albert Setchell. Washington, DC: Carnegie Institution of Washington, 1924. 275p. maps. bibliogs. (Carnegie Institution of Washington Publication, no. 341; Tortuga Laboratory Papers, vol. 20). Reprinted, New York: AMS Press, 1978.

Together, the three substantial parts of this volume, illustrated by thirty-seven black-and-white plates and fifty-seven text figures, constitute the most detailed and authoritative study of American Samoan vegetation and ethnobotany. An extensive glossary of Samoan plant names is provided in part three (p. 272-75). The background summaries are of special value, as is the account of Rose Atoll and its mapping. However, Setchell mistakenly attributes the discovery of the atoll to Louis de Freycinet, rather than to Jacob Roggeveen.

137 **The flora and vegetation of Swains Island.**
W. Arthur Whistler. *Atoll Research Bulletin*, no. 262 (1983), p. 1-25. bibliog.

Whistler maintains that Olohega (Swain's Island) is 'geographically and floristically a part of Tokelau', although politically a part of American Samoa. He visited the atoll in May 1976 spending four days there collecting plants and interviewing the Tokelauan inhabitants (see *Wildlife and wildlife habitat of American Samoa*, by A. B. Amerson Jr., W. A. Whistler, T. D. Schwaner). Vernacular names (Tokelauan and Samoan), scientific names, plant families and plant uses are given. See also 'A naturalist in the South Pacific: north to Tokelau' by W. Arthur Whistler (*Pacific Tropical Botanical Garden Bulletin*, vol. 11, no. 2 [1981], p. 29-37. bibliog.).

138 **A guide to Pacific wetland plants.**
Compiled and edited by Lani Stemmermann. Honolulu: US Corps of Engineers Honolulu District, 1981. 116p. maps. bibliog.

Eight types of wetland and indicative plant species in American Samoa, the Hawaiian islands, Guam, the Northern Mariana Islands and the high Caroline Islands are described and illustrated by excellent colour photographs. The work also includes a glossary, and an index covering family, genera, species, English and some vernacular names and synonyms.

139 **Plants of the Manu'a Islands.**
T. G. Yuncker. Honolulu: Bernice P. Bishop Museum, 1945. 73p. map. bibliog. (Bulletin, no. 184).

A systematic scientific description of the plant species found in the islands of Ofu, Olosega and Ta'ū in the Manu'a District of American Samoa.

140 **Rose Atoll, American Samoa.**
Alfred G. Mayor. *Proceedings of the American Philosophical Society*, vol. 60, no. 2 (1921), p. 62-70.

Mayor spent twenty-four hours on Rose Atoll, on 5-6 June 1920, in the company of Warren Jay Terhune, governor of American Samoa, and made the first survey of the geology and vegetation of the atoll. See also Alfred G. Mayor, 'Rose Island (*Nu'u o manu*)' (*O le Fa'atonu* [Pago Pago], vol. 18, no. 7 [July 1920]), his report to the governor, in both Samoan and English.

141 **The vegetation of Eastern Samoa.**
W. Arthur Whistler. *Allertonia*, vol. 2, no. 2 (1980), p. 45-190. map. bibliog.

An exhaustive botanical description and classification of the grasses, shrubs and trees of Tutuila, Manu'a, Rose Atoll and Swain's Island. See also *Botanical inventory of the proposed Tutuila and Ofu units of the National Park of American Samoa* by W. Arthur Whistler (Honolulu: National Park Service; 1994).

Western Samoa

142 **Plants of cropland in Western Samoa with special reference to taro.**
E. Sauerborn, J. Sauerborn. Stuttgart, Germany: Margraf, 1984. 331p. bibliog. (Universität Hohenheim PLITS 1984/2(4)).

This truly impressive scientific handbook covers all species of plants (including 'weeds') found on cultivated land, identifying species, plant habit, plant anatomy and uses. *Talo* (*Colocasia esculenta*) is discussed in considerable detail, for its special importance in the Samoan diet.

143 **Vegetation and flora of the Aleipata Islands, Western Samoa.**
W. Arthur Whistler. *Pacific Science*, vol. 37, no. 3 (1983), p. 227-49. bibliog.

This beautiful, virtually unspoiled nature reserve comprises Nu'utele, Nu'ulua and other small islands and rocks off the southeastern tip of 'Upolu.

144 **Vegetation of the montane region of Savai'i, Western Samoa.**
W. Arthur Whistler. *Pacific Science*, vol. 32, no. 1 (1978), p. 79-94. bibliog.

A detailed description of the vegetation of inland Savai'i, notable for its extinct or dormant volcanoes and its large northward lava flows.

Prehistory and Archaeology

Pacific

145 **Changes over time: recent advances in dating human colonisation of the Pacific Basin area.**

Roger C. Green. In: *The origins of the first New Zealanders.* Edited by Douglas G. Sutton. Auckland, New Zealand: Auckland University Press, 1994, p. 19-51. 3 maps. bibliog.

This absorbing 'brief summary' of our present understanding of the peopling of the Pacific Basin concludes that the Polynesians and the Polynesian languages evolved in West Polynesia through a period of over a thousand years. The basic elements of an Ancestral Polynesian Society were established in the first few centuries BC in Tonga, Samoa, Futuna and Uvea for communities speaking a proto-Polynesian language and possessing an increasingly characteristic Polynesian body form. The extensive bibliography is a valuable guide to recent research on colonization and settlement in the islands, from Indonesia eastwards. See also: *The Polynesians: prehistory of an island people* by P. S. Bellwood (London: Thames & Hudson, 1978); *Man's conquest of the Pacific* by P. S. Bellwood (Auckland, New Zealand: William Collins, 1978); and *Prehistory in the Pacific islands: a study of variation in language, customs and human biology* by John Terrell (Cambridge, England: Cambridge University Press, 1986).

146 **The evolution of the Polynesian chiefdoms.**

Patrick Vinton Kirch. Cambridge, England: Cambridge University Press, 1989. 326p. 21 maps. bibliog. (New Studies in Archaeology).

First published in 1984, this is an interesting attempt to reconstruct prehistoric political structures in Polynesia, including Samoa, from archaeological evidence. Dispersal, war and competition accelerated the demographic and economic changes from which distinctive political and cultural patterns gradually evolved. See also *The Polynesians* by Patrick Vinton Kirch (Oxford: B. H. Blackwell, 1994 [The Peoples of Southeast Asia and the Pacific]).

147 **Tropical Polynesian prehistory – where are we now?**
Roger C. Green. In: *A community of culture: the people and prehistory of the Pacific.* Edited by Matthew Spriggs, Douglas E. Yen, Wal Ambrose, Rhŷs Jones, Alan Thorne, Ann Andrews. Canberra: Department of Prehistory, Research School of Pacific Studies, Australian National University, 1993, p. 218-38. bibliog.

This lucid summary of the 'modern era of archaeology' in tropical Polynesia, from Kenneth Emory's excavations in Hawai'i in 1950 to 1992, highlights the desirability of a deeper concern with continuity and with identifying major shifts in the socio-political aspects of cultures, especially where these reflect new levels of organizational complexity. This approach has only been attempted in Western Samoa, in particular by Janet M. Davidson, Jack Golson and Roger C. Green. From the immense database built in just thirty years, ten assessments of the current situation provide useful guidelines for future research. The bibliography (p. 231-38) lists the key works of the last three decades.

The prehistoric exploration and colonisation of the Pacific.
See item no. 624.

Samoa

148 **At the halls of the mountain kings: Fijian and Samoan fortifications: comparison and analysis.**
Simon Best. *Journal of the Polynesian Society*, vol. 102, no. 4 (Dec. 1993), p. 385-447. maps. bibliog.

Best reviews the historic records and the archaeological research on impressive man-made fortifications on the rugged, jungle-clad peaks of both Fiji and Samoa (especially 'Upolu). He then discusses the construction of these fortifications, with reference to representative sites, such as Tatagamatau and newly identified fortifications in Tutuila. There are maps of several forts and of fortified complexes, such as that on Mount Vaea. See also 'Fortifications in Fiji and Samoa: comparisons and predictions' by Simon Best (*Archaeology in New Zealand*, vol. 35 [1992], p. 40-44. maps. bibliog.).

149 **Samoa and Tonga.**
Janet M. Davidson. In: *The prehistory of Polynesia.* Edited by Jesse D. Jennings. Cambridge, Massachusetts; London: Harvard University Press, 1979, p. 82-109. maps. bibliog.

Davidson reviews archaeological excavations and site surveys on 'Upolu, Manono and Tutuila, noting that evidence of the earliest settlements of Samoa is still very sparse. The earliest known site in Samoa is the submerged Ferry Berth site, which yielded a radiocarbon date on shell of 940 BC ± 80. See also 'New information for the Ferry Berth site, Mulifanua, Western Samoa' by Helen M. Leach, Roger C. Green (*Journal of the Polynesian Society*, vol. 98, no. 3 [Sept. 1989], p. 319-29. 2 maps. bibliog.).

This site (indexed as SU-MU-1) is at the time of writing Samoa's only Lapita site. The authors confirm previous radiocarbon dating of circa 3,000 years ago, and describe newly found adzes of Lapita type.

American Samoa

150 **An archaeological survey of the Manu'a Islands, American Samoa.**
T. L. Hunt, P. V. Kirch. *Journal of the Polynesian Society*, vol. 97, no. 2 (June 1988), p. 153-83. maps. bibliog.

A detailed report on the Manu'a Archaeological Project of 1986, carried out under the auspices of the Burke Museum of the University of Washington. See also: 'Radiocarbon dates from two coastal sites in the Manu'a group, American Samoa' by T. L. Hunt, P. V. Kirch (*Radiocarbon*, vol. 29 [1987], p. 417-19. bibliog.); and 'Radiocarbon dates from American Samoa' by Jeffrey T. Clark (*Radiocarbon*, vol. 35 [1993], p. 323-30. bibliog.).

151 **Necromancing the stone: archaeologists and adzes in Samoa.**
Simon Best, Peter Sheppard, Roger Green, Robin Parker. *Journal of the Polynesian Society*, vol. 101, no. 1 (March 1992), p. 45-85. maps. bibliog.

Data are presented on 161 archaeological and geological basalt samples from the Fiji-Polynesian region. The focus is primarily on the characterization of the Tutuila inland quarry complex near Leone (the Tataga Matau and Leafu quarries) and its discrimination from other sources/areas both in Samoa and throughout the region. Adzes of Samoan typology, made from a fine dark basalt, and found in an area from Lau in Fiji north to Tokelau and west to the outer eastern Solomon Islands, have been shown to have originated in Samoa, some in the Leone area of Tutuila.

152 **Petroglyphs in American Samoa.**
William K. Kikuchi. *Journal of the Polynesian Society*, vol. 73, no. 1 (March 1964), p. 163-66. bibliog.

This records the first petroglyphs found in Samoa, at site ST 128 (the lagoon at Leone village, Tutuila). See also 'Additional petroglyphs from American Samoa' by William K. Kikuchi (*Journal of the Polynesian Society*, vol. 76, no. 3 [Sept. 1967], p. 372-73. bibliog.). These represent *fe'e* (octopus), *laumei* (turtle) and an incomplete human figure.

153 **Prehistoric settlement system in Eastern Tutuila, American Samoa.**
Jeffrey T. Clark, David J. Herdrich. *Journal of the Polynesian Society*, vol. 102, no. 2 (June 1993), p. 147-85. 2 maps. bibliog.

The Eastern Tutuila investigations added 176 new sites to the site inventory of American Samoa, including a ceramic residential site, basalt quarries and highland forts. Most of the site types known for Western Samoa are now known for American Samoa. There is abundant evidence of previously unsuspected complexity in the archaeological record of Tutuila, with a wealth of information yet to be uncovered. See also 'Prehistory of Alega, Tutuila Island, American Samoa: a small residential and basalt-industrial valley' by Jeffrey T. Clark (*New Zealand Journal of Archaeology*, vol. 15 [1993], p. 67-86. bibliog.).

154 **Report on the second phase of field work at the Tataga-Matau site, American Samoa, July-August 1988.**
Simon Best, Helen Leach, Dan Witter. Auckland, New Zealand: Department of Anthropology, University of Auckland, [1989]. 75p. maps. bibliog.

Provides further details of finds at Samoa's most exciting and fruitful archaeological excavations.

155 **The To'aga site: three millennia of Polynesian occupation in the Manu'a islands, American Samoa.**
Edited by Patrick Vinton Kirch, T. L. Hunt. Berkeley, California: Archaeological Research Facility, University of California at Berkeley, 1993. 248p. maps. bibliogs. (Contributions of the Archaeological Research Facility, no. 51).

This is the definitive, meticulously detailed report of the findings of excavations at To'aga on Ofu island in 1986, 1987 and 1989. Every aspect is surveyed by the nine authors, including radiocarbon chronology, ceramics, faunal assemblages, molluscs and bird bones. Each chapter has its own extensive bibliography. Radiocarbon dates extend back to *circa* 3600 cal BP. The site is potentially a major source of archaeological evidence for the reconstruction of Ancestral Polynesian Culture, with a large assemblage of one-piece fishing gear and varied ceramics.

156 **Towards an understanding of Samoan star mounds.**
David J. Herdrich. *Journal of the Polynesian Society*, vol. 100, no. 4 (Dec. 1991), p. 381-435. bibliog.

This paper on the 'star' or 'cog' mounds (*tia 'ave*) of Tutuila, American Samoa, includes a literature review, an intensive analysis of the mounds, and an exploration of likely hypotheses about their function. Herdrich argues that star mounds and related 'specialised sites' belong to a single category, and may have been used for ritual pigeon-catching. The shape of the mounds may be connected to village spatial organization and the shape of certain Samoan gods.

157 **Volcanic glass in Samoa: a technological and geochemical study.**
Jeffrey T. Clark, Elizabeth Wright. *Journal of the Polynesian Society*, vol. 104, no. 3 (Sept. 1995), p. 239-66. 2 maps. bibliog.

A technical study of the unusually abundant volcanic-glass artefacts found at 'Aoa on Tutuila. The 'Aoa assemblage is described (a sample being geochemically characterized) and compared with material from other sites in the region. The authors conclude that the 'Aoa artefacts reflect a lithic technology broadly similar to that found on other islands, and that Tutuila supplied volcanic glass to other islands in the archipelago and thus participated in an inter-island exchange network. The bibliography (p. 262-66) includes a useful selection of relevant studies. See also 'An early settlement in the Polynesian homeland: excavations at 'Aoa Valley, Tutuila Island, American Samoa' by J. T. Clark, M. G. Michlovic (*Journal of Field Archaeology*, vol. 23, no. 2 [1996], p. 151).

Western Samoa

158 **Archaeological excavations in Western Samoa.**

Jesse D. Jennings, Richard N. Holmer, with sections by Nancy Hewitt, Gregory Jackmond, Joel Janetski, Ernest Lohse. Honolulu: Department of Anthropology, Bernice P. Bishop Museum, 1980. 155p. maps. bibliog. (Pacific Anthropological Records, no. 32).

Provides detailed reports on archaeological sites on 'Upolu and Manono, excavated in 1976 and 1977. Earlier findings for the Mt. Olo village complex, first excavated in 1974, are given in *Excavations on Upolu, Western Samoa* by Jesse D. Jennings, Richard N. Holmer, Joel C. Janetski, Howard L. Smith (Honolulu: Department of Anthropology, Bernice P. Bishop Museum, 1976. 115p. [Pacific Anthropological Records, no. 25]), which includes an appendix by W. R. Dickinson. See also 'The Ferry Berth site, Mulifanua district, Upolu' by Jesse D. Jennings in *Archaeology in Western Samoa*, edited by Roger C. Green, Janet M. Davidson (Auckland, New Zealand: Auckland Institute and Museum, 1974, vol. 2, p. 176-78. bibliog. [Bulletin, no. 7]).

159 **Archaeology in Western Samoa.**

Edited by Roger C. Green, Janet M. Davidson. Auckland, New Zealand: Auckland Institute and Museum, 1969-74. 2 vols. (Bulletins, nos. 6-7).

These volumes are typical of the 'modern era of archaeology' in tropical Polynesia in their caution, reliance on meticulous excavation of individual sites, on radiocarbon dating and on similar modern techniques, eschewing the diffusionist theories of earlier periods. Volume one includes Jack Golson's 'Preliminary research: archaeology in Western Samoa, 1957' (p. 14-20) and 'Further details on excavations at Va-1 in 1957' (p. 108-10). Volume two contains: Davidson's 'The upper Falefa Valley project: summaries and conclusions' (p. 155-62); Green and Davidson on 'A radiocarbon and stratigraphic sequence for Western Samoa' (p. 212-24); Davidson's 'Samoan structural remains and settlement patterns' (p. 225-44); Green's 'A review of portable artifacts from Western Samoa' (p. 245-75); and the editors' joint 'Conclusion' (p. 278-82).

160 **Radiocarbon dates for Western Samoa.**

Roger C. Green, Janet M. Davidson. *Journal of the Polynesian Society*, vol. 74, no. 1 (March 1965), p. 63-69. bibliog.

Provides radiocarbon dates for the 'Upolu areas of Vailele, Luatuānu'u and Lotofaga, with a discussion of the data. The earliest charcoal sample, at a *suga* mound in Vailele, was dated at 1950 ± 70 years before 1950.

History

Pacific history

161 **Americans in Polynesia, 1783-1842.**
W. Patrick Strauss. East Lansing, Michigan: Michigan State University Press, 1963. 187p.

This erudite study of a relatively little known period in Polynesian history contains three chapters on the United States Exploring Expedition. These include Charles Wilkes' observations on Tutuila and other islands of Samoa. See also *American relations in the Pacific and the Far East, 1784-1900* by James Morton Callahan (New York; Washington, DC; London: Praeger Publishers, 1969. 177p. bibliog.). This contains chapters on 'The United States Exploring Expedition, 1839-43' (p. 49-59); and 'Relations in Samoa' (p. 135-48). There is a facsimile reprint of the original edition: Baltimore, Maryland: Johns Hopkins Press, 1901 (Johns Hopkins University Studies in Historical and Political Science. Series 19, no. 1-3).

162 **The great powers in the Pacific.**
W. P. Morrell. London: Routledge & Kegan Paul, for the Historical Association, 1963. 35p. bibliog. (Historical Association pamphlet, G. 54).

An exceptionally lucid outline of imperialist rivalries and expansion in the Pacific area. Samoa was the 'thorniest problem' of the late 19th century, resolved by the Samoa Convention of November 1899. Set in the perspective of global conflicts, the Samoan 'imbroglio' now assumes relatively minor importance, despite the persistence of political dependence of American Samoa. See also *Britain in the Pacific islands* by W. P. Morrell (Oxford: Clarendon Press, 1960. 454p. maps. bibliog.), in which Morrell puts in context 'the crimes staining the British record in the Pacific', without condonation. This scholarly overview of the spread of British influence outlines the pre-contact situation; subsequent exploration; trade; settlement; and the establishment of Christian missions. There are particularly valuable accounts of the London Mission in Samoa; the labour trade; the House of Godeffroy and the Samoan imbroglio (p. 205-38); and the partition of Samoa. See also *British policy in the South Pacific*

(1786-1893): a study in British policy towards the South Pacific islands prior to the establishment of governments by the Great Powers by John M. Ward (Sydney, Wellington, London: Australasian Publishing Co., 1948. 364p. 3 maps. bibliog.).

163 **Historical dictionary of Polynesia.**
Robert D. Craig. Metuchen, New Jersey: Scarecrow Press, 1993. 326p. maps. bibliogs. (Oceanian Historical Dictionaries, no. 2).

'An introductory chapter illuminates the particular Polynesian character of these islands and shows how they are ethnically and culturally related. The history of each island state is summarized, with special emphasis upon events since European contact and especially during the last decade'. Samoa is covered reasonably adequately, though with inexplicable omission of many individuals and events of note. The dictionary is arranged alphabetically, and contains useful brief bibliographies.

164 **The Journal of Pacific History.**
Canberra: Research School of Pacific Studies, Australian National University, 1976- . biannual.

Initially published quarterly, but now twice yearly, this wide-ranging, scholarly journal 'serves historians, prehistorians, anthropologists and others interested in the study of mankind in the Pacific Islands ...'. It publishes articles, annotated and previously unpublished manuscripts, notes on source material, and comments on current affairs. The annual, supplementary *Bibliography* is an indispensable aid to research and to current awareness, listing by subject and territory theses, books, articles and chapters of books relating to the islands.

165 **Pacific history journal bibliography.**
Compiled by Clive Moore. Canberra: Pacific Manuscripts Bureau, Research School of Pacific Studies, Australian National University, 1992. 445p.

A comprehensive list of articles on Pacific history in seventeen major academic journals. Entries are arranged alphabetically by author, then chronologically. Fields and periods are indicated (*e.g.* AmSamoa, Samoa, WstSamoa). Articles with multiple authors and translators are cross-referenced to the first author. 'Appendix two: obituaries' is arranged alphabetically by decedent. There are references to many articles on Samoa, but the use only of given name initials and lack of any geographical index make them hard to find – unless one already knows the author's name. Works by the same author may be widely separated, according to how many initials are cited, e.g. J. Davidson and J. W. Davidson; and Te'o Fairbairn, who has published as I., I. J., T. I., and T. I. J. Fairbairn.

166 **The people from the horizon: an illustrated history of the Europeans among the South Sea islanders.**
Philip Snow, Stefanie Waine. Oxford: Phaidon Press, 1979. 296p. maps. bibliog.

This splendidly illustrated, perceptive account of the impact of Europeans on island societies, from the very first contacts to the present day, is soundly based in wide reading and informed by first-hand knowledge of the region. It is one of the most readable and enlightening of all popular introductions to Pacific history.

167 **Understanding Pacific history: the participant as historian.**
James W. Davidson. In: *The feel of truth: essays in New Zealand and Pacific history presented to F. L. W. Wood and J. C. Beaglehole on the occasion of their retirement.* Edited by Peter Munz. Wellington: A. H. & A. W. Reed, for the Victoria University of Wellington, 1969, p. 25-40. bibliog.

This opening lecture of the Waigani Seminar on the History of Melanesia, held at Port Moresby between 30 May and 5 June 1968, considers the relationship between personal experience and intellectual discipline. 'Every Pacific historian who belongs to the islands or has lived in them for a substantial time is, in a sense, a participant'. Davidson discusses the implications of such participation in relation to the writing of his book *Samoa mo Samoa* (q.v.) and his own involvement in Samoan public life and politics.

168 **Where the waves fall: a new South Sea islands history from the first settlement to colonial rule.**
K. R. Howe. Honolulu: University of Hawai'i Press, 1988. 403p. maps. bibliog. (Pacific Islands Monograph Series, no. 2).

First published in 1984, this island-centred 'new history' of the Pacific islands focuses on the interaction between foreigners and islanders. In his chapter on Samoa (p. 230-54), Howe considers the special features of social organization; the early European contacts; the influence of John Williams ('one of the LMS's most aggressive pioneers'); the consequences of religious conversion and the nature of Samoan Christianity; internecine warfare; the growth of Āpia as a port town; the Steinberger Government; and the dénouement in the partition of the islands. Though their experience during the period of culture contact brought Samoan leaders eventually to see the need to unite politically, in order to protect themselves against foreigners, they achieved little success, 'mainly because their social and political organisation was too inherently localised and factionalised – a situation that various European interest groups exploited to Samoa's disadvantage'.

Voyages of exploration

169 **Ignoble savages and other European visions: the La Pérouse affair in Samoan history.**
Jocelyn Linnekin. *Journal of Pacific History*, vol. 26, no. 1 (June 1991), p. 3-26. bibliog.

Essential reading for students of Samoan history, this is a revisionist view of the events of 11 December 1787 at Fagasā (when P.-A. Fleuriot de Langle and eleven French officers and men died in a sudden and still unexplained attack by Samoans), and a study of how hostile stereotypes of Samoans were gradually reversed. Linnekin suggests that anti-French feeling was influential in bringing about the rehabilitation of the Samoans in European opinion.

170 **La Pérouse: explorateur de Pacifique.** (La Pérouse: Pacific explorer.)
John Dunmore. Paris: Payot, 1986. 311p. map. bibliog.

A magisterial biography of La Pérouse, to mark the bicentenary of the disappearance of his expedition, by Dunmore, the author of *Who's who in Pacific navigation* (Honolulu: University of Hawai'i Press, 1991. 312p. bibliog.). See also: 'Lapérouse: marin et voyageur au siècle des lumières' (La Pérouse: sailor and traveller of the Enlightenment) by Alain Barrès (*Revue de Tarn*, vol. 3, no. 117 [1985], p. 5-35); 'Le bicentenaire d'une tragique entreprise scientifique: la disparition de l'expédition Lapérouse' (The bicentenary of a tragic scientific project: the disappearance of the La Pérouse expedition) by François Bellec (*Acta Geographica*, vol. 61/62 [1985], p. 1-13); 'Il y a deux cent ans: l'expédition Lapérouse' (Two hundred years ago: the La Pérouse expedition) by Danielle Fauque (*Revue d'Histoire des Sciences et de leurs Applications*, vol. 38, no. 2 [1985], p. 149-60); and 'Fleuriot de Langle et l'expédition de Lapérouse' (Fleuriot de Langle and the La Pérouse expedition) by Philippe Henwood (*xviii siècle*, no. 19 [1987], p. 245-62. bibliog.). (Paul-Antoine Fleuriot de Langle [1744-87] was one of the twelve seamen killed on Tutuila on 11 December 1787.)

171 **Lapérouse in the Pacific, including searches by d'Entrecasteaux, Dillon, Dumont d'Urville: an annotated bibliography.**
Ian F. McLaren. Parkville, Victoria: Baillieu Library, University of Melbourne, 1993. 285p. maps.

A near-definitive bibliography of works dealing with the voyages of Jean-François de Galaup, Comte de La Pérouse (1741-88), in Pacific waters and the searches made after his disappearance. References to accounts of the tragic encounter with Samoans on Tutuila in 1787 are included.

172 **Narrative of the United States Exploring Expedition during the years 1838-42.**
Charles Wilkes. Ridgewood, New Jersey: Gregg Press, 1970. 5 vols. maps.

A facsimile reprint of the full first edition (Philadelphia: Lea & Blanchard, 1845. 5 vols. & atlas). There have been several other editions, including London: Wiley & Putnam, 1845, and an abridged version, Papakura, New Zealand: R. McMillan, [n.d.]. 372p. (Reprint of London: Whittaker, 1845). See also *The United States Exploring Expedition, 1838-1842, and its publications, 1844-1874: a bibliography* by Daniel C. Haskell (New York: New York Public Library, 1942. 188p.). This definitive bibliography of the cartography and many scientific works resulting from the Expedition led by Charles Wilkes is reprinted with additions and corrections from the *Bulletin of the New York Public Library*, February 1940, January 1941, July 1941, October 1941, and prefaced with a three-page illustrated index. See also *Ethnology and philology* by Horatio Hale (Ridgewood, New Jersey: Gregg Press, 1968. 666p. maps. [United States Exploring Expedition (1838-1842), vol. 6]), a facsimile reprint of the first edition (Philadelphia: Lea & Blanchard, 1846. 666p.). Hale is a notably thorough and competent linguist and ethnologist: his accounts of Samoan and Tokelauan cultures and languages represent the first scientific descriptions, and so have great historical value.

173 **Rose de Freycinet: stowaway world traveller.**
Eugenie Stapleton. St. Mary's, New South Wales: St. Mary's Historical Society, 1982. 74p.

A straightforward, short biography of the namesake of Rose Island, American Samoa, with a brief account of Louis de Freycinet's Samoan sightings.

General Samoan history

174 **History of Samoa.**
John William Hart, Glen Wright, Allan D. Patterson. Pesega, Apia: Church Schools of Western Samoa, The Church of Jesus Christ of Latter-day Saints, 1972. 2nd ed. 137p.

A general history for school use, which provides information on the Mormon Church in Eastern and Western Samoa. The second edition includes a short section entitled 'The Church of Jesus Christ of Latter-day Saints, 1888', p. 74-75.

175 **History of Samoa.**
Fred Henry. Apia: Commercial Printers, 1992. 216p.

This is the first systematic traditional history of the Samoans, compiled by Brother Fred Henry of Tutuila. It is divided into five periods: prehistoric time, from 400 BC to 1250 AD; from the Tongan War to the arrival of John Williams, 1250 to 1830; from 1830 to the beginning of Great Power rivalry, about 1870; Samoa under consular influence, 1870 to 1900; and 1900 to 1930. The work was originally published in 1958 from Brother Henry's foolscap typescript, by K. R. Lambie, Director of Education, Western Samoa, with a Samoan-language edition translated by Pastor Faleto'ese. The typewritten format was continued until 1983.

176 **Lagaga: a short history of Western Samoa.**
Edited by Malama Meleisea, Penelope Schoeffel Meleisea. Suva: Institute of Pacific Studies, University of the South Pacific; Apia: Western Samoan Extension Centre of the University of the South Pacific, 1987. 225p. maps. bibliog.

A useful outline history, by thirteen authors, mainly of the 19th and 20th centuries. For greater detail and analysis see Malama Meleisea's *The making of modern Samoa* (q.v.). Earlier works of importance include: *Samoa and its story* by James Cowan (Christchurch, New Zealand: Whitcombe & Tombs, 1914. 63p. map), an outline, in pamphlet format, of Samoan history to the outbreak of the First World War, published on the occasion of the overthrow of German colonial rule by the New Zealand Expeditionary Force in 1914; *History of Samoa* by Robert Mackenzie Watson (Wellington: Whitcombe & Tombs, 1918. 147p. map), a useful general history, which concludes with chapters on 'Germany in Western Samoa', 'America in Eastern Samoa', and 'The British military occupation'; and *Samoa shi, jō* (Samoan history. Part I: to 1900) by Y. Iwasa (Tokyo: Nippon Taiheiyo Kyokai, 1970. 173p. maps. bibliog.), an illustrated history, mainly of the 19th century, in Japanese.

177 **The making of modern Samoa: traditional authority and colonial administration in the history of Western Samoa.**

Malama Meleisea. Suva: Institute of Pacific Studies, University of the South Pacific, 1987. 280p. bibliog.

This meticulously documented work provides, from a Samoan viewpoint, an historical explanation of the problems resulting from the contradictions of two sources of authority, *fa'a-Sāmoa* and Western legal traditions. Extensive use is made of case-studies, oral evidence, and court records as Meleisea discusses traditional authority; land alienation and civil wars, 1828-1900; the Solf administration and Samoan government, 1900-03; the Land and Titles Commission, 1903-14; the New Zealand military administration, 1914-21; and Samoan nationalism under the New Zealand civil administration, 1921-61. The sections entitled 'The mixed-race community in Samoan affairs' (p. 155-82), 'The Land and Titles Court' (p. 183-207), and 'The legacy of the century after independence' (p. 208-35) are mandatory reading. A particularly valuable feature of this wide-ranging scholarly history is Meleisea's reinterpretation of earlier works, by F. M. Keesing, J. W. Davidson and R. P. Gilson.

178 **The riddle in Samoan history: the relevance of language, names, honorifics, genealogy, ritual and chant to historical analysis.**

Tuiatua Tupua Tamasese. *Journal of Pacific History*, vol. 29, no. 1 (June 1994), p. 66-79.

In this important essay, Tamasese wonders whether historians of Samoa and anthropologists have 'quite understood' the cultural roles of such Samoan devices as the riddle, camouflage, and even propaganda and the nature of genealogy. He examines critically statements by R. P. Gilson, Augustin Krämer and J. W. Davidson, and corrects misunderstandings. There are five explanatory *gafa* (pedigrees), including those of the Malietoa line from Tia, Tupua and Salamāsina.

179 **Samoa under the sailing gods.**

Newton A. Rowe, with an introduction by Lloyd Osbourne. London; New York: Putnam, 1930. 339p. bibliog.

Rowe was District Inspector in Savai'i in the early years of the New Zealand mandate, and writes with authority on the painful story of an administration characterized, in Lloyd Osbourne's words, by 'stupidity and despotic power'. Samoan history is outlined from the first European contacts to the killing of Tamasese and ten others on 28 December 1929, an event related in 'cool, deadly sentences'. Illustrations depict Tuimaleali'ifano, Tamasese, O. F. Nelson, and Major-General Sir G. S. Richardson. The appendices include the petition, signed on 15 November 1929 by twenty-three Samoan chiefs, asking that King George V allow the Mandate to be transferred from the Government of New Zealand 'to the sole and direct control' of His Majesty.

180 **Samoa (Western Samoa and American Samoa).**

Maria Chiara. In: *International dictionary of historic places. Volume five: Asia and Oceania.* Edited by Paul E. Schellinger, Robert M. Salkin. Chicago; London: Fitzroy Dearborn Publishers, 1996, p. 723-26. map. bibliog.

A competent outline of Samoan history.

Early history

181 Sacred women chiefs and female 'headmen' in Polynesian history.
Niel Gunson. *Journal of Pacific History*, vol. 22, no. 3 (July 1987), p. 139-71. bibliog.

Includes discussions of the Samoan marriages of the Tu'i Tonga, and of the celebrated female ruler Salamāsina. A chart of descent lines from the Tupu Tupua is provided. See also 'Rank, gender and politics in ancient Samoa: the genealogy of Salamāsina *o le Tafa'ifā*' by Penelope Schoeffel (*Journal of Pacific History*, vol. 22, no. 4 [Oct. 1987], p. 174-93. bibliog.), which contains genealogical charts of the first of Salamāsina's progenitors, Tu'i Tonga, and of her descendants.

182 Salamasina: Bilder aus altsamoanischer Kultur und Geschichte.
(Salamāsina: scenes from ancient Samoan culture and history.)
Augustin Krämer. Stuttgart, Germany: Strecker & Schröder, 1923. 245p.

Based soundly on Samoan legends of Salamāsina, this is a popular account, treated almost as a novel. Salamāsina was the first royal ruler of Samoa, called *tafa'ifā*, holding the four supreme titles *Tuiā'ana*, *Tuiatua*, *Tamasoali'i* and *Gatoaitele*. She lived in Satupa'itea on Savai'i. There is an English version, *Salamasina: scenes from ancient Samoan culture and history* by Augustin Krämer, translated into English by Bro. Herman (Pago Pago: Association of the Marist Brothers' Old Boys, 1958. [not seen]).

183 Samoa: an early history.
Fred Henry, revised by Tofa Pula, Nikolao I. Tuitelelapaga. Pago Pago: Department of Education, 1980. 196p. 4 maps. bibliog.

Brother Fred Henry, a Marist Brother, worked in Samoa from 1912 to 1945, and had a vast knowledge of Samoan traditions and cultures. Tofa Pula was American Samoa's first Director of Education. This detailed work is based on oral traditions, mainly of the pre-contact centuries, and covers climactic events such as the first civil war ('The war between brothers' – c. 900 AD) and the Tongan war (c. 1250 AD). The chronological account is illustrated by legends, myths, genealogies, poems and songs.

184 The Tonga-Samoa connection 1777-1845: some observations on the nature of Tongan imperialism.
Niel Gunson. *Journal of Pacific History*, vol. 25, no. 2 (Dec. 1990), p. 176-87. bibliog.

This essay explores what is known of the connection between Tonga and Samoa until the coming of Christianity, especially in Manono, Savai'i and Ā'ana on 'Upolu. Intermarriage, paramountcy, wars and the *lotu Toga* are all discussed. Gunson concludes: 'Involvement or dominance in Samoan politics by Tongan chiefs was only likely when Samoan chiefs related to them by marriage or by traditional alliances called on them for support'.

19th century: 'imbroglio' and partition

185 **Bismarck's imperialism: the case of Samoa, 1880-1890.**
Paul M. Kennedy. *The Historical Journal*, vol. 15 (1972), p. 261-83. bibliog.

A meticulous analysis of German imperial policy and practice at the height of Great Power rivalry in the South Pacific, when coaling stations and coconut oil were of great importance to Britain, Germany and the United States.

186 **Bully Hayes: South Sea buccaneer.**
James A. Michener, A. Grove Day. In: *Rascals in paradise*. James A. Michener, A. Grove Day. London: Secker & Warburg, 1957, p. 223-58, 370-71. bibliog.

An account of the enigmatic American seaman, William Henry Hayes (1829-77), who terrorized the South Pacific in the mid-19th century. The authors summarize what is reliably known of 'this unbelievable man', concluding that it is almost impossible to separate fact from legend. 'In spite of his many ruffianisms, some of which were of so gross a nature as to preclude mention, Hayes had many friends, even among those whom he had swindled, at all events in Samoa'. (He even bested the redoubtable Theodor Weber of the Godeffroy Company!) The only portrait of Hayes (who had only one ear and the stump of the other) that may be authentic is a colour sketch made in 1912 by the Australian novelist and artist Norman Lindsay. See also *Captain Bully Hayes: blackbirder and bigamist* by Frank Clune (London: Angus & Robertson, 1971. 177p. map. bibliog. First published, Sydney: Angus & Robertson, 1970).

187 **Bully Hayes: South Sea pirate.**
Basil Lubbock. London: Martin Hopkinson, 1931. 322p. map.

This is a fictionalized but very well documented account of the American seaman, William Henry Hayes (1829-77). Louis Becke, who knew Hayes well, described him as 'an extraordinary combination of bravery, vice, kind-heartedness, and savagery'. Āpia was his base for a while, his twin daughters being reared there by his fourth wife, Emily Mary Butler. Hayes was found guilty of stealing men and women ('blackbirding') at Āpia in February 1870, but escaped aboard a brig captained by another notorious American, Ben Pease. Appendix A (p. 313-18) reproduces official letters regarding Hayes, published in the Queensland Government *Gazette* of 28 August 1875. Appendix B, 'The descendants of Bully Hayes' (p. 319-20), quotes W. B. Churchward's *My Consulate in Samoa* (q.v.): 'Hayes' legitimate wife, a New Zealand lady, was residing in Apia in 1881 with two lovely daughters and one son ...'.

188 **The Catholic hero of Samoa: Mata'afa, King of Samoa.**
J. G. Leigh. *The Month*, vol. 95 (Feb. 1900), p. 163-76.

A fervently partisan appreciation of Mata'afa Iosefo (the *bête noire* of the German colonialists in the internecine wars of the late 19th century), on whom the title of Malietoa Mata'afa was conferred during the exile of Malietoa Laupepa, and who was appointed as king, with Malietoa Laupepa as vice-king. Despite widespread support, this arrangement was annulled by the consuls of the foreign powers, thereby precipitating further warfare. See also *Mata'afa: der Held von Samoa* (Mata'afa: the hero of Samoa) by F. Albert Druck (Strassburg, Germany [now Strasbourg, France]: F. X. Le Roux, 1906).

189 **A footnote to history: eight years of trouble in Samoa.**
Robert Louis Stevenson. London: Cassell, 1892. 322p. map; Leipzig, Germany: Bernhard Tauchnitz, 1892. 254p. map. Reprinted, London: Dawson of Pall Mall, 1967. Reprinted, with an introduction by Malama Meleisea, Auckland, New Zealand: Pasifika Press, 1996. 161p.

Keenly observing the internecine warfare and the Great Power intrigues, which were still going on as he wrote, Stevenson considered his 'sketch' to be 'a piece of contemporary history in the most exact sense'. He affirms: 'Apia, the port and mart, is the seat of the political sickness of Samoa'. Stevenson's vivid, partisan descriptions of events and of the protagonists in them are essential reading for an understanding of 'the Samoan tangle' and, especially, the *furor consularis* of 1888-89. Chapter ten describes the mighty hurricane of 16 March 1889, with 'formidable ships reduced to junk': this disaster brought about the Congress and Treaty of Berlin. See also *War in Samoa* by Robert Louis Stevenson (London: Reprinted from *The Pall Mall Gazette* of September 1893. 27p.), a further account of the internecine warfare in Samoa, with some incisive comments on the part played by the three foreign powers in fomenting and sustaining it.

190 **Grass huts and warehouses: Pacific beach communities of the nineteenth century.**
Caroline Ralston. Canberra: Australian National University Press, 1977. 268p. 7 maps. bibliog.

An examination and comparison of five small port towns in the 19th century, including notably Āpia, in terms of their political, economic and social development. An indication of the lawlessness of the early beach community in Āpia is given by plate 7 (facing p. 84), entitled 'Lynch law in Samoa, 1877', and showing a man hanged by the neck from a coconut tree.

191 **Les îles Samoa ou des Navigateurs et l'arrangement anglo-allemand-américain.** (The Samoan or Navigators' Islands and the Anglo-German-American arrangement.)
Louis Vossion. Paris: Augustin Challemel, 1900. 27p. map.

A contemporary, and critical, French view of the tripartite agreement by the three Great Powers of 1889, resulting in the partition of Samoa. See also 'The Samoan agreement in plain English' by Basil Thomson (*Blackwood's Edinburgh Magazine*, vol. 166 [1899], p. 847-51). Sir Basil Home Thomson (1861-1939) is realistic and caustic in his assessment of the background and effects of the *modus vivendi* of the Berlin Treaty of 1889, 'one of the most fatuous schemes ever devised for governing a country'.

192 **The Ladrones and our other Pacific islands.**
Trumbull White. In: *Our new possessions....* Trumbull White. Chicago; Philadelphia: Monarch Book Company, 1898, p. 271-90.

'If we only had the Carolines' laments the author of this exultant survey of 'the tropic islands of the sea which have fallen under our sway': the Philippine Islands, Puerto Rico, Cuba and the Hawaiian Islands. The Ladrones, Carolines and Samoa are discussed in terms of United States strategic and commercial interests, and White also outlines (p. 286-90) the early development of Pango-Pango [sic] as a vital US Navy coaling station. Of the 'international complications' stemming from the tripartite Treaty of Berlin (1889), he prophesies: 'The natives ... execrate the Germans and are fond of Americans, so that the threatened attempt of the European nation to seize the whole of the group is likely to be the cause of considerable diplomatic correspondence, and certainly is doomed to final defeat'. See also *Greater America: the latest acquired insular possessions* (Boston, Massachusetts: Perry Mason, 1900. 189p.), which is profusely illustrated and contains chapters on Eastern Samoa, Guam, Hawai'i, Midway and the Philippines. This exultant book, written in the aftermath of the Spanish-American War, reflects the imperialistic and expansionist attitudes then current in the United States.

193 **Life in the Pacific fifty years ago.**

Alfred P. Maudslay, with an introduction by T. A. Joyce. London: George Routledge & Sons, 1930. 261p. map.

Noted also for his archaeological excavations in Central America between 1881 and 1894, Maudslay served in Fiji, Samoa and Tonga, becoming British Consul in Āpia on 12 March 1878, after the death of the mentally ill Mr Liardet. Extracts from his letters give an account of the Puletua chiefs' confinement in the consulate, the attitudes of the German and American consuls, and the 'most lawless state' of the country: 'The so-called Government is merely a collection of chiefs of the successful side in the last war, and they know nothing and do nothing about governing'. Maudslay's description of his visit to the relatively little known islands of Manono and Apolima are of particular interest. In a reference to the cession of the islands, T. A. Joyce states: 'The young Maudslay obtained the concession from the paramount chiefs for this country by his own personal influence and tact, only to find that an agreement had been concluded by the home cabinets which robbed him of a great diplomatic achievement'.

194 **The majesty of colour: a life of Sir John Bates Thurston.**

Deryck Scarr. Canberra: Australian National University Press, 1973-80. 2 vols. maps. bibliog. (Pacific Research Monographs, no. 4).

A comprehensive biography of J. B. Thurston (1836-97), High Commissioner for the Western Pacific, and as such influential in Samoan affairs. Volume one, *I, the very bayonet*, extends to 1875. Volume two, *Viceroy of the Pacific*, covers the period from 1875 to Thurston's death in 1897, and contains extensive accounts of his negotiations in and regarding Samoa. Thurston viewed German activities in Samoa as deplorable and concerned only with commercial advantage.

195 **Maori and Polynesian: race and politics: the racial argument in support of New Zealand's interests in Polynesia.**

Angus Ross. In: *Anthropology in the South Seas: essays presented to H. D. Skinner.* Edited by J. D. Freeman, W. R. Geddes. New Plymouth, New Zealand: Thomas Avery & Sons, 1959, p. 221-33. bibliog.

New Zealand interests in the Pacific in the 19th century were religious, economic and political in character. The first of the New Zealand imperialists to appreciate the possibility of using the kinship of Maori and Polynesian to extend these interests was Sir George Grey. In 1872 William Seed of the New Zealand Customs Department suggested to Sir Julius Vogel that New Zealand should assume control of Samoa, with

Pago Pago as a coaling station and naval depot. New Zealand's experience in governing the Maoris was invoked as a supporting argument then, and through to 1919. By 1927, proponents such as Sir Apirana Ngata were questioning their earlier assumptions.

196 **Moors of Samoa: Stevenson's friend.**
Percy S. Allen. Honolulu: Bernice P. Bishop Museum, 1926. 16p. (Pacific Pamphlet, no. 161).

A brief biography of Harry Jay Moors (1854-1928?), American trader in Āpia and confidant of Robert Louis Stevenson.

197 **My consulate in Samoa: a record of four years' sojourn in the Navigators Islands, with personal experiences of King Malietoa Laupepa, his country, and his men.**
William B. Churchward. Folkestone, England; London: Dawsons of Pall Mall, 1971. 404p.

A facsimile reprint of the original edition (London: Bentley, 1887). Churchward was Acting British Consul in Āpia from 1881 to 1885. Stylish, vivid and often humorous (he described Bully Hayes as 'very like a Bishop'), his calm account of complex events and devious personalities conveys a realistic picture of the Samoan kingdom, and provides a sound historical context for the later, less dispassionate accounts by Stevenson, Harry Moors and others. From his experience as Deputy Commissioner for the Western Pacific, Churchward later wrote an important study of the infamous labour traffic: *Blackbirding in the South Pacific* (London: Swan Sonnenschein, 1888. 255p.).

198 **New Zealand aspirations in the Pacific in the nineteenth century.**
Angus Ross. Oxford: Clarendon Press, 1964. 332p. map. bibliog.

This painstaking book describes and explains New Zealand's relations with her Pacific Island neighbours, which were 'interesting in themselves' and controversial in New Zealand, Paris, Berlin, Washington and London. Samoa was a major focus of attention, and there are enlightening accounts of the political designs of Sir Julius Vogel, 1870-77; of the climactic period from 1883 to 1891; and of the outspoken imperialism of Richard John Seddon, who became New Zealand's premier in 1893.

199 **Opening and penetration of foreign influence in Samoa to 1880.**
Joseph W. Ellison. Corvallis, Oregon: Oregon State College, 1938. 108p. bibliog. (Oregon State Monographs. Studies in History, no. 1).

Written at a time when there were only a few sketchy accounts of the history of Samoa, this monograph presents a close study of the nature and tactics of economic imperialism and the conduct of international relations, as revealed in American, British and German state papers and other documents relating to Samoa. The background is set in 'The Samoan islands and their people' and 'The discovery of Samoa and the introduction of Christianity'. 'Beginnings of British, German, and American interests in Samoa' leads on to 'Steinberger's first mission to Samoa, 1873-1874', 'Steinberger's second mission to Samoa' and 'The treaties and increased foreign control of Samoa, 1877-1880'.

200 **The origins of international rivalry in Samoa, 1845-1884.**
Sylvia Masterman, with a foreword by A. P. Newton. London: George Allen & Unwin, 1934. 233p. maps. bibliog.

Now a classic of literature on Samoa, Masterman's history retains its value, especially for the earlier part of its period. See also *An outline of Samoan history* by Sylvia Masterman (Apia: Commercial Printers, 1980. 79p.). Originally prepared for the Western Samoan Department of Education ([n.d.]. 25p.), this book, produced from the author's typescript, contains seventeen chronological chapters which span the history of Samoa from prehistory onwards. Appendix 6 provides a 'Chronological history of Western Samoa' (p. 13-23).

201 **Queen Emma: the Samoan-American girl who founded a commercial empire in 19th century New Guinea.**
R. W. Robson. Sydney: Pacific Publications, 1971. 239p. map.

Originally published in 1965, this is an entertaining historical account of the adventures, marriages and business concerns of Samoan-born Emma Eliza Coe Kolbe (1850-1913), a prominent and influential entrepreneur in German New Guinea. Her father, Jonas Myndersse Coe, lived in Samoa from his arrival as a shipwrecked cabin boy in 1838 until his death in 1891. For several years he was the official representative of the United States in Samoa. Emma's mother was Le'utu, a Malietoa.

202 **The Royal Navy and the Samoan civil war 1898-1899.**
Paul M. Kennedy. *Canadian Journal of History/Annales Canadiennes d'Histoire*, vol. 5, no. 1 (March 1970), p. 57-72. bibliog.

A searching, dispassionate study of the not wholly creditable role played by the Royal Navy at a climactic point in Samoan domestic affairs and internecine conflict. Soundly based on official records, it provides more detail than does Kennedy's subsequent book *The Samoan tangle* (q.v.).

203 **Samoa 1830 to 1900: the politics of a multi-cultural community.**
Richard Phillip Gilson, with an introduction and conclusion by J. W. Davidson. Melbourne: Oxford University Press, 1970. 457p. 6 maps. bibliogs.

R. P. Gilson (1925-63) ransacked the world for every scrap of evidence relevant to the subject of his superb historical study of 19th-century Samoa, completed by Miriam Gilson and Davidson after his death. Political scientist and anthropologist, Gilson learned the Samoan language in order to follow debates in the village *fono* and to question his Samoan friends, with perception and empathy. There is a bibliography of Gilson's published works (p. xiii) and an invaluable bibliography (p. 433-45) of manuscript sources, private papers and official records in eight countries, including Samoa itself.

204 The Samoan 'imbroglio': a select bibliography.
H. G. A. Hughes. Afonwen, Wales: Gwasg Gwenffrwd, 1992. 32p. map.

An unannotated listing by author of works relating to the complex imperialist rivalries and machinations of the 'shameful period' before the partition and annexation of the Samoan islands, in 1899, by Germany and the United States of America.

205 The Samoan tangle: a study in Anglo-German-American relations 1878-1900.
Paul M. Kennedy. St. Lucia, Queensland: University of Queensland Press; [Dublin]: Irish University Press, 1974. 325p. 3 maps. bibliog.

This meticulously documented study complements Sylvia R. Masterman's *The origins of international rivalry in Samoa 1845-84* (q.v.). It has as its main aim 'to place the lengthy dispute over Samoa in a wider diplomatic and imperial context', as one of the most interesting examples of Great Power rivalries. The select bibliography (p. 307-15) includes a useful list of unpublished sources in Britain, Germany and the United States and of the private papers of leading participants in the Samoan 'imbroglio'. See also 'The partition of Samoa: a study of imperialism and diplomacy' by Joseph W. Ellison (*Pacific Historical Review*, vol. 8, no. 3 [1939], p. 259-88. bibliog.), a first-rate, meticulously researched account of the external factors at work in the 'Samoan tangle', made up of duplicity, deceit, intrigue and gunboat diplomacy. Ellison is especially enlightening as to the motivation of the American government. Another authoritative account of American interests in Samoa is 'Part of a paper on the partition of Samoa and the past relations between that group and the United States' by Harold Marsh Sewall (*Annual Report of the Hawaiian Historical Society*, 7th [1900], p. 11-27). Sewall was a participant in the affairs discussed, as United States consul in Apia.

206 Slavers in paradise: the Peruvian labour trade in Polynesia, 1862-1864.
H. E. Maude. Canberra: Australian National University Press, 1981. 244p. 12 maps. bibliog.

Unlike Tokelau which lost forty-seven per cent of its estimated population in 1862, Samoa escaped the Peruvian slave raids. Only seven people were taken to Peru, seized from canoes at sea. See chapter eight (p. 55-62, 204-05): 'Niue and the Samoan Islands'. A mission meeting held at Matāutu on Savai'i assured the LMS directors in London that there was 'no fear but that the Samoans will be prepared to defend their liberties'.

207 Steinberger of Samoa: some biographical notes.
Martin Torodash. *Pacific Northwest Quarterly*, vol. 68, no. 2 (1977), p. 49-59. bibliog.

Albert Barnes Steinberger (1840-94) was actually only in Samoa from 1873 to 1876, but he was involved in Samoan politics for much longer, from New Zealand, England and Massachusetts, after his deportation to Fiji in 1876. From his birth on Christmas Day 1840 in Minersville, Pennsylvania, until his arrival in Samoa at the instance of US President Ulysses S. Grant (and, probably, of William H. Webb, shipbuilder and Pacific entrepreneur), little is known of his life. Torodash discusses this and other lacunae in Steinberger's biography.

208 **Tamafaigā – shaman, king or maniac?: the emergence of Manono.**
Tui Atua Tupua Tamasese. *Journal of Pacific History*, vol. 30, no. 1 (June 1995), p. 3-21. 2 maps. bibliog.

This exploration of the traditional and cultural reference points of Manono political motivation and power is of exceptional value in that its distinguished author has been able to enlist the help of many Samoan custodians of knowledge. The main protagonist, Tamafaigā, was the dominant political figure in 19th-century Samoa, rooted in the Salamāsina inheritance. Tamafaigā's descent from Salamāsina is shown in a long genealogy. The Manono régime tried to retain the Tamafaigā legacy (even though he was generally regarded as a monster) through regular re-assertion of arms.

209 **1889: Wendepunkt der amerikanischen Aussenpolitik: die Anfänge des modernen Panamerikanismus – die Samoakrise.** (1889: turning-point of American foreign policy: the beginnings of modern Panamericanism – the crisis in Samoa.)
Hans-Ulrich Wehler. *Historische Zeitschrift* (Munich), vol. 201, no. 1 (August 1965), p. 57-109. bibliog.

Wehler sets United States interest in Samoa in the context of the growth of Panamericanism and expansionism, from the world economic crisis of 1873-78 onwards. Using government papers, he also provides a scholarly summary of the tangled diplomatic, consular and political intrigues of the last decade of the 19th century. To the '*furor consularis*' was added the '*furor navalis*', when gunboats stood ready for war in Āpia bay. This article represents an important source on German interpretations of American policy.

210 **The trial of consul Pritchard.**
Andrew E. Robson. *Journal of Pacific History*, vol. 30, no. 2 (Dec. 1995), p. 173-93. bibliog.

William Thomas Pritchard (1829-1909), son of George Pritchard, the British consul in Tahiti and later in Samoa, succeeded his father as acting consul in Samoa in 1856, serving for nine months until his appointment as consul in Fiji in 1858. This is a meticulous review of his trial for alleged financial irregularities and interference in Fijian native affairs. Robson describes the commission's proceedings as 'a travesty' and considers that Pritchard's reputation and career deserve reassessment. For a lively account of his life in Samoa as a young man, see *Polynesian reminiscences, or life in the South Pacific islands* by W. T. Pritchard, with a preface by Dr Berthold Seemann (London: Chapman & Hall, 1866. 428p. Reprinted, London: Dawsons of Pall Mall, 1968. 428p.). See also *The Pritchard family tree, researched and compiled by Zella A. Moss, 1974-1989* by Zella A. Moss ([Auckland, New Zealand]: Z. Moss, 1989. 2 vols. [iv, 197 leaves]. maps). The Samoan connexions of the Pritchard family are thoroughly documented in this meticulous genealogical work, illustrated by many portraits and by a coat of arms. There is a copy in the New Zealand National Library.

211 **The typhoon that stopped a war.**
Edwin Palmer Hoyt. New York: D. McKay, 1968. 244p. maps.

A detailed, and dramatic, account of the great storm of 1889 which wrecked German and American warships at anchor in Āpia Bay. Hoyt considers that, but for this disaster, Great Britain, Germany and the United States might have soon been at war over their rival claims to hegemony and commercial advantage in Samoa. See also 'Samoan hurricane' by L. A. Kimberly (Washington, DC: Naval Historical Foundation, 1965. 22p. map). Rear Admiral L. A. Kimberly, USN was the commander-in-chief of the Pacific station, and was aboard the USS *Trenton* in Āpia Bay during the 1889 hurricane. Six illustrations and a chart indicating the relative positions of the American, British and German warships supplement Kimberly's authoritative, vivid recollection of the doomed ships' struggle to survive. Another interesting work on the subject is *The first commission of H.M.S. Calliope, January 25th 1887-April 30th 1890: written on the occasion of the 50th anniversary of the memorable hurricane at Apia, Samoa, March 16th, 1889* by Ernest William Swan (Newcastle upon Tyne, England: Privately printed, 1939. 124p.), which contains several plates of historical interest, and is the authentic story of 'the one that got away'. HMS *Calliope* was the only warship which managed to sail out of Āpia bay during the hurricane.

German Samoa, 1900-14

212 **Das deutsche Reich in der Südsee (1900-1921): eine Annäherung an die Erfahrungen verschiedener Kulturen.** (The German empire in the South Seas [1900-1921]: an approach to the experiences of different cultures.)
Hermann Joseph Hiery. Göttingen, Germany; Zürich, Switzerland: Vandenhoeck & Ruprecht, 1995. 353p. maps. bibliog. (Veröffentlichungen des Deutschen Historischen Instituts London, Bd. 37).

Hiery's well researched history of German colonialism in the Pacific seeks to elucidate what contact with Germans actually entailed for native peoples, notably the Samoans. The interaction of colonizers and colonized had consequences which still influence life in Western Samoa. More detail will be found in *Handbuch der deutschen Südsee*, edited by Hermann Joseph Hiery (Paderborn, Germany, 1997; in press).

213 **Erinnerungen an Samoa.** (Memories of Samoa.)
Erich Schultz-Ewerth. Berlin: August Scherl, 1926. 171p.

Dr Schultz-Ewerth (1870-1935) was the second, and last, governor of German Samoa. His memories of Samoa blend history and anthropology in vivid vignettes, illustrated by fifty-nine contemporary photographs. These include a frontispiece portrait of the author, a portrait of Mata'afa (opposite p. 65) and a photograph by A. Tattersall of Āpia of New Zealand infantry taking control of the town on 29 August 1914. Of particular interest are the governor's opinion of Lauati, who marched on Āpia in January 1909, with over a thousand armed warriors: 'Lauati war samoanischer Patriot' (Lauati was a Samoan patriot), and his assessment of Mata'afa and Suatele (p. 72-75).

214 **Former German possessions in Oceania.**
Great Britain. Historical Section, Foreign Office. London: H.M. Stationery Office, 1920. 98p. bibliog. (Peace Handbooks, no. 146).

Provides succinct, factual descriptions of former German colonies in the Pacific, including German (Western) Samoa. The work covers physical and political geography; political history; social and political conditions; communications; industry; commerce; and finance. Of particular value is the appendix (p. 89-94) which contains extracts from the texts of six agreements between Great Britain and Germany, 1885-99, including the Final Act of the Conference on the Affairs of Samoa, signed at Berlin on 14 June 1889, and the tripartite Convention signed at Washington, DC, on 2 December 1899.

215 **Germans in the tropics: essays in German colonial history.**
Edited by Arthur J. Knoll, Lewis H. Gann. Westport, Connecticut: Greenwood Press, 1987. 178p. bibliog. (Contributions in Comparative Colonial Studies, no. 24).

Nine historians present a critical updating of research on Germany's colonial record in Africa and the Pacific, following the opening to scholars of the records of the Reichskolonialamt at Potsdam. German Samoa is among the colonies discussed. The German colonial enterprise was carried out with extremely limited funding and personnel. Economic exploitation was the prime motivation, but the more far-sighted and humane German colonial officials, such as Dr Wilhelm Solf and Dr Erich Schultz-Ewerth in Samoa, left a beneficial legacy of infrastructures and knowledge.

216 **Imperialismus und Kolonialmission: kaiserliches Deutschland und koloniales Imperium.** (Imperialism and colonial mission: imperial Germany and colonial empire.)
Edited by Klaus J. Bade. Wiesbaden, Germany: Steiner Verlag, 1982. 336p. maps. bibliog.

This historical symposium sheds a great deal of light on why and how Germany acquired its colonies in the late 19th century. John Moses contributes a study on Samoa's governor Wilhelm Solf, analysing his strategies and subtle manoeuvres which were aimed at keeping a balance between the London Missionary Society and the Marist Mission (headed by the formidable Bishop Broyer).

217 **Ein Jahrzehnt in Samoa, 1906-1916.** (A decade in Samoa, 1906-16.)
Frieda Zieschank. Leipzig, Germany: Haberland, 1918. 160p. Reprinted, Leipzig, Germany: Max Möhring, [n.d.].

These observant, homely reminiscences of her life in German Samoa, by the wife of a German physician, reflect a sense of loss. This nostalgia finds expression, too, in the author's *Ein verlorenes Paradies: ein Samoa-Roman* (A paradise lost: a novel about Samoa) (Reprinted, Leipzig, Germany: Max Möhring, [n.d.]).

218 **Der Kampf um Deutsch-Samoa: Erinnerungen eines Hamburger Kaufmanns.** (The struggle for German Samoa: recollections of a Hamburg trader.)
Otto Riedel. Berlin: Kauffmans Deutscher Verlag, 1938. 251p.

These rose-coloured memories of German Samoa are pervaded with nostalgia for the lost colonial empire, but also contain impressions of historical value regarding German policies and interaction with rival interests.

219 **Lauaki Namulau'ulu Mamoe: a traditionalist in Samoan politics.**
J. W. Davidson. In: *Pacific Islands portraits*. Edited by J. W. Davidson, Deryck Scarr. Canberra: Australian National University Press, 1970, p. 267-99, 331-34. bibliog.

A sympathetic study of the life and achievements of the celebrated Savai'i chief who was exiled to Saipan in April 1909, for his opposition to German rule. Lauaki (Lauati) died on 15 November 1915 as he was returning from exile.

220 ***Manuia Samoa!*: samoanische Reiseskizzen und Beobachtungen.** (Happy Samoa!: Samoan travel sketches and observations.)
Richard Deeken. Oldenburg, Germany: Gerhard Stalling, 1901. 240p.

This greatly overstated panegyric of Germany's new colony in Samoa induced many Germans of exiguous capital to settle there, hoping to prosper from plantation ownership. Deeken settled in Samoa in 1902, founding the Deutsche Samoa Gesellschaft (DSG) in competition with the DH & PG. He was an advocate of colonial exploitation and of forced labour, and soon clashed with the more enlightened Wilhelm Solf, first governor of German Samoa. Solf blamed Deeken and his planter clique for stirring up the 'hornet's nest' of the Lauaki *Mau*. Deeken left Samoa, finally, in February 1910.

221 **The neglected war: The German South Pacific and the influence of World War I.**
Hermann Joseph Hiery. Honolulu: University of Hawai'i Press, 1995. 388p. maps. bibliog.

An enlightening scholarly overview of the German colonies in Melanesia, Micronesia and Polynesia, and of their loss as a consequence of Germany's defeat in the First World War of 1914-18. Hiery challenges the view that the change of colonial masters had little effect on the islanders they ruled. From a wide range of official sources, Hiery makes a detailed analysis of colonial policies and islander reactions to them, including those of Samoans to the administration of the new mandatory power, New Zealand.

222 **Samoa gestern: eine Dokumentation mit Fotografien von 1890-1918 und Text von Erich Scheurmann.** (Samoa yesterday: a document with photographs from 1890-1918 and text by Erich Scheurmann.)
Erich Scheurmann, edited by André Grab. Zollikon, Switzerland: Tanner & Staehelin, 1978. 51p. 38 leaves of plates. (Materialen zum *Papalagi*, vol. 1).

Produced in connexion with the continuing cult vogue of *Der papalagi* (q.v.), this reprint of the 1927 edition published by See-Verlag, Zürich, is distinguished by its fascinating and rare photographs spanning the existence of German Samoa. See also *Samoa: ein Bilderwerk* (Samoa: a picture-book) by Erich Scheurmann (Konstanz, Germany: See-Verlag, 1926. 171p. [32p. text + 139p. illustrations]), a fascinating collection of photographs, many of great historical interest.

223 **A select bibliography relating to Germany in the Pacific and Far East, 1870-1914.**
John A. Moses. In: *Germany in the Pacific and Far East 1870-1914*. Edited by John A. Moses, Paul M. Kennedy. St. Lucia, Queensland: University of Queensland Press, 1977, p. 384-412.

This is among the best bibliographies on German colonies in the Pacific, with many references to Samoa.

224 **The Solf regime in Western Samoa: ideal and reality.**
John A. Moses. *New Zealand Journal of History*, vol. 6, no. 1 (1972), p. 42-56.

A careful and balanced consideration of the policies of the first governor of German Samoa, a scholarly man with considerable respect for indigenous culture and customs. Moses looks behind Solf's paternalism and shows that German colonial rule was exploitative and arbitrary. Faced by the essentially reasonable demands for independence of *Mau a Pule*, Solf's response was to exile Lauaki (Lauati) and other leaders to Saipan in the Mariana Islands.

225 **Stevenson's Germany: the case against Germany in the Pacific.**
Charles Brunsdon Fletcher. London: Heinemann; New York: Scribner, 1920. 230p.

A strident continuation of the anti-German polemic begun in Fletcher's *The new Pacific: British policy and German arms* (London: Macmillan, 1917. 325p. bibliog.), and his *The problem of the Pacific* (London: Heinemann, 1919. 254p. map). Fletcher is especially concerned with Samoa, and seeks 'to place Robert Louis Stevenson before the world as an important witness in the case'. The history of Germany's 'thirty years of intrigue and tergiversation', before Stevenson reached Samoa, 'has to be told'.

226 **Wilhelm Solf: Botschafter zwischen den Zeiten.** (Wilhelm Solf: ambassador between times.)
Eberhard von Vietsch. Tübingen, Germany: Rainer Wunderlich Verlag Hermann Leins, 1961. 403p. bibliog.

Solf was the scholarly first governor of German Samoa. The events of his term of office are soberly outlined (p. 42-101), with particular reference to relations with the representatives of Britain and the United States of America, the years from 1900 to 1906, and the Lauati rebellion of 1907-10. The first four documents (p. 349-66) in the appendix consist of letters and first-hand reports by Solf himself, a portrait of whom constitutes the book's frontispiece. A portrait of Lauati appears opposite p. 96. See also 'Wilhelm Heinrich Solf: good governor of German Samoa' by Joseph Theroux (*Pacific Islands Monthly*, vol. 54, no. 7 [1983], p. 52-56; vol. 54, no. 8 [1983], p. 55-58), a generally sympathetic view of Solf's character and ability.

American Samoa, 1900-

227 **American Samoa.**
Michael Eastly. *Pacific Magazine*, vol. 18, no. 4/100 (July/August 1993), p. 34-37.

A dispassionate, factual survey of major economic, social and political events and trends since 1978, when Peter Tali Coleman took office as the first elected governor of American Samoa. Efforts to build a strong economic base have been hampered by intense political rivalry, natural disasters, and executive and legislative stalemates over key policies and issues. Early in 1993, governor A. P. Lutali (pictured in this article) spoke of American Samoa's 'desperate financial condition'.

228 **American Samoa or Eastern Samoa?: the potential for American Samoa to become freely associated with the United States.**
Edward J. Michal. *The Contemporary Pacific*, vol. 4, no. 1 (Spring 1992), p. 137-60. bibliog.

An analysis of American Samoa's unique status as the only US territory that is both unincorporated and unorganized. Persons born there become non-citizen US nationals, instead of US citizens, unless one or both parents are US citizens. Michal reviews the basis of US sovereignty according to American Samoans, according to the US executive branch, and according to the US legislative branch. He concludes that the acts of cession (not considered by the US government to be treaties) 'empower American Samoans to assert their right to explore alternative political statuses – even those, such as free association, that might restore Samoan sovereignty'.

229 **Amerika Samoa: a history of American Samoa and its United States Naval Administration.**

John Alexander Clinton Gray, with a foreword by Felix M. Keesing. Annapolis, Maryland: United States Naval Institute, 1960. 295p. maps. bibliog.

A highly readable, well researched history of 19th-century Samoa and of the United States Naval Administration established in Eastern Samoa by President William McKinley. Originally intended to end with the transfer of administrative responsibility to the US Department of the Interior by President Harry S. Truman in 1951, the story is brought to 1960 in a brief concluding chapter. A history of Swain's Island (p. 211-19), an annotated bibliography (p. 270-82), a list of ships (p. 283) and the Samoan and English texts of the Deed of Cession of 2 April 1900 (p. 112-17), giving the island of Tutuila to the United States, complement the virtues of Gray's unequalled history of the lesser known part of the Samoan archipelago. For the Second World War period of US Marine Corps occupation of Samoa, see *March to the sound of the drums* by Harold L. Oppenheimer (Danville, Illinois: Wabash Press, 1966. 333p.). Oppenheimer is a Harvard anthropologist whose USMC service included command of the American Samoan Marines. He blends autobiography and fiction in highly sophisticated tales of love and work in American Samoa. More factual are his 'Samoan grammar' (chapter fifteen; p. 199-222) and 'Command of native troops' (chapter fourteen; p. 179-98), the latter being a minor military classic.

230 **Raising the Stars and Stripes over Swains Island.**

Quincy F. Roberts. *Journal of Geography*, vol. 31 (April 1932), p. 148-55.

Quincy F. Roberts, of the American Consulate, Suva, Fiji, summarizes the history of the island, of the Jennings dynasty, and of its *matai* system of government. After prolonged dispute with Britain as to sovereignty, the island was annexed by the USA on 4 March 1925, by Presidential approval of Public Resolution No. 75 of the Sixty-eighth US Congress. 'Henceforth the inhabitants would have protection and they would no longer fear that some other government would turn them out of their homes'.

231 **Some perspectives on American Samoa's political relationship with the United States.**

Eni F. H. Faleomavaega. *Pacific Studies*, vol. 13, no. 2 (March 1990), p. 119-23.

American Samoa's congressional delegate to the United States House of Representatives reviews his country's experience in drafting a territorial constitution, and the implications of the 1900 and 1904 'treaties' of cession. He declares that, given its present status, Samoa's constitution 'is nothing more than an extension of the presidential authority of the Secretary of the Interior'. Faleomavaega proposes a convention to deliberate the provisions of the 1900 and 1904 acts of cession, a formal union of Tutuila and Manu'a, and the drafting of a mutually agreeable treaty between Samoa and the USA, followed by the creation of a government 'based on the terms and principles outlined in the treaty, not the U.S. Constitution'. See also *American Samoa: a descriptive and historical profile* by William R. Tansill (Washington, DC: Congressional Research Service, 1974).

Western Samoa, 1914-

232 **Aggie Grey of Samoa.**

Nelson Eustis. Adelaide, South Australia: Hobby Investments, 1979. 216p. 2 maps.

Eustis blends local history with the story of the Swann family which had its origins in Āpia. William J. Swann, a migrant pharmacist from Lincolnshire, came to Samoa in 1889. He treated the Stevenson family of Vailima for tropical ailments, and became a close friend of the writer. In 1891 Swann married Pele of Toāmua, and Agnes Genevieve Swann, one of three daughters, was born on 31 October 1897. 'Aggie' is arguably the most celebrated hotelier of the South Seas, and her status and contribution to the growth of tourism were recognized by the government in August 1971, when she was portrayed on a Western Samoa postage stamp. Besides Swann family portraits, this entertaining account of 'a legend in her lifetime' has many valuable photographs, including those of A. J. Tattersall, August Nelson, William Willis, the *Mau* bandstand office, and a leaflet dropped by a New Zealand seaplane during the *Mau* troubles in February 1930.

233 **Aggie Grey: a Samoan saga.**

Fay G. Calkins. Honolulu: Mutual Publishing, 1988. 342p. bibliog.

The strength of this particularly well informed biography of the legendary hotelier of Āpia lies in the great attention given to Samoan history since Aggie Grey's birth in 1897, and especially to Samoan social life and customs. The author is well placed to set her subject in social context, and to draw upon Samoan (rather than only European) recollections of Grey's colourful career. Calkins is an American woman who married into a Samoan family, an experience described in her book *My Samoan chief* (q.v.). Reprints of both these books bear the author's name as Fay Ala'ilima or Fay Calkins Ala'ilima.

234 **Coping with Samoan resistance after the 1918 influenza epidemic: Colonel Tate's problems and perplexities.**

Mary Boyd. *Journal of Pacific History*, vol. 15, no. 3 (July 1980), p. 155-74. bibliog.

Using unpublished papers of Colonel Robert Ward Tate (Administrator of Western Samoa, 1919-23), this study illuminates a little known aspect of New Zealand rule in Samoa. Boyd outlines Tate's efforts to smash the Toea'ina Club and its satellite company and to subdue unrest in the aftermath of the First World War and the tragic influenza epidemic. She concludes: 'Samoa during the interregnum between military occupation and civil administration was seething with discontent and all Tate could achieve was a lull'.

235 **Correspondence relating to the occupation of German Samoa by an expeditionary force from New Zealand.**

London: HMSO, 1915. 14p. (Cd. 7972).

On 6 August 1914 HM Government telegraphed to the Governor of New Zealand: '... if his Ministers feel able to seize the German wireless station at Samoa, His Majesty's Government would regard this as a great and urgent Imperial service ...'. This publication contains the communications exchanged from that date to 23 October

1914, including revealing reports by Colonel Robert Logan, Administrator of Samoa, especially with regard to the 'menace' of the Chinese indentured coolies, numbering about 3,000: 'I have found it necessary to allow the German planters to retain their arms for self-protection, considering it better that we should run some risk in this direction rather than that a European family should be placed at the mercy of the Chinese'.

236 **The decolonisation of Western Samoa.**

Mary Boyd. In: *The feel of truth: essays in New Zealand and Pacific history presented to F. L. W. Wood and J. C. Beaglehole on the occasion of their retirement.* Edited by Peter Munz. Wellington: A. H. & A. W. Reed, for the Victoria University of Wellington, 1969, p. 61-76. bibliog.

This perceptive essay on how Western Samoa achieved its 'unqualified independence' on 1 January 1962 shows that Peter Fraser and other New Zealand leaders deliberately set a middle course for self-government in Western Samoa. Boyd traces the ebb and flow of negotiations, and the acceleration of Samoan political development. She concludes that Western Samoa will stand out as 'a classic example of political evolution' of a trust territory to independence. See also *The decolonization of Oceania: a survey 1945-70* by James W. Davidson (Wellington: Institute of International Affairs, 1971. 28p.). Davidson, author of *Samoa mo Samoa* (q.v.), traces and compares the different paths to political independence in Pacific islands (including Samoa) over the twenty-five postwar years.

237 **Fetaui Mata'afa: an autobiography.**

Fetaui Mata'afa. Auckland, New Zealand: Pasifika Press, 1997. 200p.

Western Samoa's High Commissioner to New Zealand tells the story of her life, against the background of her country's struggle for political independence. Wife of the first Prime Minister of Western Samoa, Fetaui Mata'afa is a strong advocate of women's rights and an influential figure in Samoan affairs.

238 **'O le gafa o Talo'olema'agao o Satalo.**

P. J. Epling. *Journal of Pacific History*, vol. 5 (1970), p. 164-75.

The Samoan text of the traditional family history of Talo'olema'agao Avagalu, *matai* of the cognative kin group *'āigasatalo*, is annotated, with a translation into English. It was dictated in Samoan and recorded verbatim in May 1961 at Mālifa, Western Samoa. The linguistic style is formal, using *tautala lelei*. See also 'Lay perception of kinship: a Samoan case study' by P. J. Epling (*Oceania*, vol. 37 [1967], p. 260-80. bibliog.).

239 **Gods who die: the story of Samoa's greatest adventurer, as told to Julian Dana.**

George E. L. Westbrook. New York: Macmillan, 1935. 320p.

The engrossing story of George Edgerton Leigh Westbrook, an English wanderer and trader in the Caroline Islands, Marshall Islands, and the Ellice Islands from the 1870s. He settled in Āpia as a trader, living there for forty-three years, and became deeply involved in Samoan politics. He stood firmly with O. F. Nelson and other leaders of the *Mau* movement, and was an outspoken critic of the New Zealand administration, in countless letters to newspapers and in his pamphlet, *An appeal to the bishops and clergy of New Zealand* (1929). With O. F. Nelson and Edwin Gurr, Westbrook founded the newspaper, *Samoa Guardian.* His manuscripts, preserved at the Alexander Turnbull Library, Wellington, provide a vivid record of the struggle to assert Samoan rights.

240 **King Malietoa Tanumafili II.**
Veronica Maclean. In: *Crowned heads: kings, sultans and emperors: a royal quest.* Veronica Maclean. London: Hodder & Stoughton, 1993, p. 371-98.

Malietoa Tanumafili II became sole Head of State of Western Samoa, for life, in 1963 upon the death of Tupua Tamasese, joint Head of State since the achievement of independence in 1962. Though possessing some of the attributes and powers of a constitutional monarch, Malietoa Tanumafili II is neither 'king' nor 'crowned head' as this Eurocentric work assumes. Maclean presents an interesting profile of an impressive man in the *fa'a-Sāmoa* mould.

241 **The military administration of Western Samoa, 1914-1919.**
Mary Boyd. *New Zealand Journal of History*, vol. 2 [1968], p. 148-64. bibliog.

A painstaking study, based on official archives, of the five years separating the civil administrations of German Samoa and New Zealand's mandate. The occupation authorities made use of German administrative structures to a considerable extent. The period is now remembered for the controversial actions of the Administrator, Colonel Robert Logan (1914-19), and for the influenza epidemic of 1918 (for which Logan was widely blamed). See also: 'The seizure and occupation of Samoa' by S. J. Smith, in *The official history of New Zealand's effort in the Great War. Volume four: the war effort of New Zealand*, edited by H. T. B. Drew (Auckland, New Zealand: Whitcombe & Tombs, 1923, p. 23-41. bibliog.), the definitive record, from official sources, of the military occupation of German Samoa, 1914-20; and *New Zealanders in Samoa* by L. P. Leary (London: William Heinemann, 1918. 248p.).

242 ***Samoa mo Samoa*: the emergence of the independent state of Western Samoa.**
James W. Davidson. Melbourne: Oxford University Press, 1967. 467p. maps. bibliog.

'This book is concerned with the changes in the political structure, thought, and activity of Samoa resulting from its contact with the Western world. It analyses in detail, and so far as possible from the point of view of the indigenous people, one example of a historical phenomenon of almost world-wide occurrence' (Introduction, p. ix). The main sections cover: the country and the problem; political history to 1946; approach to self-government, 1946-58; transition to independence, 1958-62; and the independent state of Western Samoa. There is a glossary of Samoan terms. *Samoa mo Samoa* (Samoa for the Samoans) is a 20th-century slogan expressing 'an attitude that has dominated Samoan thinking since the arrival of the first Europeans'.

243 **A Samoan chronology.**
H. G. A. Hughes. Afonwen, Wales: Gwasg Gwenffrwd, 1996. 2nd ed. 50p. map. bibliog.

A revised, updated (up to 1996) and considerably enlarged version of the chronology of American Samoa and Western Samoa first published in 1950, as part of the author's preparations for the Linguistic Survey of Samoa. See also *A chronology of Western Samoa: being principally a record of chief events since its first European discovery in 1722*, compiled by C. G. R. McKay (Apia: J. W. Liston, *Western Samoa Mail*, 1937. 47p. 2 maps), which covers events from Roggeveen's discovery of the islands in 1722 to the election of Tamasese as *Mau* president on 16 December 1936.

244 **Tamasese: architect of West Samoan independence.**
James W. Davidson. *Pacific Islands Monthly*, vol. 33 (May 1963), p. 41-47.

A warm memorial tribute to Tupua Tamasese, joint Head of State of independent Western Samoa from 1962 to his death in 1963. Davidson outlines Tamasese's eventful career, emphasizing his constructive role in the evolution from internal self-government to full political independence. See also 'Tupua Tamasese, C.B.E., Christian statesman: a portrait of a friend' by Alan McKay (*Marist Messenger*, vol. 33, no. 7 [1963], p. 18-19).

245 **West Samoans between Germany and New Zealand 1914-1921.**
Hermann Hiery. *War & Society*, vol. 10, no. 1 (1992), p. 53-80. bibliog.

New Zealand's occupation of German Samoa in 1914 was soon followed by what Samoans felt to be arbitrary rule. Price inflation and the catastrophic influenza epidemic of 1918 strengthened Samoan resentment. Hiery holds that New Zealand's administration of Western Samoa was 'disaster and blundering, aggravated by racist attitudes'. This view is documented by New Zealand, Australian and German government archives, the records of the Archdiocese of Samoa, the Tate papers, diaries, and a wide range of secondary sources.

246 **Western Samoa.**
Norman Douglas. *Pacific Magazine*, vol. 18, no. 4/100 (July/August 1993), p. 113-15.

In a special report for *Pacific Magazine*'s 100th issue, Norman Douglas coolly reviews the progress and problems of independent Western Samoa since 1962. Besides successive natural disasters, the most intractable problems were the constitutional controversy over the legality of the *matai* franchise, the sharp decline in agriculture, the highest suicide rate in the world among young Samoan men, growing unemployment and emigration (now become an economic necessity). 'In an ironic way, by leaving their country, Samoans are doing it the most good, because only by doing so can they hope to alleviate conditions in the "cradle of Polynesia" '.

247 **Western Samoa: a New Zealand trust territory.**
W. E. H. Stanner. In: *The South Seas in transition: a study of post-war rehabilitation and reconstruction in three British Pacific dependencies.* W. E. H. Stanner. Sydney; Wellington, London: Australasian Publishing Company, 1953, p. 259-367. maps. bibliog.

Part three of this well researched book by an eminent Australian anthropologist provides an objective and critical discussion of the Trust Territory of Western Samoa under the control of New Zealand. After an examination of Samoan life and the 'riddle' of Samoan personality, there is a section dealing with the constitutional struggle and post-1945 developments, with accompanying statistics. Stanner is particularly interesting in his analysis of the racialist myths which grew apace under New Zealand rule.

Issues and events, 1988-

248 **Polynesia in review: issues and events, 1 July 1988 to 30 June 1989.**
The Contemporary Pacific, vol. 2, no. 1 (Spring 1990), p. 162-81. bibliog.

Contains 'American Samoa' by Bill Legalley (p. 162-63), and 'Western Samoa' by Ioane Lafoa'i (p. 178-81). This periodic review of issues and events is a prime source of informed, dispassionate comment.

249 **Polynesia in review: issues and events, 1 July 1989 to 30 June 1990.**
The Contemporary Pacific, vol. 3, no. 1 (Spring 1991), p. 191-211. bibliog.

Contains 'American Samoa' by Bill Legalley (p. 191-92), and 'Western Samoa' by Iosefa Maiava (p. 208-11). The devastation wrought by Cyclone Ofa was the most dramatic event of 1989-90 in Samoa. The economy of Western Samoa became far more dependent as a result of the cyclone, and the 'hand-out' mentality was further entrenched: 'In terms of self-sufficiency, the cyclone has put Samoa back many years'.

250 **Polynesia in review: issues and events, 1 July 1990 to 30 June 1991.**
The Contemporary Pacific, vol. 4, no. 1 (Spring 1992), p. 191-208.

'American Samoa' by Bill Legalley (p. 191-92) discusses the continuing government financial crisis, with a mounting budget deficit and allegations of abuse of public office. Congressman Faleomavaega Eni Hunkin was re-elected to the US Congress by an impressive majority of votes.

251 **Polynesia in review: issues and events, 1 July 1991 to 30 June 1992.**
The Contemporary Pacific, vol. 5, no. 1 (Spring 1993), p. 150-69.

'American Samoa' by Bill Legalley (p. 150-52) discusses Hurricane Val, which ravaged the Samoan Islands for three days, 7-10 December 1991, resulting in more than 9,500 damage claims. By the end of June 1992, the American Samoan administration again faced bankruptcy, attributed to the politics of dependency and, some would say, greed.

252 **Polynesia in review: issues and events, 1 July 1992 to 30 June 1993.**
The Contemporary Pacific, vol. 6, no. 1 (Spring 1994), p. 177-200.

'American Samoa' by Bill Legalley (p. 177-79) covers 'elections, continuing financial crises, department director rejections and resignations, and investigations of white collar crime'. A. P. Lutali was elected as governor, defeating Peter Tali Coleman. In 'Western Samoa' (p. 198-200), Morgan A. Tuimaleali'ifano reports on the closure of the Western Samoan embassy in Washington, DC, financial scandals, the opening of Television Western Samoa, and the silver jubilee of the University of the South Pacific. Western Samoa's population was predicted to double to 313, 981 by the year 2021.

253 **Western Samoa.**
Morgan A. Tuimaleali'ifano. *The Contemporary Pacific*, vol. 7, no. 1 (Spring 1995), p. 170-76.

A review of issues and events, from 1 July 1993 to 30 June 1994. The author focuses on the Lona village execution, the antigovernment demonstration of 2 March 1994 (against the unpopular goods and services tax), the allegations of national bankruptcy, the charges of nepotism in the Public Works Department, the mismanagement in government departments, the taro leaf blight, and the alarming incidence of suicide among young Samoans. On a per capita basis, Western Samoa in 1981 led the world with seventy-nine suicides. There were thirty-nine suicides in 1992, and thirty-seven in 1993, mainly in the fourteen to twenty-four age group. The most common methods used are paraquat, shooting and hanging, in that order.

Population

Censuses and statistics

South Pacific

254 **Population statistics.**
Compiled by Deborah Carter-Gau, Gerald Habercorn. Nouméa, New Caledonia: South Pacific Commission, 1995. 69p. (SPC Statistical Bulletin, no. 42).

Covering all the island states in the SPC area, including Western Samoa and American Samoa, this is the most up-to-date and authoritative source of demographic data. See also 'Oceania' by Doreen S. Goyer, Eliane Domschke, in *The handbook of national population censuses: Latin America and the Caribbean, North America, and Oceania*, edited by Doreen S. Goyer, Eliane Domschke (Westport, Connecticut; London: Greenwood Press, 1983, p. 403-595. 21 maps), which provides detailed data on the national population censuses of South Pacific states and territories, including American Samoa and Western Samoa. The topics covered in the various censuses are summarized and the quality of each census is evaluated. Most usefully, the national repositories for census data are indicated, with a selection of repositories in the USA. Another useful article is 'Demographic pressures on health, education, and employment resources in the South Pacific region' by Dennis A. Ahlburg (*Pacific Studies*, vol. 12, no. 2 [March 1989], p. 23-31. bibliog.). Population projections by age and sex for Western Samoa and five other South Pacific states are used to generate projections of the school-age population and the potential labour force. Very sharp increases in demand for infant and child health services, school places and jobs are likely, partly mitigated in Western Samoa by the effects of migration.

Samoa

255 **Samoa.**

Norma McArthur. In: *Island populations of the Pacific*. Norma McArthur. Canberra: Australian National University Press; Honolulu: University of Hawai'i Press, 1968, p. 98-161. map. bibliog. (p. 355-72).

An authoritative discussion of pre-censal population estimates and census enumerations for both Western Samoa and American Samoa. The chapter covers growth of population in the 20th century; age and sex composition; registration of births and deaths; analyses of mortality; and analyses of fertility. McArthur suggests, contrary to the widespread belief in the decrease of population following European discovery and settlement, that 'it might reasonably be doubted that the numbers of Samoans changed much from year to year before 1875, and probably increased in most years from then onwards'.

American Samoa

256 **The American Samoa territorial household survey of 1985: description, evaluation and preliminary analysis of demographic data.**

W. G. F. Groenewold, S. P. de Jong. Groningen, Netherlands: Geographical Institute, Groningen State University, 1986. 145p.

The 1985 survey, restricted to Tutuila and 'Aunu'u, aimed to provide information on migration, remittances, employment, health and major demographic variables. Among the specific data analysed are population growth, age and sex structure of the population, marital status, fertility and mortality.

257 **Census of population and housing, 1990, social, economic and housing characteristics: American Samoa.**

United States. Commerce Department. Census Bureau, Economics, and Statistics Administration. Washington, DC: Government Printing Office, 1992. 392p.

Consists chiefly of statistical tables and appendices on data gathered by the 1990 census.

258 **Population of American Samoa.**

Chai Bin Park. Bangkok: Economic and Social Commission for Asia and the Pacific (ESCAP); Nouméa, New Caledonia: South Pacific Commission, 1979. 78p. 4 maps. bibliog. (ESCAP/SPC Country Monograph Series, no. 7.1).

A comprehensive history of population trends in American Samoa, with an analysis of the current demographic situation and future projections. Statistical and other data (many longitudinal) are provided on population distribution, internal migration and migration to and from American Samoa. Compare this study with *Population profile of American Samoa (1980 census)* by Vai Filiga, Michael J. Levin (Washington, DC: Government Printing Office, 1988. 206p. maps. bibliog.), an exhaustive analysis of the demographic data collected by the 1980 census in American Samoa, with projections.

Western Samoa

259 **Ländliche Bevölkerung in West-Samoa: eine sozialökonomische Analyse.** (Rural population in Western Samoa: a socioeconomic analysis.)
Barbara Möhlendick. Saarbrücken, Germany: Breitenbach, 1988. 334p. map. bibliog. (Bonner Studien zur ländlichen Entwicklung in der Dritten Welt, Bd. 14).

A major work in the prestigious series of Bonn Studies on Rural Development in the Third World, with an in-depth analysis of land use and tenure, rural economic and social conditions, urbanization and migration. Möhlendick pays special attention to the status of Samoan women in the rural economy.

260 **Population growth in the Pacific islands: the example of Western Samoa.**
Peter Pirie. In: *Man in the Pacific islands: essays on geographical change in the Pacific islands.* Edited by R. Gerard Ward. Oxford: Clarendon Press, 1972, p. 189-218. bibliog.

Western Samoa shows a moderate decline in population from 1830 and an early recovery about 1860, followed by rapidly accelerating subsequent growth. Pirie attributes this in part to the decline in infant mortality after the 'spectacular results' achieved by the women's committees in each village, from 1918 onwards. Population projections are 'ominous', somewhat mitigated by emigration. See also *The population of Western Samoa: a preliminary report based on the 1956 census* by Peter Pirie (Canberra: Department of Geography, Australian National University, 1960. 74p. bibliog.); and 'Western Samoa: population, production and wealth' by Peter Pirie, G. W. Barrett (*Pacific Viewpoint*, vol. 3, no. 1 [1962], p. 63-96. bibliog.).

261 **Western Samoa: report of the census of population and housing, 1986: general report of the population census.**
Apia: Department of Statistics, [n.d.]. 170p. map.

An exhaustive analysis of the census data, providing an authoritative presentation of all salient demographic indicators. The population of Western Samoa totalled 157,158 (males 83,247; females 73, 911). Savai'i had a population of 44,930, 'Upolu and its smaller islands 112,228. The economically active population numbered 45,635 (males 37,054; females 8,581). Of these, 29,023 were engaged in agriculture, hunting, forestry and fishing. See also *Western Samoa: a population profile for the eighties* by Pamela Thomas (Canberra: National Centre for Development Studies, Australian National University, 1986. 30p. bibliog.), which is based on the latest census data, and provides a summary presentation of the demographic facts, such as the marked trend towards a predominantly youthful population, and a sober discussion of the implications. Overpopulation and insufficiency of natural resources are to be expected. Earlier studies include: 'Population expansion in Western Samoa' by Kathleen M. Jupp (*Journal of the Polynesian Society*, vol. 70, no. 4 [Dec. 1961], p. 401-09. bibliog.), an analysis of the data of the 1956 census, with population projections for 1956-76; and *The population of Western Samoa* by the United Nations, Population Division, Department of Social Affairs (New York: United Nations, 1948. 61p. map. bibliog.), an analysis which is still of interest, relating as it does to a period of relative population stability.

Migration and settlement

Samoa

262 **The Samoan exodus.**

Paul Shankman. In: *Contemporary Pacific societies: studies in development and change.* Edited by Victoria S. Lockwood, Thomas G. Harding, Ben J. Wallace. Englewood Cliffs, New Jersey: Prentice Hall, 1993, p. 156-70. bibliog. (p. 335-60).

According to the author, 'Samoans are migrating overseas in an exodus of significant proportions'. 'People have become Western Samoa's most valuable export'. Shankman analyses the background, process and effects of migration, and of the remittances sent home by migrants. Restrictions imposed by New Zealand since 1976 on migration from Western Samoa, and the prospects for return to Samoa are assessed, highlighting the problems of readjustment to island life. On balance, the exodus has been a 'mixed blessing', and Western Samoa has become economically more vulnerable as 'a recession overseas or restricted migration worsens the situation in the islands'.

263 **Selective migration from Samoa: a longitudinal study of pre-migration differences in social and psychological characteristics.**

Joel M. Hanna, Maureen H. Fitzgerald, Jay D. Pearson, Alan Howard, JoAnn Martz Hanna. *Social Biology*, vol. 37, no. 3-4 (1990), p. 204-14. bibliog.

In 1981 extensive questionnaire and interview data were collected on one hundred young Samoan adults. In 1986 it was found that thirty-five of these had migrated. The 1981 data were reviewed, to contrast the answers given by the migrants with those of the sixty-five who had remained in Samoa. Migrants reported a higher degree of peer-reliance and more community involvement. The findings support a hypothesis that migrants are pre-selected to fit into migrant communities and do not appear to be misfits who are unhappy with life in Samoa.

264 **A world perspective on Pacific islander migration: Australia, New Zealand and the USA.**
Edited by Grant McCall, John Connell. Kensington, New South Wales: Centre for South Pacific Studies, University of New South Wales in association with the Bureau of Immigration Research, 1993. 386p. bibliogs. (Pacific Studies Monograph, no. 6).

This fact-filled symposium is essential for understanding the phenomenon of migration from American Samoa, Western Samoa, Tokelau, Tonga and Micronesia. Particularly worthy of note are: 'A gathering of saints: the role of the Church of Jesus Christ of Latter-day Saints in Pacific islander migration', Max E. Stanton (p. 23-37); 'Becoming a competent migrant community: the case of American Samoans in California', Alexander F. Mamak (p. 149-59); 'Movement networks and "relative" economies in Samoa and Micronesia', Robert W. Franco (p. 161-70); 'Urban native American Samoans in the USA: employment, human services and organisational development issues', Alexander F. Mamak (p. 171-75); 'Samoan women in the workforce: a case study', Wendy Larner, Richard Bedford (p. 194-201); and 'Effects of migration on Western Samoa: an island viewpoint', Leulu Felise Va'a (p. 343-57).

American Samoa

265 **Return migration from the United States to American Samoa: evidence from the 1980 and 1990 censuses.**
Dennis A. Ahlburg. *Pacific Studies*, vol. 17, no. 2 (June 1994), p. 71-84. bibliog.

An investigation of census data found that return migration decreased between 1980 and 1990. Return migrants had greater economic success in American Samoa in 1980 and 1990 than non-migrants, although the extent of their advantage declined over the decade. Without better migration data, the benefits of migration and return migration cannot be estimated with certainty.

Western Samoa

266 **Changing patterns of commitment to island homelands: a case study of Western Samoa.**
Cluny Macpherson. *Pacific Studies*, vol. 17, no. 3 (Sept. 1994), p. 83-116. bibliog.

Macpherson uses remittances as a measure of the commitment of migrants and their children to their communities of origin. The volume and sustainability of such migrant remittances are immensely important factors in Western Samoa's social and macroeconomic policy. Four case-studies of Samoans resident in New Zealand are analysed, to establish how and why remittances fluctuate or decline. Employment, distribution of family, spouses' attitudes to remittances, and migrants' aspirations all influence decisions. Some migrants remit primarily to kin while others remit both to kin and community projects; declining remittance levels do not signal declining support for Samoan custom and practice. Migrants' children represent a source of potential replacement remitters, but the author claims that it is imperative to reduce Western Samoa's dependence on remittances in the near future.

267 **Economic and political restructuring and the sustainability of migrant remittances: the case of Western Samoa.**
Cluny Macpherson. *The Contemporary Pacific*, vol. 4, no. 1 (Spring 1992), p. 109-35. bibliog.

Pacific island states are continually seeking new sources of revenue and unless one or more such sources can be found, remittances are likely to remain important despite some negative social and economic consequences for economic development. The possibility that remittances might decline is discussed in this paper, in the case of remittance flows between New Zealand and Western Samoa. Samoan families in New Zealand find their discretionary income shrinking. The stock of new migrants will be further restricted, with adverse effects in Samoa, including political volatility. The reinstatement of the social and economic foundations of earlier, higher levels of self-sufficiency will become difficult.

268 **Migration and underdevelopment: the case of Western Samoa.**
Paul A. Shankman. Boulder, Colorado: Westview Press, 1976. 129p. map. bibliog. (Westview Special Studies in Social, Political, and Economic Development).

A comparative study of the relationship between migration, remittances and underdevelopment, based on a case-study of a Western Samoan village. Particular attention is paid to the kinds of economic ties that migrants maintain with the people who are left behind. Disagreeing with David C. Pitt (*Tradition and economic progress in Samoa*, q.v.), Shankman holds that 'as migration and remittances become more important at both national and local levels, they may *perpetuate* underdevelopment. That is, by more closely integrating islanders into a wider political economy, the effects of migration and remittances may prevent economic development'. Samoan well-being will continue to be crucially linked with migration and remittances.

269 **The Western Samoan kinship bridge.**
Evelyn Kallen. Leiden, Netherlands: E. J. Brill, 1982. 148p. bibliog. (Monographs and Theoretical Studies in Sociology and Anthropology in Honour of Nels Anderson, no. 18).

Kallen, a Canadian anthropologist, analyses the relationships between social change and migration, and the development of new criteria of ethnicity. Six months' fieldwork in Western Samoa in 1976, the contemporaneous New Zealand Immigration Survey and Western Samoan Migration Survey, participant observation and family profiles are all used in a sober consideration of how kinship networks facilitate chain migration from Western Samoa to New Zealand and, on a much smaller scale, to the United States of America. See also 'Samoan representations of World War II and military work: the emergence of international movement networks' by Robert W. Franco, in *The Pacific theater: island representations of World War II*, edited by Geoffrey M. White, Lamont Lindstrom (Honolulu: University of Hawai'i Press, 1989, p. 373-94. bibliog. [Pacific Islands Monographs, no. 8]).

Australia

270 **Migrants and their remittances: results of a household survey of Tongans and Western Samoans in Sydney.**
Richard Brown, Adrian Walker. Kensington, New South Wales: Centre for South Pacific Studies, University of New South Wales, 1995. 100p. bibliog. (Pacific Studies Monographs, no. 17).

'This research monograph presents the results of the largest survey yet to have been conducted among Pacific island migrants anywhere in the world. It is part of an ongoing series of studies on migration and remittances in the South Pacific through which a sizeable primary data base has been compiled from a number of household surveys among both remittance-receiving households in Tonga and Western Samoa and remittance-sending migrant households in Australia'.

Fiji

271 **Samoans in Fiji: migration, identity and communication.**
M. A. Tuimaleali'ifano. Suva: Institute of Pacific Studies; USP Extension Centres, University of the South Pacific, 1990. 247p. bibliog.

The author, a Samoan, considers aspects of Samoan resettlement in Fiji. These include: the oral traditions linking the Samoan and Fijian cultures; the Samoan community in Wailekutu; kinship co-operation and reciprocity; the Samoan church in Fiji; language and power; *fa'a-Sāmoa* in Fiji; Fijian-Samoan relations; and multiple identities in the Pacific context.

United States of America

272 **The northeast passage: a study of Pacific islander migration to American Samoa and the United States.**
Dennis A. Ahlburg, Michael J. Levin. Canberra: National Centre for Development Studies, Research School of Pacific Studies, Australian National University, 1990. 94p. bibliog. (Pacific Research Monographs, no. 23).

An ahistorical analysis of Pacific islander migration, discussed in terms of increasing dependence of sending countries. The considerable value of this study lies in its wealth of statistical data from previously unpublished tabulations of the 1980 US census, or from the 1980 American Samoan enumeration. See also *How many Samoans?: an evaluation of the 1980 census count of Samoans in the United States* by Geoffrey R. Hayes, Michael J. Levin (Washington, DC: Government Printing Office, 1983. 28p. bibliog.), a report prepared for the US Department of Labor, which examines estimates of the Samoan population in the USA and compares them with data provided by the 1980 federal census, by censuses in American Samoa, Western Samoa and New Zealand, and with migration statistics.

273 **Pacific Islander Americans: an annotated bibliography in the social sciences.**
Paul R. Spickard, Debbie Hippolite Wright, Blossom Fonoimoana, Dorri Nautu, Karina Kahananui Green, Tupou Hopoate Pau'u, David Hall, John Westerlund. La'ie, Hawai'i: Institute for Polynesian Studies, Brigham Young University-Hawai'i; Polynesian Cultural Center, 1995. 91p.

A briefly annotated bibliography of 390 items, including many on Samoans in the USA. Arranged by author and indexed by entry numbers, this is a valuable guide to elusive books, articles, theses and dissertations. See also *The Samoans: a selected bibliography* by Ramsay Leung-Hay Shu (Chicago: Pacific/Asian American Mental Health Research Center, 1981. 33p.), a general bibliography, including items on Samoans in New Zealand and the USA.

California

274 **The elder Samoan.**
Wesley H. Ishikawa, Vaosa Aifili, Alaisea Epati Tuitele, Pauga V. Fai'ivae. San Diego, California: Campanile Press, for the San Diego State University Center on Aging, 1978. 44p. bibliog.

Part of a cross-cultural study of minority elders in San Diego in 1974-76. Characteristic life-styles and customs, primary interactional networks, and attitudes toward formal assistance programmes were all surveyed, by means of a thirteen per cent sample of an estimated 300 over-60s in an estimated Samoan population in San Diego County of 13,800. Illness and lack of income were the areas of greatest need, with the family member as first recourse. Appendix A (p. 35-38) comprises a 'Brief history of the Samoan people and impressions of the elderly in San Diego County'.

275 **An illustrated history of Samoans in California.**
Daniel Pouesi. Carson, California: KIN Publications, 1994. 86p. maps.

This fascinating selection of rare photographs illustrates a well researched account of the gradual creation of Samoan immigrant communities, from San Diego (where many American Samoans served in the United States Navy) north to San Francisco. See also 'From Polynesia to California: Samoan migration and its sequel' by Gordon R. Lewthwaite, Christiane Mainzer, Patrick J. Holland (*Journal of Pacific History*, vol. 8 [1973], p. 133-57. map. bibliog.), which discusses the consequences of the decision to shift the naval base at Pago Pago to Hawai'i. This move resulted in the settlement of many Samoans in California.

276 **Migration, social change, and health: a Samoan community in urban California.**
Craig Robert Janes. Stanford, California: Stanford University Press, 1990. 197p. map. bibliog.

This penetrating study of the Samoan migrant community in the San Francisco area, 1982-85, focuses on the stress-health relationship in the conflict-ridden process of adaptation, and on the role of the church and other institutions. The forms of institutions have been changed to meet new circumstances, but the functions have remained largely unaltered. Directed social change is needed. The bibliography (p. 183-92) is up-to-date and wide-ranging. See also *The Samoan community in southern California: conditions and needs* by Ramsay Leung-Hay Shu, Adele Salamasina Satele (Chicago: Asian American Mental Health Research Center, 1977. 121p. bibliog. [Occasional Paper, no. 2]), a review of immigration history, followed by a discussion of Samoan households and their social and economic problems, especially with regard to medical services and care for elderly people.

277 **Radical chic *and* Mau-mauing the flak catchers.**
Tom Wolfe. London: Michael Joseph, 1971; London: Cardinal, 1989. 153p.

These essays reflect the social turmoil and anarchic spirit of the 1970s in urban America. 'Mau-mauing the flak catchers' is set in San Francisco, the main port of entry for immigrants from all over the Pacific, with eighty-seven ethnic minorities, all 'circling around the poverty program'. Samoans, 'big huge giants' with Tiki canes, were among the militants who clashed with the liberal white establishment bureaucrats (the 'flak catchers'), developing a highly refined technique of confrontation – mau-mauing – as the only possible way of winning recognition and getting the system to work.

Migration and biocultural adaptation: Samoans in California.
See item no. 489.

Hawai'i

278 **International movement and Samoan marriage in Hawaii.**
Robert W. Franco. In: *The business of marriage: transformations in Oceanic matrimony.* Edited by Richard A. Marksbury. Pittsburgh; London: University of Pittsburgh Press, 1993, p. 205-44. bibliog.

Franco presents an overview of Samoan kinship and marriage based on ethnographic accounts and then focuses on Honolulu, a key node of the Samoan network of international movement that links Australia, New Zealand, Western Samoa, American Samoa and the fifty states of the USA. In Hawai'i, a relatively high proportion of Samoan households headed by women, increasing youth discipline problems, a substantial degree of out-marriage, and homelessness, suggest that major transformations in Samoan marriage are under way.

279 Pacific island peoples in Hawaii.

Edited by Paul Spickard, Karina Kahananui Green. *Social Process in Hawaii*, vol. 36 (1994). 107p. maps. bibliog. (special issue).

Seven papers on Pacific island migrants (including Samoans) discuss barriers to social services; family dynamics; ethnic images and social distance; and 'La'ie: land and people in transition'. 'Influences of oral traditions on the language learning of Samoans and Tongans in Hawaii' by Lynne Hansen-Strain (p. 41-69. bibliog.) asserts that Tongans and Samoans focus on interpersonal involvement in their ESL speaking and writing, and that they use difficult structures more frequently and correctly in the spoken modality than in the written. The author proposes a model of discourse variability which takes into account speech modality, degree of planning, and level of interpersonal involvement. See also *The peopling of Hawaii* by Eleanor C. Nordyke (Honolulu: University of Hawai'i Press, 1989. 2nd ed. 329p. bibliog.). This revised edition of an authoritative study of ethnic groups in Hawai'i, and of the complex demographic statistics relating to them, expands and updates its discussion and data on Samoan immigrants, and highlights some problems of economic dependence.

280 Samoans in Hawai'i: a bibliography.

Proserfina A. Strona. Honolulu: Hawai'i State Library, 1991. 10p.

A selection of the works on Samoan settlers in Hawai'i held by the Hawai'i and Pacific Section of the Hawai'i State Library. This is one of a series of short bibliographies, each concerned with an immigrant ethnic group, such as Blacks, Puerto Ricans and Micronesians. See also *Samoans in Hawaii: selected readings* edited by Nancy Foon Young (Honolulu: General Assistance Center for the Pacific, College of Education, Educational Foundations, University of Hawai'i, 1977. 59p.), a selection of twenty lectures, essays and articles from newspapers and journals, on the lives and aspirations of Samoans in Hawai'i, their problems of adaptation to Hawaiian society and their contributions to it. Fourteen recommendations by the 1973 Samoan Heritage Conference focus on how to improve conditions in Hawai'i for resident Samoans. Another useful work is *The Samoans in Hawaii: a resource guide* by Nancy Foon Young (Honolulu: Ethnic Research and Resource Center, 1973. 47p. maps. [Publication, no. 1]), a highly selective bibliography, with introductory chapters dealing with the migrations from Samoa before and after 1950; problems of housing, medical services, education and employment; and the recommendations of the earlier 1972 Samoan Heritage Conference.

281 Samoans in Hawaii: a demographic profile.

Robert W. Franco. Honolulu: East-West Population Institute, East-West Center, 1987. 22p. bibliog.

A statistical analysis based on the 1980 census, intended for use by social service providers, health care workers and educators. Franco discusses cultural responses to mobility patterns and to problems of housing, employment and income. See also 'American Samoans in Hawaii: a short summary of migration and settlement patterns' by Ted Jay Born (*Hawaiian Historical Review*, vol. 12 [1968], p. 455-59. bibliog.), a useful outline of the history of migration from American Samoa to Hawai'i since 1888, with special reference to the attraction exerted by the LDS Temple at La'ie, by Brigham Young University-Hawai'i, and by the Polynesian Cultural Center.

New Zealand

282 The changing contours of Samoan ethnicity.

Cluny Macpherson. In: *Nga take: ethnicity and racism in Aotearoa/New Zealand.* Edited by Paul Spoonley, David Pearson, Cluny Macpherson. Palmerston North, New Zealand: Dunmore Press, 1991, p. 67-84. bibliog.

Macpherson discusses how remittances to Samoa may shrink with each new generation, as may direct commitment to Samoa. Interests become centred in New Zealand, in the religious, political and family activities that have developed among Samoan migrants. The ties of ethnicity subtly change, and may be weakened in the struggle to succeed in a hostile society. See also 'The future of Samoan ethnicity' by Cluny Macpherson, in *Tauiwi: racism and ethnicity in New Zealand*, edited by Paul Spoonley, Cluny Macpherson, David Pearson, Charles Sedgwick (Palmerston North, New Zealand: Dunmore Press, 1984. bibliog.).

283 Emerging pluralism: the Samoan community in New Zealand.

David Pitt, Cluny Macpherson. Auckland, New Zealand: Longman Paul, 1974. 147p. bibliog.

A pioneering sociological study of the urbanization of the Samoan migrant community in Auckland, and elsewhere in New Zealand. The traditional social structure (*fa'a-Sāmoa*) has proved remarkably flexible and adaptive. Two key institutions, the extended family (*'āiga*) and the Samoan church, have significantly assisted community distinctiveness and welfare. However, problems and social instability arise outside the *fa'a-Sāmoa* boundaries, in two areas of migrant interaction – work and school. The authors feel that European ignorance of Samoan institutions, and official insistence on integration, may lead to racial problems. See also Pitt's 'Social change in post-war New Zealand' (*Anspac Quarterly*, vol. 3, no. 2 [1971]). For housing problems see 'A Samoan migrant solution to housing limitations in urban New Zealand' by Cluny Macpherson, in *Home in the islands: housing and social change in the Pacific*, edited by Jan Rensel, Margaret Rodman (Honolulu: University of Hawai'i Press, 1997 [in press]).

284 Fa'aSamoa: the world of Samoans.

Feleti E. Ngan-Woo. [Auckland, New Zealand]: Office of the Race Relations Conciliator, 1985. 68p.

An informed, lucid introduction to Samoan attitudes, customs and life-styles, especially as they are encountered in New Zealand, intended to promote inter-communal understanding and mutual tolerance. Other studies include: *The Anisi family: Samoans in New Zealand* by Siobhan Prince ([Auckland, New Zealand: North Shore Teachers College, 1982]. 38p.), an intimate story of a Samoan migrant family, illustrated with portraits and genealogical tables, and intended for school use; 'Attitudes to Samoans in Auckland' by A. D. Trlin (*Australian Quarterly*, vol. 44, no. 3 [Sept. 1972], p. 49-57. bibliog.), a rather bleak picture of the degree of acceptance of Samoans by other residents of the Auckland urban area; 'Those strangers, our neighbours' by A. D. Trlin (*Comment*, no. 38 [1969], p. 26-32. bibliog.); 'Dimensionality of attitudes towards immigrants: a New Zealand example' by A. D. Trlin, R. J. Johnston (*Australian Journal of Psychology*, vol. 23, no. 3 [1973], p. 183-89. bibliog.); and *Ethnic & cultural issues* ([Auckland, New Zealand]: Auckland District Law Society, [1992]. 33p.

[Continuing Legal Education Programme]), which provides study notes on the legal implications and practical judicial problems created by the settlement in New Zealand of Samoans and other Pacific Islanders.

285 **The future of Western Samoan migration to New Zealand.**
Leulu Felise Va'a. *Asian and Pacific Migration Journal*, vol. 1, no. 2 (1992), p. 313-32. bibliog.

A sober appraisal of possible trends in Samoan migration southwards. The crucial determining factors are the general health of the New Zealand economy, demand for unskilled or semi-skilled labour and unemployment (with attendant xenophobia and restriction of immigration). No clear perspective is as yet discernible, but any increase in the annual immigration quota for Samoans seems unlikely. See also 'Samoan migration to New Zealand: the general background and some economic implications for Samoa' by Ian Fairbairn (*Journal of the Polynesian Society*, vol. 70, no. 1 [March 1961], p. 18-30. bibliog.), which summarizes and analyses data on Samoans in New Zealand, from the Annual Reports of the Samoan Administration, New Zealand censuses 1921 to 1956, and other official sources.

286 **Migration between Polynesia and New Zealand 1971-1981: who are the migrants?**
Richard D. Bedford, G. Lloyd. *New Zealand Population Review*, vol. 8, no. 1 (1982), p. 35-43. bibliog.

Western Samoa, Cook Islands and Niue are the main countries of origin of migrants to New Zealand, with Western Samoa leading by far in numbers. The authors present detailed statistics, and discuss the various types of migrant (such as students) and their motivations and networks. See also 'Pacific islanders in the New Zealand workforce: a comment' by Richard D. Bedford, Robert Didham, in *Economic restructuring and migrant labour in the South Pacific* (Wellington: Social Science Research Fund Committee, 1989, p. 91-96). Western Samoan men, usually unskilled or semi-skilled, are mainly to be found in manual occupations, women in factories and, especially, in hospital work.

287 **Samoan people in New Zealand: a statistical profile.**
Wellington: Statistics New Zealand, 1995. 55p. map.

Provides reliable facts on virtually every aspect of Samoan life in New Zealand. See also: *The challenge of change: Pacific island communities in New Zealand, 1986-1993* by Vasantha Krishnan, Penelope Schoeffel, Julie Warren (Wellington: New Zealand Institute for Social Research and Development, 1994. 100p. bibliog.), a thoughtful overview of the establishment of sizeable settled communities of non-Maori Polynesians, notably of Samoans and Tokelauans; *Students who come from Western Samoa to attend New Zealand secondary schools* by Helen Norman, Jacqui Kerslake, Alan Taylor (Wellington: Research and Statistics Division, Department of Education, [1986]. 35p.), an illustrated study of the motivations and the social and scholastic problems of young Samoans who seek their secondary education in New Zealand schools; 'Western Samoan marriage patterns in Auckland' by A. D. Trlin (*Journal of the Polynesian Society*, vol. 84, no. 2 [June 1975], p. 153-75. bibliog.), a detailed statistical study of in-group and out-group marriage involving Western Samoan immigrants resident in the Auckland urban area; *Samoan in the New Zealand curriculum: draft/Ta fala mo le gagana Samoa i Niu Sila: tusitusiga fa'ata ita i* (New

Zealand Ministry of Education. Wellington: Learning Media, Ministry of Education, 1994. 88p.), which puts forward practical proposals for promoting the study and use of Samoan in New Zealand schools and colleges; and *Report on the Samoan language in the New Zealand educational context* by Bernard Spolsky (Wellington: B. Spolsky, 1988. 29p.), a thoughtful discussion of the linguistic needs of Samoan children and young people resident in New Zealand.

288 **Talking past each other: problems of crosscultural communication.**
Joan Metge, Patricia Kinloch. Wellington: Victoria University Press; Price Milburn, 1978. 56p. bibliog.

Based on a joint paper presented to the New Zealand Organisation for Economic Co-operation and Development conference on Early Childhood Care and Education in February 1978, this is a study of aspects of crosscultural misunderstandings. A number of behavioural traits linking Maoris and Samoans, and distinguishing both ethnic groups from Pakehas, are explained. Differences in cultural behaviour and states of mind, likely to engender misunderstanding, are then analysed. This work has been criticized for its lumping together of Maori and Samoan, and for its stereotyping of Samoan behavioural characteristics. See also *Gender, culture, and morality: a comparative study of Samoans and Pakehas in New Zealand* by Barbara Reid (Chapel Hill, North Carolina: University of North Carolina, 1986).

Language

Bibliographies

289 **Austronesian and other languages of the Pacific and South-East Asia: an annotated catalogue of theses and dissertations.**
William G. Coppell. Canberra: Department of Linguistics, Research School of Pacific Studies, Australian National University, 1981. 521p. (*Pacific Linguistics*, series C, no. 64).

Includes theses and doctoral dissertations, from all parts of the world, relating to Polynesian languages including Proto-Samoan and Samoan. Bare details of many of the entries may be found in other bibliographies, but Coppell's compilation is of special value for its helpful annotations.

290 **The Samoan language: a guide to the literature.**
H. G. A. Hughes. Afonwen, Wales: Gwasg Gwenffrwd, 1994. 100p. maps. bibliog.

A comprehensive, unannotated listing by author of books, articles and theses on the Samoan language, together with selective lists of bibliographies on Oceanic linguistics and of works on the Polynesian language family generally. See also *Bibliography of Oceanic linguistics*, compiled by H. R. Klieneberger (London: Oxford University Press, 1957. 144p. [SOAS. London Oriental Bibliographies, vol. 1]), based in part on an extensive, unpublished 'Bibliography of Oceanic languages' (1954) by H. G. A. Hughes.

Dictionaries and phrase books

291 **Dictionnaire samoa-français-anglais et français-samoa-anglais précédé d'une grammaire de la langue samoa.** (A Samoan-French-English and French-Samoan-English dictionary preceded by a grammar of the Samoan language.)
Louis-Théodore Violette. Paris: Maisonneuve, 1879. 468p.

A valuable and still useful trilingual dictionary and extensive grammar. See also 'Grammaire samoane' (Samoan grammar) by Louis-Théodore Violette (*Revue de Linguistique et Philologie Comparative*, vol. 12 [1879], p. 379-454).

292 **English and Samoan vocabulary (*O le faasologaupu Peritania ua faa-Samoaina*): being part III of the Grammar and dictionary of the Samoan language.**
J. E. Newell. Mālua, German Samoa: London Missionary Society, 1905. 4th edition (enlarged and revised). 158p.

A separately published part of J. E. Newell's 4th edition revision of Pratt's *Grammar and dictionary* (q.v.), which is still useful.

293 **English-Samoan dictionary.**
Edited by Robert T. Littrell. [Pago Pago]: Division of Elementary Education, Department of Education, Government of American Samoa, 1954. 2 vols. Revised and corrected edition, 1955.

Compiled for school use with the special assistance of Talusa Tuitele and the Elementary Education Supervisors. This list of high-frequency English words and their Samoan equivalents (unfortunately without indication of context, register or usage) contains 'all the basic English words set forth by Laubach, Ogden and Richards'.

294 **Kurzes Vokabularium deutsch-samoanisch und samoanisch-deutsch.** (A short German-Samoan and Samoan-German vocabulary.)
E. Heider. Mālua, German Samoa: London Missionary Society Press, 1911. 70p.

Heider also published academic studies on Samoan words for death and dying; chiefs' language; children's games; proverbs; and numerals. See also: *Deutsch-samoanisches Taschenwörterbuch* (German-Samoan pocket dictionary) by F. Otto Sierich (Hamburg, Germany: Arnold Ebert, 1890); and *Kurze Anleitung zum Verständniß der samoanischen Sprache: Grammatik und Vokabularium* (Short guide to the understanding of the Samoan language: grammar and vocabulary) by B. Funk (Berlin: Ernst Siegfried Mittler und Sohn, 1893. 82p.).

295 **A lexicon of foreign loan-words in the Samoan language.**
Horst Cain. Cologne, West Germany; Weimar, East Germany; Vienna: Böhlau Verlag, 1986. 233p. bibliog. (Kölner Ethnologische Mitteilungen, Band 7).

An invaluable survey, with ample definitions, of the hundreds of words taken into Samoan usage since first contact with Europeans. It is based on fifteen months' ethnolinguistic fieldwork in Samoa in the early 1980s, and has an excellent bibliography (p. 226-33) of works in and about Samoan. See also 'Mots et concepts étrangers dans la langue de Samoa' (Foreign words and concepts in the Samoan language) by George Bertram Milner (*Journal de la Société des Océanistes*, vol. 13, no. 4 [1957], p. 51-68), a discussion of borrowed words and ideas in Samoan, and how they are assimilated.

296 **Samoan dictionary: Samoan-English, English-Samoan.**
George Bertram Milner. London: Oxford University Press, 1966. 465p. bibliog. Reprinted, Auckland, New Zealand: Polynesian [Pasifika] Press, 1993.

The standard dictionary of Samoan, based on extensive field research. Words are listed in the alphabetical order of the base, but with generous use of cross-references. Glottal stop and vowel length are indicated, and terms of respect are marked and differentiated according to their usage. The grammar which was to have accompanied this indispensable dictionary has not been published. For an account of the project see 'The Samoan dictionary project' by George Bertram Milner (*Quarterly Bulletin of the South Pacific Commission*, vol. 8, no. 3 [1958], p. 34-36). See also 'The linguistic situation in Samoa in 1952' by H. G. A. Hughes (*Rongorongo Studies*, vol. 1, no. 2 [1991], p. 43-49), a summary of the unpublished report (100p.) to the School of Oriental and African Studies, University of London, on the preliminary linguistic survey of Western Samoa and American Samoa, carried out by Hughes preparatory to the compilation of a new Samoan dictionary and grammar.

297 **Samoan phrase book.**
Alexander Hough. [Mālua], Samoa: London Missionary Society, 1924. 124p.

The Rev. Alexander Hough of the London Missionary Society writes in his preface: 'This book is not an attempt to teach the Samoan language'. It is a typically 19th-century phrasebook, arranged by topics such as numerals, education, quadrupeds and birds, the care of horse or cow, how to engage a servant, and how to pay customary compliments (*'O le fa'alupega; 'O le fa'aaloalo*). Used selectively, it is still serviceable. See also *O le faamatalaga o le gagana Samoa* (Introduction to the Samoan language) by Alexander Hough (Mālua, Samoa: London Mission Press, 1923. 3rd and revised edition). The 2nd edition of this guide was prepared by Sidney Alexander Beveridge and published by the LMS Printing and Bookbinding Establishment at Mālua in 1905.

298 **A simplified dictionary of modern Samoan.**
Ronald W. Allardice. Auckland, New Zealand: Polynesian (Pasifika) Press, 1985. 228p.

The Rev. R. W. Allardice is the author of several textbooks in Samoan and of a bilingual history of the Methodist Church in Samoa. This two-way dictionary, 'for students and others', has over 16,000 entries (Samoan-English, about 7,375; English-Samoan, about 9,160), printed in a two-column format. Lacking extended definitions and illustrations of usage, it is essentially only a wordlist, and the descriptions of pronunciation and grammar are unsatisfactory in some respects. Professor Albert J. Schütz of the University of Hawai'i, in a review (*Oceanic Linguistics*, vol. 30, no. 2 [Winter 1991], p. 272-75. bibliog.), wrote that, though not beyond redemption, Allardice's dictionary 'takes Samoan studies and lexicography a giant step backwards'.

299 ***'O le tusi pī*: a Samoan language picture dictionary.**
Illustrated by Fatu Feu'u. Auckland, New Zealand: Polynesian Press, 1991. 32p.

A colourful vocabulary of eighty-five Samoan words, illustrating the Samoan alphabet, numbers and colours. The powerful artwork combines traditional and contemporary styles, with the simplicity characteristic of Fatu Feu'u. He was born in Poutasi, Western Samoa, emigrated to New Zealand in 1966, and became a professional artist in 1988. See also *Pī faitau: Samoan alphabet* (Auckland, New Zealand: Pacific Islands Education Resource Centre, 1993. 4 picture friezes in colour, 19 × 72 cm. folded to 19 × 38 cm.), a colourful presentation, for very young children, of the Samoan alphabet. *Pī* (alphabet) is also the name of the letter *-p-*.

Grammars and course books

300 **Everyday Samoan: Samoan grammar elucidated by the use of numerous examples from ordinary conversation in the Samoan language.**
Evelyn A. Downs. Devonport, New Zealand: *North Shore Gazette*, 1949. 2nd ed. 140p. errata & addenda sheet.

First published in 1942, this is a formal treatment of Samoan in terms of parts of speech and verbal paradigms. It is well exemplified with phrases and sentences from everyday contexts, followed by chapters on: idiomatic sentences in common use; polite speech; and sentences for practice. There are three vocabularies: English-Samoan; Samoan-English; and verbs vocabulary, Samoan to English. The author was principal of Papauta School, Āpia.

301 ***Gagana Samoa*: a Samoan language coursebook.**
Galumalemana Afeleti L. Hunkin, cover design by Fatu Feu'u, photographs by Sāle Jessop. Auckland, New Zealand: Polynesian (Pasifika) Press, 1988. 143p. bibliog. accompanying cassette.

Written by a trained and experienced teacher, and illustrated with lively photographs of the Samoan community in New Zealand (including rugby star Ivasefulu Tolu), these thirty-one basic lessons are 'particularly aimed at young Samoans born in New Zealand, and other countries, who are searching for their true identity in an adopted land'. Designed for personal or classroom use, the book is eminently practical and has over 950 exercises (with answers). Glottal stop and vowel length are indicated throughout.

302 **A grammar and dictionary of the Samoan language: with English and Samoan vocabulary.**
George Pratt. Papakura, New Zealand: R. McMillan, 1984. 416p.

A reprint of the third edition of this still valuable work, as revised by the Rev. George Pratt of the London Missionary Society himself and published by the LMS, London, in 1892. The first edition appeared in 1862. Pratt served as a missionary in Samoa for upwards of forty years. The Rev. J. E. Newell of Mālua Institution, who edited a fourth edition (q.v.), said of him: 'He was a very accomplished speaker in the vernacular, and possessed a full and remarkable knowledge of other Polynesian dialects ...'.

303 **Grammar and vocabulary of the Samoan language; together with remarks on some of the points of similarity between the Samoan and the Tahitian and Maori languages.**
Heinrich Neffgen, translated from the German by Arnold B. Stock. New York: AMS Press, 1978. 155p.

A translation of *Grammatik der samoanischen Sprache* (1903), reprinted from the edition published by Kegan Paul, Trench, Trubner & Co, London, 1918. An extensive English-Samoan and Samoan-English vocabulary (p. 100-45) is complemented by 'Words in general use systematically arranged' (p. 146-55), with twenty groups of English words and their Samoan equivalents.

304 **Let's speak Samoan: an introduction and guide to the Samoan language for missionaries of the Church of Jesus Christ of Latter-day Saints.**
Alan P. Johnson, Lillian E. Harmon, revised by F. Ronald Haymore. [Pesega, Western Samoa: Church of Jesus Christ of Latter-day Saints], 1962. 469p. Reissued by the LDS Auckland Distribution Center in 1970, 1972 and 1976.

A practical course in everyday spoken Samoan, with exercises. Glottal stop and vowel length are indicated throughout. There is also a very useful Samoan-English word list (p. 412-69).

305 **Pratt's grammar & dictionary of the Samoan language.**
Revised and enlarged by J. E. Newell. Mālua, Western Samoa: London Missionary Society, 1911. 637p. (variously paginated).

The Rev. J. E. Newell served the London Missionary Society in Samoa for twenty-nine years. He added 'a considerable number of words' to the Rev. George Pratt's original work and also made use of the collection of Samoan proverbs by Dr Schultz, Judge of the Supreme Court of Samoa. The very important 'Samoan poetry' and 'Samoan proverbial sayings' are enlarged, and a wholly new article on 'Samoan chief's language' added. This fourth edition is, substantially, distinct.

306 **Samoan.**
Masahiro Oda. Tokyo: Institute for the Study of Languages and Cultures of Asia and Africa, Tokyo Gaikokugo Daigaku, 1976. 48 leaves. (Asian & African Grammatical Manual, no. 16).

An outline of Samoan grammar, prepared for the 'Bunpo chosahyo' Kyodo Kenkyu Project. See also *Samoago nyūmon* (Samoan primer) by Yoshinori Iwasa (Tokyo: Tairyusha, 1987), an introductory grammar of Samoan, in Japanese.

307 **A Samoan grammar.**
Spencer Churchward. Melbourne: Spectator Publishing Co., for the Methodist Church of Australasia, Samoa District, 1951. 2nd revised & enlarged edition. 227p. bibliog.

'Written in the first place for the use of Methodist missionaries', this is a substantially changed version of the author's *A new Samoan grammar* (Melbourne, 1926). Very much in the tradition of classical grammars (using terms such as 'crasis', 'principal parts' and 'parataxis'), it nevertheless remains a serviceable grammar. There is a thorough general index, an index of Scripture references and a Samoan index.

308 **Samoan language: a manual for the study and teaching of the Samoan language as taught by Peace Corps/W. Samoa.**
John F. Mayer. Apia: United States Peace Corps, 1976. 396p. bibliog.

A practical course in everyday Samoan, based in part on the 'Silent way' method. There are three sections: how to use the book for maximum benefit; a full course in the Samoan language, presented as a step by step teacher's manual; and a section including Samoan-English glossary, English-Samoan word list, idiomatic expressions, Samoan grammar and bibliography. It is a complete instructor's manual and a student's reference book combined. See also *Silent way: Samoan language* by John F. Mayer (Apia: United States Peace Corps, 1974).

309 **Samoan reference grammar.**
Ulrike Mosel, Even Hovdhaugen. Oslo: Scandinavian University Press; Institute for Comparative Research in Human Culture, 1992. 819p. bibliog.

This formidable descriptive grammar of modern Samoan was based on fieldwork and on extensive analysis of written sources. The introduction surveys the history of the Samoan language and of Samoan linguistics. The differences between *tautala lelei* ('*t* Samoan') and *tautala leaga* ('*k* Samoan') are explained. All words in the text are brought together in 'Word list' (p. 775-96) where glottal stop and vowel length are marked in conformity with G. B. Milner's *Samoan dictionary* (q.v.). The extensive bibliography (p. 809-19) includes many elusive works in and about Samoan. Criticism of many errors and of some analyses may be found in a review by Kenneth W. Cook (*Oceanic Linguistics*, vol. 33, no. 2 [Dec. 1994], p. 567-81. bibliog.).

310 **Samoanskii iazyk.** (The Samoan language.)
V. D. Arakin. Moscow: Nauka, 1973. 87p. map. bibliog. (Iazyki Narodov Azii i Afriki).

A concise, systematic introduction to the Samoan language, in Russian.

311 **Teach yourself Samoan.**
C. C. Marsack. London: English Universities Press, 1962. 178p. (Teach Yourself Books).

A helpful self-tuition course in Samoan prepared by a judge of Western Samoa's Land and Titles Court with the 'very great help' of the Court's registrar, Auelua F. Enari. The twenty lessons cover the grammatical categories conventionally used for European languages, which are at times at variance with the facts of Samoan usage. Chapter twenty deals with 'Language of courtesy'. There are keys to exercises and to translations, a table of principal parts of the more common verbs, Samoan-English and English-Samoan vocabularies, and a list of words adopted from other languages.

Linguistic studies

312 **The *cia* suffix as a passive marker in Samoan.**
Kenneth William Cook. *Oceanic Linguistics*, vol. 35, no. 1 (June 1996), p. 57-76. bibliog.

A discussion of the *cia* suffix, which is, according to Cook, 'a passive suffix in impersonal passives with a transitive verb stem, and in personal passives without such a stem'. See also: 'The Samoan *cia* suffix as an indicator of agent defocusing' by Kenneth William Cook (*Pragmatics*, vol. 12 [1991], p. 145-67. bibliog.); and *Patientive absolutive verbal morphology and passive in Samoan* by Kenneth William Cook (Washington, DC: Educational Resources Information Center, 1987).

313 **Ergativity in Samoan.**
Ulrike Mosel. Cologne, Germany: Institut für Sprachwissenschaft, 1985. 145p. bibliog. (AKUP, no. 61).

A linguistic examination of the grammatical relationship between sentences in Samoan, where the subject of one sentence corresponds to the object of another, the new subject of which causes rather than performs the action. See also: 'Ergative and passive in Basque and Polynesian (Samoan)' by George Bertram Milner (*Oceanic Linguistics*, vol. 15, no. 1-2 [1976], p. 93-106. bibliog.); and 'Transitivity and reflexivity in Samoan' by Ulrike Mosel (*Australian Journal of Linguistics*, vol. 11 [1991], p. 175-94. bibliog.).

314 **Forschungen über die Sprachen der Inseln zwischen Tonga und Saamoa.** (Investigations on the languages of the islands between Tonga and Samoa.)
Akihisa Tsukamoto. Münster, Germany; Hamburg, Germany: Lit Verlag, 1994. 81p. bibliog. (Austronesiana: Studien zum austronesischen Südostasien und Ozeanien, no. 2).

This careful, convincing history covers the six languages of Samoa, Tonga, Niuee, Niuafo'ou, Uvea and Futuna, the earliest settled region of Polynesia. Futuna is linguistically closest to Samoa. In a review (*Oceanic Linguistics*, vol. 35, no. 1 [June 1996], p. 146-48), John U. Wolff declares: 'It should be basic reading for all students of the history of the Austronesian languages and deserves a translation into English to give it widespread accessibility' (p. 148).

315 **It is aspect (not voice) which is marked in Samoan.**
G. B. Milner. *Oceanic Linguistics*, vol. 12 (1973), p. 621-39. bibliog.

A paper of considerable importance in Polynesian descriptive linguistics. Milner convincingly establishes that the grammatical category of 'voice', used in the early missionary grammars of Samoan, is inapplicable and needs to be replaced by that of 'aspect'. See also 'Active, passive, or perfective in Samoan: a fresh appraisal of the problem' by George Bertram Milner (*Journal of the Polynesian Society*, vol. 71, no. 2 [1962], p. 151-61. bibliog.).

316 **A scheme for describing Samoan grammar.**
Andrew K. Pawley. *Te Reo*, vol. 4 (1961), p. 38-43. bibliog.

Pawley presents a practical method of recording Samoan grammatical usage. See also: 'The person-markers in Samoan' by Andrew K. Pawley (*Te Reo*, vol. 5 [1962], p. 52-56. bibliog.); 'Aspects of Samoan phonemics' by Andrew K. Pawley (*Te Reo*, vol. 3 [1960], p. 47-50. bibliog.); 'Samoan phrase structure: the morphology-syntax of a Western Polynesian language' by Andrew K. Pawley (*Anthropological Linguistics*, vol. 8, no. 5 [1966], p. 1-63. bibliog.); *Case marking and grammatical relations in Polynesian* by Sandra Chung (Austin, Texas: University of Texas Press, 1978. 415p. bibliog.); and 'Samoan pronominalization' by Paul Chapin (*Language*, vol. 44 [1970], p. 366-78. bibliog.).

317 **Vowel lengthening in Samoan.**
Even Hovdhaugen. In: *Pacific island languages: essays in honour of G. B. Milner*. Edited by Jeremy H. C. S. Davidson. London: School of Oriental and African Studies, University of London; Honolulu: University of Hawai'i Press, 1990, p. 95-103. bibliog. (Collected Papers in Oriental and African Studies).

An examination of vowel length and reduplication in Samoan phonology and morphophonology, using examples from a formal variety of the language. See also: 'Locative accent in Samoan' by Iovanna D. Condax (*Oceanic Linguistics*, vol. 29, no. 1 [Summer 1990], p. 27-48. bibliog.); and 'Phonetic vowel length in Samoan' by Even Hovdhaugen (*Oceanic Linguistics*, vol. 31, no. 2 [Winter 1992], p. 281-85. bibliog.), a rejoinder to criticisms by Iovanna D. Condax.

Language acquisition and development

318 **Code switching and conflict management in Samoan multiparty interaction.**

Alessandro Duranti. *Pacific Studies*, vol. 14, no. 1 (Nov. 1990), p. 1-30. bibliog.

Provides case-studies, with transcripts, of night-time arguments, which are characterized by code switching between the two phonological registers called, respectively, *tautala lelei* ('good speech') and *tautala leaga* ('bad speech').

319 **Culture and language development: language acquisition and language socialization in a Samoan village.**

Elinor Ochs, with a foreword by Shirley Brice Heath. Cambridge, England: Cambridge University Press, 1988. 255p. map. bibliog. (Studies in the Social and Cultural Foundations of Language, no. 6).

An exploration of the complex interaction of the processes whereby Samoan children learn to be competent members of their society and, simultaneously, to be competent speakers of their language. See also: 'The impact of stratification and socialization on men's and women's speech in Western Samoa' by Elinor Ochs, in *Language, gender and sex in comparative perspective*, edited by S. U. Philips, S. Steele, C. Tanz (Cambridge, England: Cambridge University Press, 1987, p. 50-70. bibliog.); 'Talking to children in Western Samoa' by Elinor Ochs (*Language in Society*, vol. 11 [1982], p. 77-104. bibliog.); 'Children's insults: America and Samoa' by Claudia Mitchell-Kernan, Keith T. Kernan, in *Sociocultural dimensions of language use*, edited by Mary Sanches, Ben G. Blount (New York: Academic Press, 1975, p. 307-15. bibliog.), an inventory, discussion and comparison of the colourful, often scabrous, insults favoured by children in Samoa and in the USA; and 'Ergativity and word order in Samoan child language: a sociolinguistic study' by Elinor Ochs (*Language*, vol. 58, no. 3 [1982], p. 646-71. bibliog.).

320 **On the acquisition of the t- and k- languages by Samoan children.**

Even Hovdhaugen, Hanne Gram Simonsen. In: *Papers from the tenth Scandinavian Conference of Linguistics*. Edited by V. Rosén. Bergen, Norway: Department of Linguistics and Phonetics, University of Bergen, 1988, vol. 2, p. 1-15. bibliog.

The article addresses the question of how Samoan children learn the two different phonological systems of the two sociolects of their language. It is argued that the system of the k- language is learned first. Only later do children discover the sociolectally conditioned phonological variation (t-), and before they distinguish the two systems phonologically, they may go through a phase of using two phonetically different variants – one velar, one dental – of a k- based phonological system.

321 **Samoan linguistic acculturation in San Francisco.**
Muriel Myers. *Anthropological Linguistics*, vol. 20, no. 9 (1978), p. 395-406. bibliog.

A professional study of changes occurring in the Samoan language to meet the needs of a new and alien environment. See also 'Phonological innovations of bilingual Samoans in San Francisco' by Muriel Myers (*Anthropological Linguistics*, vol. 23, no. 3 [1981], p. 113-34. bibliog.).

Traditional usages

322 **From grammar to politics: linguistic anthropology in a Western Samoan village.**
Alessandro Duranti. Berkeley, California: University of California Press, 1994. 208p. 2 maps. bibliog.

While studying Samoan grammar and ceremonial speech in the 'Upolu village of Falefā in 1978-79 and 1988, Duranti became 'irresistibly involved' in village politics. He found how traditional oratory is shaped by the needs of the political process and how language insulates ceremonial speakers from the perils of everyday conversational confrontation. In the *fono*, 'the choice of particular linguistic forms is a significant part of a wider organization of semiotic resources that include spatial arrangements and ceremonial drinking'. This innovative combination of linguistic and political anthropology vividly describes the formal order and ceremonial speech of council meetings, and the identification of political acumen with verbal skills.

323 ***Lāuga* and *talanoaga*: two speech genres in a Samoan political event.**
Alessandro Duranti. In: *Dangerous words: language and politics in the Pacific*. Edited by D. L. Brenneis, F. R. Myers. New York; London: New York University Press, 1984, p. 217-42.

Discusses the characteristics of a formal meeting (*fono*) in the village of Falefā on 'Upolu, governed by traditional rules as to seating arrangement of *matai*; temporal boundaries (*'ava* ceremony followed by *lāuga*, *talanoaga*, concluded by *'ava* ceremony); etiquette; order of speaking; use of the ceremonial language appropriate for *matai*; ceremonial speech (*lāuga*); and discussion (*talanoaga*). The ceremonial *lāuga* is the most sophisticated form of verbal art in Samoa. Some ranked Samoan orators feel that speaking at ceremonial events may jeopardize the power they already possess, and so use representatives or hire orators to speak for them.

324 **Lāuga: Samoan oratory.**
Tātupu Fa'afetai Matā'afa Tu'i. Suva: Institute of Pacific Studies, University of the South Pacific; Apia: USP Western Samoa Extension Centre; National University of Western Samoa, 1987. 111p. bibliog.

'This is a study in the concept of social communication through the formal structure of Lāuga, Samoan oratory'. Tu'i explains the nature and anatomy of oratory, and presents the Samoan texts of actual speeches. The translations and analysis 'reveal levels of meaning and significance'. Based on the author's University of Auckland MA thesis (1985), this is an essential introduction to Samoa's most complex art form. See also: 'Ceremonial language (Samoa)' by Edward Tregear (*Transactions of the New Zealand Institute*, vol. 27 [1895], p. 593-97); and *'O le tusi fa'alupega o Samoa 'atoa* (ceremonial greetings for all Samoa) (Samoan Methodist Church. Apia: Wesley Methodist Printing Press, 1985).

325 **The Samoan *fono*: a sociolinguistic study.**
Alessandro Duranti. Canberra: Department of Linguistics, Research School of Pacific Studies, Australian National University, 1981. 195p. map. bibliog. (*Pacific Linguistics*, series B. vol. 80).

A very detailed analysis of the language and styles of speaking traditionally employed in the *fono* (council), the most characteristically Samoan of all Samoan institutions. Duranti explores the language of respect, honorific terms, the subtleties and nuances of words, and the social and political context and roles of the institution. See also 'Doing things with words: conflict, understanding and change in a Samoan *fono*' by Alessandro Duranti, in *Disentangling: conflict discourse in Pacific societies*, edited by K. Watson-Gegeo, G. White (Stanford, California: Stanford University Press, 1990, p. 459-89. bibliog.).

326 **Samoan oratory.**
Lowell D. Holmes. *Journal of American Folklore*, vol. 82 (1969), p. 342-52. bibliog.

An outline and discussion of the main traditional features of *lāuga*, Samoa's characteristic and most highly developed art form: the making of ceremonial speeches. See also: 'Heteroglossia in Samoan oratory' by Alessandro Duranti (*Pacific Studies*, vol. 15, no. 4 [Dec. 1992], p. 155-75), which discusses and illustrates the relationship between art and politics in *lāuga*, and reconsiders the role of formalized language in the reproduction of the existing social order; and 'Two Samoan ceremonial speeches' by J. E. Buse (*Bulletin of the School of Oriental and African Studies*, vol. 24, no. 1 [1961], p. 104-15. bibliog.), a structural and linguistic analysis of the Samoan texts of typical *lāuga*.

327 **Samoan plantation pidgin.**
Peter Mühlhäusler. In: *Papers in pidgin and creole linguistics, no. 1.* Edited by L. Todd and others. Canberra: Research School of Pacific Studies, Australian National University, 1978 (reprinted 1980), p. 67-120. (*Pacific Linguistics*, PLA 054).

Mühlhäusler reviews in depth what is known of the stable Samoan plantation pidgin (SPP), born of the contact in 19th-century Samoa of Melanesian pidgin English (MPE) with a Micronesian type of pidgin English already in use on the plantations. These

Samoan plantations were instrumental in establishing pidgin English in German New Guinea – particularly the Bismarck Archipelago – as a lingua franca among labourers returning from Samoa in the 1880s and later. See also: Mühlhäusler's article, 'Samoan plantation pidgin English and the origins of New Guinea pidgin: an introduction' (*Journal of Pacific History*, vol. 11, part 2 [1976], p. 122-25); and 'New evidence of a Samoan origin of New Guinea Tok Pisin (New Guinea Pidgin English)' by Ulrike Mosel, Peter Mühlhäusler (*Journal of Pacific History*, vol. 17, no. 3 [July 1982], p. 166-75. bibliog.), which includes statistics of labour recruitment for Samoa and a discussion of Samoan Plantation Pidgin English as a prestige variety.

328 **The Samoan vocabulary of respect.**
G. B. Milner. *Journal of the Royal Anthropological Institute*, vol. 91, no. 2 (1961), p. 296-317. bibliog.

A study of honorific and ceremonial language usage, made as part of the research for the author's *Samoan dictionary* (q.v.). See also: *'O le vāfealoa'i: a missionary handbook on the respect language of the Samoan people* by George Thomas Murdock, Jr. (Pesega, 'Upolu: Samoan Mission of the Church of Jesus Christ of Latter-day Saints, 1965. 78p.), an introduction, for missionary use, to the Samoan language in its various styles, which includes a concise Samoan-English dictionary; and 'Lenguaje honorífico y comportamiento reverente en Samoa y Tonga' (Honorific language and respectful behaviour in Samoa and Tonga) by Olaf Blixen (*Comunicaciones Antropológicas del Museo Nacional de Historia Natural de Montevideo*, vol. 1 [1966], p. 1-39. bibliog.), a comparison of language of respect and of reverent and deferential behaviour in the two Polynesian countries, based largely on secondary sources.

329 **Speechmaking and the organisation of discourse in a Samoan *fono*.**
Alessandro Duranti. *Journal of the Polynesian Society*, vol. 90, no. 3 (Sept. 1981), p. 357-400. bibliog.

'Oratory is probably the most sophisticated art form in Samoa and certainly one of the most well-preserved aspects of ancient Polynesia'. A *failāuga* (speechmaker) is a highly respected individual, and often indispensable to his kin and allies in economic transactions and social crises of every kind. Duranti presents a detailed case-study of speechmaking in a meeting held in the village of Falefā, 'Upolu, using transcriptions of recordings made there. See also 'Samoan speechmaking across social events: one genre in and out of a *fono*' by Alessandro Duranti (*Language in Society*, vol. 12 [1983], p. 1-22. bibliog.).

330 **'O le tusi fa'alupega o Samoa: Savai'i, 'Upolu, Tutuila ma Manu'a.**
(The book of Samoan ceremonial styles and addresses: Savai'i, 'Upolu, Tutuila and Manu'a.)
Auckland, New Zealand: Pasifika Press, 1997. 80p.

'Fa'alupega are the ceremonial exchanges made when members of one Samoan community formally meet those of another. These greetings have been handed down from generation to generation, and form an essential part of Samoan culture'. This collection covers all Samoa and presents annotations to the primary oral text, giving detailed explanations for the often idiosyncratic formula of the greetings. This essential work is entirely in Samoan. See also *'O le tusi fa'alupega o Samoa* (The book of Samoan ceremonial styles and addresses) (Apia: London Missionary Society Press, 1930. 97p. Reprinted, Apia: Mālua Printing Press, 1958).

Names

331 **Captain Cook's problem: an experiment in geographical semantics.**
Jerome Kirk, P. J. Epling, Paul A. Bick, John Paul Boyd. In: *Linguistics and anthropology: in honor of C. F. Voegelin.* Edited by M. Dale Kinkade, Kenneth L. Hale, Osward Werner. Lisse, Netherlands: The Peter De Ridder Press, 1975, p. 445-64. bibliog.

From Cook onwards, Europeans have been confused by Polynesian directional terms. Using a sample of twenty-one native Samoans in Sātalo, southern 'Upolu, local terms were matched with compass bearings. These terms are compared with usage in North Carolina, South Carolina and Yucatán, as cross-cultural validation of the method used. The authors enjoy the speculation that the inhabitants of Bougainville's 'Navigators' Islands' may be unusually *poor* navigators, and that their traditional reckoning system was one of triangular coordinates, based on the wind system: *la'i* (westerly wind), *toga* (southerly wind) and *to'elau* (easterly wind).

332 **Fish names of Western Polynesia: Niue, Samoa, Tokelau, Tonga, Tuvalu, Wallis and Futuna, Outliers.**
Honolulu: East-West Center, University of Hawai'i at Mānoa, 1993. 2 vols. maps. bibliog.

A most comprehensive guide to Polynesian fish names, with vernacular names accompanied by their scientific equivalents. Its importance for fishermen is amply matched by its value to lexicography. A very similar compilation is *Fish names of Western Polynesia: Futuna, Niue, Samoa, Tokelau, Tonga, Tuvalu, Uvea, Outliers* by Karl Heinz Rensch (Canberra: Archipelago Press, 1994. 311p. map). This gives vernacular names and English translations, with a Latin finder-list.

333 **Folk plant nomenclature in Polynesia.**
W. Arthur Whistler. *Pacific Studies*, vol. 18, no. 4 (Dec. 1995), p. 39-59. bibliog.

An interesting and useful review of Polynesian linguistics as it relates to folk names of plants. Whistler discusses and tabulates name changes resulting from a variety of factors, in Samoan, Tongan, Tahitian, Rarotongan and Hawaiian. Tables of widespread folk names and their cognates are provided, and there is a discussion of the process of coining new names. See also: 'Polynesian plant names: linguistic analysis and ethnobotany, expectations and limitations' by K. H. Rensch, in *Islands, plants, and Polynesians*, edited by P. A. Cox, S. A. Banack (Portland, Oregon: Dioscorides Press, 1991, p. 97-112. bibliog.); and 'Annotated list of Samoan plant names' by W. Arthur Whistler (*Economic Botany*, vol. 38, no. 4 [1984], p. 464-89. bibliog.).

334 **Geographical nomenclature of American Samoa.**
William Churchill. *Bulletin of the American Geographical Society*, vol. 45 (1913), p. 187-93.

An inventory of place-names on Tutuila, 'Aunu'u, Ofu, Olosega and Ta'ū, with etymological and linguistic notes.

335 **The meaning of the name Sāmoa.**
Joseph C. Finney. *Journal of the Polynesian Society*, vol. 82, no. 3 (Sept. 1973), p. 301-03. bibliog.

Most explanations of the meaning of Samoa are utterly implausible. One suggestion is *Sā* (tribe of) plus *Moa*, said to be the family name of the early Tui Manu'a. Proceeding from Tongan Ha'amoa to a conjectural Proto-Polynesian (PPN) **Sa'amoa*, Finney speculates that Sāmoa means 'people of the deep sea' (*Sā* + *moana*). See also 'Origin of the name "Samoa" ' by William Wyatt Gill (*Journal of the Polynesian Society*, vol. 4 [1895], p. 155).

336 **Teachers' handbook to fauna of Western Samoa: a vernacular listing.**
David F. Garlovsky. Alafua, Western Samoa: South Pacific Regional College of Tropical Agriculture, 1970. 118p.

A valuable, extensive list of Samoan faunal and zoological terminology, with many names which are not to be found in the Pratt and Milner dictionaries (qq.v.).

Samoan shorthand

337 **Saute Sapolu's shorthand system in Samoan language.**
Saute Sapolu. Auckland, New Zealand: Voka Saute Sapolu, 1985.

A system of shorthand devised for Samoan.

Religion

General

338 **Beyond the reef: records of the Conference of Churches and Missions in the Pacific, Malua Theological College, Western Samoa, April 22-May 4, 1961.**
London: International Missionary Council, 1961. 114p.

Held at the very beginning of the process of decolonization in the South Pacific, this important conference clarified the perspectives for the development of truly autonomous island churches. There is also a French record of this conference: *La route du soleil: conférence de Samoa, 1961* (Paris: Société des Missions Évangéliques, 1961. 157p.).

339 **The Joe Gimlet or Siovili cult: an episode in the religious history of early Samoa.**
J. D. Freeman. In: *Anthropology in the South Seas: essays presented to H. D. Skinner*. Edited by J. D. Freeman, W. R. Geddes. New Plymouth, New Zealand: Thomas Avery & Sons, 1959, p. 185-200. bibliog.

Based largely on the manuscript journals and letters of the early missionaries to the Samoan Islands, this is a study of the improving cult established at 'Eva, in the district of Ātua on the northern coast of 'Upolu, early in 1830. Siovili, a native of that village, had visited Tonga and Tahiti with Captain Samuel Henry, and was later believed by his followers to have voyaged to Botany Bay, Britain and Heaven itself. Despite strong mission opposition, the visionary and prophet attracted many thousands of believers, in 'Upolu, Savai'i and Tutuila. The cult flourished for more than thirty years, but had dwindled by 1865 to only a few adherents. Freeman concludes: 'At its height it had been of a kind and scale comparable to many of the major cults of twentieth century Melanesia'.

340 **Maori, Samoan, Tongan & Pakeha ways of celebrating Christian festivals.**

Wellington: Methodist Education Division, [1985]. 16p.

Provides interesting comparative notes, with illustrations and plans, on the diverse styles of observance of Christian festivals, such as Easter, Pentecost and Christmas.

341 **Pacific Journal of Theology: Journal of the South Pacific Association of Theological Schools.**

Suva: Pacific Journal of Theology, series 2, 1989- . 2 per year.

'The *Pacific Journal of Theology* seeks to stimulate and strengthen theological reflection by Christians living in the Pacific Islands, and to share these reflections with others, both within and beyond the Pacific region'. It includes articles relating theology to Pacific cultures and contemporary issues, and publishes artistic expressions of the Christian faith from various South Pacific contexts. No. 6 (1991), the 30th anniversary issue, was *Focus on Samoa*, and no. 14 (1995), *The legacy of Christian mission in the Pacific*, commemorating 200 years' work by the London Missionary Society. See also *PCC News: Pacific Council of Churches* (Suva: Pacific Council of Churches, 1973- . quarterly), which covers current events, religious topics, church and PCC Secretariat news of interest to member churches, including those of Samoa. It is distributed free of charge, with a circulation of about 750 copies.

342 **Religion and social organization in central Polynesia.**

Robert W. Williamson, edited by Ralph Piddington, with a preface by Raymond Firth. Cambridge, England: Cambridge University Press, 1937. 340p. bibliog.

A continuation of Williamson's *Religious and cosmic beliefs of central Polynesia* (q.v.), updated and with excellent additional material by Ralph Piddington. There is a summary account of the 'Island gods' of Samoa (p. 74-84).

343 **Religious and cosmic beliefs of central Polynesia.**

Robert W. Williamson. Cambridge, England: Cambridge University Press, 1933. 2 vols. bibliog.

Samoa is discussed in depth in this still indispensable survey of traditional Polynesian beliefs. Another excellent comparative study of Polynesian worldviews is *Polynesian religion* by E. S. C. Handy (Honolulu: Bernice P. Bishop Museum, 1927. 342p. bibliog. [Bulletin no. 34]). See also 'Perspectives in Polynesian religion' by E. S. C. Handy (*Journal of the Polynesian Society*, vol. 49 [1940], p. 309-27. bibliog.).

344 **Religious cooperation in the Pacific islands.**

Edited by Kerry James, Akuila Yabaki. Suva: Institute of Pacific Studies, University of the South Pacific, 1989. 219p. map. bibliog.

Following the religious tension and segregation of the past, a new spirit of inter-faith cooperation is emerging. This symposium of essays by prominent religious leaders describes regional organization, regional cooperation in media and communication, education and research. There is information on American Samoa's Kanana Fou Theological Seminary, the Archdiocese of Samoa-Apia, the Bahá'i faith, Congregational Church, Methodist Church, Muslims in Samoa, Seventh-day

Adventists, and Samoan students at the Pacific Regional Seminar (PRS), Suva. An appendix (p. 185-211) presents an alphabetical directory of denominations and organizations, with essential data.

345 **The Samoan White Sunday: a conjecture.**
Alan P. F. Sell. *Journal of Pacific History*, vol. 26, no. 1 (June 1991), p. 94-97. bibliog.

In Samoa the second Sunday of October is observed as White Sunday, when baptisms and processions take place, and when children are in every way prominent. Sell investigates when and why the festival was moved from May or June to October, and what *kind* of festival was moved. He suggests that the celebration of Pentecost gradually took on characteristics of the 19th-century innovation, the Sunday School Anniversary, thereby making possible the removal of the festival to October. The processions are likened to the Whit Walks of Lancashire, a county familiar to James Edward Newell and four other LMS ministers in Samoa. Tradition has it that the LMS brought White Sunday with it. For an eye-witness account of the present-day White Sunday, see 'Transformation of Christian ritual in the Pacific: Samoan White Sunday' by Elizabeth M. Roach (*Missiology*, vol. 16, no. 2 [1988], p. 173-82), in which Roach outlines some of the ways in which this popular annual celebration is being modified.

346 **Samoa's struggle against foreign oppression and its implication for the mission of the Methodist Church in Samoa (1800-1960-1980s).**
Eteuati L. Tuioti. Seoul: [n.p.], 1988. 138p.

Tuioti bleakly reviews the history of Samoan resistance to foreign domination, concluding that the Methodist Church must be genuinely independent and in harmony with the best of Samoan traditions.

347 **Some *aitu* beliefs of modern Samoa.**
Richard A. Goodman. *Journal of the Polynesian Society*, vol. 80, no. 4 (Dec. 1971), p. 463-79. bibliog.

The purpose of this fascinating paper is to examine the present forms of belief in ghosts or spirits, their variety, and their influence on the behaviour of modern Samoans. Data were gathered in Western Samoa, 1968-69, and from American and Western Samoans in the San Francisco Bay area. *Aitu* beliefs persist in both Samoas, but are far stronger in Western Samoa, 'where custom and tradition have greater vitality'. Goodman discusses *aitu* and archaeological remains; *aitu* in the *tala anamua* (ancient stories); *aitu* of deceased persons; *aitu* possession (*ma'i aitu*); contemporary named *aitu*; *aitu* and the Church; popular stories about *aitu*; and ethical and psychological functions. See also 'Continuity and shape-shifting: Samoan spirits in culture history' by Jeannette Marie Mageo, in *Spirits in culture, history and mind*, edited by Jeannette Marie Mageo, Alan Howard (London; New York: Routledge, 1996, p. 29-54. bibliog.).

348 **A theology for justice and peace in the Pacific.**
Suliana Siwatibau. In: *The Gospel is not Western: Black theologies from the Southwest Pacific*. Edited by Garry W. Trompf. Maryknoll, New York: Orbis Books, 1987, p. 192-97, 213.

The Fijian author of this chapter sees the main forces transforming island societies as socioeconomic changes, based on individualism, new beliefs, new ideas and new value systems, and the growing militarization of the region, accompanied by subtle political domination by those who wield both economic and military power. Siwatibau presents her Christian response, especially to nuclear weapons. Christians must advocate peace, and resist injustice: 'We must take the way of nonviolence, confronting and absorbing violence, and wielding power redemptively'. Of the 'desecration of our environment', she insists: 'We cannot hurt our world without hurting ourselves'. See also 'A search for soil for the mustard seed: the impact of ecumenical social thought in Fiji and the Pacific' by S. Siwatibau, W. Flannery (*Ecumenical Review*, vol. 40, no. 2 [1988], p. 233-40), a thoughtful consideration of the influence on island churches of ecumenical views on social problems and of the programmes of the World Council of Churches.

349 **Winds of change: rapidly growing religious groups in the Pacific Islands.**

Manfred Ernst. Suva: Pacific Conference of Churches, 1994. 357p. maps. bibliog.

This impressive book aims to document and account for the explosive growth of twenty-eight new religious groups and sects across the Pacific. Some long-established denominations, such as the Mormons and the Seventh-day Adventists, are included because of their theological conservatism and strongly American profile. Each denomination is surveyed, with membership statistics providing the key indicator of success or failure. There is an excellent profile of Western Samoa, including important information on the mainstream churches, some of it unflattering. The established churches have been rocked by scandals, and are seen as too involved with ruling oligarchies. The book was reviewed by John Barker: *Contemporary Pacific*, vol. 8, no. 1 (Spring 1996), p. 234-36. See also 'The politics of denominational organization in Samoa' by Sharon W. Tiffany, in *Mission, church and sect in Oceania*, edited by James A. Boutilier, Daniel T. Hughes, Sharon W. Tiffany (Ann Arbor, Michigan: University of Michigan Press, 1978, p. 423-56. bibliog. Second printing: Lanham, Maryland: University Press of America).

Conversion to Christianity

350 **The decision to *lotu*: new perspectives from whaling records on the sources and spread of Christianity in Samoa.**

Rhys Richards. *Pacific Studies*, vol. 17, no. 1 (March 1994), p. 29-43. bibliog.

In the early years of the 19th-century whalers, rather than traders, brought most foreign goods, techniques and customs to Samoa. In attracting British and American warships, the whalers also did Samoans a disservice by exposing them to Great Power rivalries. Whaling records give new insights on the Samoan decision to *lotu* – to pray to the new God. Christianity arrived in Samoa simultaneously from several separate sources, and the conversion decision had 'a high indigenous content'. The 'striking' contribution of beachcombers' '*lotu* sailor' (e.g. Siovili) is discussed, as is the uneven spread of Christianity. See also *Samoa's forgotten whaling heritage* by Rhys Richards (q.v.).

351 **People movements in southern Polynesia: studies in the dynamics of church-planting and growth in Tahiti, New Zealand, Tonga, and Samoa.**

Alan R. Tippett. Chicago: Moody Press, 1971. 288p. maps. bibliog.

A scholarly analysis and historical reconstruction of how and why Christianity took hold in southern Polynesia. The substantial sections on Samoa illuminate the interaction of missionary expansion from Tahiti and Tonga. There is a valuable bibliography (p. 270-79) which focuses on anthropology and mission history. A general index, geographical index, persons index, and Polynesian classificatory terms index make this absorbing study of a complex process remarkably easy to use.

352 **Reasons for the acceptance of Christianity in Western Samoa in 1830.**

D. J. Inglis. In: *Dialogue on religion: New Zealand viewpoints.* Edited by Peter Davis, John Hinchcliff. Auckland, New Zealand: Auckland University Press, 1977, p. 10-14. bibliog.

Contemporary missionary accounts of the spread of Christian beliefs from Tonga and Tahiti to Savai'i inform this discussion of why conversions took place. Samoan rivalries and struggles for political ascendancy were often of greater significance than any yearning for a new faith. Beachcombers and Samoans returning from journeys abroad also played a part, as intermediaries or as initiators of change (as in the Siovili movement). See also 'The transition to Christianity in Samoa' by R. F. Watters (*Historical Studies*, vol. 8 [1959], p. 392-99. bibliog.), an analysis of the transition to Christianity and an attempt to explain its extraordinary rapidity, especially in Tutuila. Watters concludes: 'While the sincerity of many converts cannot be doubted, the reasons for the success of the missionaries lay mainly in the calculating policy of a stable society that planned to increase its material prosperity and its regional prestige. This conclusion does not impugn the virtue of the mission work; its real rewards were, however, postponed to the future'.

Missions

353 **Aux Antipodes: les premiers missionnaires des Samoa (Archipel des Navigateurs).** (At the Antipodes: the first missionaries in Samoa [Navigators' Archipelago].)

A. Monfat. Lyon, France; Paris: Emmanuel Vitte, 1923. 336p. map.

Book one (p. 1-176) provides an excellent general account of Samoan traditional society, concluding with a denunciation of the 'calumnies' of Protestant missionaries. Book two (p. 177-325) traces the history of the Marist Mission in Samoa from the first visits from Wallis and Futuna and the first mass celebrated on Savai'i on 15 September 1845, to about 1861. See also *Le missionnaire des Samoa, Mgr. L. Elloy ... vicaire apostolique des Navigateurs et de l'Océanie centrale* (Mgr. L. Elloy, missionary to Samoa, Vicar Apostolic of the Navigators' Islands and Central Oceania) by A. Monfat (Lyon, France; Paris: Emmanuel Vitte, 1928. 462p. reprint of 1890 edition).

354 **Aux Îles Samoa: le forêt qui s'illumine.** (In the Samoan Islands: the shining forest.)
Joseph Darnand. Lyon, France; Paris: Emmanuel Vitte, 1934. 209p. bibliog.

Mgr. Joseph Darnand SM (b. 1879) describes Samoan traditional society, outlines the history of the Marist Mission in Samoa, and recalls his own part in it. He became Vicar Apostolic of the Navigators' Islands (Samoa) in 1919, as Titular Bishop of Polemonium. Earlier accounts of the Marist endeavour include: *Les Îles Samoa ou archipel des Navigateurs: étude historique et religieuse* (The Samoan Islands or Navigators' Archipelago: a historical and religious study) by A. Monfat (Lyon, France; Paris: Emmanuel Vitte, 1890. 414p. map), an outline of Samoan pre-contact and 19th-century history, of Samoan religious beliefs, and of the ascendancy of Christianity in its Protestant and Roman Catholic varieties; and 'Notes d'un missionnaire sur l'archipel de Samoa' (Notes of a missionary on the Samoan Archipelago) by Louis Violette (*Les Missions Catholiques* [Lyon], vol. 3 [1870], p. 71-215 [in 15 instalments]). Father Louis-Théodore Violette SM (1811-87) is the author of a useful trilingual dictionary of Samoan (q.v.) and of an extensive grammar of the language (q.v.).

355 **Beyond the reefs: the life of John Williams, missionary.**
John Gutch. London: Macdonald, 1974. 165p. 2 maps.

A brisk biography of the London Missionary Society pioneer, John Williams (1796-1839), solidly based on LMS archives and on family letters and journals. The eighteen photographs include John and Mary Williams in their early days on Raiatea, the *Duff*, the *Messenger of Peace*, the massacre of de Langle and his men by the Samoans, John Williams (from an engraving by John Snow), the *Camden*, *John Williams I*, and *John Williams VII*. See also *Memoirs of the life of the Rev. John Williams: missionary to Polynesia* by Ebenezer Prout (London: John Snow, 1843. 618p.), a eulogy of John Williams, written within a few years of his murder. The print of Williams is by George Baxter, the engraver, who illustrated *A narrative of missionary enterprises in the South Seas islands ...* by John Williams (London: John Snow, 1837. 589p.).

356 **Bibliographie des publications de la Mission Mariste des Îles Samoa, 1862-1976.** (Bibliography of the publications of the Marist Mission in the Samoan Islands, 1862-1976.)
Patrick O'Reilly, Joseph Allais. Paris: The Authors; Papeete, Tahiti: Libraire Pureora, 1977. 53p.

The definitive bibliography, including vernacular publications. Father Patrick O'Reilly SM, Secretary of the Société des Océanistes, is noted for the exceptionally rigorous standards of his bibliographical work.

357 **Church and state in German Samoa: the Solf-Broyer dispute.**
Hugh Laracy. *New Zealand Journal of History*, vol. 12, no. 2 (1978), p. 158-67. bibliog.

A 'blow-by-blow' commentary on the intense dispute between German governor Wilhelm Solf and Pierre Broyer SM (1846-1918), Vicar Apostolic of the Samoan Islands (from 1896) and Titular Bishop of Polemonium. At the heart of the matter was disagreement as to the relative authority of the colonial administration and the Roman

Catholic Church, the prerogatives of the Church, the control and language of education, and the employment of German teachers. See also 'Kulturkampf in Übersee: katholische Mission und deutscher Kolonialstaat in Togo und Samoa' (Cultural conflict overseas: Catholic mission and German colonial state in Togo and Samoa) by Horst Gründer (*Archiv für Kulturgeschichte*, vol. 69 [1987], p. 453-72. bibliog.), in which Gründer examines the disagreements and tensions regarding policies which arose between Catholic missionaries and the German colonial administrators in Togo and German Samoa in the years prior to the outbreak of the First World War in 1914.

358 **The conflict between the London Missionary Society and the Wesleyan Methodists in 19th century Samoa.**

John Garrett. *Journal of Pacific History*, vol. 9 (1974), p. 65-80. bibliog.

Garrett unravels the story of Tongan political schemes, LMS-Wesleyan skirmishing, and the re-opening in 1857 of the WM Samoan Mission, by the 'reluctant but effective architect of the restored cause', Martin Dyson. See also *My story of Samoan Wesleyanism: or, a brief history of the Wesleyan mission in Samoa* by Martin Dyson (Melbourne: Ferguson & Moore, 1875). Later, in 1908, Dyson described the Samoan venture as 'plainly a denominational hobby, to please some 2000 or 3000 at most *adult* Samoans, or *more accurately a few hundred prejudiced chiefs*' (MS Autobiography, Mitchell Library, Sydney, 58f.). See also 'Samoa and the Samoans' by Martin Dyson (*Victoria Review*, vol. 6 [1882], p. 299-311).

359 **For Jesus and His Church: Malua Theological College – a historical survey of 150 years of theological education, 1844-1994.**

Featuna'i Liua'ana. *Pacific Journal of Theology*, series 2, no. 14 (1995), p. 52-65. bibliog.

A detailed account, based largely on London Missionary Society archives, of the difficult evolution of the Samoan Mission Seminary, from its foundation in 1844, to the greatly respected Mālua Theological College of today. The article is illustrated by an engraving of Mālua's classroom and cottages of the students, from *Nineteen years in Polynesia* by George Turner (London: John Snow, 1861).

360 **Forty years' mission work in Polynesia and New Guinea, from 1835 to 1875.**

A. W. Murray. London: James Nisbet, 1876. 505p. maps.

This history of the early work of the London Missionary Society is largely devoted to Samoa. Murray had a hand in framing the Tutuila code of law. See also: *Missions in Western Polynesia: being historical sketches of these missions, from their commencement in 1839 to the present time* by A. W. Murray (London: John Snow, 1863, p. 450-68); *Wonders in the western isles: being a narrative of the commencement and progress of mission work in Western Polynesia* by A. W. Murray (London: Yates & Alexander, 1874. 344p.); 'A missionary's work in Samoa' by Samuel James Whitmee (*The Congregationalist*, vol. 7 [1878], p. 474-86); and *Samoa, past and present: a narrative of missionary work in the South Seas* by Charles Phillips (London: John Snow, 1890. 96p.).

361 **The founding of the Roman Catholic Church in Oceania, 1825-1850.**
Ralph M. Wittgen. Canberra: Australian National University Press, 1979. 610p. maps. bibliog.

This outstanding, richly illustrated work of definitive historical scholarship is solidly based on the extensive archives of the societies active in the Pacific in 1825-50, spreading from the east by way of Hawai'i and the Gambier Islands. By 1850, Apostolic vicariates covered most of the area, and were being divided into bishoprics. Wittgen examines the controversies attending the establishment of boundaries, not least in the case of the Samoan archipelago. See also 'Centenary of the Church in Samoa' by Charlotte M. Kelly (*Studies* [Dublin], vol. 35 [1946], p. 111-17), which outlines the establishment and growth of the Roman Catholic Church in Samoa.

362 **The founding of the Samoan Mission.**
Ralph Lanier Britsch. *Brigham Young University Studies* (Provo, Utah), vol. 18, no. 1 (Fall 1977), p. 12-26.

Relates the story of the earliest days of the LDS (Mormon) Mission in Samoa. The basic history of the Church in the Pacific is *Unto the isles of the sea: a history of the Latter-day Saints in the Pacific* by Ralph Lanier Britsch (Salt Lake City, Utah: Deseret Book Co., 1986). There is an unpublished *Samoa Mission history* by R. Carl Harris (1983), updated by John W. Hart in 1988, copies of which are available at Brigham Young University libraries. A summary of this unpublished history is to be found in *Unto the isles of the sea.*

363 **The great Samoan awakening of 1839.**
Alan Gavan Daws. *Journal of the Polynesian Society*, vol. 70, no. 3 (Sept. 1961), p. 326-37. bibliog.

A record of a brief period of revivalist fervour in the early years of the London Missionary Society's work on Tutuila. The awakening showed a remarkable formal similarity to 18th- and early 19th-century revivals in Britain. Daws bases his outline on missionary journals, especially those of A. W. Murray and G. A. Lundie. See also *Missionary life in Samoa, as exhibited in the journals of the late George Archibald Lundie, during the revival in Tutuila in 1840-1841* by George Archibald Lundie, 'edited by his mother' (Edinburgh: W. Oliphant & Sons, 1846. 294p.). Son of a Scottish Presbyterian minister, G. A. Lundie (-1841) was an LMS helper resident on Tutuila in 1840-41, where he witnessed the great religious 'awakening' of those years.

364 **In the Samoan group.**
R. Wardlaw Thompson. In: *My trip in the "John Williams"*. R. Wardlaw Thompson. London: London Missionary Society, 1900, p. 187-208.

The London Missionary Society's steamer *John Williams I*, first of several modern vessels of the same name, 'cost a great deal to build, and she costs twice as much as the old barque to maintain', but was considered 'necessary if the work of the Mission is to be properly done'. Thompson gives an informative account of a pastoral visit to 'Upolu, Savai'i, Manu'a and Tutuila, including Papauta boarding school for girls; Leulumoega, 'one of the oldest stations in the Mission'; and Mālua training college, 'the centre of the Mission', 'from whence have gone out all the pastors of the Samoan

Churches, and also a great company of missionaries to the Tokelau, Ellice, and Gilbert groups, and to New Guinea'. The illustrations include Vailima; the Jubilee Hall at Mālua; Papauta; Fa'amu, daughter of Malietoa; Sapapali'i church; and Leone Bay.

365 **John Williams.**

Gavan Daws. In: *A dream of islands: voyages of self-discovery in the South Seas*. Edited by Gavan Daws. New York; London: W. W. Norton, 1980, p. 22-69.

The news of the murder, on Erromanga in the New Hebrides, of John Williams (1796-1839) evoked sadness in Samoa, which he had opened up to the work of the London Missionary Society and where he had a house on 'Upolu. It inspired a widespread, immediate religious 'awakening', resulting in many conversions. This thoughtful outline of the pioneer missionary's work in Polynesia considers that: 'Williams had reached the conclusion that the best way for the LMS to proceed was by a gradual approach to conversion, by an accommodation to Polynesian culture, rather than a frontal attack on heathenism. But that was not how he personally wanted to proceed with his life and work. He was not made for the gradual. He thought of himself late in his life as able to accomplish anything, in voyages that were great sweeps of action. And so he came to Erromanga'.

366 **The legacy of Christian mission in the Pacific.**

Suva: South Pacific Association of Theological Schools, 1995. (*PJT* special issue).

Comprises the London Missionary Society Bicentenary Commemorative Issue of *Pacific Journal of Theology*, with ten articles on aspects of the work of the LMS, a tribute to the late Sione Latukefu, first Pacific islander academic historian, and a bibliography of Latukefu's writings. Among essays of direct relevance to Samoa are: 'After 200 years: the LMS legacy' (Bernard Thorogood); 'Malua Theological College: a historical survey' (Featuna'i Liua'ana); 'Catholic-Protestant encounters in the Pacific' (John Garrett); and 'The calling, preparation and appointment of an LMS missionary' (Bruce Deverell).

367 **The life and times of early Latter-day Saint missionaries in Polynesia: Samoa.**

R. Wayne Shute. [Salt Lake City, Utah]: Corporation of the President of the Church of Jesus Christ of Latter-day Saints, 1980. 6p. (World Conference on Records: Preserving Our Heritage, August 12-15, 1980. Series 829a).

Shute traces the history of the Dawning, the first phase of the LDS mission in Samoa. This began with the arrival at 'Aunu'u of Kimo Belio and Samuela Manoa on 24 January 1863 and continued to the Second World War. There followed a thirty-year period of 'significant visibility and growth', to the early 1970s. Other accounts include: *Adventures in Samoa* (Los Angeles: Wetzel Publishing Co., 1940. 224p.), by Henry Lawrence Bassett, a Mormon missionary from 1890 to 1893 in Samoa, where he met Robert Louis Stevenson; *Years in the sheaf: the autobiography of William Alfred Moody* by William Alfred Moody (Salt Lake City, Utah: Granit Publishing Co., 1959. 219p.), a description, by the president of the Mormons' Samoan Mission from 1908 to 1910, of the attempt to establish gathering places at Sāuniatu (Western

Samoa) and Māpusaga (American Samoa) and the development of mission plantations; and *Armed with the spirit: missionary experiences in Samoa* by William Karl Brewer (Provo, Utah: Young House, 1975. 237p.).

368 **A man like Bati: the Rev. Reginald Bartlett, O.B.E.: the story of his missionary work in Papua and Samoa, as told in his letters home.**
Compiled and edited by T. Wemyss Reid. London: Independent Press, 1960. 208p.

The London Mission Society in 1929 assigned Bartlett to Mālua Theological College, as Principal. He referred to this as 'a strange job', 'the very best joke to date'. His actual task was to act as a companionable reconciler during the *Mau* revolt. He spoke at the funeral of the murdered Tupua Tamasese Lealofi III, *Mau* leader and deacon in the LMS church. Bartlett was a successful and respected mediator during his two years in Samoa.

369 **The Marist Brothers in New Zealand, Fiji & Samoa 1876-1976.**
Pat Gallagher, with an introduction by Brother Romuald Gibson, FMS. Tuakau, New Zealand: New Zealand Marist Brothers' Trust Board, 1976. 211p. bibliog.

A detailed centennial history of the educational work of the Marist Brothers in the three island territories, based on mission archives and school records. Brothers first arrived at Āpia (Mulivai) on 14 April 1871, withdrawing in September 1877, until reestablishment on 18 August 1888. Schools were set up in Āpia, Lotopā, Moamoa, Sāfotulāfai and Palauli. In American Samoa, work was begun in 1905, at Leone: schools were established at Leone, Ātu'u and Leala. There is a brief chronology (p. 200) of each establishment in Western Samoa and American Samoa, and a photograph (between p. 96-97) of 'Brothers in Samoa, 1906'.

370 **Messengers of grace: evangelical missionaries in the South Seas, 1797-1860.**
Niel Gunson. Melbourne: Oxford University Press, 1978. 437p. 8 maps. bibliog.

An indispensable introduction to the history of Protestant missionary activity in the late 18th and early 19th centuries. It is usefully supplemented by: *A century in the Pacific*, edited by James Colwell (Sydney: William H. Beale, 1914. 781p. bibliog.); *Modern missions in the South Pacific* by John Wear Burton (London: Livingstone Press, 1949. 224p. bibliog.); *A missionary survey of the Pacific islands* by John Wear Burton (London: World Dominion Press, 1930. 124p.); *Histoire des missions françaises* by Jean-Marie Sédès (Paris: Presses Universitaires de France, 1950. 128p. bibliog. ['Que Sais-Je?']); and by two remarkable ecumenical works which bring the story of South Pacific missions up to the Second World War: *To live among the stars: Christian origins in Oceania* by John Garrett (Geneva: World Council of Churches; Suva: Institute of Pacific Studies, University of the South Pacific, 1982. 412p. maps. bibliog.); and *Footsteps in the sea: Christianity in Oceania to World War II* by John Garrett (Suva: Institute of Pacific Studies, University of the South Pacific; Geneva: World Council of Churches, 1992. 517p. maps. bibliog.). The growth of independent churches is outlined in *The island churches of the South Pacific: emergence in the twentieth century* by Charles W. Forman (Maryknoll, New York: Orbis Books, 1982. 285p. bibliog. [American Society of Missiology Series, no. 5]). All of these important books have extensive sections on or relevant to Samoa.

371 **The Methodist story in Samoa, 1828-1984.**

R. W. Allardice. Malifa, Apia: Methodist Conference of Samoa, 1984.

A concise history and celebration of Wesleyan Methodism in Samoa since it was first brought from Tonga. See also: 'Samoa' by Benjamin Danks, in *A century in the Pacific*, edited by James Colwell (Sydney: William H. Beale; London: Chas H. Kelly, 1914, p. 477-505. bibliog.), a concise history of Wesleyan Methodism in Samoa, slightly tinged by resentment of the London Missionary Society; *Overseas missions of the Australian Methodist Church* by Alfred Harold Wood (Melbourne: Aldersgate Press, 1978. 3 vols); and *The black knight of the Pacific* by Charles Brunsdon Fletcher (Sydney: Australasian Publishing Company, 1944. 181p.), a competent, journalistic biography of the Rev. Dr George Brown (1835-1917), Methodist missionary to Samoa and Melanesia.

372 **Mgr. Bataillon et les missions de l'Océanie centrale.** (Mgr. Bataillon and the missions of Central Oceania.)

A. M. Mangeret. Paris: Lecoffre, 1884. 2 vols.

A well documented though rather reverential study of the Marist missionary Pierre-Marie Bataillon (1810-77), the first Vicar Apostolic of Central Oceania. In 1842, Bataillon was appointed Bishop of Central Oceania, which included Samoa. Marist missionaries were sent to Samoa in 1845.

373 **A mission tour in the Southwest Pacific.**

Rev. Mother Mary Rose, edited by Rev. Charles F. Decker. Boston, Massachusetts: Society for the Propagation of the Faith, 1942. 214p. 10 maps.

The author toured Samoa and the Solomon Islands in 1934, visiting Roman Catholic religious and surveying schools and clinics. Her observations and meditations illuminate a decade of some difficulty for the Roman Catholic Church in the islands. See also *Pearls of the Pacific: an account of the visit of the Apostolic Delegate to the Catholic missions of Fiji, Samoa and Tonga* by W. M. Collins (Melbourne: Advocate Press, 1925. 54p. map), which records the first visit to the islands by a Papal representative, Mgr. Cattaneo.

374 **Missionsliteratur von Australien und Ozeanien, 1525-1950, no. 1-1410.** (The literature of missions in Australia and Oceania, 1525-1950, no. 1-1410.)

Robert Streit, Johannes Dindinger. Freiburg im Breisgau, Germany: Verlag Herder, 1955. 796p. bibliog. (Bibliotheca Missionum, vol. 21).

An exhaustive bibliography, of Roman Catholic missions only. It comprises biographical details of missionaries and religious, their careers, their correspondence, and their linguistic, ethnographic and vernacular publications. Five sections are arranged by century, and the appendix (to 1909) by religious order. This exemplary work is superbly indexed, by author, person, subject, place and ethnic name, and language and represents the essential *point de départ* for research on Roman Catholicism in the South Pacific, including Samoa.

375 **Mormons in the Pacific: a bibliography. Holdings at the Brigham Young University-Hawaii campus, Brigham Young University-Utah campus and the Church Historical Department.**
Compiled by Russell T. Clement. La'ie, Hawai'i: Institute for Polynesian Studies, 1981. 239p.

This essential, specialized bibliography of Polynesia, Micronesia and Melanesia contains 2,877 items, some lightly annotated, arranged alphabetically by author or title and numbered serially. There are many references to works about Samoa and to Samoan vernacular publications, which are indexed by geographic area/subject, and by name. The Mormon Church (LDS), in the Pacific since 1844, and the Reorganized Church of Jesus Christ of Latter Day Saints (RLDS), since 1873, are both represented. It complements the monumental *A Mormon bibliography 1830-1930* by Chad. J. Flake (Salt Lake City, Utah: University of Utah Press, 1978), which lists over 10,000 items pertaining to the first century of Mormonism.

376 **Pacific Bahá'i communities 1950-1964.**
Graham Hassall. In: *Pacific history: papers from the 8th Pacific History Association conference*. Edited by Donald H. Rubinstein. Mangilao, Guam: University of Guam Press; Micronesian Area Research Center, 1992, p. 73-95. bibliog.

An 'initial survey' of the spread of the Bahá'i faith in the South Pacific, including Samoa, and of its pioneers and organizational forms. From one local assembly in Āpia in 1959, there were nine by 1963, including Pago Pago. A National Spiritual Assembly of Samoa was established in 1970. There is a Bahá'i temple in the outskirts of Āpia.

377 **Pastels from the Pacific.**
Frank Lenwood. London: Humphrey Milford, Oxford University Press, 1917. 224p. 2 maps.

Charmingly illustrated by Lenwood's own pastel sketches and line drawings, this account of a tour of investigation includes 'Samoa and its ceremonies' (p. 46-64) and 'Samoan problems' (p. 65-87). Lenwood comments favourably on Commander John M. Poyer, US Naval Governor of American Samoa, 1915-19, and unfavourably on the pressure exerted on missions in German Samoa to teach German in their schools. He says of the London Missionary Society: 'We are the unofficial equivalent of an Established Church, and suffer many of the disadvantages of establishment'. Lenwood regrets 'that the Samoans are socialists', which, in his view, discourages ability, handicaps initiative, and breeds fear of responsibility.

378 **Polynesian paradise.**
Ronald William Taylor. Mountain View, California; Omaha, Nebraska; Portland, Oregon: Pacific Press Publishing Association, 1960. 136p. (An Authors' Awards Book).

Behind the trite title lies a fascinating account of the work and experiences of an American Seventh-day Adventist missionary, at the Si'ufaga mission station on Savai'i and at the Vailoa Missionary College, Sāluafata, which has trained SDA 'Christian soldiers' since 1930. Taylor's knowledge of Samoan in the period described was minimal, but he is observant (of the reception accorded the mission journal *Tala Moni*, Signs of the Times, for instance) and provides some excellent accounts of ceremonies and customary practices. Yet he is firm in his resolve to remain himself, a foreigner, 'because of the unique message he bears'. The Mission Station and Vailoa College are among the thirty-five photographs.

379 **Samoa: land of legends.**
Seiuli LeTagaloatele Fitisemanu, Viola C. Kelley. Apia: Privately Printed, 1960. 267p.

Discusses the history and legends of Samoa, including migration legends and the Book of Mormon. There is also an autobiography (p. 26-35) of S. L. Fitisemanu, a Samoan member of the Mormon Church, and an extensive glossary of Samoan words (p. 231-67).

380 **The Samoan journals of John Williams 1830 and 1832.**
Edited, with an introduction, by Richard M. Moyle. Canberra: Australian National University Press, 1984. 302p. maps. bibliog.

These journals, rich in ethnographic detail, provide the earliest extensive accounts of Samoa when European influence was still in its infancy. The 1830 journal should be considered as written jointly with Charles Barff. Although Williams' visits in 1830 and 1832 totalled only thirty days, his detailed descriptions of Samoan customs and practices remain unequalled.

381 **The Samoan version.**
A. W. Murray. In: *The Bible in the Pacific.* A. W. Murray. London: James Nisbet, 1888, p. 37-52.

The first-hand story of the translation of the Holy Bible into Samoan, starting with a 'very imperfect' version of the *Gospel according to Matthew* (*Mataio*), made by Samuel Wilson. The *Gospel according to John* was printed by J. B. Stair in 1841. The whole Bible was translated by late 1855, in five volumes. A revised, one-volume edition was completed by the end of 1859.

382 **Sauniatu, Western Samoa: a special purpose village, 1904-34.**
Kenneth W. Baldridge. *Journal of the Polynesian Society*, vol. 87, no. 3 (Sept. 1978), p. 165-92. bibliog.

Sāuniatu, eleven miles south-east of Āpia, was the Western Samoan 'gathering place' selected by the Church of Jesus Christ of Latter-day Saints. Baldridge traces the history of the village from LDS records and from interviews and letters. Since 1934 only the Mormon school remains, preserved (though uneconomic) because of its historical significance. See also: 'Sauniatu' by David O. McKay (*The Improvement Era*, vol. 69 [1966], p. 364-66); and 'Mormonism's "gathering": an American doctrine with a difference' (*Church History*, vol. 23 [1954], p. 248-64. bibliog.).

383 **South Seas: Samoa.**
Norman Goodall. In: *A history of the London Missionary Society 1895-1945*. Norman Goodall. London: Oxford University Press, 1954, p. 352-80. map. bibliog.

Foreign secretary of the LMS from 1936 to 1944, Norman Goodall presents a balanced account of the Society's Samoan mission since 1895, based on official records. There are other references to Samoa *passim* throughout the book: 'The ships' (p. 409-11) describes mission vessels from *Duff* onward to *John Williams V*; and Appendix III (p. 595-623) is a register of 'Missionaries in the Society's service from 1895'. See also the bilingual publication *Tala fa'asolopito o le Ekalesia Samoa (L.M.S.)/A history of the Samoan Church (L.M.S.)* by Kenape T. Faleto'ese (Malua, Western Samoa: Malua Printing Press, 1961).

Samoan foreign missions

384 **Pioneers and patriarchs: Samoans in a nonconformist mission district in Papua, 1890-1917.**
David Wetherell. *Journal of Pacific History*, vol. 15, no. 3 (July 1980), p. 130-54. bibliog.

A fascinating study of the Samoan pastors of the London Missionary Society in Papua. They were the pioneer foreign settlers in most places they went to, establishing themselves by 'a considerable degree of physical mastery' and muscular energy. C. W. Abel came to look upon them as a 'scourge', comparing Samoan mission stations to trees which had contracted a disease. Papuan villagers seem to have regarded the Samoan pastors as 'good men', despite their physical assertiveness and assumption of racial superiority.

385 **Polynesian missions in Melanesia: from Samoa, Cook Islands and Tonga to Papua New Guinea and New Caledonia.**
Edited by Ron Crocombe, Marjorie Crocombe. Suva: Institute of Pacific Studies, University of the South Pacific, 1982. 144p. maps. bibliogs.

From John Williams' first use of native agents as pioneers in 1821, and the London Missionary Society's first despatch of Polynesian missionaries to the Torres Strait Islands in 1871, a missionary tradition has become firmly established in Polynesia, not least in Samoa. The eight essays include: 'Pacific Islanders as international missionaries' by Sione Latukefu, Ruta Sinclair (p. 1-5. bibliog.); 'Preparation for mission: the Samoan *faife'au*' (p. 7-15. bibliog.); and 'Samoans in Papua' by Ruta Sinclair (p. 17-38. map. bibliog.).

Social Structure

Polynesian societies

386 **Caste: a comparative study.**

A. M. Hocart. London: Methuen, 1950. 157p. bibliog.

First published in French in 1938, this is a detailed comparison of social life, customs and ceremonies in Samoa, Tonga and Fiji. It is still of considerable interest despite its rather dated theoretical framework. See also 'Chieftainship and the sister's son in the Pacific' by A. M. Hocart (*American Anthropologist*, vol. 17 [1915], p. 631-46. bibliog.).

387 **The dilemma of the South Pacific islands: states, tradition, ethnicity.**

Sachiko Hatanaka. *Journal de la Société des Océanistes*, no. 93 (1991), p. 163-72. bibliog.

A Japanese scholar discusses the seemingly intractable ethnic problems of Fiji and the dilemma stemming from traditional social stratification in Western Samoa since 1945.

388 **Melanesians and Polynesians: their life-histories described and compared.**

George Brown. London: Macmillan, 1910. 451p.

The seventeen thematic chapters of this invaluable work embrace every aspect of Polynesian (i.e. mainly Samoan, except where otherwise stated) life, culture and belief. Brown resided in Samoa for fourteen years continuously, from 1860 to 1874, and often visited the group in later years. He came to speak Samoan well. 'The information given of Samoan customs was acquired during my residence there, and subsequently confirmed and added to by my friend, the late Rev. George Pratt'. The comparisons are mainly with the Melanesian peoples of New Britain in the Bismarck Archipelago, and more particularly of the Duke of York group.

389 **Our primitive contemporaries.**
George P. Murdock. New York: Macmillan, 1949. 613p. bibliog.

First published in 1934 (when the outmoded and inaccurate term 'primitive' was still in use), this anthropological world tour contains an interesting overview of Samoan society and culture (p. 48-84) largely based on published sources.

390 **The social and political systems of central Polynesia.**
Robert W. Williamson. Cambridge, England: Cambridge University Press, 1924. 3 vols. bibliog.

Now a standard work, this is still the most comprehensive account of traditional social organization throughout central Polynesia, including Samoa. See also *Essays in Polynesian ethnology* by Robert W. Williamson, edited by Ralph Piddington (Cambridge, England: Cambridge University Press, 1939. 373p. bibliog. Reprinted, New York: Cooper Square Publishers, 1975).

391 **Social stratification in Polynesia.**
Marshall D. Sahlins. Seattle, Washington; London: University of Washington Press, 1958. 306p. bibliog. 6th printing, 1972. (Publications of the American Ethnological Society).

A study of adaptive variation in culture, the change and variety brought about by adaptation to material, social and other contexts and needs. Variations in social stratification are related to variations in technological and environmental conditions. The degree of stratification in Samoa is established from early missionary accounts and from anthropological studies, and is compared with data for other Polynesian societies.

Samoan social organization, customs and ceremonies

392 **American Samoa: decline of a culture.**
Arnold H. Leibowitz. *California Western International Law Journal*, vol. 10, no. 2 (1980), p. 220-71.

An American lawyer presents revealing evidence to support his bleak view that traditional Samoan culture and way of life are losing ground to 'modernization', money economy, and some of the less attractive influences of the 'American way'. This is a sober, thoughtful analysis of the inexorable erosion of self-sufficiency and self-reliance. See also 'Trouble in paradise' by Tait Trussell (*Nation's Business*, vol. 56, no. 7 [July 1968], p. 82-87), in which the author argues: 'Being pampered by the federal government has proved a mixed blessing to the once self-reliant natives of Samoa ... American Samoa is now plagued with malnutrition, unemployment, increasing juvenile delinquency and crime and a growing dependence on the welfare state benefits instituted by the federal government'.

393 **Aspects of social organization in three Samoan communities.**
Maureen H. Fitzgerald, Alan Howard. *Pacific Studies*, vol. 14, no. 1 (Nov. 1990), p. 31-53. bibliog.

Long recognized as the basic unit of Samoan social structure and as one of Samoan society's most stable features, the *'āiga* (extended family) is undergoing changes in its structure, function and accessibility. A shift toward nuclear households and a change in the authority structure of both households and *'āiga* in migrant communities have been noted. Based on survey data and interviews conducted in Savai'i, Tutuila and Honolulu during 1986-87, this paper confirms a shift away from traditional Samoan social organization, in all three research sites. The rate of change varies from slowest in Savai'i, rapid in American Samoa, to fastest in Honolulu.

394 **Elite communication in Samoa: a study of leadership.**
Felix M. Keesing, Marie M. Keesing. Stanford, California: Stanford University Press; London: Geoffrey Cumberlege, Oxford University Press, 1956. 318p. maps. bibliog. (Stanford Anthropological Series, no. 3). Reprinted, New York: Octagon Books, 1973.

A case-study of communication among leaders, persons 'who wield influence in negotiation, public-opinion formation, and decision-making', in a traditional society which is undergoing dynamic modification. One conclusion reached is that effective communication stems from 'personalized and intimate interaction among group-responsible individuals'. This appears in a highly stylized form in Samoan society. Annex II, 'Linguistic aspects of communication' (p. 269-74), discusses several hundred Samoan terms directly associated with communication behaviour.

395 **Ferocious is the centipede: a study on the significance of eating and speaking in Samoa.**
Jeannette Marie Mageo. *Ethos*, vol. 17 (1989), p. 387-427. bibliog.

Oratory and feasts are salient features of Samoan traditional culture. Mageo considers how these ritualized practices serve to consolidate social and political relationships at all levels. See also 'L'orateur Samoan' (The Samoan orator) by Louis Schwehr (*Journal de la Société des Océanistes*, vol. 8 [1952], p. 117-36), which investigates the place of the orator in the Samoan social system, the art of oratory, and the salient points of the ceremonies accompanying it.

396 **Hawaii, Ostmikronesien und Samoa: meine zweite Südseereise (1897-1899) zum Studium der Atolle und ihrer Bewöhner.** (Hawaii, East Micronesia and Samoa: my second South Sea journey [1897-99] to study the atolls and their inhabitants.)
Augustin Krämer. Stuttgart, Germany: Strecker & Schröder, 1906. 585p. maps. bibliog.

Provides ethnographic observations, descriptions of material culture, and texts of traditional legends and songs. The Samoan imbroglio was coming to its climax while Krämer was in Samoa, but is not the prime concern of this scholarly work.

397 **Hierarchy and happiness in a Western Samoan community.**
Martin Orans. In: *Social inequality: comparative and developmental approaches.* Edited by Gerald D. Berreman, Kathleen M. Zaretsky. New York: Academic Press, 1981, p. 123-47. bibliog.

Based on fieldwork in 1978 in the Western Samoan community of Salamumu, which was founded by immigrants from the village of Sale'aula, Savai'i, destroyed by a volcanic eruption in 1908. Orans presents an analysis of the internal structure and hierarchy of Salamumu, and of income sources and distribution. Using a questionnaire on self-evaluations of 'happiness' and 'satisfaction', Orans seeks to relate hierarchy and sense of well-being, inconclusively.

398 **The *ifoga*: the Samoan practice of seeking forgiveness for criminal behaviour.**
La'aulu A. Filoiali'i, Lyle Knowles. *Oceania*, vol. 53, no. 4 (1983), p. 384-88. bibliog.

Describes and explains the Samoan practice of *ifoga*, a ceremonial request for forgiveness made by an offender and his kinsmen to those injured. In the case of very grave injury or offence, the ceremony may take on the character of self-abasement by the petitioners.

399 **An introduction to Samoan custom.**
F. J. H. Grattan. Apia: Samoa Printing and Publishing Company, 1948. 189p. map. bibliog. New edition, Papakura, New Zealand: R. McMillan, 1985. 189p. map. bibliog.

This is an exceptionally well informed and sympathetic introduction to contemporary Samoan culture and customs, by an anthropologist who became Secretary of Samoan Affairs in the New Zealand Administration. The subject is presented 'as simply as possible' and the approach is not anthropological. Grattan describes the organization of Samoan society; the *malaga* (village visit); the welcome ceremony; a Samoan village; quarters for visitors; food and meals; ceremonial presentations of food; dances and entertainments; religion in Samoa; and present-day society. There is an extensive glossary of Samoan words (p. 179-82).

400 **An introduction to Samoan custom.**
C. G. R. McKay. *Journal of the Polynesian Society*, vol. 66, no. 1 (March 1957), p. 36-43.

McKay spent twenty-four years in Western Samoa, ten of them as Secretary of Samoan Affairs. This address to an official orientation course brilliantly outlines the salient facts of Samoan custom. He believes that the underlying Samoan motivation continues to be pride – pride of self, of family and of race. 'Inherently, a people who are proud set value upon dignity, and expect recognition, both from strangers and in the daily round among themselves. Dignity and recognition being accepted values, Samoa is thus a land of courtesy.'

401 **Die Lichtbringer: die Geschichte vom Niedergang eines Naturvolkes.** (Bringers of light: the story of the decline of a primitive people.)
Erich Scheurmann. Oberhof, Germany: Maien-Verlag, 1928. 236p.

Loosely based on Samoan traditions and myths, this is a series of scenes depicting the process of decline of Samoan society under Western pressures. There is also a French-language edition: *Messagers de lumière: récit, en dix-neuf tableaux, de la dégénerescence d'un peuple primitif*, translated by Berthe Médici-Cavin (Geneva: Liège, 1934. 246p.).

402 **The modern Samoan family.**
Lowell D. Holmes. Wichita, Kansas: Wichita State University, 1967. 10p. bibliog. (Bulletin, vol. 43, no. 2. University Studies, no. 71).

A succinct outline of the characteristics of the traditional *'āiga*, and especially of the changes taking place in it because of the growth of the money economy, urbanization and migration.

403 **Old Samoa: or, Flotsam and jetsam from the Pacific Ocean.**
John Bettridge Stair. London: Religious Tract Society, 1897. 296p. map.

Available as a facsimile reprint (Papakura, New Zealand: R. McMillan, 1983), this is an exceptionally valuable contribution to the ethnography of early Samoa. Its abundant facts on Samoan customs and culture were purposefully collected between 1838 and 1845, when J. B. Stair (1815-98) served the London Missionary Society, on 'Upolu, first as a printer then as an ordained minister. Most of the descriptive material relates to the Ā'ana district of 'Upolu. Stair's commentary is perceptive, and his discernment is far beyond his time, as with his interpretation of Samoan child-rearing practices.

404 **Oral family traditions in the Pacific islands: a Western Samoa case study.**
Fetaui Mata'afa. [Salt Lake City, Utah]: Corporation of the President of the Church of Jesus Christ of Latter-day Saints, 1980. 12p. (World Conference on Records: Preserving Our Heritage, August 12-15, 1980. Series 834).

Mata'afa describes the ceremony and vocabulary of a Lotofaga *fono* meeting and an *'ava* ceremony. She then explains names and legends associated with her own family traditions: *inati*, *lemauga*, *sa'opapa*, *fiame*. For example, *inati* is the customary and hereditary allotment of food portions at a feast. Also included in this short work is a *fono* seating plan, a Lotofaga genealogy of the Fiame title, and a history of that title. Fetaui Mata'afa has also contributed papers on Samoan family history to Series 808 and Series 823.

405 **The political economy of an early state: Hawaii and Samoa compared.**
Martin A. VanBakel. *Political and Legal Anthropology*, vol. 8 (1991), p. 265-90.

The author discusses the structure of the two indigenous, agrarian states, which was very similar from the 16th century to the 19th century, but divergent in that Hawai'i supported an élite class of nonproducers, while all classes in Samoa made some contribution to subsistence.

406 **Sala'ilua: a Samoan mystery.**
Bradd Shore. New York: Columbia University Press, 1982. 338p. maps. bibliog.

Shore, American anthropologist and Samoa specialist, lived in the village of Sala'ilua, in western Savai'i, over a period of six months. He takes the notorious murder of Tuatō Tualevao Fatu, one of the village's two senior *matai*, by the son of the other, as the starting point of 'an interpretive ethnography cast as a mystery story'. The village is brought to the brink of war and its political integrity is undercut. Moves toward reconciliation reveal the political ramifications of the murder and enable Shore to analyse, in impressive detail, village organization, the *matai* system, the roles of *fono* and of titles, and the structures of social control and conflict resolution. This meticulous account of a remarkable Savai'i community is truthful and accurate. Sala'ilua may be taken as a microcosm, representative of the evolving, traditional rural society of Samoa. Seven concluding chapters illuminate the complex 'meanings' which underlie social action; the duality of Samoan social order; and the contrast between intimate and formal aspects of experience. See also 'Book review forum. Bradd Shore. *Sala'ilua: a Samoan mystery*. (1982)' by Thelma S. Baker, James R. Bindon, Jacob Wainwright Love (*Pacific Studies*, vol. 7, no. 1 [Fall 1983], p. 118-56. bibliogs.), which contains three critical reviews (p. 118-45), and a detailed response by Bradd Shore (p. 145-56).

407 **Samoa.**
George Brown. In: *George Brown, D.D.: pioneer-missionary and explorer: an autobiography*. George Brown. London: Hodder and Stoughton, 1908, p. 27-65.

The Rev. George Brown's reminiscences of Samoa in the latter half of the 19th century reveal the depth of his understanding of and sympathy with the traditional culture of the Samoan people, especially in the two main western islands. His Wesleyan Methodist circuit consisted of the whole of Savai'i, taking five to six weeks to visit by sea. In his fifteen years' service there, Brown experienced the great hurricane of 26 January 1865 and the war between Satupa'itea and Tufu. In 1890, he travelled from Sydney to Tonga in the company of the Rev. James Chalmers of New Guinea and Robert Louis Stevenson, an acquaintanceship which 'ripened into lasting friendship to the day of his death'. The eighteen photographs include Vailima, a magnificent *tuiga* head-dress made of human hair, a *tulāfale* with staff and fly-whisk, and two warriors in full costume.

408 **Samoa a hundred years ago and long before.**
George Turner. Suva: Institute of Pacific Studies, University of the South Pacific, 1984. 266p. map. Reprinted, 1986, 1989.

A reprint of the first edition (London: Macmillan, 1884), omitting the preface by E. B. Tylor and the notes on twenty-three other islands. This edition contains only the chapters on Samoa, covering every aspect of traditional society clearly and with understanding. In common with other pioneers of the London Missionary Society in Samoa, Dr Turner wished to put on record the essential characteristics of a traditional society likely soon to change in many respects after embracing Christianity. The 1884 edition has been translated into Samoan as *Samoa o anamua; tusia e Siaosi Tana, lomia i le tausaga 1884; faaliliuina e Semisi Ma'ia'i* (Wellington: Islands Education Division, Department of Education, 1962). See also the account of Samoa in *Nineteen years in Polynesia: missionary life, travels, and researches in the islands of the Pacific* by George Turner (London: John Snow, 1861, p. 95-355).

409 **The Samoa Islands: an outline of a monograph with particular consideration of German Samoa.**
Augustin Krämer, translated by Theodore Verhaaren. Honolulu: University of Hawai'i Press, 1994-95. 2 vols. maps. bibliog.

This is certainly the most scholarly and, at some 1,354 pages in all, the biggest work on Samoan traditional society and culture, originally published in German in 1902-03. The translation, too, greatly improves on earlier versions. Volume one contains, with Samoan texts and English translations, traditions of the origin of Samoa; *fa'alupega* (ceremonial greetings); and *gafa* (pedigrees) of Savai'i, 'Upolu, Tutuila and Manu'a. Volume two comprises a history of the scientific exploration of Samoa; anthropology and sociology; medicine; plants and cookery; fishery; men's work; ornamentation and dress; women's work; recreation and war; flora; and fauna. The bibliography, though extensive, lacks essential details, such as publishers and pagination.

410 **The Samoan culture and government.**
Aiono Fana'afi Le Tagaloa. In: *Culture and democracy in the South Pacific*. Edited by Ron Crocombe, Uentabo Neemia, Asesela Ravuvu, Werner Vom Busch. Suva: Institute of Pacific Studies, University of the South Pacific, 1992, p. 117-38.

This exceptionally interesting paper maintains that the *fa'amatai* is the most appropriate social organization for the Samoan people and culture. It discusses the rights and responsibilities of heirs of *matai* titles; decision-making (*soalaupule*); Samoan suffrage; non-alienation of customary land; the *matai* title and roll of electors; and the office of Head of State. 'Appendix I: The Electors Register, 28 January 1988' surveys forty-one constituencies, indicating total numbers of electors, the numbers and percentages of women electors, and listing the *matai* titles (*fai 'upu*) held by women. There is also a photograph of the *Fono* (Parliament). See also 'The ancient Samoan government' by Samuel Ella (*Proceedings of the Australasian Association for the Advancement of Science*, vol. 6 [1895], p. 596-603), a valuable account, based on oral traditions, of how pre-contact Samoa was governed. Samuel Ella went to Samoa as a LMS mission printer in 1848 and afterwards entered the ministry.

411 **The Samoan dance of life: an anthropological narrative.**
John Dixon Copp, Fa'afouina I. Pula, with a preface by Margaret Mead. Boston, Massachusetts: Beacon Press, 1950. 176p.

A serious, anthropologically sound account of Samoan culture and village life as they actually are, based on Copp's eight years' residence in Samoa and on the lifetime knowledge of his Samoan collaborator, a young Tutuila student. The 'novelistic' form used is a first-person narrative, with a great deal of dialogue, by Loa, 'a composite but typical Samoan boy'. Loa grows up, takes a woman, and raises his own family in a still traditional way of life assailed by change. As Margaret Mead states in the preface: 'The style is a charming primitive idiom, rich in concrete figures, naive in its unashamed frankness. The book is wholly Samoan in its attitude'.

412 **The Samoan *kava* ceremony: its form and function.**
Lowell D. Holmes. *Science of Man*, vol. 1 (June 1961), p. 46-51, 57. bibliog.

A thorough description and analysis of the ritual of the *'ava* ceremony, its participants, priorities, seating arrangement, language and social significance. See also '*Kava* drinking ceremonies among the Samoans and a boat voyage round 'Opolu Island, Samoa' by S. Percy Smith (New Plymouth, New Zealand: Avery, 1920. 21p. [*Journal of the Polynesian Society* Supplement]). Stephenson Percy Smith (1840-1922) was the first secretary of the Polynesian Society from its formation in 1892, editor of the *Journal of the Polynesian Society* for thirty years, and, in the early 1900s, Government Resident on Niue Island. His discussion of the *'ava* ceremony is based on personal observation. The circumnavigation of 'Upolu was full of incident and is of interest for its impressions of rural life under New Zealand military government.

413 **The Samoans.**
Margaret Mead. In: *Cooperation and competition among primitive peoples*. Edited by Margaret Mead. New York: McGraw-Hill, 1937, p. 282-312. bibliog.

Based upon fieldwork carried out in the Manu'a group in 1925-26 and upon published material for all of the Samoan islands, this succinct overview of Samoan culture deals with economic life, ownership of property, the place of skill, rivalry activities, war, sanctions, religion, the Samoan ideal man, education and the channelling of opposing tendencies. There is a tabular summary (p. 502-03), in Mead's 'Interpretive statement'.

414 **The social organization of Manu'a.**
Margaret Mead. Honolulu: Bernice P. Bishop Museum, 1969. 2nd ed. 237p. map. bibliog. (Bulletin, no. 76).

An extended reprint of the classical anthropological study of the three Manu'a islands of Ofu, Olosega and Ta'ū, first published by the Bishop Museum in 1930. It includes new material by Mead outlining her current thought on the original. Participants in the worldwide Freeman-Mead controversy have re-evaluated this study, and have found little to criticize in it, in sharp contrast to Mead's *Coming of age in Samoa* (q.v.). See also '*Social organization of Manu'a* (1930 and 1969), by Margaret Mead: some errata' by Derek Freeman (*Journal of the Polynesian Society*, vol. 81, no. 1 [March 1972], p. 70-78. bibliog.), an examination of the linguistic inadequacies and actual errors found in the first edition of Mead's book (and left uncorrected in the second, 'revised' edition). There is a long list of errata in Samoan words, many of them due to Mead's not having indicated either glottal stop or vowel length.

415 **Status und Macht in Samoa: das *matai*-System und die Dialektik des Nehmens und Gebens.** (Status and power in Samoa: the *matai* system and the dialectic of give and take.)
Werner Hennings. Bielefeld, Germany: Forschungsschwerpunkt, Universität Bielefeld, 1993. 19p. bibliog. (Entwicklungssoziologie Arbeitspapiere, no. 199).

An outline of the traditional Samoan social system, in which village *matai* control political and economic activity, division of labour, and the associated ceremonies. The reciprocity and compromises inherent in the system are discussed in detail. For an aspect of the modern system see *A title bestowal in Western Samoa,* photographs by Glenn Jowitt, text by Jennifer Wendt (Auckland, New Zealand: Longman Paul, 1987. 16p.). Jowitt's excellent photographs (some in colour) of the ceremonial conferring of a Samoan title are expertly interpreted and explained by Jennifer Wendt.

416 **Ta'u: stability and change in a Samoan village.**
Lowell D. Holmes. Wellington: Polynesian Society, 1958. 80p. map. bibliog. (Reprint, no. 7).

A now classic study of Ta'ū village in the district of Manu'a, American Samoa, originally published in *Journal of the Polynesian Society* (vol. 66, no. 3 [Sept, 1957], p. 301-38. map. bibliog.; vol. 66, no. 4 [Dec, 1957], p. 398-435. bibliog.). See also *Samoan village* by Lowell Holmes (New York: Holt, Rinehart & Winston, 1974. 111p. bibliog.), a study of Fitiuta, Ta'ū, which contains additional data collected in 1962-63 and in 1974.

417 **Transformation of exchange valuables in Samoa.**
Matori Yamamoto. *Man and Culture in Oceania*, vol. 6 (1990), p. 81-98. bibliog.

A study of the gradual trend towards replacing valuable objects (such as *'ie tōga* fine mats), traditionally given in ceremonial exchange of gifts, by more utilitarian articles. Tools, even sums of money, are among 'modern' substitutes. See also 'Social reproduction: towards an understanding of aboriginal Samoa' by Jan Hjarnø (*Folk*, vol. 21-22 [1979-80], p. 73-123. bibliog.), a study of marriage strategies and customs in Samoa, and of gifts in the making of alliances between *'āiga*. Hjarnø discusses gifts of mats and food, and claims that fine mats were crucial in the formation of political alliances through the hypergamous marrying strategies of lower-ranking chiefs (*matai*).

418 **Urbanisation of the chiefly system: multiplication and role differentiation of titles in Western Samoa.**
Matori Yamamoto. *Journal of the Polynesian Society*, vol. 103, no. 2 (June 1994), p. 171-202. bibliog.

Yamamoto outlines the model *matai* system, characterized by its relatively autonomous territorial organization. He also presents an overview (with statistics) of the recent urbanization of Western Samoa, and discusses title-splitting and the increase of non-resident titleholders. He concludes: 'It is true that title multiplication has degraded *matai* prestige and may cause the collapse of the chiefly system at some time in the future but, at the same time, it allows the chiefly system to adapt to the socio-economic conditions of the world system'. See also: 'A chief system urbanized: role differentiation among the title holders in Western Samoa' by Matori Yamamoto (*Bulletin of the National Museum of Ethnology*, no. 6 [1989], p. 301-29. bibliog.), an important study of how the *matai* system is being modified and 'fragmented' as more and more Samoans adopt an urban way of life; and 'The territorial organization of Faleata: a case study of the title system in Samoan society' by Matori Yamamoto (*Senri Ethnological Studies*, vol 21 [1987], p. 205-37. bibliog.).

419 **Western Samoa: the sacred covenant.**
Aiono Fana'afi. In: *Land rights of Pacific women.* Suva: Institute of Pacific Studies, University of the South Pacific, 1986, p. 102-10.

An outline of women's place in the *fa'amatai* system. *Tama'ita'i* (daughters of *matai*) are the most privileged group within the extended family, and within the village. As female heirs to *matai* titles they have rights equal to male heirs concerning access to and use of the family or customary lands held in trust by the *matai*. Women owners of freehold land (in or close to Āpia) are mainly widows. Aggie Grey was probably the most substantial woman freeholder. *Tama'ita'i* rights to *'āiga* lands through *matai* titles are customarily strong and legally binding.

Land tenure

420 **From corporate to individual land tenure in Western Samoa.**
J. Tim O'Meara. In: *Land, custom and practice in the South Pacific.* Edited by R. Gerard Ward, Elizabeth Kingdon. Cambridge, England: Cambridge University Press, 1995, p. 109-56. 7 maps. bibliog. (p. 265-79).

An extensive discussion of Samoa's traditional system of land tenure precedes an account of court-induced and 'grassroots' changes. Case-studies of contemporary practices focus on the villages of Vaegā and Neiafu on Savai'i, and Malie on 'Upolu, using data gathered between 1979 and 1984, and in 1993. Maps for each village show types of tenure. O'Meara seeks to explain change to individual tenure, and highlights the role of the Land and Titles Court as 'a conservative influence in some respects, as court decisions have tended to ossify land claims in more or less customary form ...'. The popularity of individual tenure is evidenced by the high demand for freehold land, especially around Āpia. O'Meara concludes: 'Samoans have been individualising their land tenure on their own terms and at their own, accelerating pace for at least a century. Ironically, the individualistic principles and practices that villagers embrace today are almost precisely those against which their grand-parents rebelled in 1926. It is more ironic still that with *fa'aSamoa* now protected against interference from outside, it must now be protected against interference from inside' (p. 154).

421 **Land tenure and social organisation in Western Samoa.**
R. R. Nayacakalou. *Journal of the Polynesian Society*, vol. 69, no. 2 (June 1960), p. 104-22. bibliog.

The Fijian anthropologist reviews and analyses documentary material on Samoan communal land ownership, land use and labour. He concludes that *matai* titles and land titles are inextricably interwoven, mediated through the notion of *pule* (the exclusive right given to the *matai* to make decisions regarding the allocation and administration of land). See also 'Der Landbesitz der Eingeborenen auf der Insel Savaii' (Indigenous land tenure on Savai'i) by Wilhelm von Bülow (*Globus*, vol. 81 [1902], p. 85-87), a survey of Samoan land ownership on Savai'i in the early years of German rule.

Personality, gender and sexuality

422 ***Aga/amio* and the *loto*: perspectives on the structure of the self in Samoa.**
Jeannette Marie Mageo. *Oceania*, vol. 59 (1989), p. 181-99. bibliog.

In every Samoan there is tension, even conflict, between three guides to behaviour: the *aga* or local customary usage; *āmio*, the view of right conduct formed by personal drives and urges; and *loto*, fleeting feelings and emotions. Mageo considers how the three interact in individuals. See also: 'Samoan moral discourse and the *loto*' by Jeannette Marie Mageo (*American Anthropologist*, vol. 93 [1991], p. 405-20. bibliog.), a study of the sources of public and private morality, and of the role of personal emotions and attitudes; and 'Aspects of Samoan personality' by Peggy Fairbairn-Dunlop (*Pacific Perspective*, vol. 12, no. 2 [1984], p. 24-29. bibliog.), a thoughtful attempt to arrive at a rational assessment of what character traits make up the Samoan personality, which has often been ludicrously romanticized and stereotyped.

423 **Coming of age in Samoa: a psychological study of primitive youth for Western civilization.**
Margaret Mead, with a foreword by Franz Boas. New York: William Morrow, 1928. 297p. bibliog.; London: Jonathan Cape, 1929. 297p. bibliog.

Greatly admired for very many years, this study of young people in Manu'a, American Samoa, maintains that adolescence in Samoa is free of stress because of the traditional nurture and upbringing of children. Mead's thesis, and the validity of her fieldwork, have since been challenged, by Derek Freeman and others in a debate which centres on nature versus nurture. There have been numerous reprints, notably that by the American Museum of Natural History, New York, 1973. 170p. See also 'South Seas hints on bringing up children' by Margaret Mead (*Parents' Magazine*, vol. 4, no. 9 [Sept. 1929], p. 20-22, 49-52). Using her fieldwork experience in Ta'ū, Manu'a, Mead discusses the ways in which the Samoan *'āiga* (extended family) influences its children: 'Life and death and sex are no mysteries to the growing child in Samoa'. Another article by Margaret Mead is 'Samoan children at work and play' (*Natural History* [New York], vol. 28 [1928], p. 626-36).

424 **Effects of climate on certain cultural practices.**
John W. M. Whiting. In: *Explorations in cultural anthropology: essays in honor of George Peter Murdock.* Edited by Ward H. Goodenough. New York: McGraw Hill, 1964, p. 511-44. bibliog.

Male circumcision is almost entirely restricted to Africa and the Insular Pacific. The possibility that certain ecological factors may account in part for this biased distribution is explored, with the conclusion that exclusive mother-infant sleeping arrangements, a long postpartum sex taboo, and patrilocal residence are involved. Temperature and rainy tropical climate (associated with protein deficiency) also influence these practices. The accompanying Table 9 includes Samoa.

425 **Gender and sexuality in hierarchical societies: the case of Polynesia and some comparative implications.**
Sherry B. Ortner. In: *Sexual meanings: the cultural construction of gender and sexuality.* Edited by Sherry B. Ortner, Harriet Whitehead. Cambridge, England: Cambridge University Press, 1981, p. 359-409. bibliog.

This comparative essay seeks 'to develop a general and systematic interpretation of Polynesian society that will account for as many as possible of the salient (and apparently contradictory) features of Polynesian gender culture'. The references to Samoa are from Margaret Mead's *The social organization of Manu'a* (q.v.) and *Coming of age in Samoa* (q.v.).

426 **Hairdos and don'ts: hair symbolism and sexual history in Samoa.**
Jeannette Marie Mageo. *Man*, vol. 29 (1994), p. 407-32. bibliog.

An analysis of what motivates how Samoans do their hair, and a glimpse of the sexual connotations.

427 **Incest prohibitions and the logic of power in Samoa.**
Bradd Shore. *Journal of the Polynesian Society*, vol. 85, no. 2 (June 1976), p. 275-96. bibliog.

'An account of Samoan incest (*mata'ifale*) prohibitions viewed as part of a more comprehensive system of cultural symbols, ideas and beliefs'. The first part is primarily descriptive and ethnographic, accompanied by several case-studies. The more analytical and abstract second part attempts to correlate the Samoan incest prohibition with aspects of Samoan ideology and social organization. The emphasis is on the brother-sister relationship and the particular form of power relations which it manifests. Adoption is also important in social organization. See 'Adoption, alliance, and political mobility in Samoa' by Bradd Shore, in *Transactions in kinship: adoption and fosterage in Oceania*, edited by Ivan Brady (Honolulu: University of Hawai'i Press, 1976, p. 164-99. bibliog. [ASAO Monograph, no. 4]).

428 **Inhibitions and compensations: a study of the effects of negative sanctions in three Pacific cultures.**
Jeannette Marie Mageo. *Pacific Studies*, vol. 14, no. 3 (July 1991), p. 1-40. bibliog.

The sanctions considered are teasing, scaring and punishment, in Bali, Tahiti and Samoa. Samoans tease, scare and punish their children: beating is continued until the child demonstrates submission gesturally. Mageo concludes: '... the result of Samoan punishment is an inhibiting feeling that encourages children to assume both the physical and the psychological elements of that submissive bearing earlier exacted by force'.

429 **Male transvestism and cultural change in Samoa.**
Jeannette Marie Mageo. *American Ethnologist*, vol. 19, no. 3 (1992), p. 443-59. bibliog.

A coolly scientific view of Samoan men who live and dress as women, *fa'afāfine*; their role in traditional society and in the new 'global' culture which is emerging; and attitudes towards them. See also 'Samoa: where men think they are women' by Abigail Haworth, photographs by Ian Berry (*Marie Claire* [London], no. 57 [May 1993], p. 50-53), a sympathetic account of American Samoan men who live *fa'afāfine*, brought up from an early age as girls with the support and often encouragement of their families. Haworth claims that 'as many as one family in five has a son who lives as a woman. They are totally accepted by society, are usually highly educated and hold many key jobs.'

430 **Rage and obligation: Samoan emotion in conflict.**
Eleanor Ruth Gerber. In: *Person, self, and experience: exploring Pacific ethnopsychologies*. Edited by Geoffrey M. White, John Kirkpatrick. Berkeley, California: University of California Press, 1985, p. 121-67. bibliog.

Gerber discusses the role concepts of emotion play in Samoan ethnopsychology, examined in the light of ethnographic data and research on affect. Emotions serve to reinforce important social values, and are linked with inborn patterns of affective arousal. In Samoan culture, where attention is turned outward to social and interactional cues, individuals may not be able to express inner experience directly, while intense anger toward social superiors is culturally impermissible. The glossary contains a useful list of Samoan terms for emotions.

431 **Sexuality and gender in Samoa: conceptions and missed conceptions.**
Bradd Shore. In: *Sexual meanings: the cultural construction of gender and sexuality*. Edited by Sherry B. Ortner, Harriet Whitehead. Cambridge, England: Cambridge University Press, 1981, p. 192-215. bibliog.

Explores, within the Samoan cultural context, 'the implications of the symbolic intermediacy of women in relation to nature and culture'. Reproductive sexuality, psychological sexuality, gender, sexual relations, male and female status, transvestism, and the associated vocabulary are all examined and interpreted. Shore's analysis helps to clarify many key terms in Samoan society, such as *tāupou*, *'aumāga* and *aualuma*. Dualism, exemplified by the dichotomy between *aga* and *āmio*, which represent the socially controlled and uncontrolled aspects, respectively, of human existence, is shown to pervade Samoan thought and culture.

432 **The sleep-crawling question.**
Marvin Harris. *Psychology Today*, vol. 17, no. 5 (May 1983), p. 24-27. bibliog.

A review article on the practice of *moetotolo*, which is possessing or attempting to have sexual intercourse with a woman while she is sleeping at night, and on the sanctions applicable in Samoan custom.

433 **Tonga and Samoa: images of gender and polity.**
Edited by Judith Huntsman. Christchurch, New Zealand: Macmillan Brown Centre for Pacific Studies, University of Canterbury, 1995. 122p. map. bibliog.

'Chieftainship, hierarchy, social stratification and gender are among the topics reflected upon by four long-term scholars of Tonga and Samoa: Malama Meleisea, Phyllis Herda, Kerry James and Penelope Schoeffel. The four essays are introduced and commented upon – and thus linked – by Judith Huntsman'. See also 'Gender, status and power in Samoa' by Penelope Schoeffel (*Canberra Anthropology*, vol. 1, no. 2 [1978], p. 69-81. bibliog.), an assessment of the relative standing of men and women in Samoan society, with its pervasive system of titles which reflect status and confer power of various kinds. Women can be titleholders, but traditionally the overwhelming majority are men.

Sexuality in Samoan art forms.
See item no. 816.

Social problems

434 **Alcohol in Oceania.**
S. Casswell. Auckland, New Zealand: Alcohol Research Unit, Department of Community Health and General Practice, University of Auckland, 1986. 98p.

Casswell examines all aspects of the supply and use of alcohol in Pacific communities, focusing especially on Western Samoa, Tonga, Fiji, Vanuatu and Papua New Guinea. Alcohol-related problems are seen as a potential threat to the well-being of developing societies, and possible ameliorative methods are suggested. See also *The place of alcohol in the lives of some Samoan women in Auckland* by Sene Neich, Julie Park (Auckland, New Zealand: Department of Anthropology, University of Auckland, 1988. 40p. [The Place of Alcohol in the Lives of New Zealand Women: Project Report, no. 12]), which provides case-studies of social drinking and alcoholism among Samoan women living in Auckland, together with a discussion of reasons for such behavioural choices.

435 **The mixed blood in Polynesia.**

Ernest Beaglehole. *Journal of the Polynesian Society*, vol. 58, no. 2 (June 1949), p. 51-57.

This paper, presented at the Seventh Pacific Science Congress in February 1949, compares the position and problems of people of mixed blood in Western Samoa with those in French Oceania and the Cook Islands. Beaglehole declares that German, British and New Zealand administrations introduced into Samoa 'the racial consciousness and prejudice of Anglo-Saxon colonial society'. Before the German administration of Samoa, little, if any, stigma was attached to the mixed-blood. Samoa stands out as 'an unfortunate exception to a more humane, wiser, general Polynesian pattern of behaviour towards the mixed-blood'.

436 **Rassenmischung im kolonialen System: zur deutschen Kolonialpolitik im letzten Jahrzehnt vor dem ersten Weltkrieg.**

(Racial integration in the colonial system: on German colonial policy in the last decade before World War I.)

Franz-Josef Schulte-Althoff. *Historisches Jahrbuch* (West Germany), vol. 105, no. 1 (1985), p. 52-94. bibliog.

Mixed marriages and the cohabitation of German settlers and natives in the former German colonies of Southwest Africa and Samoa were not uncommon. However, in order to preserve German dominance, the colonial administration prohibited mixed marriages and deprived their offspring of civil rights, equating them legally with natives. This important study of the period 1900-14 is based on primary sources.

437 **The Samoan conundrum.**

Paul A. Shankman. *Canberra Anthropology*, vol. 6, no. 1 (1984), p. 38-57. bibliog.

A review of Samoan social problems, notably including that of suicide and attempted suicide among young people. See also: 'Adolescence in Samoa, yesterday and today' by Eleanor Burke Leacock (*Samoa News* [American Samoa], June 1985); and 'Compounding the problems of Samoan youth' by Eleanor Burke Leacock (*Kaleidoscope* [City College of New York], vol. 1, no. 2 [1984]).

438 **Suicide and attempted suicide in contemporary Western Samoa.**

John R. Bowles. In: *Culture, youth, and suicide in the Pacific: papers from an East-West Center conference*. Edited by Francis X. Hezel, Donald H. Rubinstein, Geoffrey M. White. Honolulu: East-West Center, 1985, p. 15-35. bibliog. (Pacific Islands Studies Program, Working Paper Series).

An overview of the phenomenon of self-destruction among young people in both parts of Samoa. See also the *Annual summary of activities and narrative report*, by The Lifeline Team (Apia: Suicide Prevention Programme, Catholic Relief Services, 1984-).

439 **Suicide in Micronesia and Samoa: a critique of explanations.**
Donald H. Rubinstein. *Pacific Studies*, vol. 15, no. 1 (March 1992), p. 51-75. bibliog.

Rubinstein critically examines the theoretical dialogue among a small group of researchers seeking explanations for the rapid and extraordinary increase in youth suicide rates. He analyses the theories of loss of traditional family functions; structural change towards the nuclear family; blocked opportunity; and changes in adolescent socialization structures and goals. See also 'Reducing suicide in Western Samoa' in *Culture, youth, and suicide in the Pacific: papers from an East-West Center conference*, edited by Francis X. Hezel, Donald H. Rubinstein, Geoffrey M. White (Honolulu: East-West Center, University of Hawai'i, 1985, p. 74-87. bibliog. [Pacific Islands Studies Program. Working Paper Series]).

440 **Suicide in Western Samoa: a sociological perspective.**
Cluny Macpherson, La'avasa Macpherson. In: *Culture, youth, and suicide in the Pacific: papers from an East-West Center conference.* Edited by Francis X. Hezel, Donald H. Rubinstein, Geoffrey M. White. Honolulu: East-West Center, 1985, p. 36-73. bibliog.

A searching investigation into the thwarted expectations, personal frustrations and despair which motivate the frequent and often horrific suicides among young Samoans. See also 'Toward an explanation of recent trends in suicide in Western Samoa' by Cluny Macpherson, La'avasa Macpherson (*Man* [NS] vol. 22, no. 2 [1987], p. 305-30. bibliog.).

Old age

441 **Aging and change in Samoa.**
Lowell Holmes, Ellen Rhoads. In: *Growing old in different societies: cross-cultural perspectives.* Edited by Jay Sokolovsky. Belmont, California: Wadsworth, 1983, p. 119-29. bibliog. (p. 238-53).

This essay on aging and social change in American Samoa concludes that, despite an emergency programme of US aid, the arrival of several industries, and Americanized education programmes begun in the 1960s, adjustments to change have been made without destroying key social institutions linked to the high status of the aged, most crucially the *matai* system. 'The *matai* system, combined with open-air housing and a lack of age-segregated work activities, has made it almost impossible for the aged to disengage from Samoan society'.

442 **The impact of modernization on the aged in American Samoa.**
Ellen C. Rhoads. *Pacific Studies*, vol. 7, no. 2 (Spring 1984), p. 15-33. bibliog.

A report on research conducted in 1976, when interviews with eighty-five aged Samoans plus participant observation revealed that their status remained relatively high, though with signs of potential problems. Rhoads concludes: 'A major consideration in planning services for Samoan elders should be recognition of the effective support network of the Samoan family and its role in the retention of this high status by the aged'. See also 'Mapuifagale, Western Samoa's home for the aged: a cultural enigma' by Ellen C. Rhoads, Lowell D. Holmes (*International Journal of Aging and Human Development*, vol. 13, no. 2 [1981], p. 121-35. bibliog.).

443 **The role and status of the aged in a changing Samoa.**
Lowell D. Holmes. In: *Aging and modernization*. Edited by Donald O. Cowgill, Lowell D. Holmes. New York: Appleton-Century-Crofts, 1972, p. 73-89. bibliog.

According to this chapter: 'Samoa is not an unpleasant place in which to grow old'. Climate, open *fale*, the concept of time, the *matai* system, the extended family, status and prestige, all mitigate the harsher aspects of growing old. Special tasks can be assigned to old people without threatening the sense of well-being of younger folk. Old age can be meaningful and respected. Holmes concludes: 'It would appear that in spite of 150 years of contact with the western world the traditional Samoan value system and world view have supported a recognition of the aging process as a desirable and well-honored phenomenon'. The ancient custom, no longer practised, of 'live burial' is explained as a means of honouring aged men in their lifetime.

444 **Western Samoa's elderly people: is their lifestyle changing?**
Keith Cernak. *Pacific Health*, no. 12 (1979), p. 6-9.

Cernak suggests that life-styles of old people in rural villages remain relatively unchanged, apart from new sources of entertainment such as radio (and television where available). However, in urban areas, old people suffer some degree of isolation and diminution of prestige and influence, and are less actively involved in community activities other than religious observance.

Margaret Mead

445 **Blackberry winter: my earlier years.**
Margaret Mead. London; Sydney: Angus & Robertson, 1973. 305p.

Margaret Mead's recollections of her childhood and education, of her career as an anthropologist among seven South Sea peoples – Samoans, Manus, Arapesh, Mundugumor, Tchambuli, Balinese and Iatmul – illuminate a period which understood 'anthropology as a salvage operation'. Mead 'knew that we must get to the old men and old women who alone knew about the old ways which, once destroyed, could never be reconstructed'. Yet it was not as 'an antiquarian' that she worked in Eastern Samoa in 1925-26; she went there 'to find out more about human beings, human beings like ourselves in everything except their culture', the end purpose being: 'so that Americans might better understand themselves'. 'Samoa: the adolescent girl' (p. 137-54, 155-57) candidly recalls how she grasped the challenges of her first fieldwork.

446 **Letters from the field 1925-1975.**
Margaret Mead. London; New York: Harper & Row, 1977. 343p. (World Perspectives, vol. 52).

The seemingly interminable debate regarding the truth of Mead's field research in Manu'a lends special relevance to her letters to friends and relations. Letters about Samoa appear in the chapters covering her apprentice years, from 1925 to 1930. Despite the intrinsic interest of these early letters, little new light is shed on the validity of her theories and conclusions as published in *Coming of age in Samoa* (q.v.) and in articles on her work in American Samoa.

447 **Margaret Mead: a life.**
Jane Howard. London: Harvill Press, 1984. 527p. bibliog.

An exceptionally well sourced and soundly documented biography by an accomplished journalist whose research includes accounts and recollections of Mead by some 300 persons worldwide. Four extensive bibliographies supplement the work: 'Selected bibliography'; 'Selected Margaret Mead books'; 'Selected Margaret Mead articles'; and 'Recent articles concerning Mead-Freeman controversy'. See also *Margaret Mead: the complete bibliography, 1925-1975*, edited by Joan Gordan (The Hague: Mouton, 1977. 202p.), which includes not only major books and journal articles but also many elusive, fugitive and ephemeral items.

Margaret Mead and Samoa.
See item no. 937.

The Mead controversy

448 **Confronting the Margaret Mead legacy: scholarship, empire, and the South Pacific.**
Edited by Lenora Foerstel, Angela Gilliam. Philadelphia: Temple University Press, 1992. 298p. bibliog.

A highly controversial, angry and accusatory collection of essays mostly excoriating Margaret Mead for her alleged romanticization of Samoan and other Pacific cultures, sensationalism, erroneous ethnography, 'Freudian' orientation and much, much more. Stereotypical images of 'sex, savages, and spears' are said to owe much to the continuing legacy of Margaret Mead. The editors have an explicitly political purpose: 'It is the duty of social scientists everywhere to expose the problems faced by Pacific peoples as they resist destruction and extinction' (p. xxviii).

449 **The height of her powers: Margaret Mead's Samoa.**
Bonnie A. Nardi. *Feminist Studies*, vol. 10, no. 2 (1984), p. 323-37. bibliog.

Nardi, an anthropologist who has conducted field research in Samoa, considers that both Margaret Mead and her critic, Derek Freeman, have made erroneous generalizations about Samoan culture and that a third view is required. Freeman is criticized for his attack on Mead's sex, age and stature – an easy target, symbolizing sexual and intellectual freedom for women.

450 **Mālosi: a psychological exploration of Mead's and Freeman's work and of Samoan aggression.**
Jeannette Marie Mageo. *Pacific Studies*, vol. 11, no. 2 (March 1988), p. 25-65. bibliog.

Aggression has always had a focal place in Samoan culture. The only pre-Christian divinity worshipped throughout the archipelago was Nāfanua, a war goddess. In this closely argued article Mageo tries to clarify the nature and the place of aggression in Samoan social life, as evident in religious history and the language. This investigation is 'a pressing matter' because of confusion about the Samoan psyche and aggression arising from the Mead/Freeman controversy. After an evaluation of the psychological biases of the two scholars, Mageo considers the link between childhood punishment and the desire to hold titles (with its clear political dimension).

451 **Margaret Mead and Samoa: the making and unmaking of an anthropological myth.**
Derek Freeman. Cambridge, Massachusetts; London: Harvard University Press, 1983. 379p. bibliog.

Margaret Mead's *Coming of age in Samoa* (q.v.) portrayed a culture in which 'the storm and stress of adolescence' did not exist. Freeman holds that Mead's 'proof' is false, and he challenges the doctrine of cultural determinism. In so doing the work of Franz Boas, Alfred Kroeber and Ruth Benedict is also brought into the controversy. Mead's account of Samoan culture and character is described as 'fundamentally in error', and as 'misconstrued'. Freeman presents an alternative analysis, based on research extending from 1940 onwards. See also 'Book review forum: Derek Freeman. *Margaret Mead and Samoa* (1983)' by Fay Ala'ilima, Tuaopepe Felix S. Wendt, Nancy McDowell (*Pacific Studies*, vol. 7, no. 2 [Spring 1984], p. 91-196. bibliogs.), which contains three critical reviews (p. 91-140), and a detailed response by Derek Freeman (p. 140-96).

452 **Not even wrong: Margaret Mead, Derek Freeman, and the Samoans.**
Martin Orans. Novato, California: Chandler & Sharp, 1996. bibliog.

This is the only book on the Mead-Freeman controversy that makes use of Mead's field materials, to subject the claims of Mead and Freeman to the standards of verifiability of science. Orans' findings are 'a rebuke to the nonscientific practices of anthropologists who claim to be doing science', and to those who judge anthropological works 'on the basis of ideological virtue rather than correspondence with empirical observations'. He demonstrates that Mead understood Samoan restrictions of female sexuality. This work was not seen by the author of this bibliography whose abstract was based on *ASAO Newsletter*, no. 94 (April 1996), p. 25.

453 **Quest for the *real* Samoa: the Mead/Freeman controversy & beyond.**
Lowell D. Holmes, with a postscript by Eleanor Leacock. South Hadley, Massachusetts: Bergin & Garvey Publishers, 1987. 212p. map. bibliog.

Holmes seeks 'the reality of Samoa', by comparing his own fieldwork, conducted in Ta'ū (Manu'a) in 1954, with the earlier findings by Margaret Mead and with the criticisms of them by Derek Freeman. He identifies the major differences between the three sets of data, and concludes that Mead's Samoan research 'is by and large reliable'. Freeman's critique has ideological and geographical roots. Eleanor Leacock adds to the debate with 'The problems of youth in contemporary Samoa' (p. 177-88), based on a visit to Samoa in 1985. She stresses the need to study the effects of school failure, unemployment and loss of cultural identity on adolescents and young people in Samoa.

454 **The Samoa controversy: a select bibliography.**
Canberra Anthropology, vol. 6, no. 1 (1983), p. 86-97.

An extensive unannotated list, arranged alphabetically by author, of published reviews of Derek Freeman's controversial *Margaret Mead and Samoa* (q.v.).

455 **The Samoa reader: anthropologists take stock.**
Edited by Hiram Caton. Lanham, Maryland; New York; London: University Press of America, 1990. 351p. bibliog.

This is *not* an anthropological survey of Samoa, merely some sixty selected opinions on the Mead-Freeman problem. The bibliography comprises two parts: 'Selected writings relevant to the Samoa controversy' (p. 333-42); and 'Recent research on Samoa' (p. 342-45). A letter from Derek Freeman to Lowell D. Holmes, written in 1967, is published for the first time (p. 316-20). This makes scandalous allegations about Mead's personal conduct on Ta'ū in 1925-26, gravely impugning her character. This regrettable book is of use only to embattled anthropological polemicists.

Women

456 **The exception, not the rule: a comparative analysis of women's political activity in Pacific Island countries.**
Jean Drage. *Pacific Studies*, vol. 18, no. 4 (Dec. 1995), p. 61-93. bibliog.

Twenty-one Pacific Island states, including American Samoa and Western Samoa, are covered in this examination of overall trends in women's political participation. Drage uses the concepts of supply and demand to investigate why women's electoral success is low, and suggests this is because of traditional and cultural restraints. Women are more active in non-government organizations and community groups. Western Samoa had (1994) two women as elected members of the National *Fono*: Matamumua Moana Vermullen and Fiame Naomi Mata'afa, a Cabinet Minister. In American Samoa, Fiasili Haleck was re-elected in 1992 to the twenty-seat House of Representatives. Western Samoa has a Women's Affairs Ministry, set up in 1991. See also *Commonwealth Regional Workshop for Women in Small Island States (Communication and Community Mobilisation), 2nd, Apia, Western Samoa, 20-26 September 1981, report* (London: Commonwealth Secretariat, 1981. variously paginated), a report on discussions on training women to become involved in major national and international issues.

457 **The origin and development of women's associations in Western Samoa, 1830-1977.**
Penelope Schoeffel. *Journal of Pacific Studies*, vol. 3 (1977), p. 1-21. bibliog.

According to this article, groups of women traditionally helped in various economic activities, including gardening. Missionaries and, later, New Zealand administrators encouraged women to concentrate on children, health care and sanitation control. Women participate collectively in subsistence food production and in production and sale of handicrafts. Women's committees are ubiquitous and socially important. See also *Women's associations in the rural economy of the South Pacific: case studies from Western Samoa and East New Britain province, Papua New Guinea* (Nouméa, New Caledonia: South Pacific Commission, 1983. 47p. [SPC Occasional Paper, no. 19]).

458 **Pacific women's directory: a guide to 500 women's organisations in the South Pacific.**

Edited by Roslyn Sharp. Nouméa, New Caledonia: Pacific Women's Resource Bureau, South Pacific Commission, 1993. 199p. map.

An update of one section of the *Resource kit for Pacific women*, published by the Pacific Women's Resource Bureau (PWRB) in 1988. The PWRB hopes that annual publication may be possible. Coverage includes American Samoa (p. 1-8) and Western Samoa (p. 177-85), with addresses, telephone and fax numbers, objectives and activities of each organization. See also *Directory of national focus points for the advancement of women in Asia and the Pacific* (Bangkok: ESCAP, 1995. 4th edition. 198p. map), an update of the revised edition of 1989.

459 **Women in the Pacific: a guide to the records on microfilm written by, or about, women in the Pacific copied by the Pacific Manuscripts Bureau.**

Compiled by Gillian Scott. Canberra: Pacific Manuscripts Bureau, Australian National University, 1992. 54p.

Among microfilmed records of Samoan interest are: PMB 586, PMB 588, PMB 589 – Private correspondence of Dr Wilhelm Heinrich Solf, 1899-1934; PMB 24 – Journal and letters, 1855-74 of John Chauner Williams, British Consul in Samoa from 1858 to 1873; and PMB 718 – LDS missions (including Samoa), 1851-60.

460 **Women in Samoan history: a further critique of Derek Freeman.**

Eleanor Burke Leacock. In: *Sex and gender hierarchies*. Edited by Barbara Diane Miller. Cambridge, England; New York; Melbourne: Cambridge University Press, 1993, p. 351-65. bibliog.

Writing from a feminist standpoint, Leacock takes Freeman to task for his understatement of the role of women in Samoan history and culture.

461 **Women in the South Pacific: a bibliography.**

Donita Vasiti Simmons, Sin Joan Yee. Suva: University of the South Pacific, 1982. 124p.

This wide-ranging survey, mainly of articles, book chapters and reports, consists essentially of the references for South Pacific territories and states from a USP work of general reference: *Women: a bibliography* by Donita Vasiti Simmons, Sin Joan Yee (Suva: University of the South Pacific, 1982. 213p.).

Gender, culture and tourism development in Western Samoa.
See item no. 103.

Western Samoa: the sacred covenant.
See item no. 419.

Women and agriculture in Western Samoa.
See item no. 601.

The role of women in small-scale fisheries in the South Pacific.
See item no. 615.

South Pacific women in distance education: studies from countries of the University of the South Pacific.
See item no. 685.

Medicine and Health

Medical education

462 **Medical and socio-medical studies in the Pacific islands: a catalogue of theses and dissertations.**
William George Coppell. *Ethnomedizin*, vol. 4, no. 3/4 (1976/77), p. 315-40.

A guide to unpublished research on clinical medicine, health services, epidemiological studies, traditional medicine, etc. in the islands. American Samoa and Western Samoa are well represented.

463 ***Misi Utu*: Dr D. W. Hoodless and the development of medical education in the South Pacific.**
M. W. Guthrie. Suva: Institute of Pacific Studies, University of the South Pacific, in association with the South Pacific Social Sciences Association, 1979. 60p.

An outline history written by the daughter of Dr Hoodless, the founder in 1929 and first Principal (1929-46) of the Medical School at Suva, which was established to train medical personnel for South Pacific territories. Particularly valuable for its lists of graduates, it complements *Central Medical School* by D. W. Hoodless (Suva: Public Relations Office, Medical Department, 1947. 24p.).

464 **Pacific Health Dialog: Journal of Community Health and Clinical Medicine for the Pacific.**
Auckland, New Zealand: Resource Books, 1994- . 2 pa.

This journal is produced in a newsletter format. Vol. 1, no. 2 (1994) focuses on Pacific child health, including Samoa.

Somatology

465 **A contribution to Samoan somatology; based on field studies of E. W. Gifford and W. C. McKern.**
Louis R. Sullivan. Honolulu: Bernice P. Bishop Museum, 1921. 20p. bibliog. (Memoirs, vol. 8, no. 2; Bayard Dominick Expedition Publication, no. 1).

A pioneering study of the physical characteristics of Samoans, based on measurement and observation. See also *Marquesan somatology, with comparative notes on Samoa and Tonga; based on field studies of E. S. Craighill Handy and Willowdean C. Handy* by Louis R. Sullivan (Honolulu: Bernice P. Bishop Museum, 1923, p. 137-249. bibliog. [Memoirs, vol. 9, no. 2; Bayard Dominick Expedition Publication, no. 6]).

Indigenous medicine

466 **Is lactation Nature's contraceptive? data from Samoa.**
Maureen H. Fitzgerald. *Social Biology*, vol. 39, no. 1-2 (1992), p. 55-64. bibliog.

Data from a Samoan menstruation study suggests that lactation, even intensive on-demand lactation, does not inhibit menstruation or conception. This exploration of the applied and theoretical implications of continuing to accept lactation as a universally effective fertility control mechanism concludes that such thinking can have disastrous effects for family planning programmes, especially for populations like Samoans. See also 'Traditional control of fertility in Western Samoa' by Viopapa E. Annandale (*British Journal of Family Planning*, vol. 11 [1985], p. 63-66), a well informed account of Western Samoan traditional birth control practices and methods of abortion, with details of the natural folk medicines employed.

467 **Midwives and midwifery in Western Samoa.**
Patricia J. Kinloch. In: *Healing practices in the South Pacific.* Edited by Claire D. F. Parsons. La'ie, Hawai'i: Institute for Polynesian Studies, Brigham Young University-Hawai'i, 1985, p. 199-212. map. bibliog. (p. 234-44).

A professional overview of incipient overpopulation, status of indigenous midwives, antenatal care, delivery, placenta and umbilical cord, treatment of the newborn and postnatal treatment of the mother. A distinction is made between a *fafine fa'atōsaga*, a midwife who has not attended a Department of Health course, and a traditional birth attendant (TBA), who has. A *fafine fa'atōsaga* is regarded as a specialist and a professional by herself and her community. The main difference between a *fafine fa'atōsaga* and a TBA is in the practice of antenatal care, in that the TBA sees the pregnant woman less often. See also 'Some modern Samoan beliefs concerning pregnancy, birth and infancy' by L. L. Neich, R. Neich (*Journal of the Polynesian Society*, vol. 83, no. 4 [Dec. 1974], p. 461-65. bibliog.), an account of beliefs and prohibitions commonly quoted and referred to by young Samoan married women resident in New Zealand.

468 **Missionary accounts of *fofō mo'omo'o*.**
R. J. Crawford. *Journal of the Polynesian Society*, vol. 86, no. 4 (Dec. 1977), p. 531-34. bibliog.

This article stresses the need for caution in using ethnographical accounts left by missionaries, citing as an example the word *mo'omo'o*, termed 'consumption' by Turner (1861) and 'phthisis' by Krämer (1902). Richard M. Moyle (1974) states that '*mo'omo'o* by itself refers to a type of headache affecting half the head ...'. This example 'highlights the difficulty in studying a body of indigenous knowledge, protected both by its own esoteric nature and by missionary prohibitions. The difficulty becomes acute when the only accounts of the subject are those written by the missionaries themselves'.

469 ***Morinda citrifolia* L.: use in indigenous Samoan medicine.**
A. Dittmar. *Journal of Herbs, Spices and Medicinal Plants*, vol. 1, no. 3 (1993), p. 77-92. bibliog.

A detailed account of the medicinal uses in Samoa of the Indian mulberry (*nonu*), a widespread shrub or small tree of the coffee or madder family, with large, glossy, opposite leaves, tubular white flowers, and fleshy, ovoid, white fruit. See also 'The effectiveness of *Hernandia* spp. (*Hernandiaceae*) in traditional Samoan medicine and according to scientific analyses' by A. Dittmar (*Journal of Ethnopharmacology*, vol. 33, no. 3 [1991], p. 243-51. bibliog.).

470 **Samoan folk knowledge of mental disorders.**
Dorothy C. Clement. In: *Cultural conceptions of mental health and therapy*. Edited by Anthony J. Marsella, Geoffrey M. White. Dordrecht, Netherlands; Boston, Massachusetts; London: D. Reidel, 1982, p. 193-213. bibliog.

Samoan knowledge of mental disorders includes three general causative factors: brain damage or brain abnormalities (now also incorporating drug abuse); *aitu* (spirits); and excess emotion. Common themes connect folk knowledge of mental disorders and social types. Mad persons appear not to be cultured in Samoan terms, and so are disvalued. Beliefs linking *aitu* to mental disorders are challenged by the Christian churches. See also '*Ma'i aitu*: the cultural logic of possession in Samoa' by Jeannette Marie Mageo (*Ethos*, vol. 19, no. 3 [1991], p. 352-83. bibliog.). *Ma'i aitu* is a form of mental illness, even madness, said to be caused by temporary possession of a person by a ghost or a devil. Mageo sets this belief in spirit possession in the context of traditional Samoan culture, in this respect unmodified by Christianity, which also accepts the ideas of possession and exorcism.

471 **Samoan herbal medicine: 'o lā'au ma vai fofō o Samoa.**
W. Arthur Whistler. Honolulu: Isle Botanica, for 'O le Siosiomaga Society Inc. of Western Samoa, distributed by University of Hawai'i Press, 1996. 120p. maps. bibliog.

'Today in Samoa a large segment of the population takes or is given Samoan herbal medicine sometime during their lifetime, especially during infancy and childhood'.

This volume documents the physical and herbal treatments used in traditional Samoan medicine. A glossary of Samoan medical terms is also included. See also *Polynesian herbal medicine* by W. Arthur Whistler (Lawai, Hawai'i: National Tropical Botanical Garden, 1992. 237p. map. bibliog.), which is superbly illustrated with colour photographs, taken by the author.

472 **Samoan medical belief and practice.**
Cluny Macpherson, La'avasa Macpherson. Auckland, New Zealand: Auckland University Press, 1990. 272p. bibliog.

An exemplary, sociological account of the medical beliefs and practices 'which Samoans call Samoan medicine and believe to be indigenous'. The skills of *fofō*, or healers, are examined in detail. The five sections cover: 'Some conceptual and theoretical issues'; 'Samoan indigenous medicine in its historical context'; 'The social organisation of Samoan indigenous medicine'; 'Medical belief, diagnosis, and practice in contemporary Western Samoa'; and 'Conclusion: The future of indigenous medicine in Western Samoa'. There is an extensive glossary (p. 265-69) and a valuable bibliography (p. 259-64). See also 'Samoan medicine' by Cluny Macpherson, in *Healing practices in the South Pacific*, edited by Claire D. F. Parsons (La'ie, Hawai'i: Institute for Polynesian Studies, Brigham Young University-Hawai'i, 1985, p. 1-15. bibliog.).

473 **Samoan medicinal incantations.**
Richard M. Moyle. *Journal of the Polynesian Society*, vol. 83, no. 2 (June 1974), p. 155-79. bibliog.

A thorough account of Samoan belief in spirits of several kinds, with English translations of incantations used in treating eight common ailments, such as choking, headaches, hiccoughs, carbuncles, and maladies of skin, stomach and groin. The accompanying treatments are described in considerable detail.

474 **Saving the ethnopharmacological heritage of Samoa.**
Paul Alan Cox. *Journal of Ethnopharmacology*, vol. 38, no. 2-3 (1993), p. 181-88. bibliog.

A paper presented to the Second International Congress on Ethnopharmacology, Uppsala, Sweden, 2-4 July 1992. Cox emphasizes the potential importance of Samoan traditional medicines, and the need to conserve the plants from which they are made. See also: 'Medicinal plants of Samoa: a preliminary survey of the use of plants for medicinal purposes in the Samoan islands' by G. Uhe (*Economic Botany*, vol. 28, no. 1 [1974], p. 1-3. bibliog.); *Samoan medicinal plants and their usage* by Charles R. McCuddin (Pago Pago: Office of Comprehensive Health Planning, Department of Medical Services, Government of American Samoa, 1974); and *Arzneipflanzen der Polynesier* (Medicinal plants of the Polynesians) by Bernhard Zepernick (Berlin: Dietrich Reimer, 1972).

Historical studies

475 **The influenza epidemic of 1918-19 in Western Samoa.**
Sandra M. Tomkins. *Journal of Pacific History*, vol. 27, no. 2 (Dec. 1992), p. 181-97. bibliog.

An examination of the epidemic in terms of the colonial relationship in Samoa and of Britain's imperial responsibility to try to mitigate the lethal effects of the pandemic in its colonies. Only Australia was able to send a relief ship. Samoans were blamed for thwarting European efforts on their behalf, and for 'moral failings' and 'want of determination'. Tomkins concludes: 'In fact, the handling of the epidemic was a conspicuous failure of Western science and methods'. See also 'Die Grippeepidemie auf Samoa 1918' (The influenza epidemic on Samoa 1918) by Hermann Hiery (*Geschichte Lernen*, vol. 31 [1993], p. 25-30. bibliog.), a detailed account of the course of the catastrophic epidemic in Western Samoa, with an analysis of its causes and consequences. American Samoa was virtually unaffected.

476 **The land of the talking men.**
S. M. Lambert. In: *A doctor in paradise*. S. M. Lambert. London: J. M. Dent & Sons; Melbourne: Georgian House, 1941, p. 213-33. map.

This work was first published in 1941 (Boston, Massachusetts: Little, Brown, 1941. 393p. map). From 1920 to 1939 Lambert was perhaps the best known authority on tropical diseases in the South Pacific, latterly being associated with the Central Medical School in Suva, Fiji. He investigated hookworm in Western Samoa in 1924, and yaws and poliomyelitis in 1933. He starts his recollections of 'un-romantic' Samoa with Major-General Sir George S. Richardson's *malaga* (visitation) of 1924, when medical help was refused to a woman in protracted labour: 'a diplomatic blunder'. This incident was remembered when the *Mau* rebellion broke out in 1927, and long after, ranking with the shooting of Tamasese.

477 **Researches in the Western Pacific: being a report on the results of the expedition sent from the London School of Tropical Medicine to the Ellice, Tokelau, and Samoan islands in 1921-1922.**
Francis William O'Connor. London: J. C. Phelp & Son, 1923. 57p. (Research Memoirs of the London School of Tropical Medicine, vol. 4).

The diseases studied, and illustrated by eight plates, include tuberculosis, yaws, filariasis and leprosy. This is a prime source of health information for Western Samoa in the first years of the New Zealand mandate, with which to judge later advances in containment and treatment of endemic diseases.

478 **Sanitary report on Swain's Island, 1934; Historical note on Swain's Island.**
C. S. Stephenson. *United States Naval Medical Bulletin*, vol. 35, no. 3 (1937), p. 356-61, 361-64.

The *Sanitary report* provides information on insect pests, water supply, food supply, houses, population census, health, etc.

Diseases and symptoms

479 **Acculturation and symptoms: a comparative study of reported health symptoms in three Samoan communities.**

Joel M. Hanna, Maureen H. Fitzgerald. *Social Science and Medicine*, vol. 36, no. 9 (1993), p. 1,169-80. bibliog.

The subjective perception of illness is discussed on the basis of the symptoms reported by patients in urban and rural communities. Modernization and acculturation affect life-styles and diseases, particularly among young people, where suicide is an increasingly disturbing reaction to mental health problems.

480 **Cancer incidence in Western Samoa.**

Nadir Paksoy. *International Journal of Epidemiology*, vol. 20, no. 3 (1991), p. 634-41. bibliog.

Paksoy surveys the types of cancers commonly found in the Western Samoan population and suggests how they may be related to diet and other life-style factors. Lung and stomach cancers, linked with long-term tobacco use (smoking or chewing), are reported to be increasing in their incidence.

481 **The changing Samoans: behavior and health in transition.**

Edited by Paul T. Baker, Joel M. Hanna, Thelma S. Baker. New York; Oxford: Oxford University Press, 1986. 482p. 7 maps. bibliog. (Research Monographs on Human Population Biology, no. 5).

Presents seventeen studies, conducted in 1975-84, on the demography, work, nutrition, diet, health and behaviour of Samoans in urban and rural sites in Western Samoa and American Samoa, and at four locations on O'ahu, Hawai'i. The context of these studies is described in 'Environment and exploitation' (p. 19-38) and 'Social settings of contemporary Samoans' (p. 39-62). The extensive bibliography (p. 435-71) is indispensable as a guide to recent medical, psychological and sociological publications relevant to the Samoan research.

482 **Epidemiology of subperiodic Bancroftian filariasis in Samoa 8 years after control by mass treatment with diethylcarbamazine.**

E. Kimura, L. Penaia, G. F. S. Spears. *Bulletin of the World Health Organization*, vol. 63, no. 5 (1985), p. 869-80. bibliog.

Mosquito-borne filarial infestation of blood leads to the disfiguring disease of elephantiasis, characterized by immensely swollen limbs or testicles. Filariasis has long been endemic in Samoa. This report reviews the outcome after eight years of single-dose mass treatment with diethylcarbamazine citrate.

483 **Hyperuricaemia and gout in Western Samoans.**
L. Jackson, R. Taylor, S. Faaiuso, S. P. Ainuu, S. Whitehouse, P. Zimmet. *Journal of Chronic Diseases*, vol. 34 (1981), p. 65-75. bibliog.

A summary of the findings of extensive clinical studies of inflammatory conditions resulting from excess uric acid in the blood.

484 **The interplay of culture and symptoms: menstrual symptoms among Samoans.**
Maureen H. Fitzgerald. *Medical Anthropology*, vol. 12 (1990), p. 145-67. bibliog.

'Interview data from male and female Samoans in rural Western Samoa, rapidly modernizing American Samoa, and modern Hawaii are used to explore the role of culture and culture change in explaining variations in reports of menstrual symptomatology and menstrual distress'.

485 **Leprosy in Western Samoa and the Cook Islands.**
Norman R. Sloan. Nouméa, New Caledonia: South Pacific Commission, 1954. 23p. (SPC Technical Paper, no. 69).

An outline of the history and incidence of Hansen's disease in the two territories, and of the resources and facilities available for its treatment. See also 'Epidemiology of leprosy in American Samoa' by John Alexander Clinton Gray (*United States Armed Forces Medical Journal*, vol. 4, no. 4 [1953], p. 585-98. bibliog.), in which Gray outlines the known history of leprosy in the islands of American Samoa and discusses the incidence of the disease during and immediately after the Second World War.

486 **Patterns of disease and health practice in Western Samoa, 1835-1985: implications for policy.**
Pamela Thomas. Canberra: Islands/Australian Research Project, National Centre for Development Studies, Australian National University, 1990. 21p. bibliog. (Islands/Australia Working Paper, no. 90/7).

Thomas traces the gradual change from endemic tropical diseases to introduced diseases, such as smallpox, syphilis and influenza, and to the life-style and diet-related diseases of the present day. See also 'Pacific islands of Nauru, Tuvalu and Western Samoa' by Paul Zimmet, Sunny Whitehouse, in *Western diseases: their emergence and prevention*, edited by H. C. Trowell, D. P. Burkitt (London: Edward Arnold, 1981, p. 204-24. map. bibliog.), which argues that the adoption of sedentary, modernized life-styles has resulted in high incidence of chronic degenerative diseases, such as diabetes, obesity, hypertension, hyperuricaemia, gout, coronary heart disease, appendicitis, and strokes. In the Western Samoan disease rates given, those for rural dwellers are consistently much lower than for the urban population. The authors conclude that 'only a return to traditional lifestyle can prevent their occurrence and escalation'. Also useful are: *Talking health but doing sickness: studies in Samoan health* by Patricia J. Kinloch (Wellington: Victoria University Press, 1985. 54p. bibliog.), in which Kinloch focuses on the illnesses resulting from 'modern' life-styles and diet, in Samoa and among Samoan migrants in New Zealand; and *Samoan health practices in Wellington* by Patricia J. Kinloch (Wellington: Management Services & Research Unit, Department of Health, 1980 [Occasional Paper, no. 12]).

Diet, activity and health

487 **Breadfruit, banana, beef, and beer: modernization of the Samoan diet.**

James R. Bindon. *Ecology of Food and Nutrition*, vol. 12 (1982), p. 49-60. bibliog.

A discussion of new foods and new diseases. Bindon reviews what is known of Samoans' diet in pre-contact times. He considers that reliance on locally grown vegetables and fruits, and on fish, resulted in a generally adequate level of nutrition and in good physical health. The 19th-century switch to imported foods, such as sugar and rice, brought with it new diseases, directly stemming from dietary causes, and obesity. See also: 'An evaluation of the diet of three groups of Samoan adults: modernization and dietary adequacy' by James R. Bindon (*Ecology of Food and Nutrition*, vol. 14 [1984], p. 105-15. bibliog.); 'Taro or rice, plantation or market: dietary choice in American Samoa' by James R. Bindon (*Food and Foodways*, vol. 3 [1988], p. 59-78. bibliog.); 'Life style, modernization and adaptation among Samoans' by James R. Bindon, D. E. Crews, W. W. Dressler (*Collegium Anthropologicum*, vol. 15 [1991], p. 101-10. bibliog.); and 'Changes in some health status characteristics of American Samoan men: a 12 year follow up study' by James R. Bindon, D. E. Crews (*American Journal of Human Biology*, vol. 5 [1993], p. 31-38. bibliog.).

488 **Infant feeding patterns and growth of infants in American Samoa during the first year of life.**

James R. Bindon, C. Cabrera. *Human Biology*, vol. 60 (1988), p. 80-92. bibliog.

Other studies of infant and pre-adolescent nutrition include: 'Dietary patterns of children in American Samoa: multivariate analyses of food groups and household associations' by James R. Bindon (*Ecology of Food and Nutrition*, vol. 18 [1986], p. 331-38. bibliog.); 'Patterns of growth in weight and length among American Samoan infants' by D. L. Pelletier, James R. Bindon (*Ecology of Food and Nutrition*, vol. 18 [1986], p. 145-57. bibliog.); 'Patterns of growth in weight among infants in a rural Western Samoan village' by James R. Bindon, D. L. Pelletier (*Ecology of Food and Nutrition*, vol. 18 [1986], p. 135-43. bibliog.); 'Patterns of growth in height and weight among three groups of Samoan pre-adolescents' by James R. Bindon, S. M. Zansky (*Annals of Human Biology*, vol. 13 [1986], p. 171-78. bibliog.); and 'Infant feeding and women's work in Western Samoa: a hypothesis, some evidence and suggestions for future research' by Bonnie A. Nardi, in *Infant care and feeding in the South Pacific*, edited by Leslie B. Marshall (New York: Gordon and Breach, 1985, p. 293-306. bibliog.).

489 **Migration and biocultural adaptation: Samoans in California.**
Craig Robert Janes, Ivan G. Pawson. *Social Science and Medicine*, vol. 22 (1986), p. 821-34. bibliog.

An assessment of the considerable changes in life-style entailed by settlement in western USA. See also: 'Biocultural risks in longevity: Samoans in California' by Ivan G. Pawson, Craig Robert Janes (*Social Science and Medicine*, vol. 16 [1982], p. 183-90. bibliog.); 'Massive obesity in a migrant Samoan population' by Ivan G. Pawson, Craig Robert Janes (*American Journal of Public Health*, vol. 71 [1981], p. 508-13. bibliog.); and 'The effects of modernization and migration on Samoan blood pressure' by S. T. McGarvey, P. T. Baker (*Human Biology*, vol. 51 [1979], p. 461-75. bibliog.).

490 **The relationship of energy intake and expenditure to body fatness in Western Samoan men.**
D. L. Pelletier. *Ecology of Food and Nutrition*, vol. 19 (1987), p. 185-99. bibliog.

An assessment of diet and physical activity in relation to obesity. See also: 'The effects of occupation, leisure activities, and body composition on aerobic fitness in Western Samoan males' by D. L. Pelletier (*Human Biology*, vol. 60 [1988], p. 889-99. bibliog.); 'Daily activity, energy intake and body composition among Western Samoans' by D. E. Schendel (*American Journal of Physical Anthropology*, vol. 75 [1988], p. 267); and 'Estimation of energy expenditure in Western Samoa, American Samoa and Honolulu by recall interviews and direct observation' by J. D. Pearson (*American Journal of Human Biology*, vol. 2 [1990], p. 313-26. bibliog.).

491 **The Samoans.**
Richard A. Markoff, John R. Bond. In: *People and cultures of Hawaii: a psychocultural profile*. Edited by John F. McDermott Jr., Wen-Shing Tseng, Thomas W. Maretzki. Honolulu: John A. Burns School of Medicine and the University Press of Hawai'i, 1980, p. 184-99. bibliog.

Chapter ten, in this new edition of a handbook for mental health workers first published in 1974, presents the immigration history, traditional culture, stereotypes or myths, and current situation of the Samoans now forming part of the population of the multi-ethnic and multi-cultural state of Hawai'i. Against this demographic, historical and cultural background, the authors explain, in non-technical language, the potential mental health problems commonly experienced.

492 **Social aspects of obesity.**
Edited by Igor de Garine, Nancy J. Pollock. Luxembourg: Gordon & Breach Publishers, 1995. 314p. maps. bibliogs. (Culture and Ecology of Food and Nutrition, vol. 1).

The eighteen studies in this volume (covering cultural fattening processes, physical and social aspects, and social phenomena associated with obesity) include: 'Polynesian responses to modernization: overweight and obesity in the South Pacific' by James R. Bindon (p. 227-51. map. bibliog.); and 'Activity level and obesity among Samoans' by Lawrence P. Greksa (p. 253-66. bibliog.).

493 **Vitamin A deficiency in the South Pacific.**

D. A. Schaumberg, M. Linehan, G. Hawley, J. O'Connor, M. Dreyfuss, R. D. Semba. *Public Health*, vol. 109, no. 5 (Sept. 1995), p. 311-18. bibliog.

Vitamin A is necessary for growth; shortage of it results in degenerative conditions, such as ulceration of the cornea or bone changes, and in susceptibility to disease. In the South Pacific, sources of Vitamin A include sweet potato, oranges, mango, pawpaw, water melon, green beans, green leafy vegetables, pumpkin and fish livers. Such sources are inadequate in atoll conditions, as in Tokelau, and may be underused in Samoa and other high islands, where canned foods may be preferred, to the great detriment of health, especially in children. See also *Diet and nutrition in American Samoa* by Sheila Malcolm (Nouméa, New Caledonia: South Pacific Commission, 1954. 64p. [SPC Technical Paper, no. 63]), in which Malcolm considers nutrition to be generally adequate in the more traditional rural communities. Greater reliance on imported foods (e.g. the ubiquitous *pisupo*) results in dietary imbalance and widespread conditions such as obesity, diabetes, hypertension – all diet-induced diseases of 'modernity' and urban life-styles. Also of interest is *Dental conditions in school children of American Samoa* by Raymond G. Neubarth (Nouméa, New Caledonia: South Pacific Commission, 1954. 20p. [SPC Technical Paper, no. 64]), which suggests that tooth decay becomes more serious as Samoans move away from their traditional foods.

Public health services

494 **Damned if you do and damned if you don't: dilemmas in development for Pacific health.**

Margaret Mackenzie. In: *Paradise postponed: essays on research & development in the South Pacific*. Edited by Alexander Mamak, Grant McCall. Rushcutters Bay, New South Wales: Pergamon Press, 1978, p. 225-31.

Drawing on her studies of cultural and social aspects of health and nutrition on Savai'i in Western Samoa, Rarotonga and Malekula, medical anthropologist Mackenzie pleads for 'some skepticism about the value of development for its own sake', though not all the problems experienced can be blamed on outside contact and development. 'The stress from competing for political titles among adult males in Samoa is an almost perfect parallel of the cut-throat struggle for tenure among academics in universities in the United States'. The nature and availability of health services need to be reconsidered; for example, Āpia's hospital, though very heavily used, serves only a limited area. Useful features of traditional, local medicine should be conserved.

495 **Dilemmas of modernisation in primary health care in Western Samoa.**
Penelope Schoeffel. *Social Science & Medicine*, vol. 13, no. 3 (1986), p. 209-16. bibliog.

Concern as to the financial sustainability of health care modernization, and the consequences of undue centralization of medical resources in Āpia prompt this re-evaluation of Samoan traditional medicine, and of healers, midwives and women's committees as participants in the delivery of primary health care in rural communities.

496 **The economics of public health in Western Samoa.**
Helen Lapsley. Canberra: Islands/Australia Research Project, National Centre for Development Studies, Australian National University, 1990. 16p. bibliog. (Islands/Australia Working Paper, no. 90/5).

Presents and analyses essential data on the severe economic and financial constraints on the provision of public health services in Western Samoa. See also 'State control and economic inequality in public health (Western Samoa)' by Penelope Schoeffel (*Review* [USP], vol. 14 [1986], p. 19-24), a trenchant critique of Western Samoa's public health services which focuses on the inadequacies of the Āpia-based Health Department, on undue centralization of specialist services, and on priorities inequitably accorded to wealthier communities. Officials seldom keep up regular contact with villages remote from Āpia, and most local activities are, consequently, directed by women's associations and committees. Another article on the subject is 'Aid, politics and hospitals in Western Samoa' by J. Stephen Hoadley (*World Development*, vol. 8, no. 5/6 [May-June 1980], p. 443-55), a critical research essay – and cautionary tale – which shows how the New Zealand aid project for the modernization of Āpia Hospital had the unforeseen consequences of worsening rural health services and depriving district hospitals of staff and funds.

Politics

Samoa

497 **The High Commissioner in Polynesian politics: Samoa, 1875-1899.**
Deryck Scarr. In: *Fragments of empire: a history of the Western Pacific High Commission, 1877-1914*. Deryck Scarr. Canberra: Australian National University Press; London: C. Hurst, 1967, p. 53-81. map. bibliog. (p. 341-57).

This meticulously documented account of the Samoan policies of the Western Pacific High Commission (and especially of Sir John Bates Thurston) is essential to an understanding of why Britain gave way to Germany in Samoa, preferring a free hand in Tonga. The bibliography contains details of many relevant archives. There are photographs of Tupua Tamasese, Malietoa Laupepa and Mata'afa Iosefo.

The Samoan culture and government.
See item no. 410.

German Samoa

498 **Pacific islanders under German rule: a study in the meaning of colonial resistance.**
Peter J. Hempenstall. Canberra; Norwalk, Connecticut: Australian National University Press, 1978. 265p. maps. bibliog.

Contains two excellent accounts of German Samoa: 'German Samoa: early disquiet' (p. 25-50; notes p. 223-26); and 'Lauaki versus the Solf system' (p. 51-72; notes

p. 226-27). There are photographs of Mata'afa Iosefo, Lauaki (Lauati) Namulau'ulu and his wife Sialatana; Wilhelm Solf; and Solf's opponent Richard Deeken.

499 **Resistance in the German Pacific empire: towards a theory of early colonial response.**
Peter J. Hempenstall. *Journal of the Polynesian Society*, vol. 84, no. 1 (March 1975), p. 5-25. bibliog.

This comparative study of indigenous responses to German colonial policies includes an analysis of the *'Oloa* or *Cumpani* movement in Samoa. The slump in copra prices after 1903 led the chiefs of the still existing central government to attempt to set up a Samoan co-operative to produce and market the islanders' copra. This was adamantly opposed by Solf and the DHPG in every way. See also *Protest and dissent in the colonial Pacific* by Peter J. Hempenstall, Noel Rutherford (Suva: Institute of Pacific Studies, University of the South Pacific, 1984. 200p. 2 maps. bibliog.). These five case-studies of political protest against colonial rule include a history of anti-colonial organization in Samoa, culminating in the *Mau* movement. The obduracy of colonial powers, in not responding to indigenous initiatives for political change, is well documented.

American Samoa

500 **American Samoa: *fa'a Amerika*?**
Fofo I. F. Sunia. In: *Politics in Polynesia.* Edited by Ron Crocombe, Ahmed Ali. Suva: Institute of Pacific Studies, University of the South Pacific, 1983, p. 115-28. map. bibliog. (p. 256-58). (Politics in the Pacific, vol. 2).

Sunia was the representative of American Samoa in the United States Congress in Washington, DC. He describes American Samoa as 'probably the best example of how a territory can grow politically without a plan, but with a great deal of playing by ear'. Political and educational advance, and Samoanization have been striking: 'Today, there is a college graduate in practically every village in American Samoa'. Governor and Lieutenant Governor are now elective offices. Sunia concludes by recommending a Congressionally approved constitution, independence from the US Department of the Interior, development of local political parties, local control of the judiciary, and faster economic growth. See also 'American Samoa: the 1977 gubernatorial election' by Muliufi Hannemann (*New Zealand International Review*, vol. 2, no. 6 [1977], p. 10-13), which discusses the Future Political Status Study Commission, created in 1969, which recommended the popular election of a governor and senators, and representation in the US Congress by a delegate-at-large. Three plebiscites between 1972 and 1975 rejected the idea of electing a governor, but such an election finally took place in 1977. Peter Tali Coleman (1919-), a respected Samoan government official, became the first elected governor of American Samoa, taking office in 1978.

Western Samoa

Independence struggle: *Samoa mo Samoa*

501 ***Mau*: Samoa's struggle for freedom.**
Michael J. Field. Auckland, New Zealand: Polynesian (Pasifika) Press, 1991. revised edition. 262p. maps. bibliog.

The meticulously researched story, vivid in detail, written in simple and captivating prose, of the most dramatic episode in Western Samoa's history: the struggle against New Zealand's arbitrary colonial rule waged by the *Mau*, 'a courageous and non-violent freedom movement'. Field traces the movement from its founding manifesto, drawn up in March 1927 when it was called the Samoa League, to the massacre of December 1929, with evident sympathy. The work was originally published as *Mau: Samoa's struggle against New Zealand oppression* (Wellington: A. H. & A. W. Reed, 1984).

502 **The revolt of the Samoans.**
H. E. Holland. Wellington: *Clarté* Depot, 1928. 16p.

A sympathetic account of the *Mau* resistance to New Zealand maladministration, by the first leader of the New Zealand Labour Party. Henry Edmund Holland (1868-1933), an Australian, moved to New Zealand in 1912, becoming editor of *The Maoriland Worker*. He defended the right of the people of Western Samoa to self-determination, condemned the shooting of *Mau* leaders in 1929, and befriended the exiled O. F. Nelson. See also *The stir in Samoa: an independent review* by A. B. Chappel (Auckland, New Zealand: Wilson & Horton, 1928. 62p.), in which Chappel considers that New Zealand could have done more to mitigate political tensions and to meet Samoans' legitimate aspirations.

503 **Samoa: a story that teems with tragedy.**
H. E. Holland. Wellington: *The Maoriland Worker*, [1918]. 20p.

Writing on behalf of the New Zealand Labour movement, Holland reviews the adverse impact of modern capitalism on Samoan society in the 19th century. He opposes the proposal that Samoa should be annexed to New Zealand: 'We insist on the right of every people to determine its own destiny – to choose the country under whose flag it will range itself, or to remain a separate nationality'.

504 **The truth about Samoa: a review of events leading up to the present crisis.**
O. F. Nelson. Auckland, New Zealand: National Printing Company, 1928. 95p.

The head of Samoa's most important trading firm and holder of the Sā Tupuā title of Taisi, Nelson was exiled for five years for his leading part in the *Mau* resistance movement. In May 1928 he went to Geneva to present a *Mau* petition and one of his own to the Permanent Mandates Commission of the League of Nations, but was not allowed to do so. *The truth about Samoa* records the many arbitrary decisions and actions taken by the New Zealand administration (and, especially, by Richardson,

New Zealand Administrator of Western Samoa, 1923-28) up to the mass arrests of 1928. See also *Samoa at Geneva: misleading the League of Nations* by O. F. Nelson (Auckland, New Zealand: National Printing Company, 1929. 24p.).

505 **Western Samoa's independence.**
C. G. R. McKay. *Journal of the Polynesian Society*, vol. 71, no. 1 (March 1962), p. 107-10.

'How can 110,00 people stand alone? Samoans would answer simply that "We can do it" – sincere in their belief that God will help them do it'. McKay casts a sympathetic eye over the problems facing Western Samoa on the eve of independence, and the choices to be made.

***Samoa mo Samoa*: the emergence of the independent state of Western Samoa.**
See item no. 242.

After independence

506 **Englishing my Samoan: selected speeches and letters.**
Tuiatua Tupua Tamasese Taisi Tupuola Tufuga Efi. Suva: University of the South Pacific, 1995. 124p.

An interesting selection of pronouncements, both public and private, by the veteran Western Samoan statesman, relating to important aspects of his country's political and cultural evolution.

507 **General elections in Western Samoa, 1979-1982.**
Leulu Felise Va'a. *Political Science* (New Zealand), vol. 35, no. 1 (1983), p. 78-102. bibliog.

Since attaining independence in 1962, Western Samoa attempted to reconcile the British parliamentary system with political power *fa'a-Sāmoa*, firmly based in the authority of *matai*. Western Samoan political parties tended to be 'ancestor-related' and to reject universal suffrage. Va'a analyses the electoral progress of the various parties over a four-year period of rapid change. See also 'Western Samoa's General Election 1973' by Ata Ma'ia'i (*Journal of Pacific History*, vol. 9 [1974], p. 146-52), a close analysis of the elections for the fifth Parliament, a watershed in Samoan politics. Of the forty-six members, twelve were elected unopposed (five of them newcomers to politics), eleven sitting members were re-elected, and there were twenty-eight new members. This represented a more than sixty per cent change in the composition of Parliament. Another interesting article is 'Consensus and plurality in a Western Samoan election campaign' by Fay C. Ala'ilima, Vaiao J. Ala'ilima (*Human Organization*, vol. 25, no. 3 [1966], p. 240-55. bibliog.), an exceptionally acute study of Samoan voting behaviour and of the tension between traditional authority and modern electoral practices.

508 **Leadership and change in the Western Pacific: essays presented to Sir Raymond Firth on the occasion of his 90th birthday.**

Edited by Richard Feinberg, Karen Ann Watson-Gegeo. London: Athlone Press, 1996. 480p. bibliogs. (London School of Economics: Monographs on Social Anthropology, vol. 66).

This symposium is an ethnographic and theoretical exploration of the rise of new forms of leadership at community and national levels in the politically independent states of the Western Pacific, including Western Samoa. These changes raise basic questions about leadership and tradition (as in the friction between universal suffrage and the *fa'amatai* system). Bradd Shore contributes a searching essay: 'The absurd side of power in Samoa'.

509 **Political change in Tahiti and Samoa: an exercise in experimental anthropology.**

F. Allan Hanson. *Ethnology*, vol. 12, no. 1 (1973), p. 1-13. bibliog.

This enlightening comparison considers the likenesses and differences of Samoan and Tahitian politics, and how in each case to discern the underlying processes and motivations. At the time of writing, Samoa still favoured *matai* franchise and traditional styles, while Tahitian politics had a distinctly French appearance, obscuring local differences and alignments. Hanson suggests how anthropological methods might be applied in political contexts.

510 **The Samoan culture and government.**

Aiono Fana'afi Le Tagaloa. In: *Culture and democracy in the South Pacific*. Edited by Ron Crocombe, Uentabo Neemia, Asesela Ravuvu, Werner Vom Busch. Suva: Institute of Pacific Studies, University of the South Pacific, 1992, p. 117-38. bibliog.

Aiono Fana'afi examines those elements in Samoan culture which make representative democracy hard to establish and to operate, quoting personal views by prominent people on the interaction of traditional culture and political democracy. For a broader view and comparisons with other countries in the South Pacific (notably Fiji and Tonga), see ' "A foreign flower"?: democracy in the South Pacific' by Peter Larmour (*Pacific Studies*, vol. 17, no. 1 [March 1994], p. 45-77. bibliog.). See also 'Politics and grammar: agency in Samoan political discourse' by Alessandro Duranti (*American Ethnologist*, vol. 17, no. 4 [1990], p. 646-66. bibliog.), in which Duranti examines the complexities of Samoan law, politics, social control and social conflicts from the standpoints of linguistics and of social and cultural anthropology.

511 **Tradition versus democracy in the South Pacific: Fiji, Tonga and Western Samoa.**

Stephanie Lawson. Oakleigh, Victoria: Cambridge University Press, 1996. 240p. 4 maps. bibliog.

A perceptive comparative survey of political tensions and dysfunctions in the three countries, engendered by the introduction of alien political structures. See also 'Toward the problem of studying the political systems of the independent countries of Oceania' by V. P. Nikolaev (*Soviet Studies in History*, vol. 21, no. 4 [1983], p. 70-86. bibliog.). There is a great variety of political systems in the South Pacific region, reflecting the relations of imperial powers and islanders during the colonial era. Nicolaev considers that Oceanic political systems are not yet fully evolved, as they currently '... rest on a weakly developed economic base and a backward social structure'. Western Samoa is described as 'an aristocratic republic', with a parliamentary system on the Westminster model but lacking universal suffrage.

512 **Universal suffrage in Western Samoa: the 1991 general elections.**
Asofou So'o. Canberra: Department of Political and Social Change, Research School of Pacific and Asian Studies, Australian National University, 1993. 20p. (Regime Change and Regime Maintenance in Asia and the Pacific. Discussion Paper no. 10).

Universal suffrage replaced *matai* suffrage in 1991. So'o reviews the new legislation, the results of the general elections of that year, and the implications for Samoan politics in future. See also 'Universal suffrage in Western Samoa: a political review' by Ioane Lafoa'i (*Journal of Pacific History*, vol. 26, no. 3 [1991], p. 67-73. bibliog.). The plebiscite on replacing *matai* suffrage by universal suffrage, held at the end of 1990, resulted in a two per cent majority for the latter system. This article reviews the voting patterns and considers the implications. The introduction of universal suffrage and the passing of the Village *Fono* Act (bringing these within the periphery of central government) may be seen as a sign of political maturity in Western Samoa, despite geographical difference and the very small majority. The extension of the suffrage to untitled adults and the attendant notion of 'democracy', may come to be subject to the subtle influence of *fa'a-Sāmoa*.

513 **Western Samoa: 'like a slippery fish'.**
Malama Meleisea, Penelope Schoeffel. In: *Politics in Polynesia.* Edited by Ron Crocombe, Ahmed Ali. Suva: Institute of Pacific Studies, University of the South Pacific, 1983, p. 81-112. map (p. 79). bibliog. (p. 256-58). (Politics in the Pacific Islands, vol. 2).

A perceptive account of politics in Samoa, from the traditional society, with two parties – the Victors (*Mālō*) and the Vanquished (*Vāivai*) – to the crisis of 1982. A new dimension of discontent is discernible, among the politically important younger people. 'Western notions of individual rights and freedoms have been promoted by mass education and emigration. The question is whether any government can meet these aspirations'. See also 'Titles, wealth, and faction: electoral politics in a Samoan village' by Robert Norton (*Oceania*, vol. 55, no. 2 [1984], p. 100-17. bibliog.).

From grammar to politics: linguistic anthropology in a Western Samoan village.
See item no. 322.

***Lāuga* and *talanoaga*: two speech genres in a Samoan political event.**
See item no. 323.

Constitution and Legal System

General

514 **South Pacific islands legal systems.**
Edited by Michael A. Ntumy. Honolulu: University of Hawai'i Press, 1993. 660p. map. bibliogs.

Provides overviews of the legal system of each island state, including American Samoa and Western Samoa: 'Western Samoa' by C. Guy Powles (p. 395-430, notes p. 653-54, bibliog. p. 429-30); and 'American Samoa' by Mary McCormick (p. 433-61, notes p. 654-55, bibliog. p. 460-61). See also: *Heads of State in the Pacific: a legal and constitutional analysis* by Yashi Ghai, Jill Cotterell (Suva: Institute of Pacific Studies, University of the South Pacific, 1990. 276p.), a comparative study of the status and functions of the heads of state of those states in the Pacific islands which are members of the Commonwealth; *Report of meeting of Law Officers of small Commonwealth jurisdictions: Port Vila, Vanuatu, July-August 1985* (London: Commonwealth Secretariat, 1986. 156p.), which contains papers and discussions on topics of concern to small states in the Commonwealth, including those in the Pacific Ocean; and *A bibliography of Commonwealth law reports*, edited by Wallace Breem, Sally Phillips (London: Mansell, 1991. 332p.), a descriptive bibliography of published law reports, indexed by title, subject, and jurisdictions, which includes Western Samoa, which joined the Commonwealth in 1970.

German Samoa

515 **The most important principles of Samoan family law and the laws of inheritance.**
Erich Schultz. *Journal of the Polynesian Society*, vol. 20 (1911), p. 43-53.

Erich Bernhard Theodor Schultz-Ewerth (1870-1935) was the scholarly second governor of German Samoa. This valuable summary of Samoan family and inheritance law is translated from *Die wichtigsten Grundsätze des samoanischen Familien- und Erbrechts* (Apia: Lübke, 1905. 15p.). The third edition was *Samoanisches Familien-, Immobiliar- und Erbrecht* (Apia: Lübke, 1911. 43p.).

American Samoa

516 **The High Court of American Samoa and traditional land tenure disputes in the context of modern economic development.**
William Tagupa. In: *Land issues in the Pacific*. Edited by Ron Crocombe, Malama Meleisea. Christchurch, New Zealand: Macmillan Brown Centre for Pacific Studies, University of Canterbury; Suva: Institute of Pacific Studies, University of the South Pacific, 1994, p. 183-89.

'A traditional land tenure system, by its very nature, cannot lead to intensive economic development.' This essay examines the tension between such development and the constitutional requirements for the preservation of the Samoan way of life, based on the judicial experience. Decided court cases are cited.

517 **Judicial intervention in *matai* title succession disputes in American Samoa.**
William E. H. Tagupa. *Oceania*, vol. 54, no. 1 (1983), p. 23-31. bibliog.

Provides case-studies of the application of United States law to Samoan title-succession disputes ordinarily settled by customary procedures and precedents. See also 'High Court adjudication of chiefly title succession disputes in American Samoa' by Walter W. Tiffany (*Journal of the Polynesian Society*, vol. 84, no. 1 [March 1975], p. 67-92. bibliog.). 'This article discusses how the introduced court system of American Samoa has influenced the traditional procedures and criteria by which Samoan successors to chiefly or *matai* titles are chosen in the Territory of American Samoa'. Compare with 'The Land and Titles Court and the regulation of customary title successions and removals in Western Samoa' by Sharon W. Tiffany (*Journal of the Polynesian Society*, vol. 83, no. 1 [March 1974], p. 35-57. bibliog.).

518 **Samoa comes of age: a case study.**
James K. Bishop. Washington, DC: Foreign Service Institute, 1977. 27p. bibliog.

The election of a Samoan governor of American Samoa in 1977 marked that territory's political maturity, after a half-century of US Naval administration followed, from 1951, by a quarter-century of civil government by the US Department of the Interior. Bishop succinctly outlines the successive stages in that evolutionary process, for a readership of career diplomats and administrators. He presents possible perspectives for future development, focusing on the key question of 'unincorporated' and 'unorganized' American Samoa's constitutional relationship with the USA. See also: 'American Samoa', in *Pacific constitutions. Volume one: Polynesia* (Suva: University of the South Pacific, 1983 [3rd printing 1988], p. 1-32. map), a facsimile text of the *Revised constitution of American Samoa* of 1967; and *Your Fono: a handbook of the twentieth legislature of the Territory of American Samoa* ([Pago Pago]: Legislative Reference Bureau, 1987. 120p.), a comprehensive guide to the powers, prerogatives, protocol, procedures and personnel of the Territorial *Fono* or legislative council.

Western Samoa

519 **Asia-Pacific constitutional yearbook 1993.**
Edited by Cheryl Saunders, Graham Hassall. Melbourne: Centre for Comparative Constitutional Studies, University of Melbourne, 1995. 361p. bibliog.

The first volume of a new annual publication which reviews major constitutional developments in a range of countries in the region. Guy Powles contributes a study of Tonga and Western Samoa (focusing on the introduction of universal suffrage). See also *The Westminster model in the South Pacific: the case of Western Samoa* by Yashi P. Ghai (*Public Law* [Winter 1986], p. 597-621. bibliog.), in which Ghai discusses, in terms of legal principles, the adaptation of the Westminster parliamentary model, to suit Samoan custom. The role of the head of state in the appointment and dismissal of the prime minister, his relationship with the cabinet, and his power to dissolve the legislature are among the matters regulated by Western Samoa's written Constitution. See also *Predicaments in Polynesia: culture and constitutions in Western Samoa and Tonga* by Rodney C. Hills (*Pacific Studies*, vol 16, no. 4 [Dec. 1993], p. 115-29. bibliog.), which compares the Western Samoan and Tongan constitutions, each devised with necessary compromises between tradition and modernity, in order to cope with legislative needs. Challenges to the systems of representation originally incorporated are described and evaluated. Hills considers that Western Samoa is 'more adaptable' than Tonga in face of modern political challenges.

520 **The Land and Titles Court and customary tenure in Western Samoa.**
Galumalemana Netina Schmidt. In: *Land issues in the Pacific.* Edited by Ron Crocombe, Malama Meleisea. Christchurch, New Zealand: Macmillan Brown Centre for Pacific Studies, University of Canterbury; Suva: Institute of Pacific Studies, University of the South Pacific, 1994, p. 169-81. bibliog.

The Land and Titles Court is 'the battleground' for disputes and its power is 'pervasive in every niche of society'. It has become the ultimate forum in disputes of national importance, regarding potentially rich areas for development, such as Ātua District. It has become an equalizing agent, by intervening in customary succession and appointments. More and more frequently, the Court resolves disputes equitably, disregarding differences in customary status and hereditary prerogatives. Gradually *matai* are coming to find that, before the law, they have only the same rights and duties as all other citizens. See also 'Lawyers and customary land: the Western Samoa Land and Titles Court' by Aeau Semi Epati (*Pacific Perspective*, vol. 10, no. 1 [1981], p. 65-71), which traces the history of the Land and Titles Court from its inception. The Court derives from the Land and Titles Commission established in 1903 by Dr Wilhelm Solf. A case is made for greater involvement of qualified lawyers in this 'most important' court, vital to the maintenance of Samoan social structure. Another useful work is *Notes on the practice of the court and the principles adopted in the hearing of cases affecting (1) Samoan matai titles; and (2) land held according to customs and usages of Western Samoa* by C. C. Marsack (Apia: Land and Titles Court, 1958. 27p.), an excellent introduction to the complexity and quirks of the *matai* system, and to Samoan customary land tenure, by a long-serving judge well versed in Samoan language and culture.

521 **Law, status and citizenship: conflict and continuity in New Zealand and Western Samoa (1922-1982).**
William Tagupa. *Journal of Pacific History*, vol. 29, no. 1 (June 1994), p. 19-35.

Tagupa reconsiders 'the colonial and post-colonial policies and assumptions attendant on the issue of New Zealand citizenship and Western Samoans'. The focal points addressed are: the lawsuit against Falema'i Lesa (one of many cases brought to arrest the tide of Polynesian immigration); subsequent Court of Appeal decisions; and the relevant *Mau* cases of the 1920s. The issues were resolved by the *Citizenship (Western Samoan) Act, 1982*. Tagupa asserts that its enactment marks the true achievement of Western Samoan independence.

522 **The Lesa case and the Citizenship (Western Samoa) Act, 1982.**
Barrie Macdonald. In: *New Zealand and international migration.* Edited by Andrew D. Trlin, Paul Spoonley. Palmerston North, New Zealand: Department of Sociology, Massey University, 1986, p. 73-80. bibliog.

An account of the Lesa *cause célèbre*, involving Western Samoans' right to New Zealand citizenship. The Privy Council ruling of July 1982, in London, that all Western Samoans born between 1924 and 1949, and their male children, were entitled to that citizenship, was annulled by the New Zealand and Western Samoan governments. Illegal immigrants already in New Zealand would be allowed to apply for citizenship, and a quota of 1,100 migrants a year would be accepted by New Zealand. See also 'New Zealand citizenship and Western Samoa: a legacy of the mandate' by F. M. Brookfield (*Otago Law Review*, vol. 5, no. 3 [1983], p. 367-96. bibliog.), which analyses the often controversial citizenship status of Samoans born in Samoa during New Zealand's administration, under the League of Nations mandate and United Nations trusteeship. The issue is discussed at length in this meticulously documented overview of the problems arising and the attempts made to find mutually acceptable resolutions.

523 **Problems of the Pacific: proceedings of the second conference of the Institute of Pacific Relations, Honolulu, Hawaii, July 15 to 29, 1927.**

Edited by J. B. Condliffe. Chicago: University of Chicago Press, 1928. 630p. maps. bibliog.

The summary of the round-table discussion on 'The Pacific mandates' (p. 192-95) and Document 28, 'Notes on certain aspects of the work of the League of Nations of interest to the Pacific countries', outline the historical background of the mandate for Western Samoa, granted to the British Empire and administered by New Zealand. This allocation was made by the Supreme Council of the Allies during the preliminary discussions which preceded the treaty of Versailles, and was later confirmed by the League of Nations, 'as a sacred trust of civilization'. Western Samoa's special political problems in the early years of the mandate (p. 523-24) are discussed. Other problems included: the total prohibition of intoxicating spirits and beverages; the use of imported Chinese labourers ('sometimes as many as three or four thousand'); and the plans of the New Zealand government to develop gradually the system of individual property in land on the islands.

524 **Western Samoa.**

In: *Pacific constitutions. Volume one: Polynesia.* Suva: University of the South Pacific, 1983 (3rd printing 1988), p. 459-517. map.

The facsimile text of *The constitution of the independent state of Western Samoa*, adopted by the Constitutional Convention on 28 October 1960. See also: 'Samoa', in *Constitutions of nations. Volume 2: Asia, Australia and Oceania* by Amos J. Peaslee, revised by Dorothy Peaslee Xydis (Dordrecht, Netherlands: Martinus Nijhoff Publishers, 1985. revised 4th edition, p. 1,259-96. bibliog.), which contains amendments made in 1963, 1965 and 1969; *The Constitution of the independent state of Western Samoa* (Apia: Administration of Western Samoa, 1960. 63p.), the original text of the Independence Constitution as presented for adoption by plebiscite; and *The plebiscite and the Constitution* (Apia: Administration of Western Samoa, 1961. 18p.).

Environmental legislation review: Western Samoa 1993.
See item no. 660.

Human Rights

525 **The protection of human rights in the Pacific region.**
Patricia Hyndman. London: Commonwealth Secretariat, 1991. 48p.

Primarily concerned with the Commonwealth states in the Pacific region, this survey examines the ways in which human rights are safeguarded. These include bills of rights, checks on and judicial reviews of executive action, and recourse to an ombudsman.

Administration and Local Government

Samoa

526 **Decentralisation in the South Pacific: local, provincial and state government in twenty countries.**

Edited by Peter Larmour, Ropate Qalo. Suva: Institute of Pacific Studies; Institute of Social and Administrative Studies, University of the South Pacific, 1985. 393p. maps. bibliog. (UNESCO Supported Series on Social Sciences in the Pacific).

These studies of the evolution of administrative districts include: 'Western Samoa' by Pamela Thomas (p. 214-31. map); and 'American Samoa' by Ropate Qalo (p. 232-36. map). The maps show, respectively, the district and sub-district names and boundaries of Western Samoa, and the county and district names and boundaries of American Samoa.

527 **Difficulties of the mandate; the American method.**

Margery Perham. *The Times* (London), (10-11 April 1930).

A shrewd comparison of the administrations of Western Samoa and American Samoa in 1929, to the advantage of the latter. A leading article, 'The art of governing Samoans', appeared on 11 April 1930.

American Samoa

528 **American Samoa: which road ahead?**

James Bishop. *Pacific Studies*, vol. 1, no. 1 (Sept. 1977), p. 47-53.

A candid and forthright discussion (based on many interviews) of American Samoa's problems and future, by a representative of the US State Department. Bishop considers that the major problems 'are not those of neglect but of administration', characterized by inadequate response. The problems are defined as: out-migration to Hawai'i and West Coast USA; in-migration from Western Samoa; a deficient education system; growth without development; a swollen bureaucracy; and disorientation.

529 **Historical sketch of the naval administration of the government of American Samoa: April 17, 1900-July 1, 1951.**
T. F. Darden. Washington, DC: United States Navy Department, Government Printing Office, [1952]. 39p.

An outline, by a USN captain, of the half-century in which American Samoa was administered by serving naval officers. It details main events and personnel, and indicates policy changes of consequence.

530 **Political advancement in the South Pacific: a comparative study of colonial practice in Fiji, Tahiti and American Samoa.**
F. J. West. Melbourne: Oxford University Press, 1961. Reprinted, Westport, Connecticut: Greenwood Press, 1984. 188p. bibliog.

Three chapters of this comparative analysis of government structures and political development are devoted to American Samoa. West suggests that, as in the other two territories, leadership and village government are inadequately developed, largely due to the superimposition of alien institutions.

Western Samoa

531 **Annual report to the League of Nations on the administration of Western Samoa.**
New Zealand. Government. Wellington: Government Printer, 1922-41. variously paged.

Although bland and often rather superficial, these reports for 1921 to 1941 provide an essential framework for historical research on the policies pursued by New Zealand as the mandatory power responsible for Western Samoa. The report for 1941 contains eleven pages.

532 **Duties of officials. Western Samoa.**
Malua, Western Samoa: [New Zealand] Administration, 1922. 39p.

This remarkable set of guidelines on what to do and what not to do for the first civil administrators in Western Samoa is indicative of New Zealand's inexperience in colonial governance and of its lack of empathy with Samoans.

533 **Equatorial acquiescence: village council and *pulenu'u* in Western Samoa.**

Paul Shankman. In: *Middlemen and brokers in Oceania.* Edited by William L. Rodman, Dorothy Ayers Counts. Lanham, Maryland: University Press of America, 1983, p. 209-32. bibliog. (p. 287-304). (ASAO Monograph, no. 9).

Most local-level decisions about village affairs in Western Samoa are made by the village council on the basis of consensus by village titleholders. There is an official representative of the central government chosen from the village: the *pulenu'u*, or 'village mayor'. Shankman examines the role of the mayor, his relations with his fellow titleholders in the council, and the indigenous system of stratification generally. The role of the *pulenu'u* is one of acquiescence to local interests, and modernization and bureaucratization may lock the village mayor further into a pattern of 'dubious responsibilities and divided loyalties'.

534 **New Zealand and the South Pacific.**

F. H. Corner. In: *New Zealand's external relations.* Edited by T. C. Larkin. Wellington: New Zealand Institute of Public Administration; London: Oxford University Press, 1962, p. 130-52.

Corner rather gloomily catalogues the deficiencies of New Zealand's external representatives and administrators, especially in Western Samoa. New Zealand's administering attitude was for many years 'a muddled one', characterized by 'a weak, unconsidered but well-meaning liberalism', and by an equally unconsidered and 'equally weak and ineffective desire for colonial prestige'. A major defect in education was the refusal to teach Samoan, and an inability to admit the validity of the indigenous culture.

535 **New Zealand's record in the Pacific islands in the twentieth century.**

Edited by Angus Ross. New York: Humanities Press, 1969. 341p. map. bibliog.

This pioneering, detailed study sets out to explain and evaluate New Zealand's colonial administration of her island dependencies – the Cook Islands, Niue, Tokelau and Western Samoa. Land policies, education and economic development are discussed clearly and objectively.

536 **The price of liberty is eternal vigilance.**

Tupuola Efi. In: *The Pacific way: social issues in national development.* Edited by Sione Tupouniua, Ron Crocombe, Claire Slatter. Suva: South Pacific Social Sciences Association, 1975, p. 235-38. Reprinted, 1983.

Contains thoughts on the 'tyranny of freedom' and on political independence and economic dependence by one of the best-known political personalities in Western Samoa. He stresses the need for balance, between social services and essential infrastructure, and between need for, and control of, foreign investment. The Samoan government invests 'substantial sums' in hotels to ensure that majority shareholding is held within the country. To safeguard political independence, high calibre leadership and high quality people are both needed.

537 **Racial attitudes of New Zealand officials in Western Samoa.**
Mary Boyd. *New Zealand Journal of History*, vol. 21, no. 1 (1987), p. 139-55. bibliog.

Boyd traces New Zealand's commercial and political interest in Samoa from 1872 to 1938, using archival records, manuscripts and published documents. Attitudes toward Samoans were shaped by 19th-century racial and imperial ideologies blended with a belief in 'noble savages'. Anthropological studies of acculturation modified these views, but the belief persisted among officials that self-government for Samoans would have to await their attainment of European standards of education and living.

538 **The record in Western Samoa since 1945.**
Mary Boyd. In: *New Zealand's record in the Pacific islands in the twentieth century.* Edited by Angus Ross. Auckland, New Zealand: Longman Paul, for the New Zealand Institute of International Affairs; London: C. Hurst; New York: Humanities Press, 1969, p. 189-270. bibliog.

New Zealand's administration of Western Samoa is analysed against the background of resurgent nationalism, from the advent of Colonel F. W. Voelcker as Administrator to 1962. 'The transition from trusteeship to independence was one of the smoothest possible, being helped by the gradual assumption of political responsibility over the past fourteen years, and by friendly co-operation with New Zealand'.

539 **The record in Western Samoa to 1945.**
Mary Boyd. In: *New Zealand's record in the Pacific islands in the twentieth century.* Edited by Angus Ross. Auckland, New Zealand: Longman Paul, for the New Zealand Institute of International Affairs; London: C. Hurst; New York: Humanities Press, 1969, p. 115-88. bibliog.

A dispassionate outline, soundly based on official documents and unpublished sources, of the New Zealand administration of mandated Western Samoa up to the end of the Second World War. Boyd sheds new light on the attitudes and abilities of the New Zealand officials of the period, not least on the 'out-and-out soldier', Major-General G. S. Richardson, often accused of 'misguided paternalism'.

540 **Report of the Commission to inquire into and report upon the organization of district and village government in Western Samoa.**
Government of Western Samoa. Wellington: R. E. Owen, Government Printer, 1951. 75p.

An essential document for understanding Samoan local government problems, and a criterion for subsequent developments. The report, which was presented to His Excellency the Acting High Commissioner on 30 November 1950, provides an excellent historical survey and makes many detailed recommendations (p. 12-49). The Commission's chairman was James Wightman Davidson of Āpia, a member of the Legislative Assembly, later the author of many academic works on Samoa. The consultants to the Commission were the two *fautua*, Tupua Tamasese and Malietoa Tanumafili, F. J. H. Grattan, Secretary of Samoan Affairs, and Thomas Robson, Resident Commissioner of Savai'i.

Foreign Affairs and Diplomacy

19th century

541 **Correspondence, treaties and conventions respecting the affairs of Samoa, 1881-99.**
Dublin: Irish University Press, 1971. 746p. map. (British Parliamentary Papers. United States of America, 50; Irish University Press Area Studies Series).

This comprehensive collection of facsimile reprints of the many Parliamentary papers (London: HMSO, 1881-99) dealing with Samoan foreign relations and internal affairs is indispensable for historical research. The original pagings are included.

542 **The foreign policy of the United States in relation to Samoa.**
George Herbert Ryden. New Haven, Connecticut: Yale University Press, 1933. 634p. bibliog.

This scholarly, highly detailed account of the American government's convoluted dealings with Samoans, and with the British and German governments and consular agents, is soundly based on official records and archives. It is still unmatched as an introduction to one major factor in the Samoan 'tangle' of the 19th century.

20th century

543 **A minor ornament: the diplomatic decisions of Western Samoa at independence.**
R. A. Herr. *Australian Outlook*, vol. 29, no. 3 (1975), p. 300-14. bibliog.

National self-interest, defence, trade, migration and meagre financial resources were among the considerations taken into account in determining the diplomatic course of independent Western Samoa. Samoa's main external representation was focused on Australia, New Zealand, USA, Germany and the European Community. Diplomatic representation in Āpia in 1995, at embassy or high commission level, was from Australia, the People's Republic of China, New Zealand and USA.

544 **Navigating the future: a Samoan perspective on U.S.-Pacific relations.**
Eni F. H. Faleomavaega. Carson, California: KIN Publications; Suva: Institute of Pacific Studies, University of the South Pacific; Honolulu: Pacific Islands Development Program, East-West Center, 1995. 146p. map. bibliog.

The author provides shrewd speculations as to the future role of the United States in Pacific affairs, and the possible repercussions on Samoa, east and west. See also the earlier discussion in *The United States and the South Pacific: a conference report, Apia, 1988* by Leon M. Slawecki (San Francisco: Asia Foundation Center for Asian Pacific Affairs, 1989).

545 **New Zealand and the South Pacific.**
Ramesh Thakur. *The Contemporary Pacific*, vol. 5, no. 1 (Spring 1993), p. 75-102. bibliog.

An essential introduction to New Zealand's South Pacific diplomacy in the 1990s, characterized by an increasing identification with the region, and by 'a responsive rather than a coercive approach to the challenges confronting the Pacific Islands, and on appropriate responses to those challenges'. An example of such a response is the NZ $2 million sent in relief to Western Samoa, which was devastated by a tropical cyclone in December 1991.

546 **The Pacific basin since 1945: a history of the foreign relations of the Asian, Australian and American rim states and the Pacific islands.**
Roger C. Thompson. London: Longman, 1994. 353p. maps. bibliog. (The Postwar World).

Though inevitably cursory, this is a well informed account of the diplomatic relationships of circum-Pacific states with their much smaller, vulnerable island neighbours, with the United States as the major regional influence.

547 **The South Pacific foreign affairs handbook.**
S. Hoadley. North Sydney: George Allen & Unwin, 1992. 258p. bibliog.

Four chapters of background political and diplomatic information on the South Pacific region are followed by detailed chapters on each state in turn, including Western Samoa. See also 'The Commonwealth in South East Asia and the Pacific' by A. S. B. Olver (*The Round Table*, no. 284 [Oct. 1981], p. 353-59), a discussion of cooperation by Commonwealth countries in the region, and of the value of meetings of Heads of Government.

548 **The South Pacific Symposium, Apia, Western Samoa, 7-11 July 1986.**
London: Commonwealth Foundation, 1986.

Comprises the first volume of a set of five reporting on progress in formation of Commonwealth NGO Liaison Units, to link governments and non-governmental organizations (NGO) and to harness the creative, flexible strengths of voluntary bodies at all levels. A summary volume, *A conspectus of the five regional symposia*, was published in 1988.

549 **Treaty with New Zealand on the delimitation of the maritime boundary between the United States and Tokelau.**
Washington, DC: Government Printing Office, 1983. 13p. map. (Senate Executive Report, no. 98-8).

The report of the Committee on Foreign Relations of the United States Senate on the proposed treaty with New Zealand concerning the disputed maritime boundaries between American Samoa and Tokelau. The treaty fixes these boundaries, and confirms United States sovereignty over Swain's Island, administered by American Samoa since 1925. An appendix cites foreign opinions of the treaty.

550 **The United Nations and Western Samoa.**
Apia: Samoa Printing and Publishing Company, 1952. 60p.

This volume, in English and Samoan, contains the full text of the *Universal Declaration of Human Rights*, with an explanatory preface, together with a selection of important resolutions and documents of the United Nations Trusteeship Council and General Assembly that most directly concern Western Samoa, with commentary.

Economy and Investment

General

551 **The future of Asian-Pacific economies: Pacific islands at the crossroads?**

Edited by Rodney V. Cole, Somsak Tambunlertchai. Kuala Lumpur: Asian and Pacific Development Centre; Canberra: National Centre for Development Studies, Research School of Pacific Studies, Australian National University, 1993. 350p. bibliogs.

Provides fourteen authoritative surveys of every aspect of economic and social development in South Pacific states (including Western Samoa, but excluding American Samoa). There is a 'Statistical summary' (p. 11-16), many other statistical tables, covering all significant indicators, and many up-to-date bibliographies of relevant official and other publications. Of particular importance is 'Socio-cultural aspects of development in the South Pacific' by Antony Hooper (p. 314-42. bibliog.) which discusses Western Samoa's collective land tenure as a factor in development. See also *Customary land tenure and sustainable development: complementarity or conflict?* edited by Ron Crocombe (Nouméa, New Caledonia: South Pacific Commission [SPC]; Suva: Institute of Pacific Studies, University of the South Pacific, 1995. 124p. maps. bibliog.), a collection of studies of the developmental problems arising from customary land tenure in the SPC states, including Samoa.

552 **Island economies: studies from the South Pacific.**

Te'o I. J. Fairbairn. Suva: Institute of Pacific Studies, University of the South Pacific, 1985. 442p. bibliog.

This imposing volume in the UNESCO supported series on social sciences in the Pacific is the most comprehensive study ever produced on Pacific Islands economies. A general overview is followed by a discussion of theories of development planning and promotion. Western Samoa is focused on in depth, with a wealth of statistics, and there are comparative case-studies of Fiji and Tuvalu. See also: *Pacific island economies: toward higher growth in the 1990s* (Washington, DC: The World Bank,

1991. 371p. [World Bank Country Study]), which includes Fiji, Kiribati, Solomon Islands, Tonga, Vanuatu and Western Samoa; and *The island states of the Pacific and Indian oceans: anatomy of development*, edited by R. T. Shand (Canberra: Development Studies Centre, Australian National University, 1980. 512p. map. [Development Studies Centre Monographs, no. 23]), based on a DSC seminar held in 1979, and containing papers on specific island states, including Western Samoa, and thematic essays on trade, education, training, transport, population and health.

553 **Oceanic economic handbook.**
London: Euromonitor, 1990. 226p. map.

A truly helpful compendium of up-to-date economic information of all kinds, with forecasts of future trends. American Samoa and Western Samoa are comprehensively covered, with detailed statistics spanning 1983-88. It is suggested that the whole Oceanic region will become more closely tied to the Asian rim nations. There are chapters on Oceania in a world context; regional interdependence; Australia; New Zealand; the South Pacific islands; future outlook; and a statistical factfile. The chapter on the South Pacific islands (p. 155-83) discusses land and people; government and political structure; structure of the economy; primary production; and external position.

American Samoa

554 **Commercialization and political change in American Samoa.**
Melvin Ember. In: *Explorations in cultural anthropology: essays in honor of George Peter Murdock.* Edited by Ward H. Goodenough. New York: McGraw Hill, 1964, p. 95-110. bibliog.

This essay seeks to provide data on the relationship of commercialization and political change, based on research in Pago Pago and Malaeloa (Tutuila, American Samoa), and in Ofu in the Manu'a group, 1955-56. Two indicators of commercialization were chosen: the proportion of people with full-time, money-earning jobs; and the proportion of houses in the village which were non-Samoan in type (i.e. with a metal roof). Pago Pago was the most commercialized, Ofu the least. There is a linear relationship of commercialization and political change in American Samoa: 'The more a contemporary village has become commercialized, the more it has discarded the traditional political system'.

555 **The first Five Year Plan for the territorial development of American Samoa: agricultural resources 1983-1987.**
Fotuali'i Uele Sutter. Pago Pago: Office of Economic Development and Planning, Government of American Samoa, 1982. 81p. maps.

Represents the first, ambitious attempt to plan the agricultural development of American Samoa, on the basis of a realistic inventory of resources.

Western Samoa

556 **Country presentation: Samoa.**
United Nations Conference on Trade and Development. Secretariat; Government of Western Samoa. New York; Geneva: United Nations, 1990. 21p. (UNCLDC II/CP.13).

An authoritative summary of the salient facts regarding Western Samoan economic development, economic policy, development planning and development aid, prepared for the 2nd United Nations Conference on the Least Developed Countries, held in Paris in 1990.

557 **The cult of custom meets the search for money in Western Samoa.**
Tim O'Meara. In: *Contemporary Pacific societies: studies in development and change*. Edited by Victoria S. Lockwood, Thomas G. Harding, Ben J. Wallace. Englewood Cliffs, New Jersey: Prentice Hall, 1993, p. 135-55. bibliog. (p. 335-60).

'Though the material signs of modernization have increased rapidly in Western Samoa since independence, internally generated development has been illusive'. The search for money is profoundly changing Samoan culture, even in the more remote and traditional villages of Savai'i. O'Meara outlines the traditional *matai* system and its control of resources; the changes in land tenure; and the effects of money and cash cropping on every aspect of economic, social, political and ceremonial life.

558 **From the outside, looking in.**
Felise Va'a. In: *The Pacific way: social issues in national development*. Edited by Sione Tupouniua, Ron Crocombe, Claire Slatter. Suva: South Pacific Social Sciences Association, 1975, p. 71-72. Reprinted, 1983.

Felise Va'a, a Western Samoan journalist, comments critically on local development planning. Most projects are suggested by public servants, there is comparatively little innovation and plans can be 'geared to the present at the expense of the future'. A more co-ordinated approach towards development planning is needed, with an independent government body to advise the cabinet on development priorities. Politicians are prone to 'decision paralysis'. See also: 'Western Samoa: the Samoan Methodist land development programme' by R. Lechte, in *Appropriate technology for development: a discussion and case histories*, edited by D. D. Evans, L. N. Adler (Boulder, Colorado: Westview Press, 1979, p. 249-62); and *Samoan values and economic development* by Vaiao J. Ala'ilima, Fay C. Ala'ilima (Honolulu: Institute of Advanced Projects, East-West Center, 1964. 13p. bibliog.), an informed discussion of Samoan traditional values, based on *fa'amatai* and on *'āiga* land tenure, as they affect modern economic development. This paper later appeared, with the same title, in the East-West Center's journal *East-West Center Review* (vol. 1, no. 3 [1965], p. 3-18. bibliog.).

559 **New Zealand and the South Pacific: a guide to economic development in the Cook Islands, Fiji, Niue, Tonga and Western Samoa.**

Edited by Anthony Haas. Wellington: Asia Pacific Research Unit, 1977. 118p. bibliog.

Also available in five parts, this is an expert survey of projects in the territories where New Zealand economic and technical aid is of crucial importance. Development problems and prospects are realistically assessed. See also: *The development of Western Samoa, 1971-1972* (Western Samoa. Department of Economic Development. Apia: Department of Economic Development, 1972. 117p.), a review of progress in 1971 and annual plan for 1972, with statistical data on economic and social development ten years on from Western Samoa's achievement of political independence; and *Un inventaire économique des Samoa occidentales* (An economic inventory of Western Samoa) by V. D. Stace (Nouméa, New Caledonia: Commission du Pacifique Sud, 1955. 146p.), an outline of the economic condition of Western Samoa ten years after the Second World War. A shorter version is available in English: *Western Samoa: an economic survey* (Nouméa, New Caledonia: South Pacific Commission, 1956. 76p. [SPC Technical Paper, no. 91]).

560 **Pacific islands: Papua New Guinea, Fiji, Solomon Islands, Western Samoa, Vanuatu, Tonga: country report.**

London: Economist Intelligence Unit, 1993. 75p.

Provides summary reports on the prevailing economic conditions, political trends, and government of each country, based on official data, and with prognostications of the likely course of development. American Samoa is excluded.

561 **Remittances and their impact: a study of Tonga and Western Samoa.**

Dennis A. Ahlburg. Canberra: National Centre for Development Studies, Research School of Pacific Studies, Australian National University, 1991. 70p. bibliog. (Pacific Policy Paper, no. 7).

A searching and well documented inquiry into the importance of remittances by migrants in these MIRAB island economies. In the case of Western Samoa, such remittances, from New Zealand and, to a lesser extent, from the United States, form a substantial part of the available money supply, at times outstripping export earnings by as much as 300 per cent.

562 **Samoan planters: tradition and economic development in Polynesia.**

J. Tim O'Meara. Fort Worth, Texas: Holt, Rinehart & Winston, 1990. 242p. maps. bibliog. (Case Studies in Cultural Anthropology).

Beautifully written and enlivened with engaging personal anecdotes, this 'reflective' ethnography is an honest (and by far the best) account of real life in a Samoan community. O'Meara presents an impressive array of data on land and household economies, on traditional and individualized land tenure, and on planters' attitudes to production, mainly in southern Savai'i. Samoan planters' decisions are rational, rather than tradition-bound, and agricultural market conditions are so bad that effort does not pay; wage labour and remittances are seen as better sources of income. See also 'Samoa: customary individualism' by J. Tim O'Meara, in *Land tenure in the Pacific*, edited by R. G. Crocombe (Suva: Institute of Pacific Studies, University of the South Pacific, 1987, p. 74-113. bibliog.).

563 Samoan village economy.

Brian Lockwood. Melbourne: Oxford University Press, 1971. 232p. maps. bibliog.

A detailed study of the change from subsistence to market economy in Western Samoa, as exemplified in 1966 by the villages Uafato, Poutasi, Utuali'i on 'Upolu, and Taga on Savai'i. Lockwood concludes: 'Although the villagers respond to market incentives in a predictable way they rarely responded as fully as they could given their resource situation'.

564 Tradition and economic progress in Samoa: a case study of the role of traditional social institutions in economic development.

David Pitt. Oxford: Clarendon Press; New York: Oxford University Press, 1970. 295p. maps. bibliog.

Pitt investigates: the 'overrated' role of Europeans in economic development; Samoan economic values; production; subsistence and sale; the economic aspect of status; property; chiefs and community; village wage labour in town; village capital formation; and trading institutions. He concludes that 'local economic development can be internally generated, achieved mainly through traditional (*fa'asāmoa*) values and institutions'. The most important dynamic in this internal generation is the strong desire for European goods. More recognition should be given to local or traditional resources, capital and incentives.

565 The Western Samoan economy: paving the way for sustainable growth and stability.

Fairbarn Pacific Consultants Pty. Ltd., Kolone Va'ai and Associates. Canberra: AIDAB, 1994. 94p. bibliog.

A critical analysis of the state and problems of the Western Samoan economy, which provides short-term and longer-term recommendations for its improvement and eventual stabilization on a sustainable basis. See also: *Western Samoa: the experience of slow growth and resource imbalance* by Shahid Yusuf, R. Kyle Peters (Washington, DC: The World Bank, 1985. 27p. bibliog. [World Bank Staff Working Papers, no. 754]), a searching analysis of economic and social conditions, in the light of virtual stagnation in agricultural production and of resource inadequacies; *A guide to investment* by the Department of Trade, Commerce and Industry, Western Samoa (Apia: Department of Trade, Commerce and Industry, [1995]. unpaginated [14 leaves]), an official outline of investment opportunities and incentives, and of the procedures to be observed; and *Indigenous entrepreneurship in Western Samoa* by C. Ross Croulet, Laki Sio (Honolulu: Pacific Islands Development Program [PIDP], 1986. 148p. bibliog.), a well documented study of Samoan business enterprises, many of them small in scale, and of the organizational problems and financial risks involved.

566 **The Western Samoan economy: prospects for recovery and long-term growth.**

Te'o Ian Fairbairn. Canberra: Australian Government Publishing Service, 1991. 57p. bibliog.

Each sector of the economy of Western Samoa is assessed, to discover signs of decline or growth, and to estimate future possibilities. Tourism is likely to develop considerably if infrastructural problems can be overcome. However, remittances may begin to decline in economic importance. In all sectors, the future appears uncertain, even precarious, despite some sporadic signs of short-term improvement. See also 'Samoa: development performances and prospects' by Te'o I. J. Fairbairn, in *Least developed countries of Asia and the Pacific* (Bangkok: ESCAP, 1990. vol. 2, p. 73-107. bibliog.), a thorough appraisal of development progress and problems up to Western Samoa's Sixth Development Plan. For its aims see *Western Samoa's sixth development plan 1988-1990* by the Government of Western Samoa (Apia: Department of Economic Development, 1987). For subsequent aims see *Western Samoa seventh development plan 1992-1994* by the Government of Western Samoa (Apia: National Planning Office, 1992. 96p. [DP7]). Earlier studies include: 'The Samoan economy: some recent developments' by I. J. Fairbairn (*Journal of Pacific History*, vol. 5 [1970], p. 135-39); 'A survey of local industries in Western Samoa' by I. J. Fairbairn (*Pacific Viewpoint*, vol. 12 [1971], p. 103-22); and 'Village economics in Western Samoa' by I. J. Fairbairn (*Journal of the Polynesian Society*, vol. 79, no. 1 [March 1970], p. 54-70. bibliog.).

567 **Zum Beispiel Samoa.** (For example Samoa.)

Götz Mackensen. Bremen, Germany: Übersee-Museum Bremen, 1977. 483p. bibliog. (Veröffentlichungen aus dem Übersee-Museum Bremen. Reihe G: Bremer Südpazifik-Archiv. Band 1).

An authoritative and well documented critical history of socio-economic change in Samoa from the beginning of colonial penetration in 1830 to the establishment of Western Samoa as an independent state in 1962. Mackensen also analyses Western Samoa's development plans from 1962 to 1970. Eight appendices cover geographical data; population; a chronology; external trade, 1910-70; employment; a useful bibliography; and a glossary of Samoan terms. For an official view of the public sector in development, see *Western Samoa public sector investment programme 1992/93-1994/95* by the Government of Western Samoa (Apia: National Planning Office, Prime Minister's Department, 1992. 76p. [PSIP]).

Finance, Banking and National Accounts

American Samoa

568 **American Samoa Government. Comprehensive Annual Financial Report.**
Pago Pago: Government of American Samoa, 1951- . annual.

This indispensable serial contains detailed accounts for the preceding year, together with summaries of trends and key fiscal indicators.

Western Samoa

569 **The Development Bank of Western Samoa: a profile.**
P. G. H. Carroll. Canberra: National Centre for Development Studies, Australian National University, 1984. 61p. (Working Paper, no. 39).

A thorough examination of the structure, internal organization, financing and investment policies of the crucial agency of development in Western Samoa.

570 **Domestic and national savings of Western Samoa, 1982-1992: an empirical investigation.**
T. K. Jayaraman. Kensington, New South Wales: Centre for South Pacific Studies, University of New South Wales, 1993. 24p. (Pacific Studies Monographs, no. 10).

A senior economist of the Asian Development Bank examines the trends in savings of Western Samoa and analyses its savings behaviour during 1982-1992, using a simple econometric model. Western Samoa experienced negative domestic savings in that period, but a high rate of gross domestic investment, averaging about 25 per cent of GDP up to 1989 and around 35 per cent from 1990 to 1992. External aid contributed to exchange rate stability, so avoiding frequent currency adjustments. Jayaraman stresses the importance of remittances.

571 **Financial institutions and markets in the South Pacific: a study of New Caledonia, Solomon Islands, Tonga, Vanuatu, and Western Samoa.**

Michael T. Skully. London: Macmillan, 1987. 379p. maps. bibliog.

An expert appraisal, with case-studies and comparative data, on the institutions essential to trade, development and economic activity generally. The structural weaknesses of the Western Samoan economy are considered, in the context of its national indebtedness, vulnerable export trade, excessive imports and dependence on aid and remittances.

572 **Monetary policy formulation in Western Samoa.**

Ariya C. Randeni. *Pacific Economic Bulletin*, vol. 6, no. 2 (1991), p. 32-39. bibliog.

An outline of the role and influence of financial and credit institutions in determining Western Samoa's monetary policy. See also *World debt tables 1994-95: external finance for developing countries* (Washington, DC: The World Bank, 1995. 2 vols.) which provides complete and up-to-date information on the external debt of and financial flows to developing countries, including Western Samoa. Volume one provides analysis and summary of the data; volume two consists of country tables. This report is also available as 3½" PC-compatible data diskettes and STARS retrieval program.

573 **National accounts of Western Samoa 1984-1986.**

Asian Development Bank. Economics and Development Resource Center. Manila: Asian Development Bank, 1990. 102p. (Technical Assistance Report).

Published accounts for 1984-86 are critically analysed in order to determine the adequacy of the national accounting methods used and the value of the accounts for economic forecasting. Improved systems and methods are recommended.

574 **The national income of Western Samoa.**

Ian J. Fairbairn. Melbourne: Oxford University Press, 1973. 215p. maps. bibliog.

This detailed economic study is concerned with the national income of Western Samoa for selected years from 1947 to 1970. Estimates of income produced are given by individual sectors and these are then combined to derive tables of national income for the country as a whole. Special attention is paid to village structure, to subsistence production and, in the latter part of the period under review, to industrial development. Surveys of cash income, expenditure, subsistence production and work effort were made in the rural villages of Taga (Savai'i) and Poutasi ('Upolu). Despite many problems, much has been done to lay the foundation for economic development. Agriculture, banking and credit, and rural infrastructure need to be further strengthened.

Trade and Industry

Trade

19th century

575 **The financial adventures of J. C. Godeffroy and Son in the Pacific.**
A. E. Bollard. *Journal of Pacific History*, vol. 16, no. 1 (Jan. 1981), p. 3-19. bibliog.

The Hamburg firm J. C. Godeffroy & Sohn and its successor, the DHPG, ruled the Pacific market economies, especially Samoa and Tonga, throughout the latter half of the 19th century. This was achieved through political domination and economic efficiency. A third factor in their control was finance. The Godeffroy company promoted debased South American currencies as a medium of exchange for the Pacific, thereby dominating and exploiting the small economies. Bollard concludes: 'With an almost Machiavellian cunning, Godeffroys had bought themselves great wealth and power, and they had paid in counterfeit coin'.

576 **German firms in the Western Pacific, 1857-1914.**
Stewart Firth. In: *Germany in the Pacific and Far East, 1870-1914*. Edited by John A. Moses, Paul M. Kennedy. St. Lucia, Queensland: University of Queensland Press, 1977, p. 3-25. bibliog.

An overview of German trade in the islands, including Samoa where the economy was dominated by the DHPG. This was originally published in *Journal of Pacific History*, vol. 8 (1973), p. 10-28. bibliog.

577 **J. C. Godeffroy & Sohn: Kaufleute zu Hamburg: Leistung und Schicksal eines Welthandelshauses.** (J. C. Godeffroy & Sohn: Hamburg merchants: achievement and fate of a world trading firm.)
Kurt Schmack. Hamburg, Germany: Verlag Broschek, 1938. 312p. map. bibliog.

This authoritative history of the Godeffroy Company centres on its progress in South America and Australia, from 1837 to 1857, and in the South Seas from 1857 to 1880. Āpia became the firm's main port and its representative, Theodor Ludwig August Weber, German consul and arbiter of Samoan political life. Plates include: a view of Āpia (20); Theodor Weber (21); the German consulate in Āpia (22); the first maps (1899) of the Samoan islands (with Rose Atoll) (28); and maps of Samoa in 1910 (32). Appendices include a genealogical chart of the Godeffroy family, and the German text of the Treaty of Friendship between the German Kaiser and the Samoan Ta'imua government, signed at Āpia on 24 January 1879. An earlier study is still useful: *Das Hamburger Seehandelshaus J. C. Godeffroy und Sohn* (The Hamburg maritime trading company of J. C. Godeffroy and Son) by Richard Hertz (Hamburg, Germany: Verein für Hamburgische Geschichte, 1992 [Veröffentlichungen, Bd. 6]). See also *White falcon: the house of Godeffroy and its commercial and scientific role in the Pacific* by Florence M. Spoehr (Palo Alto, California: Pacific Books, 1963).

578 **Private interests and the origins of American involvement in Samoa, 1872-1877.**
Barry Rigby. *Journal of Pacific History*, vol. 8 (1973), p. 75-87. bibliog.

An investigation of the Samoan interests of William H. Webb, an influential New York shipowner, Captain Edgar Wakeman, and James B. M. Stewart, who had begun buying land in Samoa in 1871. Stewart set up the Central Polynesian Land and Commercial Company in San Francisco in December 1871. Wakeman arranged that the USS *Narragansett* should visit Pago Pago in 1872, where Commander Richard W. Meade signed a document with the local chief, Mauga, granting use of the harbour as a naval station to the United States. Webb recommended to President Ulysses S. Grant that Colonel Albert B. Steinberger be sent to Samoa as an official observer. Private interests thus paved the way to the American annexation of Eastern Samoa.

579 **To California and the South Seas: the diary of Albert G. Osbun, 1849-1851.**
Albert G. Osbun, edited by John Haskell Kemble. San Marino, California: Huntington Library, 1966. 233p. 2 maps.

Dr Osbun went to California to mine for gold, then organized an expedition to Samoa, Wallis Island, Fanning Island and Hermes and Pearl reefs to buy supplies for the San Francisco market. Seventy-three pages are devoted to this voyage to the South Pacific, with many details on the islands and their people.

580 **Tom De Wolf's Pacific venture: the life history of a commercial enterprise in Samoa.**
Doug Munro. *Pacific Studies*, vol. 3, no. 2 (Spring 1980), p. 22-40. bibliog.

J. S. De Wolf & Co. was a Liverpool shipping and merchant firm founded in 1840 by two Canadian brothers, John Starr and James Ratchford De Wolf. It entered the island trade in copra in the late 1870s, using Āpia as its base. Tom De Wolf arrived in Āpia on 15 June 1879 and set himself up in direct opposition to the Godeffroy company. Louis Becke was De Wolf's agent at Nanumanga for a time, and dedicated his *Pacific tales* (London: T. Fisher Unwin, 1897. 323p.) to his former employer. The firm finally wound up its affairs in 1933. See also 'Note on the De Wolf family of Nova Scotia' by Esther Clark Wright (*Pacific Studies*, vol. 3, no. 2 [Spring 1980], p. 41-42).

20th century

581 **Foreign trade statistics of Asia and the Pacific.**
Bangkok: United Nations Economic and Social Commission for Asia and the Pacific, 1987- . annual.

Formerly issued as two series, *A* and *B*, this unified annual provides, in matrix form, detailed data on regional commodity trade, with origins, destinations and trade flows. Data for each major state in the Asia-Pacific Basin (including Western Samoa) are presented individually.

582 **Forum island countries and the single European market, 1992.**
David Butcher. Wellington: Institute of Policy Studies, Victoria University of Wellington, 1993. 133p. bibliog.

An attempt to foresee likely consequences that the achievement, in 1992, of a single European market might entail for Western Samoa and other members of the South Pacific Forum (some of which are also in the ACP group covered by the Lomé Convention).

583 **Islands Business Pacific.**
Suva: Islands Business International, 1990- . monthly.

Formerly *Islands Business News*, this useful periodical covers all aspects of business activity in the Pacific, with features on specific developments, a digest of current events, and reviews of relevant publications.

584 **Produce marketing in a Polynesian society: Apia, Western Samoa.**
B. A. Lockwood. In: *Pacific market-places: a collection of essays.* Edited by H. C. Brookfield. Canberra: Australian National University Press, 1969, p. 97-114. map.

Lockwood presents a detailed study of the commercial market in Āpia, made on 30 July 1966. The circumstances were abnormal, as the hurricane of 29 January 1966 had wrought considerable damage to both cash crops and food crops throughout Western Samoa. At least 254 sellers were active, most having come into Āpia by bus, a few even from Savai'i. The total value of all commodities recorded was Samoan £754. Seventy-nine per cent of the produce on offer consisted of Samoan foodstuffs, especially *talo* (seventy-nine per cent of the whole). Nothing was sold by weight. Prices were adjusted by varying quantity. For many sellers the market was their only source of money.

585 **South Pacific trade directory 1995: Pacific ACP states and French territories.**
Suva: South Pacific Forum Secretariat, 1995. 414p.

This elaborate directory is designed to promote trade, internationally and regionally, by identifying businesses and products in each country. 'International Trade organisations' (p. 8-12) is followed by 'Country profiles' and 'Company profiles' (Western Samoa: p. 313-28), and by 'Buyers' guide' (p. 329-414), classified by product and territory. Addresses, telephone and fax numbers, and type of business are given for each firm or official body. Introductory explanations are in English and French. This represents an excellent survey of business and governmental activity in Western Samoa, with information not easily to be found elsewhere.

586 **SPEC bibliography.**
Suva: South Pacific Bureau for Economic Cooperation, 1974. 3rd ed. 76p.

This bibliography of trade and economic development in all Pacific island territories is arranged by commodity (e.g. copra, phosphate) and by country, with publications of international organizations and of SPEC member governments particularly well represented.

587 **Western Samoa national trade and investment directory.**
Compiled by John Crighton. Suva: South Pacific Bureau for Economic Cooperation (SPEC), for Commonwealth Regional Consultative Group on Trade, 1986. 57p. maps.

A comprehensive guide to governmental agencies and to major commercial concerns and financial institutions operating in Western Samoa, providing all essential access information in each case.

Industry

American Samoa

588 **La mise en conserve du thon à Pago-Pago.** (Tuna canning at Pago Pago.)
François Doumenge. In: *L'homme dans le Pacifique Sud: étude géographique* (Man in the South Pacific: a geographical study). François Doumenge. Paris: Société des Océanistes, 1966, p. 496-511. 2 maps. bibliog. (p. 593-622).

A well documented history of the establishment of tuna canning plants in Tutuila, of their financial vicissitudes, and of the consequences for Samoan society. The maps indicate the origins, in Western Samoa and American Samoa, of the workers employed and trained by the several plants. Doumenge considers that the dependence of American Samoa can only be solved by continued integration in the economy of the USA.

Agriculture, Forestry, Fisheries and Food

Land policy and management

589 **Bibliography of soil fertility and soil management in Pacific Island countries.**

Alexander Lincoln. Suva: South Pacific Commission, 1995. 212p.

Arranged by country and topic, this extensive, briefly annotated bibliography includes American Samoa and Western Samoa.

590 **Pacificland News.**

Suva: IBSRAM Pacific Regional Office, 1994- . monthly.

The bulletin of the Pacificland Network of the International Board for Soil Research and Management, which focuses on the management of sloping lands in the South Pacific. Problems of severe land erosion, as found in Western Samoa and American Samoa, are also discussed. See also *Journal for Hawaiian and Pacific Agriculture* (Hilo, Hawai'i: College of Agriculture, University of Hawai'i at Hilo, 1988- . irregular), which publishes technical reports on all aspects of agriculture in tropical areas.

591 **Western Samoa: social consequences of government acquisition.**

Pamela Thomas. In: *Land, people, and government: public lands policy in the South Pacific*. Edited by Peter Larmour, A. Taungenga, Ron Crocombe. Suva: Institute of Pacific Studies, University of the South Pacific; Lincoln Institute of Land Policy, 1981, p. 45-54. bibliog.

A critique of land acquisition by the government of Western Samoa, which focuses on the consequent social disruption and hardship. For a broader analysis, see 'Society, land and law: land policy in Western Samoa' by Pamela Thomas (*Pacific Islands Land Review* [Port Moresby], vol. 1 [1984]).

Agriculture

Traditional

592 **Cultivation in old Samoa.**
R. F. Watters. *Economic Geography*, vol. 34 (1958), p. 338-51. map. bibliog.

A study of cultivation as it was practised in Samoa about 1840, only ten years after the beginning of regular European contact. Based mainly on accounts by Charles Wilkes, J. B. Stair and George Turner, it presents a fully documented picture of indigenous practices and of the landscape before the intrusion of Western influences significantly modified their nature. Taro growing and shifting cultivation were of primary importance, and irrigation was absent. See also: 'Some forms of shifting cultivation in the South-West Pacific' by R. F. Watters (*Journal of Tropical Geography* [Singapore], vol. 14 [July 1960], p. 35-50. maps. bibliog.), which describes bush fallow farming in an environmental context, especially in Samoa and Fiji; and 'The nature of shifting cultivation: a review of recent research' by R. F. Watters (*Pacific Viewpoint*, vol. 1, no. 1 [1960], p. 59-99. bibliog.), a worldwide review which pays particular attention to the occurrence of shifting cultivation and its impact on vegetation in Fiji and Samoa. An extensive bibliography is provided and both papers contain many photographs of this mode of farming.

German Samoa

593 **German plantations in the South Seas before 1914.**
Yves Pehaut. Bordeaux, France: CRET, 1990. 218p. maps. bibliog.

Includes a detailed history and description of the extensive German-owned plantations on 'Upolu and Savai'i, especially those of the DHPG. See also 'German plantations in Samoa: report dated August 15, 1888, in Samoa' by Harold Marsh Sewall (*United States Trade Reports*, vol. 27, no. 97 [Sept. 1888], p. 409-11), a summary report by the American consul-general in Āpia which provides details of the ownership, extent, crops, productivity, management and labour force of German plantations in Samoa, with brief comments on practices good and bad. Sewall is described by Robert Louis Stevenson, in his *A footnote to history* (q.v.), as 'a young man of high spirit and a generous disposition' by no means happy with US policy, and 'grasping at every opportunity to thrust a stick into the German wheels'. See also *Pflanzung und Siedlung auf Samoa* (Plantation and settlement in Samoa), by Ferdinand Wohltmann (Berlin: Kolonialwirtschaftliches Komitee, 1904. 164p. maps), a sober, realistic analysis of the plantation economy of German Samoa and the opportunities afforded for German settlement.

American Samoa

594 **Land utilization in American Samoa.**
John Wesley Coulter. Honolulu: Bernice P. Bishop Museum, 1941. 50p. 2 maps. bibliog. (Bulletin, no. 170).

Based on fieldwork carried out in American Samoa in 1937, this is a broad survey of the interaction of human activities with the physical environment. Main factors in change identified by Coulter are an increase in population, education and Western contacts. He stresses the need for changes 'that may be thought beneficial' to be gradually effected in order that they may be properly assimilated into Samoan culture without abruptly changing the social order. A subsequent case-study is 'The copra industry of the Manua Islands and Swain's Island of American Samoa' by T. G. Hatakeyama (*Oléagineux*, vol. 24, no. 6 [June 1969], p. 357-60), the most expert and authoritative of the very few accounts of copra production in the islands of Ta'ū, Ofu and Olosega in the Manu'a group, and in Swain's Island, between Samoa and Tokelau.

Agricultural Development in the American Pacific (ADAP) Program.
See item no. 687.

Western Samoa

595 **Alafua Agricultural Bulletin.**
Alafua, Western Samoa: School of Agriculture, University of the South Pacific, 1976- . quarterly.

Provides essential reading for news and discussion of agricultural research and practice in Samoa, and elsewhere in the USP region.

596 **The cocoa rehabilitation project in Western Samoa.**
L. Andrews. Canberra: National Centre for Development Studies, Australian National University, 1987. 44p. (IA 87002).

One of Western Samoa's main cash crops, cocoa is vulnerable because of fluctuations of price on the international market, and because of pest and disease damage. Production has at times stagnated because of low profitability, and of neglect. Total production in 1990 was estimated at 1,000 metric tons. Exports of cocoa beans have declined, from 2,143,000 *tala* in value in 1989 to merely 6,000 *tala* in 1991. Andrews' study relates to the plans for rehabilitation of cocoa growing formulated just as this slide in exports began.

597 **Let us feed ourselves.**
F. S. Wendt (Tuaopepe). *Alafua Agricultural Bulletin*, vol. 7, no. 3 (1982), p. 13-18.

Professor Felix Wendt, Head of the University of the South Pacific School of Agriculture at Alafua, Western Samoa, cogently presents the case for developing local agriculture, horticulture, fisheries and animal husbandry so as to meet the food needs of the indigenous population and so obviate reliance on imported foodstuffs. See also: 'Ways of increasing food production in Western Samoa' by D. Betham (Afamasaga) (*Alafua Agricultural Bulletin*, vol. 7, no. 3 [1982], p. 27-30); 'The productivity of Samoan village agriculture' by W. J. Barratt (*Proceedings of the Minnesota Academy of Sciences* [1961], p. 73-82); 'Land tenure and agricultural productivity in Western Samoa' by Fred Opio (*Journal of South Pacific Agriculture*, vol. 1, no. 3 [1992], p. 27-33); and *Workshop on Post Harvest Losses, South Pacific, Apia, Western Samoa, 25-31 May 1983, report* (London: Commonwealth Secretariat, 1984. 125p.).

598 **Past and present practices in agriculture and fisheries in Samoa.**
A. Tolova'a. In: *Land use and agriculture.* Edited by John Morrison, Paul Geraghty, Linda Crowl. Suva: Institute of Pacific Studies, University of the South Pacific, 1994, p. 223-30. (Science of Pacific Island Peoples, vol. 2).

Tolova'a deplores sawmills, chainsaws, pesticides, insecticides and weed killers. Paraquat, the preferred means of suicide by young Samoans, is seen as wholly undesirable: 'Weed killers and fertilizers benefit the producers rather than the planters'. Outboard motors, despite their many advantages, cause some problems: fishermen venture too far from shore, and, if the engine expires, it is not easy to paddle back to land, as in a canoe. See also: 'Western Samoa and its agriculture' by M. Asghar, F. S. Wendt (*Muslim Scientist: Journal of the Association of Muslim Scientists and Engineers*, vol. 9, nos. 3 & 4 [Sept. & Dec. 1980], p. 52-84), a realistic overview of Western Samoan agriculture in 1980 (p. 52-65) and of constraints and choices (p. 66-84); 'Agriculture in Western Samoa – from a producer's point of view' by D. Betham (Afamasaga) (*Alafua Agricultural Bulletin*, vol. 7, no. 1 [1982], p. 13-17); 'The agricultural sector of Western Samoa' by R. J. Burgess (*Alafua Agricultural Bulletin*, vol. 7, no. 1 [1982], p. 18-35); and 'Changing village agriculture in Western Samoa' by J. H. Mercer, P. Scott (*Geographical Journal*, vol. 124, no. 3 [Sept. 1958], p. 347-60. maps. bibliog.), which includes information on cultivation and associated secondary vegetation, with land use-vegetation maps.

599 **Western Samoa.**
In: *South Pacific agriculture: choices and constraints: South Pacific agricultural survey 1979.* Edited by R. Gerard Ward, Andrew Proctor. Manila: Asian Development Bank; Canberra: Australian National University Press, 1980, p. 395-406. map. bibliog. (p. 503-12).

A sober, expert assessment of the state of Western Samoan agriculture in 1976-77, characterized by stagnation, and of the government's response. The importance for Samoan economic viability of the export of services through migration is highlighted. Far more important, in the quest for increased export earnings, will be the rate of growth in agriculture. The need for progression in management practices in agriculture is crucial. For a later account of developments, see 'Agricultural policy and projects in the Solomon Islands, Western Samoa, and Fiji' by J. A. Young, H. M. Gunsaekera (*South Pacific Forum*, vol. 1, no. 1 [1984], p. 1-31).

600 **Western Samoa's census of agriculture: major features and implications for development.**

Te'o Ian John Fairbairn. Kensington, New South Wales: Centre for South Pacific Studies, University of New South Wales, 1993. 26p. (Pacific Studies Monograph, no. 7).

Fairbairn analyses the census data to highlight the main characteristics of agriculture in Western Samoa. He ventures a number of predictions as to how the islands' principal economic resource may progress in future, stressing the need for sustainable and environmentally friendly development. This brief work is available free of charge on application to CSPS. See also: 'The Samoan farmer: a reluctant object of change?' by Per Ronnas (*Development and Change*, vol. 24, no. 2 [1993], p. 339-62. bibliog.); 'Current development issues in Western Samoan agriculture and the contribution of aid: lessons for the Pacific' by F. S. Wendt (Tuaopepe) (*Alafua Agricultural Bulletin*, vol. 8, no. 1 [Jan.-March 1983], p. 5-14); 'A critique of agricultural development policies in Western Samoa' by M. J. Blackie (*Alafua Agricultural Bulletin*, vol. 3, no. 2 [1978], p. 7-8); and 'Agricultural mechanization in Western Samoa' by T. Fyhri (*Alafua Agricultural Bulletin*, vol. 1, no. 2 [1976], p. 6-9).

601 **Women and agriculture in Western Samoa.**

Peggy Fairbairn-Dunlop. In: *Different places, different voices: gender and development in Africa, Asia and Latin America.* Edited by Janet H. Momsen, Vivian Kinnaird. London; New York: Routledge, 1993, p. 211-23. bibliog.

The author is an authority on Samoan agriculture, traditional and modern, and on the part played by women, which is likely to continue to grow in importance. She stresses the vital role of agricultural extension education in showing new possibilities and in equipping women with the knowledge and skills needed to meet them successfully. See also *Women's roles in South Pacific agriculture: traditional, transitional and modern roles of women with specific focus on Papua New Guinea, Fiji, Western Samoa and Tonga* by Claire Slatter (Honolulu: Institute of Culture and Communication, 1984. 55p. bibliog.), which provides enlightening comparisons of the extent to which women's roles in agriculture have changed. In Western Samoa, women continue to be active in village gardening, but have also assumed important responsibilities in marketing vegetables and other agricultural produce. See also 'The role of women in nutrition and food production: agrarian reform' by N. Simi (*Alafua Agricultural Bulletin*, vol. 8, no. 2 [1983], p. 118-20).

Forestry

American Samoa

602 **American Samoa resource management bibliography.**
Compiled and edited by P. A. Knudsen, K. D. Kluge, R. D. Volk. [Pago Pago]: Le Vaomatua, 1992. 38p.

A valuable guide to natural-resource literature, particularly relating to forests.

603 **A look at the forests of American Samoa.**
R. E. Nelson. Berkeley, California: Pacific South-west Forest and Range Experimental Station; Washington, DC: U.S. Forest Service, U.S. Department of Agriculture, 1964. 14p. (U.S. Forest Service Research Note, PSW-53).

A brief, expert description, by a forester, of forest vegetation, tree species and timber potential, particularly on Tutuila. See also *Report on forestry in American Samoa* by C. Marshall (Washington, DC: Pacific Science Board, National Research Council, 1951. 172p. bibliog.), an assessment of forest resources, extractive practices, economic potential, and conservation needs. For a visual impression of the tropical rain forest of Tutuila, see 'Forestry views of American Samoa' by R. E. Nelson, T. Annastas (*Unasylva*, vol. 20, no. 4 [1966], p. 23-27).

Western Samoa

604 **Diurnal CO_2 exchange and photosynthesis of the Samoa tropical forest.**
S. Ryan. *Global Biogeochemical Cycles*, vol. 4, no. 1 (1990), p. 69-84. bibliog.

A clear discussion of the daily chemical and biological processes in a rain forest. Though primarily scientific in purpose and language, this is a unique and vivid account of the make-up and vibrant life of the great forests which still cover most of the interior uplands of the high islands of both American Samoa and Western Samoa.

605 **Forestry development in Western Samoa.**
I. Reti. *New Zealand Journal of Forestry*, vol. 28, no. 3 (1983), p. 423-31.

An overview of forestry policy, practice and prospects. For a highly personal view of how forests are exploited, see 'Forest management in developing countries: experiences of a New Zealand forester in Western Samoa' by I. G. Trotman (*New Zealand Journal of Forestry*, vol. 24, no. 2 [1979], p. 252-60). 'Forests – an impediment to agriculture?' by S. S. Sesega (*Alafua Agricultural Bulletin*, vol. 7, no. 1 [1982], p. 55-66) is a reasoned comment on the arguments of those who advocate forest clearance, to make way for plantations and gardens. It explains the ecological and economic importance of tropical rain forests and insists on the need to protect them. Earlier discussions include: 'The Territory of Western Samoa' by T. S. Thompson (*Empire Forestry Review* [London], vol. 32 [1953], p. 309-15), which includes notes on geology, topography, climate, soils, vegetation and forest management; and *Forestry in Western Samoa* by C. Marshall, T. S. Thompson (Wellington: Government Printer, 1953. 64p. bibliog.). For an illustrated review of this work, see 'Forestry in Western Samoa' by A. H. Kroon (*Quarterly Bulletin of the South Pacific Commission*, vol. 3, no. 3 [1953], p. 29-30).

606 **A forestry scheme in Samoa.**

Paul A. Shankman. *Natural History*, vol. 84, no. 8 (1975), p. 60-69.

The Potlatch Corporation, a giant of the North American lumber industry, was given a major timber concession by the Western Samoan government, in a deal widely held to be corrupt. Shankman examines the Corporation's influence on Western Samoa, and the likely harmful effects of uncontrolled logging. An official view is given in 'Timber development in Western Samoa' (*South Pacific Bulletin*, vol. 22, no. 3 [1972], p. 33-34). See also 'Notes on a corporate "potlatch": the lumber industry in Samoa' by Paul A. Shankman, in *The world as a company town: multinational corporations and social change*, edited by Ahamed and Elizabeth Idris-Soven, Mary K. Vaughan (The Hague: Mouton, 1978, p. 375-404. bibliog. [World Anthropology]), essential reading for environmentalists and democrats alike. Anthropologists will grasp, and relish, the 'potlatch' reference, with its connotation of a ceremonial share-out of wealth and its echo of a corporation name. See also 'Indigenous control of tropical rain-forest reserves: an alternative strategy for conservation' by Paul Alan Cox, Thomas Elmqvist (*Ambio: a Journal of the Human Environment* [Royal Swedish Academy of Sciences], vol. 20, no. 7 [1991], p. 317-21. bibliog.), which discusses how logging by foreign companies is destroying Samoa's forests and forest resources. The authors propose a series of radical conservation measures based on the social participation of Samoan communities and agencies.

607 **Properties and uses of the timbers of Western Samoa: indigenous hardwoods.**

Compiled by J. A. Kininmonth. Rotorua, New Zealand: Forest Research Institute, 1982. 56p. bibliog.

A systematic survey of the hardwood trees native to Samoa, with information on the traditional and modern uses made of them. See also: 'Forest plantation species selection for Western Samoa' by E. H. Nile (*Forest Genetic Resources Information*, no. 17 [1989], p. 2-6. bibliog.), in which Nile recommends trees and shrubs suitable for reafforestation in Western Samoa; 'The Samoan diameter stick' by R. G. Dixon (*Commonwealth Forestry Review*, vol. 52, no. 3 [1973], p. 266-69), a discussion of how Samoans measure tree girth; and *Tropical trees of the Pacific* by D. Hargreaves, B. Hargreaves (Lahaina, Hawai'i: Ross-Hargreaves, 1970. 64p.), a well illustrated guide to the trees commonly found in the islands. Each tree (and, occasionally, its flowers and fruit) is described, and illustrated by a colour plate. This represents a companion volume to the authors' *Tropical blossoms of the Pacific* (1970).

608 **Wind damage in the forest of Western Samoa.**
T. W. W. Wood. *Malayan Forester*, vol. 33, no. 1 (Jan. 1970), p. 92-99. bibliog.

Recurrent hurricanes regularly cause widespread damage in Samoa's forests, east and west. This is an informed discussion of the problem, illustrated with photographs of the ravages caused by cyclonic winds.

Fisheries

19th century

609 **Samoa's forgotten whaling heritage: American whaling in Samoan waters 1824-1878: a chronological selection of extracts from primary sources, mainly whaling logbooks, journals and contemporary news items.**
Rhys Richards. Wellington: Lithographic Services, [1992]. 208p. map. bibliog.

Published under the auspices of the Western Samoa Historical and Cultural Trust, this is a superb, well illustrated anthology covering the heyday of American whaling in the seas around Samoa. This had led to the appointment of United States consular agents at Āpia in November 1839 (J. C. Williams), at Pago Pago in 1847 (Henry Gibbons) and in Savai'i in 1854. Many Samoan families bear whaler surnames, such as Coffin, Hunkin, Jennings, Gibbons, Pereira, Stowers and Slade. The *fautasi* longboats that race for village honours each Independence Day are 'stretched' copies of early American whaleboats.

Samoa

610 **Bêche-de-mer of the tropical Pacific: a handbook for fishermen.**
South Pacific Commission. Nouméa, New Caledonia: South Pacific Commission, 1979. 29p. (SPC Handbooks, no. 18).

A revised version of *Bêche-de-mer of the South Pacific islands* (Nouméa, New Caledonia: South Pacific Commission, 1974), this illustrated handbook identifies and describes commercially valuable species of bêche-de-mer, or sea cucumbers (Holothurians), with supplementary notes on their collection, processing, packing and marketing.

American Samoa

611 **La pêche asiatique aux Samoa Américaines.** (Fishing by Asians in American Samoa.)
François Doumenge. In: *L'homme dans le Pacifique Sud: étude géographique* (Man in the South Pacific: a geographical study). François Doumenge. Paris: Société des Océanistes, 1966, p. 418-21. map. bibliog. (p. 593-622).

This historical account of the development, from 1954 to 1964, of fishing by Japanese, South Korean, Taiwanese and Okinawan vessels in American Samoan waters is soundly based on the archives of the Van Camp Sea Food Company, Pago Pago. The map (p. 420) illustrates the extension of tuna fishing grounds. A Japanese vessel, renamed *Atu'E*, was acquired for training Samoans as industrial fishermen. The experiment failed because of Samoan reluctance to remain at sea for weeks at a time, and the vessel was lost, with its Korean crew, off Pago Pago in the cyclone at the end of January 1966.

612 **A selectively annotated bibliography of social, cultural and economic material relating to fishery development in Hawaii, American Samoa, and Micronesia.**
Santa Cruz, California: Center for Coastal Marine Studies, University of California, Santa Cruz, 1980. 139 leaves. maps.

This work represents a novel project: to chart the human contexts relevant to the development of fishing industries. Anthropological and sociological studies are well represented in this submission to the Pacific Marine Fisheries Commission, and indexes are included.

613 **Sport fishing in Hawaii, Guam, and American Samoa: with charts to fishing grounds and an illustrated guide to Pacific fishes.**
James L. Squire, Jr., Susan E. Smith. Rutland, Vermont: Charles E. Tuttle, 1979. 53p.

Originally compiled for the US Department of Commerce, this guide lists 237 game fish, with their scientific, common and Hawaiian names. Each fish is illustrated, and its size, colour, distribution and habitats are given. Charts indicate shore fishing areas, coral reefs, locations of fishing facilities and sportfishing boat operations.

614 **The use of nearshore marine life as a food resource by American Samoans.**
Harry Burnette Hill. Honolulu: Pacific Islands Study Center, University of Hawai'i, 1978. 170p. bibliog. (Miscellaneous Work Papers, Pacific Islands Program 1978, no. 1).

An absorbing study of food gathering along the shore and of fishing in coastal waters, with special attention to shellfish and to the *palolo* worm (relished as a seasonal delicacy).

Western Samoa

615 **The role of women in small-scale fisheries in the South Pacific: report of case studies in the Cook Islands, Papua New Guinea, Solomon Islands, Tonga, Vanuatu and Western Samoa.**
Penelope Schoeffel, Sisilia Talagi. London: Commonwealth Secretariat, 1989. 60p. maps. bibliog.

This report surveys fisheries development and the involvement of women, aquaculture, and food and nutrition, and proposes development aid for harvesting, handling, processing and marketing. See also: *The role of women in small-scale fisheries in the South Pacific: report of a Consultation, University of the South Pacific, Tonga, 18-24 October, 1989* (London: Commonwealth Secretariat, 1990. 87p.), which discusses how the Consultation sought ways of implementing the recommendations of the 1989 report, especially with regard to coordination, training and financial support; and *Fishing for answers: women and fisheries in the Pacific Islands*, edited by Elizabeth Matthews (Suva: Women and Fisheries Network, 1995. 177p. maps), a collection of studies of the involvement of women in fishing and fisheries in the islands, including Samoa.

616 **The structure and role of the Fisheries Division in Western Samoa.**
James Crossland. Honiara, Solomon Islands: Forum Fisheries Agency (FFA), 1986. 101p.

Crossland outlines the organization, duties and activities of the body responsible for fisheries protection and development in Western Samoa, a member state of the South Pacific Forum Fisheries Agency. The context is outlined in 'The politics and economics of fisheries in the South Pacific' by Geoffrey Waugh, in *Resources, development and politics in the Pacific islands*, edited by Stephen Henningham, R. J. May, Lulu Turner (Bathurst, New South Wales: Crawford House Press, 1992, p. 170-78. bibliog.), which surveys the development of 'industrial' fishing in the South Pacific, by Japan, Korea, Taiwan, Russia and the United States, from about 1897. The problem of conserving tuna resources (important for Tutuila canneries) is examined in depth. See also *The development of fisheries in the South Pacific region with reference to Fiji, Solomon Islands, Vanuatu, Western Samoa and Tonga* by Geoffrey Waugh (Canberra: National Centre for Development Studies, Australian National University, 1986. [Island/Australia Working Paper, no. 86/2]).

617 **Western Samoa fisheries bibliography.**
Robert Gillett, Taniela Sua. Suva: UNDP/FAO Regional Fishery Support Programme, 1987. 77p. (RFSP Document, no. 87-6).

This bibliography is particularly useful for its extensive listing of reports and papers published by Western Samoan official agencies, by the South Pacific Commission, the Forum Fisheries Agency, and other international and intergovernmental bodies.

Past and present practices in agriculture and fisheries in Samoa.
See item no. 598.

Food, nutrition and recipes

618 **These roots remain: food habits in islands of the central and eastern Pacific since Western contact.**

Nancy J. Pollock. La'ie, Hawai'i: Institute for Polynesian Studies, Brigham Young University-Hawai'i, 1992. 316p. maps. bibliog.

'This study addresses the question of South Pacific peoples retaining their cultural and dietary attachment to traditional food sources despite Westernization. Why does the use of root and tree starches such as taro, yams, and breadfruit persist despite the availability of other foods? Using approaches of symbolic anthropology, social ecology, and household economy, Pollock explores the values of food, not only in diet and health but also as a symbol of power and well-being that structures social life'. See also '*Masi* and *tanu'eli*: ancient Polynesian technologies for the preservation and concealment of food' by Paul Alan Cox (*Pacific Tropical Botanical Garden Bulletin*, vol. 10 [1980], p. 81-93), a discussion of how Polynesians (including Samoans) preserved and stored food for times of hardship, sometimes by burying it (*tanu'eli*). *Masi* is a preserve made with breadfruit (*'ulu*; *fuata*) left to ferment in a special pit. Also of interest are: *Friends of Samoa cookbook*, edited by Luki O'Connor (Pago Pago: Women's Hospital Auxiliary, Lyndon Johnson Tropical Medical Center, 1979. 184p.), which contains traditional Samoan recipes, and a range of recipes using local ingredients *fa'a-Amerika*, such as breadfruit chips and pizza pork chops; and 'Peace Corps involvement in food and nutrition' by C. Feinstein (*Alafua Agricultural Bulletin*, vol. 7, no. 3 [1982], p. 76-81), which reviews the ways in which Peace Corps volunteers from the USA are involved in food production and in influencing nutritional practices, with some ideas of how this involvement might be further promoted. A relevant publication is G. Jackmond's *Garden growing in Samoa* (Apia: Peace Corps, 1975).

Transport and Communications

General

619 **Pacific Panorama.**

North Ryde, New South Wales: Braynart Group, 1987- . quarterly.

This inflight magazine for Polynesian Airlines is devoted to well illustrated articles on travel to the Pacific islands served by the airline, including Samoa.

620 **Western Samoa and American Samoa: history, culture and communication.**

Ruth E. Runeborg. Honolulu: East-West Center, 1980. 83p. bibliog. (Pre-print Paper Series, East-West Communication Institute).

A useful summary of published ethnographic data introduces a study of forms of symbolic communication, as present in the *fono*, in the *'ava* ceremony, and in *ifoga* (ritual apology). All modern media of communication are discussed in turn, including cinema and satellites (particularly PEACESAT). An excellent, twenty-one page bibliography is also included.

Traditional voyaging and navigation

621 **Canoes of Oceania.**

A. C. Haddon, James Hornell. Honolulu: Bishop Museum Press, 1975. rev. ed. 884p. maps. bibliog.

Including detailed and profusely illustrated descriptions of canoe types and canoe construction in Samoa, this combination of three earlier works by the two authors also illuminates patterns of migration and settlement in the Pacific islands. The earlier works were issued as Bishop Museum Special Publications, nos. 27-29 (1936-38), with Hornell covering Polynesia (no. 27). He and Haddon jointly wrote the indispensable *Definition of terms, general survey, and conclusions* (no. 29).

622 The immigration and early seafaring of the Samoans as reflected in their mythology.

Horst Cain. *Anthropos*, vol. 76 (1981), p. 841-48. bibliog.

Faced by an apparent lack of traditions about the discovery and settlement of Samoa, Cain examines two myths of voyages to the heaven of Tagaloa, interpreting them as evidence of actual seafaring. For a discussion of Samoan canoe types and supposed voyaging over great distances, see 'Die Fahrzeuge der Samoaner' (Modes of transport of the Samoans) by Georg Thilenius (*Globus*, vol. 80 [1901], p. 167-72).

623 Indigenous navigation and voyaging in the Pacific: a reference guide.

Compiled by Nicholas J. Goetzfridt. Westport, Connecticut; New York; London: Greenwood Press, 1992. 295p. map. (Bibliographies and Indexes in Anthropology, no. 6).

This fine, annotated bibliography of 694 items is primarily concerned with journals and books in several languages 'concentrating on the multifaceted range of aspects related to indigenous navigation and voyaging in the Pacific'. The extensive coverage of Polynesia (p. 53-201) includes many works relating to Samoa. Author, geographical and subject indexes are provided.

624 The prehistoric exploration and colonisation of the Pacific.

Geoffrey Irwin. Cambridge, England: Cambridge University Press, 1992. 248p. maps. bibliog.

Using an innovative model to establish a detailed theory of navigation, Irwin suggests that 'exploration was rapid and purposeful, undertaken systematically, and that navigation methods progressively improved'. He claims that islanders expanded settlement by exploring upwind, so as to ease safe return. A paperback edition of this important, challenging work appeared in 1994.

625 Voyaging against the direction of the trades: a report of an experimental canoe voyage from Samoa to Tahiti.

Ben R. Finney. *American Anthropologist*, vol. 90 (1988), p. 401-05.

Traditional Polynesian navigational skills brought the Hawai'i-built canoe *Hōkūle'a* from Samoa against the trade winds to Pape'ete. This was one of Finney's voyages in a series designed to illuminate the possibilities of Polynesian seamanship in pre-contact times. See also: Ben Finney's account of the voyage from Samoa to the Southern Cook Islands, 'Demonstrating the possible: sailing from west to east across Polynesia' in *The wayfaring art*, edited by C. Sneider, W. Kyselka (Berkeley, California: Lawrence Hall of Science, University of California, 1986, p. 48-50); Finney's story of the whole *Hōkūle'a* saga in his *Voyage of rediscovery* (Berkeley, California: University of California Press, 1995); and the earlier account of his first voyage, *Hōkūle'a: the way to Tahiti* (New York: Dodd, Mead, 1979). These difficult voyages lend weight to the view that Pacific islanders had greater navigational abilities than hitherto supposed and that most inter-island voyages were purposeful and sustainable. Another interesting article is 'Floatsam [sic] and jetsam from the great ocean: or, summary of early Samoan voyages and settlements' by John Bettridge Stair (*Journal of the Polynesian Society*, vol. 4 [1895], p. 99-131).

Postal history and philately

626 **History of the New Zealand military postal services 1845-1991.**
R. M. Startup, Edward B. Proud. Heathfield, England: Heathfield Postal History, 1992. 377p. maps. bibliog. (Military Postal History Series).

This definitive history includes details and facsimiles of the stamps and postmarks used by the New Zealand Expeditionary Force in Western Samoa during and after the First World War. See also 'Samoa serendipity' by M. P. Bratzel, Jnr. (*Pacifica*, vol. 34, no. 134 [Jan. 1996], p. 34-37). Originally published in the June 1992 issue of the *American Philatelist*, this is an illustrated, expert study of the provisional stamp issue authorized by Colonel Logan, commander-in-chief of the New Zealand Expeditionary Force which occupied German Samoa in August 1914. Another interesting work is *G.R.I.: the postage stamps of the German colonies occupied by the British, 1914-1918* by Robert M. Gibbs (London: Christie's-Robson Lowe, 1987. 275p. maps. bibliog.), an outline (with maps) of the campaign conducted in each of the six colonies occupied: German Samoa, Marshall Islands, New Guinea, Cameroons, Togoland and Mafia. Details are given of all stamp printings, varieties and errors, together with a checklist and rarity table.

627 **Missionary letters from Samoa.**
Brian Purcell. Bristol, England: Published by the Author (1 Ashton Way, Keynsham, Bristol BS18 1JY), 1994. 20p.

A detailed study of missionaries' letters from Samoa, with Samoan and transit postage rates, explanations of all markings, and a chronological list of every recorded example of such letters. See also *Methodism in the South Pacific on stamps, covers and postmarks* (London: Methodist Philatelic Society, [n.d.] [c. 1970]. 40p. [Handbooks, no. 2]), a collector's guide to philatelic representations of Methodism by South Pacific postal administrations, including that of Western Samoa. Many commemorative stamp issues, first-day covers and slogan postmarks are shown in the black-and-white illustrations.

628 **Pacifica: Journal of the Pacific Islands Study Circle of Great Britain.**
[London]: PISCGB, 1962- . quarterly.

Contains research and news on Pacific Island postal history, postmarks and new issues of postage stamps, with frequent coverage of Western Samoa and American Samoa. The first twenty volumes are indexed in *Pacifica: Journal of the Pacific Islands Study Circle of Great Britain: Index to volumes 1-20, 1962-82*, compiled by Raymond Price ([London]: PISCGB, 1984. 125p. bibliog.), arranged in one major alphabetical sequence, by country or territory. *Pacifica* is of great importance to philately of the Pacific area. See also *U.S. Pacific Islands Bulletin* (Chorley, England: Eric Baxendale (23 Walgarth Drive, Chorley, Lancashire PR7 2QN), 1993- . quarterly), a 'reader-supported' periodical devoted to the postal history and postmarks of United States territories in the islands, including American Samoa. It does not specifically discuss postage stamps.

629 **A postal history/cancellation study of the US Pacific Islands.**
Robert T. Murphy. Webster, Texas: Published by the Author, 1974. 156p. Revised edition, 1983.

The basic work of reference for its subject, which includes the postmarks of American Samoa. It is updated from time to time in the philatelic press of several countries. See also: *Cancellation study of the U.S. territories in the Pacific; and cancellations of American Samoa* by Howard Lee, G. J. Raymond, edited by D. H. Vernon ([Worthing, England]: Pacific Islands Study Circle of Great Britain, [1970]. 21p.), with a section on 'Cancellations of American Samoa' by G. J. Raymond, covering postmarks from 1900 to 1969; and 'American Samoa: post offices of the Manu'a Islands 1981 to 1995' by Eric Baxendale (*U.S. Pacific Islands Bulletin*, no. 14 [Sept. 1996], p. 2).

630 **A postal history of the Samoan Islands.**
Richard Burge. Wellington: Royal Philatelic Society of New Zealand, 1987-89. 2 vols. bibliog.

The well illustrated, definitive history of postal services and stamp issues in pre-partition Samoa, German Samoa, American Samoa, mandated Western Samoa and independent Samoa i Sisifo/Western Samoa. Volume one extends up to 1914, and volume two covers 1914 to 1989.

631 **Samoa express.**
York, England: Barefoot (Investments), 1983. 36p. (Forgery & Reprint Guide, no. 5-6).

A guide to identification, with facsimile illustrations. See also *The Samoa express postage stamps* by R. B. Yardley (London: Royal Philatelic Society, 1916. 64p.), an illustrated inventory of known examples.

632 **Samoa: notes on the postal history, 1882-1900.**
Romney Gibbons. Sydney, New South Wales: J. H. Smyth, 1941. 28p.

Consular overprints and Samoan government issues are described and illustrated in these interesting notes on a troubled and complex phase of Samoan history. This work was first published in *Australian Stamp Journal*, 12 June 1940-12 June 1941.

633 **Samoan civil censorship during World War II.**
Nigel Sawyer. *Pacifica*, vol. 32, no. 126 (Jan. 1994), p. 27-31.

Censorship of civilian mail was first notified on 4 September 1939. Mail from Samoa was normally censored in New Zealand. All letters, or at least a sample, would be read and marked 'Opened by censor', and letters excluded from the sample were marked

'Passed by censor'. Various types of censor handstamping are illustrated and discussed in detail, with a checklist of covers. This article and its continuation (*Pacifica*, vol. 32, no. 129) were reprinted in the *Fellowship of Samoan Specialists Newsletter*. Additional information appeared in 'Samoan civil censorship during World War II' by Nigel Sawyer (*Pacifica*, vol. 34, no. 135 [April 1996], p. 76-77).

634 **South Pacific price list 1870-1985.**
Robin Linke. Wembley, Western Australia: Published by the Author, 1996. unpaginated [44p.]

Samoan Government issues, G.R.I. overprints and overprints on New Zealand stamps, and Western Samoan definitive issues are among the many stamps illustrated in colour, described and priced, with Stanley Gibbons catalogue numbers and comparative 1995 prices. See also Linke's *Australia & South Pacific price list 1995*, with SG and Scott catalogue numbers. There are also available: *Australien & Südpazifik Preisliste* (with Michel numbers); and *Australie & Pacifique Sud* (with SG and Yvert-Tellier numbers), priced respectively in Deutschmarks and French francs.

635 **Stamps of Western Samoa.**
Nelson Eustis. *South Pacific Bulletin*, vol. 21, no. 4 (1971), p. 27-30.

An illustrated history of the postage stamps issued by successive Samoan administrations. See also: 'First stamps of Samoa' by L. Hanclau (*Stanley Gibbons' Monthly Journal*, vol. 22 [15 Nov. 1910], p. 39-42), an illustrated commentary on early issues of postage stamps in Samoa; 'Notes on the first issue of Samoa' by John N. Luff (*American Journal of Philately*, 2nd series, vol. 14 [1 Oct. 1901], p. 261-62); and 'Samoa' by H. D. S. Haverbeck, in *The commemorative stamps of the British Commonwealth* (London: Faber & Faber, 1955, p. 177-79).

636 **Stanley Gibbons Commonwealth two reigns stamp catalogue: Eastern Pacific.**
London: Stanley Gibbons, 1987- . irregular.

An illustrated, priced catalogue of the postage stamps of Pitcairn, Western Samoa and Tonga, 1937-87, the first of a series. See also *Stanley Gibbons stamp catalogue. Part 1: British Commonwealth* (London: Stanley Gibbons Publications, 1865- . annual), the philatelists' indispensable reference work, with each stamp priced. Since 1992/93 this has been published in two volumes.

Labour, Employment and Manpower

General

637 **Pacific Solidarity: a Newsletter of the CTUC Pacific Trade Union Education Project.**
South Brisbane, Australia: Commonwealth Trade Union Council (CTUC), 1987- . [quarterly].

The newsletter reports on a CTUC project to promote trade union training and self-reliance in Western Samoa and other Commonwealth states in the Pacific islands.

638 **Samoan perceptions of work: moving up and moving around.**
Robert W. Franco. New York: AMS Press, 1991. 386p. bibliog.

Franco uses an ethnohistorical approach to review the perceptions of work of the rapidly growing migrant population of Samoans. A detailed description of work in traditional Samoan society and in the 'transitional' period from 1830 to 1985, provides the context for an examination of contemporary perceptions and patterns of work. The focus is on Samoans in New Zealand and in the United States, especially Hawai'i. The material on incentives is of particular interest, highlighting *tautua* (service to the kin group). Disincentives include communication problems and discrimination in the workplace.

639 **Western Samoa trade unionism: the 1981 public service strike.**
R. Snell. *New Zealand Journal of Industrial Relations*, vol. 17 (April 1992), p. 69-84. bibliog.

An expert reappraisal of independent Samoa's first strike, and of its implications for the growth of trade unionism. Snell applies the concept of mutual adjustment, in an interactive process between foreign institutions and traditional Samoan institutions and values. See also 'The strike in Western Samoa: an interpretation' by Patricia Kinloch (*Pacific Viewpoint*, vol. 23, no. 2 [1982], p. 161-72), a discussion of the strike which pays particular attention to the problem of giving meaning to the alien concept of 'strike' in Samoan culture.

640 **Western Samoa's first strike: a foreign invention which became Samoan overnight?**
Albert Wendt. *Pacific Perspective*, vol. 10, no. 1 (1981), p. 45-56.

A perceptive analysis of an unprecedented event in independent Western Samoa: the thirteen-week PSA strike, 'a surrealist happening, a fabulous beast with rainbow colours, multiple heads and faces, an enormous belly full of insatiable fire'. Wendt examines strategy, tactics, leadership, propaganda and Government intransigence, concluding that 'No one won'. Wendt claims that trade unionism is 'here to stay' in Samoa. If the right to strike is legalized, then arbitration mechanisms will have to be set up, to avoid damage from another marathon strike.

Indentured labour

641 **Compagnie et consulat: lois germaniques et emploi des travailleurs sur les plantations de Samoa, 1864-1914.** (Company and consulate: German laws and employment of labourers on the plantations of Samoa, 1864-1914.)
Stewart Firth, Doug Munro. *Journal de la Société des Océanistes*, no. 91 (1990), p. 115-34. bibliog.

This well documented article discusses how the Hamburg firm of J. C. Godeffroy und Sohn and its commercial successor, the Deutsche Handels- und Plantagen-Gesellschaft der Südsee-Inseln (DHPG), benefited from German government support and legislation in the imposition of harsh working conditions in Samoa between 1864 and 1914.

642 **The coolie labour question and German colonial policy in Samoa, 1900-1914.**
John A. Moses. *Journal of Pacific History*, vol. 8 (1973), p. 101-24. bibliog.

The plantations of German Samoa sought indentured labourers mainly in China, though some Melanesians were still recruited. Moses traces the growth in numbers of Chinese labourers, and discusses official policies and planter attitudes. See also the related study covering the period 1914-19, 'The problems of indentured labour in Samoa under the military administration' by P. S. O'Connor (*Political Science* [Wellington], vol. 20, no. 2 [1968], p. 10-27).

643 **The dragon came from afar: the Chinese in Western Samoa 1875-1985.**
Nancy Y. W. Tom. Apia: Western Samoa Historical and Cultural Trust, 1986. 112p. map. bibliog.

Based on the memories of the sixty-eight former indentured labourers still living in Western Samoa in April 1973 and on other local sources, this is a history 'in composite form', using fictitious names in most cases. The historical facts, however, are accurate, and are supplemented by numerous photographs and facsimiles of documents. For a more formal outline of the subject, see *Labour problems in the Pacific mandates* by John A. Decker (New York: Institute of Pacific Relations; London: Oxford University Press, 1940. 246p. maps. bibliog.).

644 **From company rule to consular control: Gilbert Islands labourers on German plantations in Samoa, 1867-96.**
Doug Munro, Stewart Firth. *Journal of Imperial and Commonwealth History*, vol. 16, no. 1 (1987), p. 22-44. bibliog.

Of the approximately 9,400 Gilbertese recruited during the second half of the 19th century to work on foreign plantations, twenty-five per cent went to Samoa. This study deals with the recruiting of these workers and its effect on relations between Great Britain and Germany. The work is soundly based on British and German official records, and on the archives of the London Missionary Society.

645 **German labour policy and the partition of the Western Pacific: the view from Samoa.**
Doug Munro, Stewart Firth. *Journal of Pacific History*, vol. 25, no. 1 (June 1990), p. 85-102. bibliog.

The American Civil War gave impetus to the emergence of plantation economies in the Pacific in the 1860s, but the critical limiting factor was labour. German planters in Samoa recruited indentured labourers from Melanesia and from the Gilbert Islands. The DHPG, the largest employer in Samoa, exercised a 'disproportionate influence' in Anglo-German relations, leading eventually to agreement on zones of influence, and finally to colonial partition of the Western Pacific. See also 'The last days of the Melanesian labour trade in Western Samoa' by Malama Meleisea (*Journal of Pacific History*, vol. 11, no. 2 [1976], p. 126-32. bibliog.).

646 **Planter versus protector: Frank Cornwall's employment of Gilbertese plantation workers in Samoa, 1877-1881.**
Doug Munro. *New Zealand Journal of History*, vol. 23, no. 2 (1989), p. 173-82. bibliog.

Gilbertese indentured labourers suffered ill treatment and many abuses at the hands of German, American and British plantation owners. This is a documented study of the labourers' grievances against plantation owner Frank Cornwall. The Gilbertese were not passive victims, but employed various strategies of resistance, in particular recourse to the British consular court.

647 **The present system in the South Pacific islands (a) Western Samoa.**
Persia Crawford Campbell. In: *Chinese coolie emigration to countries within the British Empire*. Persia Crawford Campbell, with a preface by the Hon. W. Pember Reeves. London: Frank Cass, 1971, p. 217-31. (Reprint of the original 1923 edition).

After the First World War, the use of Chinese indentured labour continued in Western Samoa, by express request of the Government of New Zealand and local European planters. By December 1921 there were 1,597 Chinese in the islands. Campbell uses

New Zealand records of parliamentary debates, 1919-20, to outline the political controversies which the practice evoked, and the problems experienced in Samoa.

648 **Samoan plantations: the Gilbertese laborers' experience, 1867-1896.**

Doug Munro, Stewart Firth. In: *Plantation workers: resistance and accommodation.* Edited by Brij V. Lal, Doug Munro, Edward D. Beechert. Honolulu: University of Hawai'i Press, 1993, p. 101-27. bibliog.

About 2,500 Gilbertese worked on plantations in 'Upolu and Savai'i owned by J. C. Godeffroy und Sohn, Frank Cornwall, or the DHPG (successor to the Godeffroy company). Plantation discipline was severe, with imprisonment or flogging as punishment. However, the general acquiescence to a 'reign of near-terror' was ended by strikes at Mulifanua in 1871 and 1875. Furthermore, the appointment in 1894 of the British consul as protector encouraged the Gilbertese to resist the iniquities of the plantation system more effectively.

649 ***'O tama uli*: Melanesians in Western Samoa.**

Malama Meleisea. Suva: Institute of Pacific Studies, University of the South Pacific, 1980. 57p. bibliog.

'O tama uli ('black boys') is the term still used for the Melanesians brought to Samoa as plantation labourers during the German Administration, and for their dark-skinned descendants. In 1975 only six of the original recruits were still alive in Samoa. Meleisea interviewed four of these old men, and bases most of this book on their stories. Chapter one provides a succinct history of the plantation industry from the 1850s, when Theodor Weber began to acquire large tracts of Samoa land. The treatment of many part-Melanesians was inequitable under the New Zealand administration and continued to be so in independent Samoa, where some still work on the WSTEC Mulifanua plantation. Meleisea concludes: 'The Melanesians who were brought to Samoa made a major contribution to the economy of the country'.

Human Resources and Community Development

650 **Community development in Western Samoa: survey of a project form and its implementation.**
Hans Gullestrup. Copenhagen: National Museum of Denmark, 1977. 217p. 10 maps. bibliog.

Gullestrup, a former United Nations associate economist in Western Samoa, presents a case-study of two communities and two water-supply projects. He then formulates and tests a hypothesis with regard to the interaction of community and development, suggesting that successful development is most likely where there is a high degree of social integration and social heterogeneity. There are a number of statistical tables which reflect economic and social conditions in Western Samoa.

651 **Incorporating traditional knowledge in development activities: Western Samoa.**
Nu'ufou Petaia. In: *Education, language, patterns and policy.* Edited by John Morrison, Paul Geraghty, Linda Crowl. Suva: Institute of Pacific Studies, University of the South Pacific, 1994, p. 173-89. map. bibliog. (Science of Pacific Peoples, vol. 4).

Petaia argues that development would greatly benefit from traditional knowledge and skills, and proposes that, with the help of the government, such knowledge should be systematically elicited and recorded while its possessors are still available.

652 **Report of leadership training in Upolu and Savaii, 1985.**
Young Men's Christian Association of Western Samoa. Apia: YMCA of Western Samoa, 1985. Mimeographed translation from Samoan.

This interesting outline of efforts to develop Western Samoa's human resources includes a challenging paper, 'Develop vs. social realities' by Lafi A. Sanerivi.

653 **The road to power is a chainsaw: villages and innovation in Western Samoa.**

Cluny Macpherson. *Pacific Studies*, vol. 11, no. 2 (March 1988), p. 1-24. bibliog.

Based on cases studied in 1980, this paper argues that Samoan social organization, per se, is not an obstacle to economic growth. Macpherson provides examples of entrepreneurial individuals who have adopted items of technology and strategies that have increased both productivity and profitability in village agriculture. This sector's failure to attain higher productivity stems largely from rational consideration of the costs and benefits of various economic alternatives. Declining prospects of out-migration, slow growth in the small domestic wage sector, and lower levels and reduced purchasing power of remittances may force villagers to reconsider the possibilities of agriculture. Increased agricultural production is 'the most constructive response' to the worsening situation.

654 **SPC/ILO Reports on Migration, Employment & Development in the South Pacific.**

Nouméa, New Caledonia: South Pacific Commission, 1983- . irregular.

Covers employment and unemployment in all countries and territories of the SPC region, as well as migration to other countries. Statistics relating to Samoan migration to USA and New Zealand figure prominently. This is a prime source of reliable data on the human factor in development. See also *Human resource plan* by the Government of Western Samoa (Apia: Public Service Commission, 1992).

655 **We want the forest, yet fear the spirits: culture and change in Western Samoa.**

Malama Meleisea. *Pacific Perspective*, vol. 9, no. 1 (1980), p. 21-29. bibliog.

An outline of some of the cultural constraints on use of natural resources and on modern development. An extensive analysis of the process and pressures of change, and of how Samoan society adapts its ways to meet the new challenges is presented in *Change and adaptations in Western Samoa* by Malama Meleisea (Christchurch, New Zealand: Macmillan Brown Centre for Pacific Studies, University of Canterbury, 1992. 80p. bibliog.).

Statistics

American Samoa

656 **American Samoa statistical digest 1991.**
Pago Pago: Economic Development and Planning Office, Government of American Samoa, 1991. 219p.

The standard official summary of statistics on the economic, political and social organization of the Territory of American Samoa, together with a guide to other sources of relevant statistics. Emphasis is given to the most recent available economic and social data. Published annually since 1981, it includes statistics relating to emigration and immigration.

Population statistics.
See item no. 254.

Western Samoa

657 **Key Indicators of Developing Asian and Pacific Countries.**
Manila: Asian Development Bank, 1990- . annual.

Part one of this useful compilation compares Asian and Pacific developing countries with other world regions and with industrialized countries; part two compares financial and economic performance within the Asian-Pacific region; and part three presents detailed data for each individual state, including Western Samoa.

658 **Statistical Yearbook for Asia and the Pacific.**
Bangkok: United Nations Economic and Social Commission for Asia and the Pacific, 1973- . annual.

Wide-ranging and authoritative, this annual compilation usually appears two years after the cover date. It includes sectoral data, longitudinal data for a decade, and summary tables enabling world comparisons to be made. See also *Quarterly Bulletin of Statistics for Asia and the Pacific* (Bangkok: United Nations Economic Commission for Asia and the Pacific, 1973- . quarterly), an invaluable journal which comprises all major states in the Asian-Pacific Basin (including Western Samoa). Current statistics for each country cover population and manpower, agricultural production, industrial output, transport, international trade, balance of payments, prices and wages, inflation and unemployment. Also useful is *Statistical Indicators for Asia and the Pacific* (Bangkok: United Nations Economic and Social Commission for Asia and the Pacific, 1977- . monthly), which provides current monthly data on demographic and economic trends, and is well illustrated by graphs, covering population, industrial production, transport, foreign trade, prices, finance and government accounts.

659 **World Bank atlas 1995.**
Washington, DC: The World Bank, 1994. 27th ed. 36p. maps.

Provides key social, economic and environmental data for 209 economies, including Samoa. The text is in English, French and Spanish. See also *Commonwealth factbook* (London: Commonwealth Secretariat, 1992. 5th ed. 76p.), a concise country-by-country summary of economic and social statistics, based on data from the Commonwealth Secretariat, the World Bank and other international organizations.

Population statistics.
See item no. 254.

Foreign trade statistics of Asia and the Pacific.
See item no. 581.

Environment

Ecology and environment

660 **Environmental legislation review: Western Samoa 1993.**
Clark Peteru. Apia: South Pacific Regional Environment Programme (SPREP), 1993. 113p.

This comprehensive report on Western Samoan laws in force relating to environmental protection and conservation of natural resources was prepared for SPREP and the Government of Western Samoa, as documentation in support of the National Environment and Development Management Strategies (NEMS), with financial assistance from the United Nations Development Programme (UNDP).

661 **Environmental planning for tourism in Western Samoa.**
Auckland, New Zealand: KRTA Limited, 1988. 124p. maps. bibliog.

This report to the Government of Western Samoa and to the South Pacific Regional Environment Programme (SPREP) analyses the likely environmental impact and consequences of the growing tourist trade. A viable and sustainable environmental policy, aimed at avoiding or mitigating harm, is outlined for consideration. Water resources and the pollution of coastal waters and reefs are among matters of particular concern.

662 **Environmental problems in the South Pacific: the Regional Environment Programme perspective.**
Neva Wendt. In: *Resources, development and politics in the Pacific islands.* Edited by Stephen Henningham, R. J. May, Lulu Turner. Bathurst, New South Wales: Crawford House Press, 1992, p. 185-94. bibliog.

An outline of the environmental problems faced by the South Pacific Regional Environment Programme (SPREP), written by a SPREP project officer based in Āpia. The many problems raised include: coastal erosion; scarcity of fresh water;

degradation of forests; loss of endangered species; damage to and pollution of reefs; domestic and industrial waste disposal; driftnet fishing; and climatic change and potential sea-level rise. See also *Report of the fifth intergovernmental meeting held in Apia, Western Samoa, on 14-18 September 1992* by South Pacific Regional Environment Programme (SPREP) (Apia: SPREP, 1992. 74p.), a review of current environmental problems in the South Pacific and of progress being made to resolve them.

663 **The fragile South Pacific: an ecological odyssey.**
Andrew Mitchell. Austin, Texas: University of Texas Press, 1990. 256p. bibliog.

Travel writing with a welcome difference! This is not a modish plea for 'ecotourism' but rather a serious, well illustrated (in colour) investigation of human impact on the environment, especially on the under-appreciated, endangered biota of the Pacific islands, notably including Samoa. Mitchell emphasizes that the rainforests of Samoa and elsewhere in the region contain a remarkably high proportion of unique species. Their loss 'will be felt far more than that of an equivalent area in the great rainforests of Amazonia or Southeast Asia would be'.

664 **Land-based sources of pollution of the marine environment in Western Samoa: a case study.**
Philomena Gangaiya, Inia Wele. Apia: South Pacific Regional Environment Programme (SPREP), 1994. 39p. (SPREP Reports and Studies, no. 81).

A thorough investigation of all the terrestrial souces of pollution of Western Samoan coastal waters, which reflects growing concern for the environment. Outflows of raw sewage and uncontrolled disposal of refuse are major sources of pollution of the sea near human settlements, above all off Āpia. See also *Western Samoa: land-based pollution sources and their effects on the marine environment: a report* by Pavel Klinckhamers (Apia: South Pacific Regional Environment Programme [SPREP], 1992. 48p. maps).

665 **Nature legislation and nature conservation as a part of tourism development in the island Pacific: a report covering Cook Islands, Fiji, Niue, Papua New Guinea, Solomon Islands, Tonga, Tuvalu, Vanuatu and Western Samoa.**
Dangroup International. Suva: Tourism Council of the South Pacific, 1988. 82p.

Reflecting concern at the harmful consequences of tourism development in the Pacific islands, this comprehensive study embraces nature management and conservation and relevant legislation. It discusses nature reserves, nature parks, wildlife breeding, museums, zoological and botanical gardens, and offers recommendations for environmental and conservation legislation, guidelines and facilities. It lists current laws and protected nature areas within the member states of the Tourism Council of the South Pacific.

666 **Oceania: islands, land, people.**
Geoffrey M. White, Lamont Lindstrom. *Cultural Survival Quarterly*, vol. 17, no. 3 (Fall 1993), p. 32-40. map. bibliog.

Oceania has the most to lose, culturally speaking, from the pressures of global, political and economic change. White and Lindstrom review the threats to Pacific peoples of unsustainable development, migration, tourism, even video showings (p. 32-34). Reports from individual countries include 'Samoa' by Caroline G. Sinavaiana (p. 37); Sinavaiana highlights the loss of Samoan cultural integrity in a destructive social cycle and climate of disaffection.

667 **Preserving Western Samoa's cultural heritage and environment.**
Leulu Felise Va'a. In: *Pacific history: papers from the 8th Pacific History Association conference*. Edited by Donald H. Rubinstein. Mangilao, Guam: University of Guam Press; Micronesian Area Research Center, 1992, p. 461-74. bibliog.

A survey of the changes which have taken place in independent Western Samoa since 1962, affecting the natural environment, language and culture, archives, and historical sites. The issue is 'preservation *and* development', and the establishment of a balance or middle ground between the demands of both considerations.

668 **Western Samoa: state of the environment report.**
Tu'u'u Leti Taule'alo. Apia: South Pacific Regional Environment Programme (SPREP), 1993. 76p.

This thorough survey of human ecology, environmental conditions and environmental protection in Western Samoa highlights both the considerable progress achieved and the continuing threats. These include mountain erosion after logging, the severe problems of refuse disposal, the pollution of coastal waters by sewage, and damage to coral reefs.

Settlement patterns

669 **Culture and environment in old Samoa.**
R. F. Watters. In: *Western Pacific: studies of man and environment in the Western Pacific*. Wellington: Department of Geography, Victoria University of Wellington, in collaboration with the New Zealand Geographical Society (Wellington Branch), 1958, p. 41-70. map. bibliog.

An exceptionally interesting outline of the manifold patterns of traditional Samoan culture and an analysis of the relationship of certain cultural spheres and phenomena with the physical environment. The main topics discussed are: agriculture and population pressure; forest resources; sea resources; crafts; social structure; and religion and ceremonies. The map shows 'Oceania: culture and sub-culture areas'.

670 **Faleapuna: a Samoan village.**
Glenn Cunningham. *California Geographer*, vol. 4 (1963), p. 23-34. 3 maps. bibliog.

This study in village geography (micro-geography) reveals the patterns of communal and individual use of land and water within the village area. Faleāpuna lies about fourteen miles east of Āpia on the northern coast of 'Upolu, and has functions that are both rural and urban. Although primarily a farm village (its role historically), after European contact it became a trading centre of more than local importance, the extent of which changed with alteration of the transportation pattern and the availability of a frequent bus service, to Āpia and to the populous south-east coast.

671 **Port town village organisation in Western Samoa.**
Sharon W. Tiffany. *Journal of the Polynesian Society*, vol. 88, no. 2 (June 1979), p. 127-75. 2 maps. bibliog.

This paper examines the social organization of a port town village in the Āpia urban area studied in 1969-71, using comparative material from Susan Hirsh's (1958) urban research in 1957. Āpia is then compared with other Pacific Island urban centres. See also 'The social organisation of an urban village in Samoa' by Susan Hirsh (*Journal of the Polynesian Society*, vol. 67, no. 3 [Sept. 1958], p. 266-303. maps. bibliog.).

672 **Samoan village patterns: four examples.**
Jesse D. Jennings, Richard N. Holmer, Gregory Jackmond. *Journal of the Polynesian Society*, vol. 91, no. 1 (March 1982), p. 81-102. maps. bibliog.

Attempts to determine whether identifiable social factors are reflected in the layout of 'Upolu and Savai'i villages from about AD 1200 to the present. The prehistoric sites surveyed are Mt. Olo Plantation ('Upolu), Nelson Plantation (Letolo, Savai'i) and Sapapāli'i (Savai'i); these are compared with the modern village of Fa'a'ala (Savai'i). The main conclusion is that the basic village layout and organizing social principles have changed little over the last 500 or more years, except for the difference in location of chiefly residences noted at Fa'a'ala. See also 'Settlement patterns in Samoa before 1840' by Janet M. Davidson (*Journal of the Polynesian Society*, vol. 78, no. 1 [March 1969], p. 44-82. bibliog.).

673 **Settlement in old Samoa: 1840.**
R. F. Watters. *New Zealand Geographer*, vol. 14, no. 1 (April 1958), p. 1-18. 5 maps. bibliog.

Based on 'the most thorough and penetrating' contemporary accounts, this paper attempts a geographical reconstruction of life and landscape in 1840, the earliest feasible date for this purpose. Watters outlines the physical setting; distribution of population; soils and water supply; the village; house types (with contemporary illustrations); the settlement plan; inland settlements; early missionary house types; and village functions.

Housing and architecture

674 **A *fale* in Polynesia: traditions linger in a noted *tapa* artist's Samoan home.**
J. C. Wright. *Architectural Digest* (USA), vol. 41 (July 1984), p. 82-87.

An illustrated description of the traditional Samoan house of Mary J. Pritchard, the foremost bark artist of American Samoa. No metal is used in the *fale*, the *ifilele* and breadfruit logs being filled and lashed with sennit made from coconut-husk fibre. Pritchard has a studio in the *fale*, where she develops her own contemporary designs.

675 **The ritual of architecture: the creation of Samoan guest *fale*.**
Anne Elizabeth Guernsey Allen. *Pacific Arts*, no. 9/10 (1994), p. 76-84.

Every Samoan village has a guest house, normally of distinctive traditional design. Increasing numbers of visitors and tourists oblige communities to build and equip more modern guest *fale*. Allen describes the ritualized processes along the way, from the first decision to build to the final celebration of completion.

676 **The Samoan *fale*.**
F. L. Higginson, Peter Higginson, illustrated by Philippe Lair. Apia: UNESCO Office for the Pacific States; Bangkok: UNESCO Principal Office for Asia and the Pacific, 1992. 81p. map.

Based on the expert and beautiful films, black-and-white and colour photographs, and drawings of the French architect-photographer Philippe Lair, this is a magnificent, near-definitive study of all aspects of house-building in Samoa, and of the social and ritual roles of *fale*. It covers: the layout of Samoan villages; the functions of meeting and guest houses; the building of homely *fale*, noble *fale tele* and *fale ăfolau* (with measured drawings for the latter two types); furnishings, feasts and ceremonies; the guild of builders; *fale* for non-traditional purposes; and terminology. From lashings to roof structures and their names, this is a thorough description of how and why Samoans build as they do. See also 'From houses without walls to vertical villages: Samoan housing transformations' by Robert W. Franco, Simeamativa Aga, D. Thomas Keene, in *Home in the islands: housing and social change in the Pacific*, edited by Jan Rensel, Margaret Rodman (Honolulu: University of Hawai'i Press, 1997 [in press]).

Parks and nature reserves

677 **Palolo Deep National Marine Reserve: a survey, inventory and information report.**

Edward R. Lovell. Apia: South Pacific Regional Environment Programme (SPREP), 1994. 88p. map. bibliog.

Palolo Deep is the steep-sided underwater chasm just beyond the reef off Beach Road in Āpia, designated as a marine park and reserve, with viewing platforms and rental facilities for snorkelling. This is a scientific survey of the Deep, with a listing of the many colourful fish and corals to be found there. See also: *Ocean management: a regional perspective: the prospects for Commonwealth maritime cooperation in Asia and the Pacific; Report of a Commonwealth Group of Experts* (London: Commonwealth Secretariat, 1984. 155p.), which considers all aspects of management of offshore resources; and *Marine environment survey: proposed Aleipata Islands National Park, Western Samoa* by G. J. Andrews, P. F. Holthus (Nouméa, New Caledonia: South Pacific Commission, 1989. 68p. map. [United Nations Environment Programme]), a detailed study of the marine environment in the coastal waters of the Aleipata Islands.

Education

Bibliographies and catalogues

678 **Education in the Pacific islands: a selective bibliography.**
Camilla H. Wedgwood. Nouméa, New Caledonia: South Pacific Commission, 1956. 80p. (SPC Technical Report, no. 99).

Still relevant for research on the history of education in SPC member states (including Samoa), this work provides useful coverage of official documents. It is based in part on several bibliographies (in *Oversea Education* and in private communications to the author) by H. G. A. Hughes, friend and colleague of Camilla Wedgwood.

679 **A world catalogue of theses and dissertations concerning the education of the peoples of the Pacific islands (including the New Zealand Maori).**
William George Coppell. Honolulu: University of Hawai'i, 1977. 63p. (Pacific Islands Studies Program, Miscellaneous Work Papers 1977, no. 1).

A useful finding list, by author and territory, of unpublished research on all aspects of education in the islands, including American Samoa and Western Samoa. See also *American dissertations on foreign education: a bibliography with abstracts. Volume seventeen: Pacific*, edited by Franklin Parker, Betty June Parker (Troy, New York: Whitston, 1986. 208p.), which lists, alphabetically by author, United States doctoral dissertations on education in Pacific islands with extensive abstracts and a topical index. It includes twenty-six dissertations on American Samoa and Western Samoa.

Samoa

680 American Samoa and Western Samoa.

R. Murray Thomas. In: *Schooling in the Pacific islands: colonies in transition.* Edited by R. Murray Thomas, T. Neville Postlethwaite. Oxford: Pergamon Press, 1984, p. 202-35. map. bibliog.

A succinct description of educational development in Samoa as a whole from the first missionary initiatives after 1830, followed by separate consideration of American Samoa, 1900-80s (p. 208-20) and Western Samoa, 1900-80s (p. 220-30). The two territories are then compared, 1930s to 1980s, in terms of secular education, structure of educational administration, composition of student population, and cultural sources of curriculum and teaching methods. The 1930s in both territories are labelled 'classical colonialism', and the 1980s in Western Samoa 'neocolonialism' and in American Samoa 'enlightened colonialism'.

681 Directions: Journal of Educational Studies.

Suva: Institute of Education, University of the South Pacific, 1979- . 2 pa (May and October).

The main forum for academic discussion of all aspects of education in the South Pacific, including Samoa. Topics range widely, from language maintenance and promotion and reading-literacy surveys to tensions between professionalism and bureaucracy. *Directions*, issue 30, vol. 16, no. 1 (June 1994), includes articles on education for small businesses, and on women's education. See also *USP Bulletin* (Suva: University of the South Pacific, 1967- . 192 pa (February to December). Issued irregularly until 1977, this free newsletter contains news of official and unofficial USP events, in Fiji and in the University's centres in other territories, as well as classified advertising. Its circulation is about 2,000 copies.

682 Educational Innovations in the Pacific.

Honolulu: Pacific Regional Educational Laboratory, 1994- . quarterly.

Provides serious, well informed reports on educational experiments and new developments in the Pacific region. The non-profit Pacific Regional Educational Laboratory also publishes *Pacific Education Updates*, a quarterly journal serving children and educators in American Samoa and other Pacific territories closely associated with the USA.

683 Pacific universities: achievements, problems, prospects.

Edited by Ron Crocombe, Malama Meleisea. Suva: Institute of Pacific Studies, University of the South Pacific, 1988. 427p. maps. bibliog.

This conspectus of tertiary education in the Pacific devotes four essays specifically to Samoa and also discusses Samoan problems in thematic chapters: 'Culture and communication at Alafua', Peggy Fairbairn-Dunlop (p. 155-64); 'The National University of Samoa', Tau'ili'ili Uili (p. 210-17); 'American Samoa Community College', Eneliko Sofa'i (p. 218-27); and 'National perspectives on higher education: Western Samoa', Le Mamea R. Mualia (p. 332-38). See also: 'Regionalism in educational institutions: the South Pacific Regional College of Tropical Agriculture,

Alafua' by F. S. Wendt (Tuaopepe) (*Alafua Agricultural Bulletin*, vol. 7, no. 2 [April-June 1982], p. 12-28), an informed account of the rationale, past, present and importance for the South Pacific of the SPRCTA at Alafua, Western Samoa, founded in 1966 and now the University of the South Pacific School of Agriculture; 'Alafua campus' (*Alafua Agricultural Bulletin*, vol. 7, no. 2 [1982], p. 5-88); 'National University' by T. F. S. Wendt (*Pacific Perspective*, vol. 12, no. 1 [1983], p. 49-54), a reasoned appraisal of development plans for the new National University of Samoa, and of its likely prospects and problems; and *A development plan for the National University of Samoa* by K. Back (Apia: National University of Samoa, Government of Western Samoa, 1993).

684 **South Pacific education profiles: a sourcebook on trends and developments.**
T. L. Baba, I. J. Cokanasiga, J. B. Caballes. Suva: Institute of Education, University of the South Pacific, 1992. 117p. map. bibliog.

A guide to educational data for island territories, including Samoa. The educational infrastructure is outlined in each case, and there are detailed statistics relating to educational finance, enrolment ratio, student teacher ratio and teacher qualifications. This work will be indispensable for comparative studies.

685 **South Pacific women in distance education: studies from countries of the University of the South Pacific.**
Edited by Cema Bolabola, Richard Wah. Suva: University Extension, University of the South Pacific; Vancouver, British Columbia: Commonwealth of Learning, 1995. 319p.

These student case-studies include women from Samoa. The profiles include details such as previous schooling, aspirations, choice of courses, and comments on problems experienced.

686 **UNESCO Pacific News.**
Apia: UNESCO Office for the Pacific States, 1993- . irregular.

Provides news of educational and communications development and population education in the South Pacific and neighbouring states of Asia.

American Samoa

687 **Agricultural Development in the American Pacific (ADAP) Program.**
Victor D. Phillips. *ISLA: a Journal of Micronesian Studies*, vol. 2, no. 1 (Rainy Season 1994), p. 169-76. bibliog.

'A key route to successfully achieving political stability and economic growth through agricultural development lies in fully developing the land-grant institutions in the region'. ADAP was formally organized in 1988, as a coalition of five land-grant institutions including American Samoa Community College. Agricultural research and extension programmes, and maintenance of the quality of fragile tropical ecosystems are prime objectives. This article reviews progress in staff development, crop protection, communications, database development, agro-forestry and environmental education, and future planning. Compare with 'Agricultural extension in Western Samoa' by S. T. Imo (*Alafua Agricultural Bulletin*, vol. 7, no. 1 [1982], p. 69-72), in which Imo reviews progress in extension teaching and in village development, highlighting achievements in improving cultivation and animal husbandry methods, and some of the problems yet to be overcome.

688 **American Samoa.**

R. Murray Thomas. In: *International encyclopedia of national systems of education.* Edited by T. Neville Postlethwaite. Oxford: Pergamon (Elsevier Science), 1995. 2nd revised edition, p. 19-27. bibliog.

An outline of a system which is falling short of its aim to educate for both Samoan and American needs, and which has a damaged infrastructure. See also: *Think children: annual report of the Department of Education* (Pago Pago: Department of Education, 1974- . annual); and *Instructional program* (Pago Pago: Department of Education, 1991). Earlier studies include: 'Evaluation consequences of unreasonable goals: the plight of education in American Samoa' by R. Murray Thomas (*Educational Evaluation and Policy Analysis*, vol. 3, no. 2 [1981], p. 41-50. bibliog.); and 'The rise and decline of an educational technology: television in American Samoa' by R. Murray Thomas (*Educational Communication and Technology*, vol. 28, no. 3 [1980], p. 155-67. bibliog.).

689 **Bold experiment: the story of educational television in American Samoa.**

Wilbur Schramm, Lyle M. Nelson, Mere T. Betham. Stanford, California: Stanford University Press, 1981. 244p. bibliog.

Educational television (KVZK-TV) came to American Samoa on 4 October 1964, as the central feature of an emergency aid programme designed to modernize and rapidly upgrade the entire educational system. Governor H. Rex Lee described the existing system as appalling, even by comparison with the mainland's ghettos. By 1979, Samoa's three channels were providing 174 hours of US network programming a week. The authors state that: schools at all levels were modern; that goals, values and attitudes to *fa'a-Sāmoa* had undergone significant (and not always positive) change; and that migration to the USA had greatly increased.

690 **Education in American Samoa.**

Charles F. Reid. In: *Education in the territories and outlying possessions of the United States.* Charles F. Reid. New York: Bureau of Publications, Teachers College, Columbia University, 1941, p. 348-401, 579-81. bibliog. (Contributions to Education, no. 825).

An excellent history and description of education under United States naval administration. There is an account of the work, from 1931, of the Frederic Duclos Barstow Foundation, especially its Feleti School, which attempted to solve the problems of Samoan readjustment by means of training native leaders. Reid's recommendations stress the need for federal grants to be extended to American Samoa: 'American Samoa is governed by the fiat of a Naval officer'. See also: 'Educational policy in Eastern Samoa: an American colonial outpost' by E. Beauchamp (*Comparative Education* [Oxford], vol. 11, no. 1 [March 1975], p. 23-30. bibliog.), a mildly critical view of the ethos, organization and methods of education in American Samoa, with observations on the merits and demerits of ITV (instructional television); and 'A scheme for assessing unmet educational needs: the American Samoa example' by R. Murray Thomas (*International Review of Education*, vol. 13, no. 1 [1977], p. 59-78), which describes a series of tests and studies on learning needs aimed at assessing the suitability of existing educational objectives and the degree to which they were being achieved.

691 **Educational television, enculturation, and acculturation: a study of change in American Samoa.**

Richard B. Baldauf. *International Review of Education*, vol. 27, no. 3 (1981), p. 227-45.

The transplanted American educational system was one of the few institutions which remained alien and apart from traditional Samoan culture, so was able to adopt and adapt those aspects of Western contact culture which it found necessary or desirable. This article reviews the historical and cultural place of education in Samoan society and examines the acculturative effects of educational television from 1964 to 1973 when it was phased out as the central medium of instruction.

692 **ITV in American Samoa: after nine years.**

Wilbur Schramm. Washington, DC: Information Center on Instructional Technology, 1973. 55p. bibliog. (AID Studies in Educational Technology).

This description of the reform of American Samoa's educational system through the introduction of instructional television (ITV) concludes that, even after nine years, data are insufficient for satisfactory programme evaluation. Schramm points out that allocation per student is very high, that achievement in English is marginally improved, and that resistance to ITV increases from lower to upper grades and between primary and secondary teachers.

693 **Under the Southern Cross.**

Frederic Duclos Barstow. [Honolulu]: Frederic Duclos Barstow Foundation for American Samoans, [n.d.]. 70p.

Contains impressions of Samoa by the philanthropist whose Foundation so greatly advanced education in American Samoa under US Naval administration. The Frederic Duclos Barstow Foundation was set up in 1931, in memory of a young American who had lived in Samoa. Its Committee first visited American Samoa in 1932. From the discussions with Samoans during this tour came a general plan for education. An important part of the work of the Barstow Committee was the establishment of the Feleti School, financed mainly by the Barstow Foundation. See also *Report by A. F. Judd to his colleagues of the Committee, 1937* by A. F. Judd (Honolulu: Frederic Duclos Barstow Foundation for American Samoans, 1937. 47p.).

694 **A view toward school/community-based management: perspectives of public school principals in American Samoa.**
Selina J. Ganopole. *Pacific Studies*, vol. 16, no. 2 (June 1993), p. 143-65. bibliog.

Presents the findings of an investigation of education- and culture-related factors which may be relevant to the introduction of school/community-based management (SCBM). School principals revealed 'a general lack of confidence' with respect to teachers' knowledge and skills. Principals, too, appeared 'ill prepared' to assume the responsibilities of school-based management. Despite professed enthusiasm among growing numbers of Samoan educators for SCBM, many of the conditions deemed essential for its successful implementation were not present in American Samoa. See also 'Factors contributing to the cultural stability of Samoa' by Lowell D. Holmes (*Anthropological Quarterly*, vol. 53 [1980], p. 188-99. bibliog.).

Western Samoa

695 **Daughters of the islands.**
Evelyn A. Downs. Wallington, England: Religious Education Press, 1944. 78p.

This charming picture of the London Missionary Society's Boarding School for Samoan Girls at Papauta on the slopes of Mount Vaea, above Āpia, is set against the gradual changes which have affected the life of the Samoan people in the 20th century. Opened in 1892, Papauta educated many of the wives of Samoan pastors and missionaries. There are sixty-three excellent photographs 'by courtesy of Major-General C. D. Barrett, U.S.A. Marine Corps'. Highlights of this affectionate chronicle are the long effort to build a school chapel and the appendix, 'Mother of the Southern Sea', devoted to Lakena of Nanumea, who came to Papauta in 1895 as a child, and remained for the rest of her life as a teacher, her spirit pervading the school.

696 **Decentralisation or centralisation?: education in Western Samoa 1992.**
Peggy Fairbairn-Dunlop. *Access*, vol. 11, no. 2 (1992), p. 51-57.

A cool contribution to the perennial polemic regarding the relative virtues, advantages and disadvantages of strict central control of educational institutions, curricula and resources, or of devolution of power and responsibility to district and village levels, and to individual educational establishments. Earlier studies include: 'The United Nations and educational development in Western Samoa during the trusteeship' by J. M. Barrington (*International Review of Education*, vol. 19, no. 2 [1973], p. 255-61. bibliog.), a retrospect of New Zealand educational policy and practice, UNESCO assistance and educational development in the UN trust territory of Western Samoa, 1920-61; and *Report on education in Western Samoa* by Clarence Edward Beeby (Wellington: R. E. Owen, Government Printer, 1954. 40p.), a comprehensive report prepared for the New Zealand Department of Island Territories and presented to the House of Representatives. It is frank in its assessment of educational achievements and shortcomings after three decades of New Zealand administration, and progressive in the importance it gives to education in the vernacular and to the promotion of positive Samoan cultural values.

697 **Education for economic development in the South Pacific.**
Edited by K. G. Gannicott. Canberra: National Centre for Development Studies, Research School of Pacific Studies, Australian National University, 1990. 119p. (Pacific Policy Papers, no. 6).

Five Australian economists discuss important questions with regard to the policies of aid-donor nations toward 'developing' countries, largely in quantitative terms. Each chapter summarizes recent developments in education, examines the current situation in detail, and makes recommendations for more effective use of funding. The chapter on Tonga and Western Samoa compares and contrasts policies, with Western Samoa introducing more vocational education and Tonga opting for traditional academic skills. The authors point out that 'vocationalizing' the curriculum is 'a costly and inefficient way of increasing the value of schooling'. They declare that 'the option of return to village life is viewed quite positively'. See also *Education and the socio-economic environment: recent development in Western Samoa*, compiled by Shiva Lingappa (Paris: Division of Educational Policy and Planning, UNESCO, 1977).

698 **Literacy instruction in a Samoan village.**
Alessandro Duranti, Elinor Ochs. In: *The acquisition of literacy: ethnographic perspectives.* Edited by Bambi B. Schieffelin, Perry Gilmore. Norwood, New Jersey: Ablex, 1986, p. 213-32. bibliog.

This interesting study of how children are taught to read in a traditional village in Western Samoa shows how the instructor also socializes his pupils and introduces them to new expectations in the adult-child relationship and in task accomplishment.

699 **Samoa: a teacher's tale.**
George Irwin. London: Cassell, 1965. 182p. map.

This entertaining, well illustrated account of colonial education in Western Samoa in the decade following the Second World War provides a vivid impression of village schools and Samoan customs. Irwin, a New Zealander, was Principal of the Teachers' Training College and, later, Assistant Director of Education. For Irwin, the optimistic, fiercely proud, poetic inhabitants of 'the heartland of the Polynesian Pacific' resemble Homer's dark-eyed Greeks.

700 **Western Samoa.**
T. Esera. In: *International encyclopedia of national systems of education.* Edited by T. Neville Postlethwaite. Oxford: Pergamon (Elsevier Science), 1995, 2nd revised edition, p. 1,065-71. bibliog.

A comprehensive and up-to-date presentation of authoritative information on Western Samoa's national system of education, in all its aspects. See also: 'An assessment of secondary education in a small island state: implications for agricultural education' by Lafita'i Fuata (*Directions: Journal of Educational Studies*, vol. 15, no. 2 [1993], p. 17-27); and 'Western Samoa: rebuilding the education system' (*Education Sector Review* [The World Bank, Washington, DC] [1992]).

Science and Technology

General

701 **Pacific Science.**
Honolulu: University Press of Hawai'i, 1947- . quarterly.
This respected journal publishes contributions to research on biological and physical sciences in the Pacific.

702 **Preliminary bibliography on traditional science and technology in the Pacific islands: partly annotated.**
E. Eade. Suva: Pacific Information Centre, University of the South Pacific Library, 1992. 104p.
Conceived by the Organizing Committee for the Conference on Science and Pacific Island Peoples (July 1992), this bibliography of 444 items is limited to works on traditional scientific and technical knowledge before European settlement in Melanesia, Micronesia and Polynesia. New Zealand, Hawai'i and Papua New Guinea are excluded. Numbered entries are arranged (and indexed) by subject, e.g. agriculture, boats, ecology and medicine.

Samoa

703 **The names and movements of the heavenly bodies, from a Samoan point of view.**
John B. Stair. *Journal of the Polynesian Society*, vol. 7 (1898), p. 48-49.
A brief introduction to Samoan astronomy and its nomenclature.

704 **Some Samoan observations on science and scientists.**
Cluny Macpherson, La'avasa Macpherson. In: *Man and a half: essays in Pacific anthropology and ethnobiology in honour of Ralph Bulmer.* Edited by Andrew Pawley. Auckland, New Zealand: Polynesian Society, 1991, p. 589-93. (Memoir, no. 48).

Samoans have a genuine respect for knowledge, coupled with scepticism about formal education and the sciences 'which are seen to have challenged the existence of God and his place in the explanation of the world'. A series of vignettes show Samoan reservations about science to be rationally based, with regard to practitioners, knowledge and practices. 'Samoans reflect on science in terms which are defined by their culture. Scientists reflect on Samoans in terms defined by their "culture". They do no more than to confirm the fact that all science is ethnoscience'.

German Samoa

705 **Cultural imperialism and the exact sciences: German expansion overseas, 1900-1930.**
Lewis Pyenson. New York: Peter Lang, 1985. 353p. maps. bibliog. (Studies in History and Culture, no. 1).

This scholarly account of the work of physicists and astronomers in German colonies and zones of influence includes details of research conducted in German Samoa, where one of three principal overseas scientific institutions was located. The exact sciences were largely unaffected by imperialist ideology. See also 'Cultural imperialism and exact sciences: German expansion overseas 1900-1930' by Lewis Pyenson (*History of Science*, vol. 20, no. 1 [1982], p. 1-43. bibliog.).

American Samoa

706 **A bibliography of energy literature for U.S. Micronesia and American Samoa.**
Charles W. Case. Mangilao, Guam: MARC, University of Guam, 1986. 52p.

A bibliography of works relating to the two areas in the fields of appropriate technology, energy conservation, energy policy and renewable energy sources. See also *Guidebook to alternative energy projects: American Samoa, the Commonwealth of the Northern Mariana Islands, the Federated States of Micronesia, Guam, and the Republics of the Marshall Islands and Palau* by Charles W. Case (Sausalito, California: Energy Resources International, 1987. 143p. bibliog.).

707 ***Eneti*: Samoa's Energy News.**

Pago Pago: Territorial Energy Office, 1981- . quarterly.

A Government of American Samoa official periodical devoted to news and discussion of the Territory's power resources, and of conservation and alternative energy projects. See also *Solar energy: lessons from the Pacific island experience* by Andres Liebenthal, Subodh Mathur, Herbert Wade (Washington, DC: The World Bank, 1994. 72p. [World Bank Technical Paper, no. 244]), which presents lessons learned from the success of the World Bank and other international organizations in using and maintaining solar photovoltaic (PV) systems in the Pacific islands.

708 **Pacific Ocean engineers: history of the US Army Corps of Engineers in the Pacific 1905-1980.**

Erwin N. Thompson. Washington, DC: Government Printing Office, 1985. 460p. maps. bibliog.

Though primarily concerned with Hawai'i, this also covers Corps of Engineers' assignments and projects (all of which are listed in the appendix) in other areas of the Pacific, including American Samoa.

Scientific Institutions and Research

German Samoa

709 **History of the Samoan Observatory from 1902 to 1921.**
Gustav Heinrich Angenheister, translated and edited by William Ian Reilly. Wellington: Geophysics Division, Department of Scientific and Industrial Research, 1978. bibliog.

A discussion of the Samoan Observatory, which for its first two decades of existence was a prestigious outpost of the best traditions of German astronomy and geophysical sciences, staffed by competent scientists prolific in their learned publications.

Samoa

710 **The agricultural research system in Western Samoa.**
International Service for National Agricultural Research (ISNAR); Western Samoa. Department of Agriculture and Forestry. The Hague: ISNAR, 1983. 131p. bibliog. (ISNAR R 16).

Every aspect of Samoan agriculture, agricultural research, agricultural development and agricultural policy is thoroughly presented in this invaluable study. Research policy, institutions and needs are considered and assessed, including the role of the USP School of Agriculture, Alafua, in the system. See also: 'Farming systems research: a theme for Alafua' by M. J. Blackie, R. H. Schwass, R. B. Jones (*Alafua Agricultural Bulletin*, vol. 4, no. 4 [1979], p. 3-19), in which the authors advocate greater attention to research on farming systems, such as multiple cropping; and 'Rural development in Western Samoa through farming systems research. Part 1: the problem and perspective' by M. J. Blackie, R. H. Schwass, R. B. Jones (*Fiji Agricultural*

Journal, vol. 41, no. 2 [July-Dec. 1979], p. 87-94) and 'Part 2: an approach through multiple cropping' (*Fiji Agricultural Journal*, vol. 42, no. 1 [1980], p. 1-10).

711 **A comparison of field research in Canada and Polynesia.**
Robert J. Maxwell. In: *Marginal natives: anthropologists at work.* Edited by Morris Freilich. New York; Evanston, Illinois; London: Harper & Rowe, 1970, p. 441-84. bibliog.

Part two, 'West of Pango Pango' (p. 452-81), comprises a detailed and often amusing account of research into introversion-extroversion among Samoans in the Tutuila village of Laovele and Korean fishermen in Pago Pago. One finding was that introversion increases with age. Maxwell came to regret his somewhat irreverent attitude to Samoan and *pālagi* élite groups and religious leaders. He concludes: 'I would also try to court the part-Samoan élite, too, for they seemed to take particular pride in their mythology and were not as likely to lie as the ordinary villagers were'.

712 **Developments in Polynesian ethnology.**
Edited by Alan Howard, Robert Borofsky. Honolulu: University of Hawai'i Press, 1989. 374p. bibliog.

Represents an attempt by nine experienced researchers to assess the current state of Polynesian ethnology, by reviewing the impressive quantity of work done in Polynesia since Alan Howard edited the collection *Polynesia: readings on a culture area* (Scranton, Pennsylvania: Chandler, 1971). The essays reflect the excitement and intellectual ferment in Polynesian ethnology, where virtually every issue posed in the past has been examined afresh, often with startling results. Topics discussed include: prehistory; social organization; socialization and character development; *mana* and *tapu*; chieftainship; art and aesthetics; and the early contact period. Samoa is discussed throughout, *passim*. Among the distinguished contributors Alan Howard, Patrick V. Kirch and Bradd Shore have carried out field research in Samoa. The extensive bibliography (p. 293-352) is a useful guide to research in the Pacific islands.

713 **Exploring the written: anthropology and the multiplicity of writing.**
Edited by Eduardo P. Archetti. Oslo: Scandinavian University Press, 1994. 342p. bibliog. (Oslo Studies in Social Anthropology).

A symposium of essays examining how literature relates to ethnography: '... in what way can the ethnographer make use of fiction, essays, songs, letters, poetry, drama, newspapers or autobiographies that are produced in the culture that is being studied?' The diverse, worldwide empirical case-studies include Samoa and Fiji.

714 **From Labrador to Samoa: the theory and practice of Eleanor Burke Leacock.**
Edited by Constance R. Sutton. [Arlington, Virginia]: Association for Feminist Anthropology/American Anthropological Association, in collaboration with the International Women's Anthropology Conference, 1993. 153p. bibliogs.

Includes: 'Being an anthropologist' by Eleanor Burke Leacock (p. 1-31. bibliog.); a reprint of 'The problems of youth in contemporary Samoa' by Eleanor Burke Leacock

(p. 115-30), originally written as a postscript to *Quest for the REAL Samoa: the Mead/Freeman controversy and beyond* (q.v.); and 'Bibliography of Eleanor Burke Leacock's published work' (p. 141-49).

715 **[A Japanese chief in Western Samoa: a research diary 1965-1980].**
Hisatsugu Sugimoto. Kyoto, Japan: Kokin Shoten, 1982. 200p. bibliog.

Sugimoto carried out research on the *matai* population of Samamea ('Upolu) and Fagafau (Savai'i) in 1965 and 1980. In this Japanese-language work, he highlights the increase in the total number of titleholders due to the large increase in nonresident titleholders.

716 **Leacock's Samoan research.**
IWAC Newsletter, vol. 9 (1987), p. 5-10.

An outline of the research on adolescence and on the psychological and social problems of young people carried out in American Samoa and Western Samoa by Eleanor Burke Leacock (1922-87), in order to assess the validity or otherwise of the criticisms of Margaret Mead's fieldwork made by Derek Freeman. Leacock was America's best known Marxist anthropologist, a feminist scholar, and 'one of the foremost contributors to the recasting of anthropology in a historical materialist framework'.

717 **Mediated encounters with Pacific cultures: three Samoan dinners.**
Alessandro Duranti. In: *Visions of empire: voyages, botany, and representations of nature*. Edited by David Philip Miller, Peter Hanns Reill. Cambridge, England; New York; Melbourne: Cambridge University Press, 1996, p. 326-34. bibliog.

Duranti, anthropologist and authority on the sociolinguistics of Samoan, discusses the parallels between voyages of discovery and anthropological fieldwork. He illustrates his argument with an example of a mediated encounter with Samoan domestic culture, from his own experience.

718 **New Zealand based research on the Pacific islands.**
Compiled by Melani Anae, edited by Marjorie Tuainekore Crocombe. Auckland, New Zealand: Centre for Pacific Studies, University of Auckland, 1993. 75p. bibliog.

The updated and expanded version of the 1982 *New Zealand research register: the Pacific islands*, edited by Peter Crowe and published by the Anthropology Department of the University of Auckland. It comprises an alphabetical list of researchers, with details of their publications, and is indexed by area and subject. Lack of full details in many instances diminishes its bibliographical value. There are lists of relevant theses and dissertations awarded by New Zealand universities, 1945-90 (PhD, p. 59-62; MA, p. 63-75).

719 **Social anthropology in Polynesia: a review of research.**
Felix M. Keesing. London; Melbourne; New York: Oxford University Press, 1953. 126p. map. bibliog.

Published under the auspices of the South Pacific Commission, this is an expert critical review of anthropological studies up to about 1952, grouped under economic development, social development and health. Chapter five states research needs and possibilities, and the extensive bibliography (p. 68-119) includes Samoa (p. 89-96). Asterisks indicate works of 'some importance' or of 'major significance'.

720 **South Pacific Research Register.**
Suva: Pacific Information Centre, University of the South Pacific Library, 1982- . biennial.

Arranged by author and indexed by subject, this is a detailed guide to research in progress, of any nature and anywhere, relating to the islands, and also to indigenous peoples in Australia, Hawai'i and New Zealand.

721 **Weaver of the border.**
Margaret Mead. In: *In the company of man: twenty portraits of anthropological informants.* Edited by Joseph B. Casagrande. New York; Evanston, Illinois; London: Harper & Row, 1964, p. 175-210. (Harper Torchbook).

In this work, first published in 1960, Mead writes affectionately, and with great respect, of her 'most gifted informant', Mrs Phebe Clotilda Coe Parkinson, wife and collaborator of Richard Parkinson, author of *Dreißig Jahre in der Südsee* (Stuttgart, Germany: Strecker & Schröder, 1907). Extensive extracts from Mrs Parkinson's autobiography shed light on life in her native Samoa, and on the trading empire and second 'contact culture' developed by her and her sister, 'Queen Emma', in New Britain.

Literature

South Pacific literature

722 **Indigenous literature of Oceania: a survey of criticism and interpretation.**
Nicholas J. Goetzfridt, with a foreword by Vilsoni Hereniko. Westport, Connecticut; London: Greenwood Press, 1995. 348p. map. bibliog. (Bibliographies and Indexes in World Literature, no. 47).

'For the first time, bibliographic data and short summaries of texts that comment on fiction, poetry and plays written by Pacific Islanders can be found between the covers of one book'. This splendid, painstaking, annotated guide to works of criticism in English, by people native to the islands of the South Pacific, Aotearoa (New Zealand) and Australia, has much on Samoan writers, especially Momoe Malietoa Von Reiche and Albert Wendt. It is indexed by title and author, critics and subjects.

723 ***Mana*: a South Pacific Journal of Language and Literature.**
Suva: South Pacific Creative Arts Society, 1973- . 2 pa.

This invariably interesting journal is devoted to the new literatures of the Pacific islands, including Samoan creative writing in English. The journal was originally called *Mana Review*. See also *Pacific Moana Quarterly* (Suva: South Pacific Creative Arts Society, 1978- . quarterly). Formerly published in Hamilton, New Zealand by Outrigger Publishers, and then primarily devoted to literature and literary criticism, this journal now embraces all aspects of creative arts and handicrafts in the islands of the South Pacific.

724 Silence and invisibility: a study of the literatures of the Pacific, Australia, and New Zealand.

Norman Simms. Washington, DC: Three Continents Press, 1986. 227p. map. bibliog.

Provides essays which introduce and evaluate new writing in the region, and seek to create 'Third World critics of all literature', with Albert Wendt as exemplar (p. 37-45; p. 178-80). Today's *fa'a-Sāmoa* is seen as a new construct made of the Christian morality and capitalist economy permeating the smallest villages and *'āiga*. American television beamed to Āpia from Pago Pago distorts Samoan culture into 'a spectacular, sensationalist farrago of unrequited fears and expectations', clashing with the 'puritanical power' of the Samoan church. The extensive bibliography (p. 153-224) offers a general guide to the serious study of the new literatures of the Pacific region since 1970.

725 South Pacific literature written in English: a selected bibliography.

Esther W. Williams. Suva: University of the South Pacific Library, 1979. 102p. (Selected Bibliography, no. 6).

An unannotated bibliography of 1,272 works by indigenous writers, except for those of Hawai'i and Papua New Guinea. The categories used are: research aids; general works; drama; folk-tales; interviews; poetry; reviews and criticism; short stories; and forthcoming works. Samoan writers are well represented.

726 Span: Journal of the South Pacific Association for Commonwealth Literature and Language Studies.

Christchurch, New Zealand: University of Canterbury, 1975- . bi-annual.

Span publishes scholarly comparative studies, reports of work in progress, reviews and poems. Issue 10 contains an index to nos. 1-10. Since 1988, literature in the South Pacific has also been surveyed by the twice-yearly *SPACLALS Newsletter*.

727 Writers from the South Pacific: a bio-bibliographic critical encyclopedia.

Norman Simms. Washington, DC: Three Continents Press, 1991. 184p. map. bibliog.

This alphabetically arranged, indexed by territory, encyclopaedia of writers covers Australia, East Timor, Malaysia, New Zealand and Singapore as well as the Pacific islands. In his perceptive introduction, Simms explores the achievements and problems of island writers, stressing the need to consider not just the few internationally known writers, such as Albert Wendt, but equally 'the silent and invisible authors'. These include the Samoan writers Aiava, Kelekoli, Ma'ia'i, Malifa, Meleisea, Petaia, Sa'aga, Sapolu, Simi, Taule'alo, Tui'i and Von Reiche. Albert Wendt (photograph, p. xxii) is anomalously indexed with New Zealand writers in English.

Literature in Samoan

728 **Aspects of Samoan literature I: the structure of the Samoan single story form and its uses.**
John Charlot. *Anthropos*, vol. 85, no. 4 (1990), p. 415-30. bibliog.

In this, the first of several articles on Samoan orally transmitted literature, the typical story structure is shown to consist of a title or titular sentence, an introduction, an optional time reference, a narrative, an optional conclusion, and an optional final phrase or sentence. In 'Aspects of Samoan literature II: genealogies, multigenerational complexes, and texts on the origin of the universe' (*Anthropos*, vol. 86, no. 1/3 [1991], p. 127-50. bibliog.), Charlot describes the form of genealogies and analyses texts on the origin of the universe. In the final article of the series, 'Aspects of Samoan literature III: texts on historical subjects and bodies of literature' (*Anthropos*, vol. 87, no. 1/3 [1992], p. 33-48. bibliog.), Charlot analyses the structure of a number of Samoan texts on historical subjects, and sketches a tentative outline of Samoan history.

729 **Moana: o se tusi i le gagana Samoa.** (Deep sea: writing in the Samoan language.)
Apia: Western Samoa Centre, University of the South Pacific, 1979- . annual.

The journal of the Western Samoan Writers' Association, devoted to creative writing and literature in Samoan. *Moana* sponsors a regular Samoan Story and Poem Competition and publishes the best of the poems and stories entered. This journal is not to be confused with *Pacific Moana Quarterly*.

Samoan literature in English

Studies

730 **Samoan writing: searching for the written *fāgogo*.**
Peggy Fairbairn-Dunlop. In: *Readings in Pacific literature*. Edited by Paul Sharrad. Wollongong, New South Wales: New Literatures Research Centre, University of Wollongong, 1993, p. 136-60.

Originally published (as by Peggy Dunlop) in *Pacific Islands Communication Journal*, vol. 14, no. 1 (1985), p. 41-69, this is an exploration of the emergence of Samoan written literature and of the factors which have shaped and encouraged it. The success of Albert Wendt and his courageous questioning both of alien values and emerging nationalism prompted greater confidence among Samoan writers. The author also considers the factors determining whether to write in Samoan or in English.

731 **Western influences on Samoan poetry.**
Sefulu Ioane. *SPAN*, no. 19 (Oct. 1984), p. 64-77.

Many fine Samoan poets, such as Ruperake Petaia, Momoe Malietoa von Reiche and Albert Wendt, have chosen to write in English. Their work exhibits considerable Western influence in models, style, versification, imagery and content. This is a long established phenomenon in which missionary hymnology, colonial education, radio, television and pop music have all played a part. *SPAN* is the twice yearly journal of the South Pacific Association for Commonwealth Literature & Language Studies, devoted to literary criticism (especially of post-colonial writing) and to creative writing in the region.

Anthologies

732 ***Nuanua*: Pacific writing in English since 1980.**
Selected with an introduction by Albert Wendt. Honolulu: University of Hawai'i Press, 1995. 405p. (*Talanoa*: Contemporary Pacific Literature).

This important anthology of contemporary Pacific writing in English from nine countries is a successor to *Lali* (1980), the widely read and admired anthology also edited by Albert Tuaopepe Wendt. His introduction reviews progress since 1980, highlighting the growing strength and confidence shown in fiction and poetry, and the disillusionment, irony, anger and cynicism so often expressed. Seventeen Samoan writers are represented, some living in the Samoan diaspora. They are Apelu Aiavao, Litia Alaelua, Pasitale Faleilemilo, Epi Enari Fua'au, Sano Malifa, Tasi Malifa, Ruperake Petaia, Clara Reid, Eti Sa'aga, Noumea Simi, Tate Simi, Caroline Sinavaiana, Talosaga Tolovae, Emma Kruse Va'ai, Makerita Va'i, Momoe Malietoa Von Reiche and Albert Wendt.

733 **Penny plain and two pence coloured: a collection of writing by young Samoans and New Zealanders.**
Compiled by Ronald Thomas. Palmerston North, New Zealand: Massey University, 1994. 92p.

This interesting anthology features stories and poems in English by new Samoan writers, alongside works by their New Zealand contemporaries.

734 **Western Samoa.**
In: *Lali: a Pacific anthology*. Edited and with an introduction by Albert Wendt. Auckland, New Zealand: Longman Paul, 1980, p. 243-94.

Contains two Sāpepe village stories: 'The birth and death of the miracle man' and 'A talent', both by Albert Wendt; and poems by Eti Sa'aga, Ruperake Petaia, Ata Ma'ia'i, Sano Malifa, Momoe Malietoa Von Reiche and Albert Wendt. Momoe Malietoa Von Reiche is the author of: *Solaua, a secret embryo: a collection of poems* (Suva, Āpia: *Mana* Publications, 1979); and *Pa'a Alimago on wet days* (Āpia: Samoa Printing and Publishing Company, 1979). See also *Some modern poetry from Western Samoa*, edited by Albert Wendt (Suva: *Mana* Publications, 1974. 32p. Reprinted, 1983), an anthology of verse by seven Western Samoan poets.

Individual writers

735 **Kidnapped: a cry from Western Samoa.**
Ruperake Petaia. *Cultures*, no. 33 (1983), p. 25.

An accomplished Western Samoan poet considers his cultural heritage and cultural identity. Petaia's best known work is *Blue rain* (Apia: USP Western Samoa Centre; Suva: *Mana* Publications, 1980. 34p. Reprinted, 1991). Other notable works include: *Pinnacles* by Makerita Va'ai (Suva: *Mana* Publications, 1993. 68p.), an imaginatively illustrated, first collection of verse by a talented woman poet from Sātaua, Savai'i, Western Samoa; and *Lost reality* by Fepai F. S. Kolia (Suva: *Mana* Publications, 1988. 76p.), an impressive collection.

736 ***'O le solo ia Lupe ma le i'a*: poem of Lupe and the fish.**
C. S. Figiel. *Rongorongo Studies*, vol. 4, no. 2 (1994), p. 35-43.

The winning poem (in *tautala leaga*, with English translation) in the 1994 Polynesian Literary Competition, by a Western Samoan writer from Matāuta Uta. It expresses a passionate longing for old ways and old gods, and a detestation of the 'imagesellers' from 'cold wintery Europe' and their 'messengers among the savages': *sui o galo* (messengers of forgetting). See also her first book *Where we once belonged* (Auckland, New Zealand: Pasifika Press, 1996. 236p.). This uses the traditional *su'ifefiloi* story-telling form to tell 'a modern tragicomedy of violence, the repression of women and the struggle for identity in Samoa'. Honestly and forcefully it follows the unhappy coming of age of thirteen-year-old Aloga Filiga, who lives with her family, the *'āiga* Filiga, in the village of Malaefou, near Āpia.

737 **The story of Laulii, a daughter of Samoa: giving her life, manners and customs of the islanders, peculiarities of the race, games, amusements, incidents of many kinds, and matters of interest in connection with the Samoan people. Also, a sketch of the life of Alexander A. Willis, (her husband).**
Lauli'i Willis, edited by William H. Barnes. San Francisco: J. Winterburn, 1889. 255p.

Lauli'i was the Samoan wife of Alex Willis, Āpia carpenter. She was a favourite of Robert Louis Stevenson. Fanny Stevenson said of this life story that Lauli'i 'wrote very well when she was allowed her own expressions'.

738 **Talofa ali'i.** (Greetings, Lord!)
Glen Fowler Ovard. Mapusaga, American Samoa: American Samoa Community College; [Pago Pago]: Department of Tourism, Government of American Samoa, 1979. 24p. endpaper maps.

A collection of twelve short poems in English, supplemented by twenty charming photographs, mostly in colour, and by three maps. The map of Tutuila usefully identifies fifty-nine settlements. Ovard, a professor of education at Brigham Young University in Provo, Utah, expresses 'his love and appreciation toward the South Sea Islands, especially Samoa – the land, the people and the traditions. He has tried to create a oneness with them in their expression of reverence of God and appreciation of the beautiful in the land in which they live'.

739 **Think of a garden.**

John A. Kneubuhl. *Mānoa: a Pacific Journal of International Writing*, vol. 5, no. 1 (Summer 1993), p. 106-37.

A section of the last play written by Kneubuhl, playwright, actor, director and scriptwriter (e.g. for the *Perry Mason* TV series). Set in American Samoa in December 1929, it is overshadowed by the police killing of Tamasese in Āpia: 'So much – so very much – had depended on him. A people's freedom. Our dignity and pride in being ourselves'. The complete play is included in the trilogy *Think of a garden, and other plays* by John Kneubuhl (Honolulu: University of Hawai'i Press, 1997). The other works in this volume are 'Mele Kanikau: a pageant' and 'A play: a play'.

740 **Two poems.**

Caroline Sinavaiana. *Mānoa: a Pacific Journal of International Writing*, vol. 5, no. 1 (Summer 1993), p. 227-28.

'Ianeta's dance' and 'Sā Nāfanua' reflect their author's scholarly interest in Samoan traditions and culture. An American Samoan, Sinavaiana is a teacher, lecturer on Samoan folk arts and cultural affairs, and an environmentalist. Among her scholarly publications is an authoritative study of the Samoan traditional comedy, *fale aitu*. See also: *Three Tutuila poets* by Eti Sa'aga, Caroline Sinavaiana, John Enright (Pago Pago: *'O le Si'uleo o Samoa*, 1993); and *Atauloma* by John Enright (Pago Pago: *'O le Si'uleo o Samoa*, 1993), 'an eclectic selection of poems covering many areas', by the well known American Samoan poet and Folk Arts Coordinator, American Samoa Council on Arts, Culture and Humanities.

Fata Sano Malifa

741 **Alms for oblivion.**

Fata Sano Malifa. New York: Vantage Press, 1993. 258p.

This remarkable, lyrical, 'resolutely Samoa-centred novel' has as its protagonists Pasikale, Piso'o, a sexual galloper, and Nikoloa M. ('Niko'), a man of philosophical bent. Niko spends years abroad, returning to Samoa to find himself an internal exile, unable either to conform to the *fa'a-Sāmoa* or to escape from it. His conflict reflects national polemics, the tension between tradition and modernity, the inexorable pressures of global capitalism, and the 'cancerous corruption' of Samoan politics and bureaucracy. Niko enters politics in order to expose those who, like the colonialists before them, 'just took what they wanted'.

742 **Looking down at waves.**

Sano Malifa. Suva: *Mana* Publications, 1975. 61p. Reprinted, 1991.

A first collection by the admired Western Samoan poet and novelist from Afega. See also: Sano Malifa's 'Eight poems' in *The third Mana annual of creative writing*, edited by Marjorie Tuainekore Crocombe (Suva: *Mana* Publications, 1977, p. 47-49); *Song and return* (1992); and his novel, as Fata Sano Malifa, *Alms for oblivion* (q.v.). 'The edge of his next goodbye' by P. O'Sullivan (*Mana Review*, vol. 1, no. 1 [1976], p. 79-81), discusses the poetry of Sano Malifa, especially *Looking down at waves*. The poet's travels are said to reflect a restless and 'perplexed' nature.

Albert Wendt

Works

743 **Black rainbow.**

Albert Wendt. Honolulu: University of Hawai'i Press, 1995. 272p.

'This startling novel takes the form of a fast-moving allegorical thriller. Who are the all-powerful Tribunal and President? Who are the Hunters and the Hunted, and the allies from the depths of the city? Set in a future New Zealand where only the Citizen who asks no questions can achieve happiness, a renegade hero seeks to rescue his family in the State-sponsored Game of Life'. Allegory, science fiction and fantasy are deftly blended as Wendt explores the nature of power, violence, free will, reality, time and literature itself. The novel was first published by Penguin Books in 1992.

744 **Flying-fox in a freedom tree.**

Albert Wendt. Auckland, New Zealand: Longman Paul, 1980. 149p. (Pacific Paperbacks).

First published in 1974, this is a collection of eight shrewdly observed short stories and a novella, set in a Western Samoa undergoing rapid economic, social and moral change.

745 **Inside us the dead: poems 1961 to 1974.**

Albert Wendt. Auckland, New Zealand: Longman Paul, 1976. 55p. Reprinted, 1980.

These thirty-nine elegant and impressive poems confirm Wendt's versatility as a writer. His themes range from reverent contemplation of nature to powerful satire of Western images of island 'paradises'. He is savagely critical of Western racism, Western education and Western values.

746 **Leaves of the Banyan Tree.**

Albert Wendt. Auckland, New Zealand: Longman Paul, 1979; Honolulu: University of Hawai'i Press, 1994. 424p. (*Talanoa*: Contemporary Pacific Literature).

This powerful, now classic early novel, winner of the 1980 New Zealand Wattie Book of the Year Award, is an epic spanning three generations of a family and community in Western Samoa. Rich in characters, action and emotion, it explores 'on a grand scale such universal themes as greed, corruption, colonialism, exploitation, and revenge'. It convincingly corrects the inaccurate images of Samoans that have been created by early explorers and by anthropologists like Margaret Mead.

747 **Ola.**

Albert Wendt. Honolulu: University of Hawai'i Press, 1995. 350p.

Olamai'ileoti Monroe takes her seventy-five-year-old father, Finau, on a pilgrimage to the Holy Land. Set in Samoa, New Zealand, New York and Israel, Wendt's novel opposes the modern selfishness of Ola to the older, more complex morality of Finau, and grapples with the moral problems of Jew and Christian. Wendt achieves an aesthetic success which adds to his stature as the most innovative novelist in the South Pacific region.

748 **Photographs.**
Albert Wendt. Auckland, New Zealand: Auckland University Press, 1995. 89p.

These richly diverse poems are Wendt's first collection for over a decade. 'Snapshots of the close and familiar contrast with strange and mythical sequences from a vast Pacific epic in progress and a vivid impressionistic montage of global travel in the late twentieth century'. The sequences are: 'Maungawhau'; excerpts from 'The adventures of Vela: a novel in verse'; 'Nightflight'; and 'Photographs'.

749 **Pouliuli.** (Darkness.)
Albert Wendt. Honolulu: University of Hawai'i Press, 1980. 148p.

First published in Auckland by Longman Paul (1977), this is a novel of extraordinary artistic power, and of perception of the reality of Samoan society. Seventy-six-year-old Faleasa Osovae, titled head of the *'āiga* Faleasa, wakes to an almost unbearable feeling of revulsion against all that had given meaning to his existence. Memories flood into his heart 'in an endless stream of accusing pain, and the more his pain deepened the more he was forced to confront his past'. Tradition conflicts with the corrupt politics of the new world, which 'dreams of terror'.

750 **Shaman of visions: poems.**
Albert Wendt. Auckland, New Zealand: Auckland University Press; Oxford: Oxford University Press, 1984. 59p.

Best known for his novels and short stories, Wendt is also a poet of merit, with a distinctive voice. 'Out of Pacific details, observed places, the fighting and loving of family, his poems build a passionate landscape of the mind. In technique and content they are a bridge between the Pacific Islands and international literature'. The forty poems in this collection include 'The Fuluasou river, Upolu', 'Breadfruit trees', 'Mo'o', 'Teuila', 'The season of the moon', 'Circles' and the poignant 'Shaman of visions'.

Studies

751 **Albert Wendt.**
James W. Davidson. *Meanjin*, vol. 37, no. 1 (1978), p. 109-18.

Jim Davidson, Pacific historian and chronicler of the *Samoa mo Samoa* movement, interviews Albert Wendt, emergent Samoan writer and editor, at an early stage of his career. Wendt's first novel, about Samoans in New Zealand and entitled *Sons for the return home* (Auckland, New Zealand: Longman Paul, 1973. 218p.), was made into a successful if controversial film. Wendt discusses his sources of inspiration and some of his purposes as a creative writer in English. See also: 'The artist and the reefs breaking open' by Albert Wendt (*Mana*, vol. 3, no. 1 [1978], p. 107-21); and 'The angry young men of Oceania' by Albert Wendt (*UNESCO Courier* [Feb. 1976], p. 4-11, 32). There is also a welcome reprint of *Sons for the return home* (Honolulu: University of Hawai'i Press, 1996. 224p. [*Talanoa*: Contemporary Pacific Literature]).

752 **Albert Wendt.**

Foreword by Jean-Pierre Durix. Mont Saint Aignan, France: Société d'Études des Pays du Commonwealth, n.d. [198-]. 107p. bibliog. (Échos du Commonwealth, no. 8).

A symposium of critical analyses of *Leaves of the Banyan Tree*, *Flying-fox in a freedom tree*, *Sons for the return home*, *Pouliuli* and other works by the expatriate Samoan writer. The discussion focuses on style and on content, especially the tension between Samoan traditional culture and the ways of the outside world (and the new power relations those bring). The select bibliography covers both Wendt's own writings and critical works about them.

753 **Following in her footsteps: an interview with Albert Wendt.**

Vilsoni Hereniko. *Mānoa: a Pacific Journal of International Writing*, vol. 5, no. 1 (Summer 1993), p. 51-59.

An abridged and edited version of 'A conversation with Albert Wendt', broadcast by Hawaii Public Television in 1992 in its series 'Spectrum Hawaii'. Wendt talks about his grandmother's love of stories and her influence on him; techniques of writing; the reception of his work; and problems of new literatures in English. A significant thread is the writer's love for his family and his commitment to writing that is honest and fearless, and champions the underdog. Wendt's novels are 'mainly about political power and what political power does to people. How it destroys the people who wield the power and the people who suffer that power'.

754 **An interview with Albert Wendt.**

Vilsoni Hereniko, David Hanlon. *The Contemporary Pacific*, vol. 5, no. 1 (Spring 1993), p. 112-31.

Hereniko and Hanlon interviewed the noted novelist and professor of English at Auckland University on 4 February 1992 in Honolulu, on behalf of *The Contemporary Pacific*. Topics discussed included colonialism, political corruption in Samoa, the Fiji coups, Maori self-determination and the Treaty of Waitangi, Pacific history, literature, his novels *Ola* and *Black rainbow*, the films of *Leaves of the Banyan Tree* and *Flying fox in a freedom tree*, families and homelessness. Wendt claims that the third volume in the trilogy of the *Black rainbow* will be his last book: 'Then I'm through'.

755 **Wendt's crippled cosmos: genesis and form of his novels.**

Subramani. In: *South Pacific literature: from myth to fabulation*. Subramani. Suva: Institute of Pacific Studies, University of the South Pacific, 1985, p. 117-50. bibliog.

In this perceptive study of the emergence of creative writing in English in several Pacific island states, and of indigenous and expatriate influences (the latter largely negative), Subramani gives pride of place to Western Samoa's Albert Wendt. 'His triumph is in absorbing the history, myths and other oral traditions of his country, and synthesising them with the contemporary realities and the idiosyncracies of the novel form, and imposing upon it all a vision that is his own. He has invented the Samoan novel'.

756 **'You can't go home again': the colonial dilemma in the work of Albert Wendt.**

Helen Tiffin. *Meanjin*, vol. 37, no. 1 (1978), p. 119-26.

A perceptive study of the explicit and implicit anti-colonialism of Wendt's early novels and essays, and of the personal alienation and literary conflicts stemming from the writer's keen awareness of his colonial status. See also 'Albert Wendt: an assessment' by Roger Robinson (*Landfall*, vol. 135, no. 3 [Sept. 1980], p. 275-90).

Fiction about Samoa

757 **The beach of Falesá.**

Robert Louis Stevenson, with an introduction by J. C. Furnas, illustrations by Millard Sheets. New York: Heritage Press, [1958]. 128p.

This special edition of Stevenson's story contains handsome illustrations, some in colour, and an excellent introduction by the author of one of the best books on Stevenson in Samoa. The story first appeared, under the title *Uma*, in six successive weekly issues of the *Illustrated London News*, from 2 July 1892 to 6 August 1892. An early edition is *Island nights' entertainments: consisting of The beach of Falesá* by Robert Louis Stevenson, illustrated by Gordon Browne, W. Hatherell (London, Paris; Melbourne, 1893. 277p. map). The stories in this work are 'The beach of Falesá', 'The bottle imp' (first published as a serial, in Samoa) and 'The isle of voices'.

758 **Black coconuts, brown magic.**

Joseph Theroux. Garden City, New York: Dial Press, 1983. 227p.

This unusual novel tells of an American doctor and veteran of the war in Vietnam who returns to American Samoa, where he grew up. He renews his close association with the local Samoan community, and in so doing recalls past events and past friendships. The novel is notable for its sympathetic picture of traditional culture and for its very positive view of Samoan women.

759 **Fia fia: a novel of the South Pacific.**

James Ramsey Ullman. Cleveland, Ohio; New York: World Publishing Company, 1962. 325p.

Set in American Samoa, this realistic novel traces the lives of four American expatriates, a sociologist, a nurse, a naval flyer and a hotel developer. Walk-on characters include federal officials and congressmen, who provide light relief for the tensions and tragedies stemming from American involvement in Samoan society. The projected hotel stands as a symbol of unwanted and unpredictable change.

760 **Kifanga: ein Lebens- und Sittenbild des Volkes unserer ehemaligen deutschen Kolonie Samoa.** (Kifanga: a picture of the life and customs of the people of our former German colony of Samoa.)
Emil Reche. Leipzig, Germany: Haberland, 1924. 157p. Second edition, as *Kifanga: ein Lebens- und Sittenbild aus der Südsee*, Leipzig, Germany: Max Möhring, [n.d.]. 142p.

This novella, a popular success in the Weimar Republic and likened to the best love lyrics of Goethe and Kalidasa, is a sympathetic, partly fictionalized picture of life *fa'a-Sāmoa*. The author of several works on Polynesian culture, Reche in his introduction and notes discusses linguistic usage and customs. The appendix contains the music, Samoan and German texts of six songs, including the seemingly undying song of farewell, *Tofā la'u felegi* (nowadays *Tofā mai feleni*), a boatsong from Manono, and a *vi'i* about a battle at Matāutu.

761 **The laird of Samoa: a play.**
John Cargill Thompson. Edinburgh: Diehard, 1994. 25p.

Published together with Thompson's *Port and lemon: the mystery behind Sherlock Holmes: a play* (23p.), this whimsically imagines Robert Louis Stevenson of Vailima in the role of a Scottish landowner.

762 **Louis Becke.**
A. Grove Day. New York: Twayne, 1966. 192p. bibliog.

Of all the important writers on the Pacific, Louis Becke is the most prolific, the most honest and the most realistic. His stories are soundly based in twenty years experience as a seaman and as an island trader, in Micronesia, Polynesia and Samoa (the scene of some of his best stories). Day describes the main events in Becke's colourful life and discusses in depth his fictional and factual writing. There is an extensive bibliography of Becke's published and unpublished works. See also *South Sea supercargo: Louis Becke*, compiled and edited by A. Grove Day (Honolulu: University Press of Hawaii, 1967. 194p.), a collection of twenty-two tales by Becke, the 'Kipling of the Pacific'.

763 **Mad about islands: novelists of a vanished Pacific.**
A. Grove Day. Honolulu: Mutual Publishing Co., 1987. 291p. bibliog.

A compelling and thoughtful survey of fictional literature about the Pacific, including chapters on Becke, Maugham and Stevenson, all of whom used Samoa as the scene of some of their stories.

764 **A modern buccaneer.**
Rolf Boldrewood (i.e. T. A. Browne). London; New York: Macmillan, 1895. 338p.

This often reprinted novel of the exploits of William Henry Hayston (i.e. Hayes) is largely based on a manuscript by Louis Becke who had sailed with Hayes. The seizure of Haye's brig *Leonora* in Apia bay, by the American gunboat *Narragansett*, and his trade in weapons, which the Samoans were buying in large quantities, are among the topics included. See also Louis Becke, *Bully Hayes, buccaneer* (Sydney, 1913), and his articles in *Adventure* (New York, September 1914), *The Bulletin* (Sydney, 4 February 1893) and *Lone Hand* (Sydney, March 1912).

765 **Motu tapu: stories of the South Pacific.**
Graeme Lay. Auckland, New Zealand: Polynesian Press, 1990. 172p.

The New Zealand writer, Graeme Lay, writes crisply of Pacific islanders in Auckland, struggling for acceptance, and of Europeans in the islands, uncertain of their role in post-colonial Polynesia. 'Dateline' (p. 53-59) is set in Samoa, as is 'Vailima' (p. 60-69). The latter story contains a meeting, by the tomb of Robert Louis Stevenson on Mount Vaea above Āpia, with the materialized ghost of the poet Rupert Brooke. Other modern fiction includes *The islander* by T. E. Dorman (Auckland, New Zealand: Collins, 1975. 178p.), a novel about Samoans in New Zealand. An early popular success was *Lost in Samoa: a tale of adventure in the Navigator Islands* by E. S. Ellis (London: Cassell, 1894. 248p.), containing fictional adventures very much in the late 19th-century vogue set by R. M. Ballantyne, Jules Verne, Louis Becke, and Samoa's first novelist, R. L. Stevenson.

766 **No kava for Johnny.**
John O'Grady, illustrated by 'Wep'. London: Nicholas Kaye, 1961. 239p.

By the author ('Nino Culotta') of *They're a weird mob* and *Cop this lot*, this is, purportedly, 'the story of Ioane Papatiso, Polynesian, as told by himself'. It relates Ioane's progress from his beatings of childhood in Faleālili, on the south coast of 'Upolu, to his rejection of obedience to his *matai* and to his status and independence as a capable Health Department chemist and owner of a plot of freehold land.

767 **Old Samoan days.**
Louis Becke. In: *Wild life in southern seas*. Louis Becke. London: T. Fisher Unwin; New York: New Amsterdam Book Company, 1898, p. 172-211.

Contains tales of 19th-century Āpia, the notorious beach community frequented by whalers, beachcombers, unscrupulous traders, and blackbirders and pirates of the stamp of Bully Hayes – all known at first-hand by Becke, who conveys the wild spirit of the time in inimitable style.

768 **Der papalagi: die Reden des Südseehaüptlings Tuiavii aus Tiavea.**
(The *papalagi*: discourses of the South Sea chief Tuiavii from Tiavea.) Introduction by Erich Scheurmann, afterword by Bertolt Diel, illustrations by Maxine van Eerd-Schenk. Adliswil-Zürich, Switzerland: Verlag Tanner & Staehelin, 1977. 127p.

This collection of eleven discourses, ostensibly by a Western Samoan chief, critically contrasts the cultural values and way of life of the Samoans, 'free children of sunshine and light', with those of white men in Europe. The *papālagi* have 'made God poor' and 'have no time' for anything but worship of money and material possessions. Now a left-wing 'cult' book, it was originally published in 1920 by Felsenverlag at Buchenbach, Baden, with three reprintings within two years. It was again reprinted in 1971 by Marburg students of anarchist tendency. Horst Cain, in his *Persische Briefe auf samoanisch* (q.v.), shows the actual author to be Erich Scheurmann.

769 **Persische Briefe auf samoanisch.** (*Lettres persanes* in Samoan.)
Horst Cain. *Anthropos*, vol. 70 (1975), p. 617-26. bibliog.

Cain subjects *Der Papalagi* (q.v.), ostensibly the critical views on Samoan and European cultural values of a Western Samoan chief, to detailed scrutiny. He shows it to be a work of literary camouflage, in the tradition of Montesquieu's *Lettres persanes* (1721) and Diderot's *Supplément aux voyages de Bougainville* (1775). In each case, the purpose is to criticize contemporary society in Europe. Erich Scheurmann, the actual author of *Der papalagi*, is much in sympathy with the Samoan way of life. His photographic essay, *Samoa: ein Bilderwerk* (Samoa: a pictorial work) (Konstanz, Germany: See-Verlag, 1927), is among the best of its genre.

770 **Queen Emma of the South Seas: a novel.**
Geoffrey Dutton. South Melbourne, Victoria: Macmillan, 1976. 283p.

A sensational novel based on the life of the Samoan-American Emma Eliza Coe Kolbe (1850-1913), daughter of Jonas Myndersse Coe (1822-91), US Commercial Agent in Apia, and Le'utu Taletale of the Malietoa family. 'Queen Emma' was successively known as the Princess Tui Malietoa Coe, Mrs James Forsayth, Mrs Thomas Farrell and Mrs Paul Kolbe.

771 **Rain.**
W. Somerset Maugham. In: *The world over: the collected stories*. London: William Heinemann, 1951; The Reprint Society, 1954, Volume one, p. 1-36.

Maugham's cautionary tale of ill matched travelling companions and incompatible moral codes, set in Pago Pago, has come to be a local legend, with Sadie Thompson's memory still very much alive as a lure for tourists.

772 **Wild justice: stories of the South Seas.**
Lloyd Osbourne. New York: D. Appleton, 1921. reprint. 359p.

Contains rather lurid tales based on the author's personal experiences. Osbourne spent eight years in the South Pacific, especially in Samoa during the civil wars (in which he and his step-father Robert Louis Stevenson played a role).

Children's books

773 **Children of Samoa: a true story of the children of Western Samoa.**
Marie Maddox. Sydney, New South Wales: Committee for Promotion, Methodist Mission, 1964. reprint. 63p.

A compilation of short vignettes of various aspects of village life and religious observance.

774 **Eastward sweeps the current: a saga of the Polynesian seafarers.**
Alida Sims Malkus. Winston, New York: Junior Guild, 1937. 394p. bibliog.

Fictional Samoans sail eastward in great canoes to hair-raising adventures among the Inca and Maya of South and Central America. This is a work of pure imagination, with no known basis in historical fact, written for young readers. See also *Storm over Samoa* by Dale Collins, illustrated by Vera Jarman (Melbourne, Victoria: Heinemann, 1954. 170p.), an adventure story set in Samoa.

775 **Island boy: Robert Louis Stevenson and his step-grandson in Samoa.**
Margaret Mackprang Mackay, illustrated by John Lewis. London: Harrap, 1969. 95p.

The story of Austin Strong's life at Vailima, written for young people.

776 **Jottings from the Pacific: life and incidents in the Fijian and Samoan islands.**
Emma Hildreth Adams. Oakland, California: Pacific Press, 1890. 160p. (Young People's Library).

Simply written, for children, this is a still engaging story of life in Samoa at a climactic point of the 19th century. It is rich in description and incident, rather cursory in its account of the course of events, but still of anthropological interest.

777 ***Ko te kakai o Hina ma te tuna/'O le fagogo 'ia Sina ma le tuna/*Sina and the eel; notes for teachers; English translation.**
Ester Temukisa Laban Alama. Wellington: Learning Media, 1995. 3 vols.

The traditional Polynesian story of Sina and the eel is retold as a play, in Tokelauan (*Hina*) and Samoan (*Sina*), with an English translation and suggestions for staging the play. The notes are useful for teaching aspects of Samoan language and culture, such as *fāgogo, lāuga, tautala lelei, tautala leaga* and the vocabulary of respect. See also: *Tala mo tamaiti Samoa* (Tales for Samoan children) by Fana'afi Ma'ia'i (Wellington: School Publications Branch, Department of Education, for the Department of Island Territories, 1957. 64p.), an illustrated (some in colour) collection of stories previously published in the *Samoan Journal*, selected and adapted by Fana'afi Ma'ia'i; *Stories of old Samoa* by Fana'afi Ma'ia'i (Christchurch, New Zealand: Whitcombe & Tombs, 1960. 48p.); *The pigeon with nine heads: and other fascinating legendary tales of Samoa* by David Glen Wright (Provo, Utah: Aro Publishing, 1981. 48p. [Fascinating Tales of the Pacific]); *The sacred hens: ancient history and legends of Samoa* by Glen Wright, Seiuli Le Tagaloatele Fitisemanu, Tavita Fitisemanu (Honolulu: Conch Press, 1982. 2nd edition, expanded and illustrated); and *Salamasina, queen of love: romantic mystery of the Samoan Islands* by Glen Wright (Honolulu: Conch Press, 1982). See also *The stone maiden and other Samoan fables* by Daniel Pouesi, Michael Igoe, illustrated by Michael Evanston ([Carson, California]: KIN Publications, 1994. 46p.). With a preface by emeritus professor of anthropology, Martin Orans, this is a collection of eighteen folk-tales, retold in a modern idiom.

778 **Pacific island communities.**

Bruce Stevenson, Maeve Stevenson. Auckland, New Zealand: Longman Paul, 1992. 48p. maps.

An attractive topic book which sets the scene in the Southwest Pacific, and then looks at six communities (including Sāvaia, 'Upolu) from different perspectives. Other educational texts include: *Samoa* by Alexander Wyclif Reed, illustrated by E. H. Papps (London: Frederick Warne, 1967. 17p. map. [Social Studies Readers]); *Islands of the South Pacific* by Ralph Gerard Ward (London: Educational Supply Association, 1961. 104p. maps. bibliog. [How People Live Series]), a well informed textbook covering Western Samoa and Fiji; *Michael Leyden's people of the Pacific: Samoa* by Michael Leyden (Auckland, New Zealand: M. Leyden Publications, [1988]), a boxed teaching kit comprising teacher's handbook, thirteen study prints, and a sound cassette; and *Samoa: resource pack for secondary schools* (Christchurch, New Zealand: Canterbury Education Centre, 1989. 33 sheets in portfolio; cassette; booklet [3p.]. maps), a collection of photographs, maps and portraits.

779 **Samoa: its customs and traditions.**

Samoan Committee of Culture and Customs. Pago Pago: Department of Education, 1955. 43p.

A succinct account, by Samoans of Tutuila and Manu'a, of the traditions and customs held by them to be of cardinal importance, written for use in the schools of American Samoa. This supplements *Second book of Samoan social culture for the public schools of American Samoa* by S. Fa'amausili ([Pago Pago: Education Department, Government of American Samoa], 1945. 19p.). See also *The story of Samoa* by Lowell D. Holmes (Cincinnati, Ohio: McCormick-Mathers, 1967), a general introduction to Samoan history, society and culture, for young people.

780 **A Samoan family.**

Fay C. Ala'ilima. Wellington: Islands Education Division, Department of Education, 1961. 36p.

A well informed and pleasantly written account of life in a Western Samoan extended family, for school use. The author, formerly Fay G. Calkins, married into such a family on 'Upolu, and related her experiences in a now classic work *My Samoan chief* (q.v.). See also *Family in Samoa* by Wilfred George Moore (London: Hulton Educational Publications, 1961. 82p. 2 maps. [This is Their Life]). Written for children, this is a detailed, very well informed account of the village of Lefaga, on the south-western coast of 'Upolu, centred on the everyday routine of Tuli and his sister Ani. The forty-one excellent photographs, by R. F. Rankin, for many years a teacher in Samoan schools, enhance the careful authenticity of Moore's text. This may be recommended as a simple yet sound introduction to the main features of rural life in Western Samoa. See also *Talofa means aloha: the story of a Samoan family in Waianae, Hawaii* by Nancy Foon Young (Honolulu: Office of Instructional Services, Department of Education, State of Hawai'i, 1975. 26p.), in which four Maga brothers discuss how their Samoan family is settling down to a new life in Hawai'i. This is intended for school use, with text in both Samoan and English.

Robert Louis Stevenson

Family letters and reminiscences

781 **Letters from Samoa, 1891-1895.**
Margaret Isabella [Balfour] Stevenson, edited and arranged by Marie Clothilde Balfour. London: Methuen, 1906. 340p.

A sequel to *From Saranac to the Marquesas and beyond* ... by M. I. Stevenson, edited and arranged by M. C. Balfour (New York: Scribner's, 1903. 313p.). These intimate letters by Robert Louis Stevenson's mother to her sister, Jane Whyte Balfour, concern life at Vailima (in considerable domestic detail) and momentous events outside. Mrs Stevenson includes many well observed descriptions (as of Mālua 'university city', the clearing of the Mount Vaea road, and a visit to the home of Mata'afa). The twelve photographs include Mrs M. I. Stevenson in 1848, Mata'afa, and several of and inside Vailima.

782 **Our Samoan adventure: with a three-year diary by Mrs. Stevenson now published for the first time together with rare photographs from family albums.**
Edited, with an introduction and notes, by Charles Neider. London: Weidenfeld & Nicolson, 1956. 287p.

Fanny Stevenson's diary for 1890-94, with portions cross-hatched out by a modern pen using blue ink, is held by Stevenson House in Monterey, California, an old adobe building which is now a state museum. Neider has succeeded in deciphering most of the deleted passages. Interpolated passages by Stevenson himself are from his *Vailima letters*, written to his friend Sidney Colvin (1845-1927) at the British Museum, London. Neider considers that the diary 'makes clear many of Fanny's virtues'. Four appendices comprise 'Vailima prayers', 'Letter to *The Times*' (9-12 April 1892), both by R. L. Stevenson, 'A list of over-inkings' and 'A note on the special photography' (illustrated). The contemporary photographs, many often copied, include Mata'afa, Malietoa Laupepa, Tamasese, Seumanutafa, 'chief of Apia', childhood portraits of Alex Willis and his wife Lauli'i (a great favourite of Stevenson), and Stevenson lying in state, 4 December 1894.

783 **Vailima [etc.].**

Isobel Field. In: *This life I've loved.* Isobel Field. London: Michael Joseph, 1937, p. 253-320.

Chapters thirty-five to forty-two comprise intimate memories of Robert Louis Stevenson's Vailima household, by Isobel, the daughter of his wife Fanny Osbourne Stevenson. Visitors included the artist John LaFarge and Henry Adams of Boston. Opposite p. 272 are the last photograph of Stevenson, taken in Sydney, and one of Fanny Stevenson, captioned 'Tamaitai'. An appendix (p. 311-20) contains a letter signed Isobel Strong: 'To the President and Members of the Stevenson Society of America'. There is a new edition of *This life I've loved*: New York; Toronto: Toronto University Press, 1941. See also *Memories of Vailima* by Isobel Strong, Lloyd Osbourne (Westminster, London: Archibald Constable, 1903. 151p.), compiled by two members of Robert Louis Stevenson's family, containing his 'Verses written in 1872', together with Osbourne's 'Mr. Stevenson's home life at Vailima', and Strong's 'Vailima table-talk', 'Pola' and 'Samoan songs'. This last essay (p. 139-51) describes some of the songs about *Tusitala.*

784 **Vailima letters: being correspondence addressed by Robert Louis Stevenson to Sidney Colvin. November 1890-October 1894.**

Robert Louis Stevenson. London: Methuen, 1895. 366p.

Sidney Colvin of the British Museum, London, was a close friend of Stevenson and later the editor of posthumous editions of his works. The letters, covering the first years in Āpia, provide an entertaining account of family life at Vailima, news of work in progress, and cogent comments on the international tension bedevilling Samoan life. See also *Letters and miscellanies of Robert Louis Stevenson: letters to his family and friends* by Robert Louis Stevenson, edited with an introduction by Sidney Colvin (New York: Scribner's, 1918. 2 vols.), selected from *The letters*, edited by Sidney Colvin (New York: Scribner, 1911. 4 vols.), and containing about 300 pages of letters from Samoa.

Biographies

785 **Island days.**

In: *Stevensoniana.* Edited by J. A. Hammerton. London: Grant Richards, 1903, p. 92-131.

This collection of published but elusive ephemeral writings relating to Robert Louis Stevenson in Samoa includes: a poem 'To Tusitala in Vailima', by Edmund Gosse; 'Mr. R. L. Stevenson as a Samoan chief'; 'A talk with Tusitala', by Marie Fraser, 'the well-known actress'; 'The library at Vailima'; and 'A Samoan resident's resminiscences', by Sir Berry Cusack-Smith, Judge of the British Court at Āpia during Stevenson's life there.

786 **Recollections of Robert Louis Stevenson in the Pacific.**
Arthur Johnstone. London: Chatto & Windus, 1905. 327p.

Among Johnstone's unorthodox opinions is his explicit view that Stevenson's involvement in the Samoan imbroglio was 'an indiscretion' which probably delayed settlement. He was 'unfitted by habit and education for the difficult task', and could not fully appreciate or understand the vital importance of applying the principle that 'in politics conflicting interests must be compromised ...'.

787 **Robert Louis Stevenson.**
Gavan Daws. In: *A dream of islands: voyages of self-discovery in the South Seas.* Edited by Gavan Daws. New York; London: W. W. Norton, 1980. p. 162-215.

Daws sketches Stevenson's voyages in the Pacific and his final years at Vailima. High on Mt. Vaea above Āpia, Stevenson 'lived spectacularly well' and wrote 700,000 words for publication between the beginning of 1890 and the end of 1894, driven by his 'charge of souls'. After four years he had had enough of the exotic: 'I am used to it; I do not notice it, rather prefer my grey, freezing recollections of Scotland'. While Vailima was being built, Stevenson published, as a serial, his story *The bottle imp*, about a genie who could grant wishes. This was the first piece of fiction to appear in the Samoan language, and some readers took the story to be fact: 'In the great hall at Vailima was a locked iron safe, and it was thought that the bottle imp was kept inside'.

788 **Robert Louis Stevenson: a biography.**
Ian Bell. Edinburgh: Mainstream Publishing, 1992. 295p. bibliog.

'A biographer soon discovers that Stevenson was the consummate autobiographer'. Wherever possible, Bell allows Stevenson to speak for himself, drawing upon his writings. Chapters sixteen and seventeen (p. 249-72) and 'An epilogue' (p. 273-83) soberly review the years at Vailima and events following Tusitala's death. Bell is a journalist, and does not pretend to be anything else: his achievement in this work is to have scanned the innumerable works about Stevenson, subjecting them to minute analysis and unravelling fact from myth. He praises *Voyage to windward* (q.v.) by J. C. Furnas and the several critical works by David Daiches. A more impressionistic, even lurid, perspective is to be found in Alexandra Lapierre, *Fanny Stevenson: muse, adventuress and romantic enigma* (London: Fourth Estate, 1995. 520p.).

789 **Robert Louis Stevenson: bright ring of words.**
Edited by Alanna Knight, Elizabeth Stuart Warfel. Nairn, Scotland: Balnain Books, 1994. 56p.

An anthology of personal recollections of Robert Louis Stevenson and of 'his strange influence' on the contributors' lives. Samoa is represented by Fiame Mata'afa, on several occasions prime minister of Western Samoa, and by Lloyd Osbourne, a member of the Vailima household. See also: *Robert Louis Stevenson in the South Seas: an intimate photographic record* by Robert Louis Stevenson, edited by Alanna Knight, photographs by Robert Louis Stevenson (Edinburgh: Mainstream, 1986; New York: Paragon House, 1987. 191p. map. [US title: *R.L.S. in the South Seas: an intimate photographic record*]), which contains ninety black-and-white photographs of Stevenson's voyages to Hawai'i, French Polynesia and Samoa, with excerpts from his letters; 'Gone native' by Brad Leithauser (*Art and Antiques* [USA] [May 1988],

p. 66-75, 108), in which Leithauser contrasts Paul Gauguin's restless, unfulfilled life in Tahiti with the greater and more realistic involvement of Robert Louis Stevenson in Samoan affairs; and 'Stevenson's life in Samoa' by W. H. Triggs (*Bookman*, vol. 72 [April 1931], p. 158-63), a workmanlike account of Robert Louis Stevenson's eventful years in Samoa.

790 **Robert Louis Stevenson. In the South Seas: a dramatic cassette.**
Karen Steele. Twickenham, England: Published by the Author (36 Sidney Road, St. Margaret's, Twickenham, Middlesex TW1 1JR), 1995. cassette.

Includes readings from diaries, letters and writings, narrated by Crawford Logan, Karen Steele and Laura Aitken. The selections 'best reflect the joys and trials' experienced by Stevenson and his wife Fanny during their travels in the *Casco* and *Equator*, and in Samoa. Side two presents 'Four years in Samoa' and 'Stevenson's death and burial'. (For every cassette ordered, £1 will be donated to the RLS Preservation Foundation which has restored Vailima, Stevenson's home above Āpia.)

791 **Some misconceptions about RLS.**
Joseph Theroux. *Journal of Pacific History*, vol. 16, no. 3 (July 1981), p. 164-67. bibliog.

Theroux examines some endlessly perpetuated myths about Robert Louis Stevenson in Samoa, found in biographies such as *Robert Louis Stevenson* by James Pope Hennessy (New York, 1975) and *The violent friend: the story of Mrs. Robert Louis Stevenson* by Margaret Mackay (New York, 1968). There is a rejoinder, on the meanings of *ona*, by Gavan Daws. Theroux concludes: 'The myths have replaced the facts. The tourist bureaus propagate the myths and the tourists cherish them'.

792 **Stevenson's shrine: the record of a pilgrimage.**
Laura Stubbs. London: Alexander Moring, The De La More Press, 1903. 58p. map.

This is truly a work of piety. 'I, a lover of the man, personally unknown to me, save through the potency of his pen, journeyed across the world in order to visit his grave, and to get into direct touch with his surroundings'. The pilgrimage, which focuses on Vailima and the tomb on Mount Vaea, was made in 1892-93. Laura Stubbs sees everything 'with eyes full of reverence and wonder', even the house bereft of all its furniture, and the mosquitoes. Of the tomb, she writes: 'Not an ideal structure by any manner of means, not even beautiful, and yet in its massive ruggedness it somehow suited the man and the place'. There are twelve plates of Samoan scenes and of Vailima, all often reproduced in later books.

793 **Tusitala of the South Seas: the story of Robert Louis Stevenson's life in the South Pacific.**
Joseph W. Ellison. New York: Hastings House, 1953. 297p. bibliog.

The historian of foreign influence in Samoa in the 19th century and of the partition of the islands sets his hand to the familiar story of Stevenson's experience of Polynesia and Micronesia. Ellison's account of the Vailima years is soundly based in his research on contemporary events and personalities: the warring Samoan chiefs; the manipulative consular agents of the three great powers; and prominent Āpia residents such as the enigmatic H. J. Moors. Other biographies include: *Journey to Upolu: Robert Louis Stevenson, Victorian rebel* by Edward Rice (New York: Dodd, Mead, 1974. 145p.); *Tusitala ou la vie aventureuse de Robert Louis Stevenson* (Tusitala: the adventurous life of Robert Louis Stevenson) by Rodolphe Jaquette (Paris: Seghers, 1980. 242p. bibliog. [Étonnants Voyageurs]); *Home from the sea: Robert Louis Stevenson in Samoa* by Richard Arnold Bermann, translated by Elizabeth Reynolds Hapgood (Honolulu: Mutual Publishing, 1967. 280p. bibliog. [First American edition: Indianapolis, Indiana: Bobbs-Merrill, 1939. 280p. bibliog.]); and *Trois tombes au soleil: Robert Louis Stevenson, Paul Gauguin, Alain Gerbault* (Three tombs in the sun: Robert Louis Stevenson, Paul Gauguin, Alain Gerbault) by B. Gorsky (Paris: A. Michel, 1976. 344p.).

794 **Voyage to windward: the life of Robert Louis Stevenson.**
J. C. Furnas. London: Faber & Faber, 1952. 478p. bibliog. Reprinted, Philadelphia: R. West, 1980.

The best known and most admired modern biography of Stevenson, unlikely to be significantly bettered. The section entitled 'The South Seas' (p. 265-371, 447-57) is well documented and percipient (and much used by later writers). The list of works consulted (p. 405-17) is extensive and useful though lacking full bibliographical details. There are excellent photographs, mainly of family members and friends; of Vailima, before and after extension; of the wrecks of USS *Vandalia*, *Trenton* and *Nipsic*; and of the Western Samoa one shilling postage stamp showing Stevenson's tomb. A more critical, even iconoclastic, view of Stevenson is *Portrait of a rebel: the life and work of Robert Louis Stevenson* by Richard Aldington (London: Evans Brothers, 1957. 245p. bibliog.), in which Aldington pays tribute to 'a kindness and generosity in him which more than atone for all and any of the – mostly rather harmless – faults in him …' (p. 231).

795 **With Stevenson in Samoa.**
H. J. Moors. London; Leipzig, Germany: T. Fisher Unwin, 1910. 230p.

These engaging recollections of Robert Louis Stevenson's years at Vailima also provide a participant's view of the strife which preceded the partition of the Samoan Islands, and of the main protagonists. The forty-three plates include: the wrecks of the *Trenton*, *Vandalia* and *Olga*; Stevenson's pony 'Jack'; the original Vailima cottage, and later extensions; the first number of *The Samoan Reporter* in March 1845; *The bottle imp* in Samoan (May 1891); Malietoa Laupepa; Tamasese the Elder; and Mata'afa. Further details are provided by Harry Moors' *Some recollections of early Samoa* (q.v.).

Culture and the Arts

Material culture

796 **Art and life in Polynesia.**

T. Barrow. Rutland, Vermont; Tokyo: Charles E. Tuttle, 1973. 191p. map. bibliog.

With its splendid illustrations of artefacts in collections in Europe and New Zealand, this scholarly conspectus reveals both the remarkable homogeneity of Polynesian art and its local diversity, intimately associated with social organization and religion. In the section on Samoa (p. 76-81), Barrow is perhaps unduly dismissive: 'The ornamentation of chiefly persons by tattoo, elaborate headdresses and fine ceremonial mats (which were exchanged on all important occasions), and house-building, represent the art of Samoa'. Rare photographs show traditional *tuiga* head-dresses (worn by men and women), and the process of tattooing buttocks and thighs. See also *Schmuck der Südsee: Ornament und Symbol. Objekte aus dem Linden-Museum, Stuttgart* (South Sea adornment: ornament and symbol. Artefacts from the Linden Museum, Stuttgart) by Ingrid Heermann, Ulrich Menter, photography by Uwe Seyl (Munich: Prestel-Verlag, 1990. 152p. bibliog.), a handsomely illustrated (black-and-white and colour plates), scholarly introduction to a major exhibition held in 1990-91. Samoa is represented by a *tuiga* head-dress, ornamental combs, necklaces and a red-feather 'bonnet' (*'o le 'ie 'ula*). Each artefact is catalogued and described in detail. See also *Made in the South Pacific: arts of the sea people* by C. Price (London: Bodley Head, 1979. 134p. map. bibliog.), which contains monochrome photographs only.

797 **The art of Oceania: a bibliography.**

Louise Hanson, F. Allan Hanson. Boston, Massachusetts: G. K. Hall, 1984. 539p.

This near exhaustive bibliography of 6,650 publications on Oceanic art, in English, French, German, Italian, Japanese and other languages, is divided into five main sections: Oceania generally; Polynesia; Micronesia; Melanesia; and (particularly valuable) sales catalogues. Most entries are briefly annotated. Polynesian coverage (including Samoa) is extensive, with little of importance missed.

798 **Baskets in Polynesia.**
Wendy Arbeit, photographs by Douglas Peebles. Honolulu: University of Hawai'i Press, 1990. 118p. 2 maps. bibliog. (Kolowalu Books).

Well illustrated with studio photographs, this is a practical introduction to Polynesian basketry, describing types of baskets and pandanus boxes and how they are made. Nine Samoan types are illustrated (p. 58-67). 'Techniques' (p. 97-113) deals with: coconut frond work; pandanus plaiting; coil technique knots; and three-strand lattice work. See also *Pacific basket makers: a living tradition. Catalog of the 1981 Pacific Basketmaker's Symposium and Exhibition*, edited by Suzi Jones (Fairbanks, Alaska: University of Alaska Museum, for Consortium for Pacific Arts and Cultures, Honolulu, Hawai'i, 1983. 80p. map. bibliog.). The exhibits illustrated and described in the catalogue come from Alaska, American Samoa, California, Guam and the Northern Mariana Islands. Colour photographs of each basketmaker are followed by three essays: 'The basket imperative' by Barre Toelken; 'North American and Pacific basketry' by Roger Rose; and 'Cultural preservation and pluralism' by Steven F. Arvizu. Adeline Huff and Matafesaga'i Tafao, both of Pago Pago, represent American Samoa. The Samoan artefacts shown are *'ato* (baskets made of pandanus) and *'enu* (fish traps made of *Freycinetia* aerial rootlets and coconut fibre).

799 **Cloth and human experience.**
Edited by Annette B. Weiner, Jane Schneider. Washington, DC: Smithsonian Institution Press, 1989. 431p. bibliog. (Smithsonian Series in Ethnographic Inquiry).

An absorbing investigation of the role and meanings of cloth and cloth-making in small-scale and large-scale societies, as influenced by capitalism and gender. Chapter two, by Annette B. Weiner, 'Why cloth?: wealth, gender, and power in Oceania', compares the Trobriand Islands with Samoa. See also: *Traditional arts of Pacific Island women* by Janet M. Davidson (Wellington: Museum of New Zealand *Te Papa Tongarewa*, 1993. 32p. map); and *Polynesian venture* by Truman Bailey (New York: Doubleday, Doran, 1939. 233p.). In search of native crafts to adapt to modern merchandising, Bailey visited Samoa, Cambodia, Japan, China and Korea. His experiences in Samoa take up half of the story, which is illustrated with ninety black-and-white photographs. This lively book provides an insight into the meeting of traditional crafts and commercial imperatives, and into the compromises which ensue.

800 **An inquiry into the question of cultural stability in Polynesia.**
Margaret Mead. New York: Columbia University Press, 1928. 89p. bibliog.

A historical and contemporaneous study of the relative stability or sensitivity to change of three key elements in Samoan culture: house building; canoe building; and tattooing. Methods and organization are analysed, and compared with those of Hawai'i, the Marquesas, New Zealand and Tahiti.

801 **Material culture of Western Samoa: persistence and change.**
Roger Neich. Wellington: National Museum of New Zealand, 1985. 66p. map. bibliog. (National Museum of New Zealand Bulletin, no. 23).

Neich surveys the current state of material culture in Western Samoa, differentiating between those aspects which conform to tradition and those which are subject to change. In contrast to American Samoa, traditional *fale* types prevail in rural areas. See also 'Processes of change in Samoan arts and crafts' by Roger Neich, in *Development of the arts in the Pacific*, edited by Philip J. C. Dark (Wellington: Pacific Arts Association, 1984, p. 16-47. map. bibliog. [PAA Occasional Papers, no. 1]). Neich conducted this research in Western Samoa half a century after Sir Peter H. Buck's definitive study of *Samoan material culture* (q.v.). He notes fenced houses, changing house styles, new dugout canoes, innovations in mat-making and in *siapo* production and design, new types of *'ali* (pillows and headrests) and new fashions in art and aesthetics. In all fields traditional Samoan structuring principles persist, along with choice from a wider range of artefactual competence. This paper was first presented at the 15th Pacific Science Congress, 1983. See also: 'Western Samoa: living in a museum' by Philippe Lair (*Museums*, vol. 42, no. 1 [1990], p. 46-47), which provides impressions of the considerable extent to which Samoa's traditional material culture and its artistic expressions remain evident in everyday life, 'outside museums'; and 'Samoan material culture in the 1980s' by Adrienne L. Kaeppler (*Pacific Arts*, no. 3 [1991], p. 17-21. bibliog.), containing studies of Samoan artefacts, and focusing on changes in materials, techniques and designs.

802 **Samoan house building, cooking, and tattooing.**
E. S. C. Handy, W. C. Handy. Honolulu: Bernice P. Bishop Museum, 1924. 26p. (Bulletin, no. 15).

Provides ethnological notes, with illustrations and seven plates, on the construction of traditional *fale*, on cooking methods (including the *umu* earth oven), and on the methods, implements and patterns of male and female tattooing.

803 **Samoan material culture.**
Te Rangi Hiroa [i.e. Peter Henry Buck]. Honolulu: Bernice P. Bishop Museum, 1930. 724p. map. bibliog. (Bulletin, no. 75). Reprinted, New York: Kraus Reprint, 1971.

The Māori scholar's meticulous survey of all aspects of material culture, such as houses, tools and carving, is particularly interesting in its examination of three types of Samoan double canoes and four types of plank-built canoes (p. 371-417). Some of the data in this pioneering work have been reinterpreted or expanded by Roger Neich (q.v.). A perceptive critique of Te Rangi Hiroa's views on Samoan culture is 'Sir Peter Buck and the Samoans' by Helen M. Leach (*New Zealand Journal of Archaeology*, vol. 15 [1993], p. 57-66. bibliog.). See also 'Zhizn' i byt samoantsev (po kollektsiiam MAE)' (Everyday life and culture of the Samoans [based on MAE collections]) by I. K. Fedorova (*Sbornik Muzeia Antropologii i Etnografii* [Leningrad: Izdatel'stvo "Nauka"], vol. 39 [1984], p. 78-98. bibliog.), an interesting discussion in Russian (with seventeen illustrations) of Samoan material culture, based on artefacts in the collections of the Museum of Anthropology and Ethnography (MAE) of the Academic of Sciences of the USSR. The items discussed are inventoried and described (p. 94-98).

804 ***Siapo*: bark cloth art of Samoa.**
Mary J. Pritchard. Honolulu: University of Hawai'i Press, in association with American Samoa Council on Culture, Arts and Humanities, 1984. 80p. bibliog. Reprinted, Auckland, New Zealand: Pasifika Press, 1995.

A study of the Samoan art of *siapo*, a woven and painted bark cloth, based on Pritchard's own experience as a *siapo* artist and teacher of the craft. She traces the history of *siapo* as a cultural art form and discusses all stages of production, from the paper mulberry plant itself, the plant dyes used, and the way in which traditional symbols and motifs are transferred on to the bark. The various processes, and examples of work by her and other artists are illuminated by 245 photographs and illustrations (198 of them in colour). See also: *Patterns of Polynesia: Samoa* by Ailsa Robertson (Auckland, New Zealand: Heinemann Education, 1989. 32p. map); *Polynesian tapa: siapo Samoa and ngatu fakatonga* by Donald Cole, Shari Cole (Rotorua, New Zealand: Pacific Projects, 1986. 16p. + 45 slides [35mm]); *Tapa in Polynesia* by Simon Kooijman (Honolulu: Bernice P. Bishop Museum, 1972. 498p. bibliog.); and 'Die Tapa-Bereitung' (Preparation of *tapa*) by W. von Bülow (*Internationales Archiv für Ethnologie*, vol. 12 [1899], p. 66-75).

805 **Western Polynesia: a study of cultural differentiation.**
Edwin G. Burrows. Dunedin, New Zealand: University Book Shop, [n.d.]. 192p. map. bibliog.

Originally published in 1938 by the Göteborg Ethnographical Museum as volume 7 of its *Etnologiska Studier*, this scholarly compilation uses the culture area approach to reconstruct culture history from distributional evidence of culture traits in Western Polynesia, defined as 'the region centering in Samoa and Tonga', and including Uvea and Futuna. Distribution diagrams are provided for fish-hooks, bonito hook points, food pounders, bark cloth techniques, fabric techniques, stone adzes, house construction, canoe hulls, canoe lashing techniques, outrigger attachment, sail types, carved human figures, club types, composite dart and musical instruments, *kava* complex and chiefs' language, kinship terminology and usages, religious beliefs, sacred structures, native calendar and cultural groupings in Polynesia.

Traditional art forms

Fale aitu

806 **Clowning as political commentary: Polynesia, then and now.**
Vilsoni Hereniko. *The Contemporary Pacific*, vol. 6, no. 1 (Spring 1994), p. 1-28. bibliog.

'Every chief needs a clown. Thus, in Tonga and Samoa, two Polynesian societies marked by hierarchy in the social order, chiefs had in their retinues one or two clowns who were an integral part of their courts'. Hereniko examines the nature and role of clowning as a critique of chiefly authority and of foreigners and foreign influences in

Polynesia. He insists that 'clowning was and is an antidote to the abuse of power, and how needed it is in modern Polynesia'. Secular and ritual clowning are contrasted, and both are found to have a levelling effect. In Samoa, the *fale aitu* is a male domain, and an institution in its own right, and could serve as trenchant political commentary in a society become corrupt and oppressive.

807 **Comic theater of Samoa: an interview with John A. Kneubuhl.**
Vilsoni Hereniko. *Mānoa: a Pacific Journal of International Writing*, vol. 5, no. 1 (Summer 1993), p. 99-105.

This 1990 interview focuses on Samoan comic theatre, *fale aitu*. John A. Kneubuhl (1919-92), son of a German father and Samoan mother, defines *fale aitu* as 'a spirit house that is used for performing comedic sketches', as 'not an aesthetic experience, but a psychosocial experience. It tends more towards politics than art'.

808 **Traditional performance in Samoan culture: two forms.**
Victoria Kneubuhl. *Asian Theatre Journal*, vol. 4 (1987), p. 166-76. bibliog.

An analysis of ritual and secular *fale aitu* sketches, often performed within the frame of a *pōula*, 'teasing night', held during a *malaga*. Kneubuhl states that *aitu* are associated with chaos, wilderness, danger and darkness. *Fale aitu* are important in that they release tension through laughter and provide relief from the constraints of a regimented daily routine. See also 'Ghosts and government: a structural analysis of alternative institutions for conflict management in Samoa' by Bradd Shore (*Man* [NS], vol. 13 [1978], p. 175-99. bibliog.), which focuses on the aspects of social satire and criticism of authority.

809 **Where the spirits laugh last: comic theater in Samoa.**
Caroline Sinavaiana. In: *Clowning as critical practice: performance humor in the South Pacific*. Edited by William E. Mitchell. Pittsburgh, Pennsylvania; London: University of Pittsburgh Press, 1992, p. 192-218. bibliog. (ASAO Monograph, no. 13).

Founder, Director and Resource Consultant in Intercultural Communications for the Pacific-Asia Institute for the Arts and Human Sciences, Pago Pago, American Samoa, Dr Sinavaiana studies the integral role in public celebrations and performances often played by spontaneous or scripted clowning. A reflexive form of expression, traditional Samoan comedy uses devices such as satire, parody and slapstick to effect a dramatic inversion or reversal of normative status roles in society. A central persona may have the conventional characteristics of a ghost or transvestite. The comedy sketch (*fale aitu*) implies an indigenous critique of forms of Western culture, thereby, by contrast, tacitly acknowledging and reinforcing customary values. The chapter is based on Sinavaiana's ASAO conference paper, 1989: *Fale aitu ('house of spirits'): text and context in Samoan clowning*. See also 'Comic theater in Samoa as indigenous media' by Caroline Sinavaiana, in *The arts and politics*, edited by Karen Nero (*Pacific Studies*, vol. 15, no. 4 [1992], special issue, p. 199-210. bibliog.).

Song and dance

810 **An annotated bibliography of Oceanic music and dance.**
Mervyn McLean. Wellington: Polynesian Society, 1977. 252p. (Memoir, no. 41). Supplement, 1981. 74p.

A comprehensive annotated guide to published descriptions, arranged alphabetically by author. Each area has a code (e.g. Western Polynesia OU; Samoa: OU 8), and an area index arranged by codes refers to authors and publication dates.

811 ***Fa'a-Sāmoa*: the Samoan way ... between conch shell and disco. A portrait of Western Samoa at the end of the twentieth century.**
Ad Linkels. Tilburg, Netherlands: Mundo Étnico Foundation, 1995. 94p. bibliog. discography.

This interesting account of modern Samoan music, translated from the original Dutch edition of 1991, is based on fieldwork carried out in 1982, the aim of which was to collect songs and dances and to study the social and cultural contexts in which they were performed. Particular attention is paid to traditional modes.

812 **Folk ballads of Samoa and culture change.**
Vernon W. Williams. *Cultures* (Paris), vol. 1, no. 3 (1974), p. 95-116.

An interesting description of popular songs in Western Samoa and American Samoa, and of how traditional music is affected by social and cultural change. Williams too readily attributes what he sees as the 'swift and efficient extinction' of traditional music to acculturation. He considers that 'the movement away from the past in Samoa becomes more rapid daily' – a patently preposterous view. See also: *Samoan song book* by Alfred Leta Hunkin (Auckland, New Zealand: Pacific Islanders' Educational Resource Centre, 1979), a varied collection of well known Samoan songs, traditional and modern; *Samoan songs for children* by Alison Matai'a (Auckland, New Zealand: Alison Matai'a, 1992); and *Polynesian music from Hawaii, New Zealand, Tahiti, the Cook Islands, Fiji & Samoa: words and music for 63 songs* (Wellington: Seven Seas Publishing Company, 1966. 83p.), a collection of well loved songs, mainly in modern styles, with ukulele tuning and finger charts.

813 **Polynesian music and dance.**
Richard M. Moyle. Auckland, New Zealand: Centre for Pacific Studies, University of Auckland, 1991. 64p. map. bibliog.

Intended essentially as a first-year Pacific Studies textbook introducing Polynesian song and dance, this is a superlative conspectus of musical life, music systems, instruments, composition and teaching, song styles and dance movements. Moyle shows that the islands of Western Polynesia (including Samoa) form a distinctive culture and music area. See also: 'Samoan song types' by Richard M. Moyle (*Studies in Music* [Nedlands, Western Australia: University of Western Australia Press], vol. 6 [1972], p. 55-67. bibliog.); and *Polynesian sound-producing instruments* by Richard M. Moyle (London: Shire Ethnography, 1990. 64p. map. bibliog.).

814 ***Samoa I Sisifo*: muziek en dans op Samoa.** (Western Samoa: music and dancing on Samoa.)
Ad Linkels, Lucia Linkels. *Verre Naasten Naderbij*, vol. 2 (1980), p. 38-58.

An illustrated account, in Dutch, of various types of Western Samoan songs and dances. See also: 'The native music of American Samoa' by Frances Densmore (*American Anthropologist*, vol. 34 [1932], p. 415-17); and 'The dance cultures of Tonga and Samoa' by Rue Hinton in *Dimensions of Polynesia*, edited by Jehanne Teilhet (San Diego, California: Fine Arts Gallery of San Diego, 1973, p. 170-76. bibliog.).

815 **Sāmoan variations: essays on the nature of traditional oral arts.**
Jacob Wainwright Love. New York; London: Garland Publishing, 1991. 327p. bibliog. (Harvard Dissertations in Folklore and Oral Tradition).

A superb investigation of variation in the oral arts of Samoa, by means of quantitative and statistical techniques. Love discusses the interface between speaking and singing, types of songs, variation in the tones of a song, and the mechanisms of change in Samoan music over time. Most of the interviews on which Love's research is based were conducted in the village of Faleālupo in north-west Savai'i. The extensive bibliography (p. 299-320) cites relevant works up to 1990.

816 **Sexuality in Samoan art forms.**
Richard M. Moyle. *Archives of Sexual Behavior*, vol. 4, no. 3 (1975), p. 227-47. bibliog.

An exploration of manifestations of sexuality in Samoa as revealed through songs, poetry, dance, gestures, verbal expressions, stories and games. For each of these art forms, texts and translations of original material are presented. Moyle concludes: 'Sexuality in Samoa is far from free in its modes of expression, but rather adheres to traditional formalized patterns which determine its occasions, participants, and verbal and kinetic limits. ... As an element of verbalized group sentiment, it is a positive assertion of Samoan values, a statement of social solidarity'.

817 **Traditional Samoan music.**
Richard M. Moyle. Auckland, New Zealand: Auckland University Press; La'ie, Hawai'i: Institute for Polynesian Studies, Brigham Young University – Hawai'i, 1988. 271p. 4 maps. bibliog.

'An introduction to Samoan music is an introduction to the Samoan people as a whole'. Moyle sets song and dance in social context as he analyses each type of composition and performance, past and present. The introduction traces the history of study and collection of Samoan songs and dances, from the vivid accounts by the Reverend John Williams in 1830 and 1832. A particularly valuable chapter (p. 24-54) describes traditional musical instruments. Melodies are given in Old Notation and words in both Samoan and English. 'In looking to the past for a degree of stability and to the present for its subject matter and occasions for performance ... Samoan music continues its progressive development in a way which seems certain to ensure its social relevance and stylistic integrity'.

Tattooing

818 **Die Tatowirung beider Geschlechter in Samoa/The tattooing of both sexes in Samoa.**

Carl Marquardt, English translation by Sibyl Ferner. Papakura, New Zealand: R. McMillan, 1984. 79p.

First published in 1899, and now available in a well illustrated, bilingual edition, Marquardt's important study explains the significance of tattooing in Samoan culture, and discusses the techniques and patterns used. See also *Tatau: the mark of a man* by Donald Cole, Shari Cole (Rotorua, New Zealand: Pacific Projects, 1986. 10p. + 30 slides [35mm]). Every aspect of *pe'a* (tattooing) is illustrated clearly in these photographs taken in American Samoa and Western Samoa. There are close-up photographs of designs, including the *malu* tattoo (worn by an eighty-year-old Samoan woman). See also *Wrapping in images: tattooing in Polynesia* by Alfred Gell (Oxford: Clarendon Press, 1993. 358p. bibliog.). Breaking new ground in Pacific history and the anthropology of Polynesia, this modern comparative analysis shows that tattooing formed part of 'a complex array of symbolic techniques for controlling sacredness and protecting the self'. This framework is used to elucidate the iconographic meaning of tattoo motifs, as well as the rich corpus of associated mythology, and the complex rituals accompanying the tattooing operation.

Design and ornamentation

819 **Samoan figurative carvings and *taumualua* canoes.**

Roger Neich. *Journal of the Polynesian Society*, vol. 100, no. 3 (Sept. 1991), p. 317-27. bibliog.

The *taumualua* (two bows) canoe, traditionally used in war and later for transport, had its bow and stern posts decorated with carved figures of birds, shells or humans. Neich studies four examples in German museums, all collected in Samoa in the late 1880s and 1890s. See also: 'Samoan figurative carvings and Samoan canoes' by Roger Neich (*Journal of the Polynesian Society*, vol. 93, no. 2 [June 1984], p. 191-97. bibliog.); 'A human image from Samoa: some observations' by Stuart D. Scott (*Journal of the Polynesian Society*, vol. 91, no. 4 [Dec. 1982], p. 589-92. bibliog.), which describes a figure, perhaps from Tutuila, in the Peabody Museum, Salem, Massachusetts; 'The wooden image from Samoa in the British Museum: a note on its context' by Janet Davidson (*Journal of the Polynesian Society*, vol. 84, no. 3 [Sept. 1975], p. 352-55. bibliog.). This figure, presented by Queen Victoria, was twice seen in 1836 in the 'Upolu village of Āmaile, by Aaron Buzacott of the LMS and later by the Methodist missionaries Peter Turner and Matthew Wilson.

Colonial photography

820 **Bilder aus dem Paradies: koloniale Fotografie aus Samoa, 1875-1925.** (Pictures from paradise: colonial photography from Samoa, 1875-1925.)
Edited by Jutta Beate Engelhard, Peter Mesenhöller. Marburg, Germany: Jonas Verlag, 1995. 176p. map. bibliog. (*Museumsausgabe und Ethnologie*, Neue Folge, Band 19).

A truly magnificent publication, comprising the catalogue of an international exhibition of photographs taken in colonial Samoa, supplemented by eight erudite essays. The authors are Jutta Beate Engelhard, Alison Devine Nordström, Jan Lederbogen, Virginia-Lee Webb, Hermann Hiery, Elizabeth Edwards and Peter Mesenhöller. They show how photography served imperial and racial purposes, and created the image of a 'paradise'. A particularly important essay discusses the Samoan photographs by the Rev. George Brown.

821 **Early photography in Samoa: marketing stereotypes of paradise.**
Alison Devine Nordström. *History of Photography*, vol. 15, no. 4 (1991), p. 272-86. bibliog.

A thorough exploration of the way in which 19th-century photographers often tended to emphasize the exotic aspects of Samoan life, commercializing them to create the still persistent myth of an idyllic South Sea paradise. This theme is developed in 'Paradise recycled: images of Samoa in changing contexts' by Alison Devine Nordström (*exposure: Journal of the Society of Photographic Education*, vol. 28, no. 3 [Spring 1991], p. 8-15. bibliog.), a discussion of classic Samoan photographs by Thomas Andrew, Josiah Martin, Alfred John Tattersall and John David. Nordström shows how the photographs were misappropriated (by authors such as Lewis R. Freeman) and manipulated 'to conform to a few manageable and marketable clichés of "an unchanging Eden" '. See also: 'Lebende Bilder aus Samoa: das Reisealbum S.M.S. >*Bussard*< (1893-95) im Agfa Foto-Historama' (Living pictures from Samoa: the travel album of S.M.S. *Bussard* [1893-95] in the Agfa Foto-Historama) by Peter Mesenhöller (*Kölner Museums-Bulletin*, no. 1 [1993], p. 38-50. map); and *Burton brothers: photographers in New Zealand, 1866-1898* by Paul Faber, Anneke Groeneveld, Hardwicke Knight (Amsterdam: Fragment, 1987. 88p. bibliog.), an annotated catalogue of an exhibition of photographs, taken in New Zealand, Fiji, Samoa and Tonga by Walter John Burton and Alfred Henry Burton, held at Rotterdam's Museum voor Land- en Volkenkunde, 21 November 1987 to 13 January 1988.

822 **Picturing paradise: colonial photographs of Samoa, 1875 to 1925.**
Edited by Casey Blanton. Daytona Beach, Florida: Southeast Museum of Photography, Daytona Beach Community College, 1995. 149p. map. bibliog.

Although relating to the same international exhibition as *Bilder aus dem Paradies* (q.v.), this is a distinct publication, appreciably reduced in some respects (e.g. catalogue, bibliography, essays) and expanded in others. The essays by Lederbogen and Hiery are omitted, replaced by forewords by Tofilau Eti Alesana and A. P. Lutali, and by 'Letter from Apia' by Momoe Malietoa von Reiche (p. 69-70), which includes her poem, 'The reluctant traveller'. There are omissions and additions in the illustrations. A notable addition is a colour reproduction of G. Pieri Nerli's painting, 'A friend of the Stevenson household' (c. 1892).

Contemporary arts

823 **Art in the new Pacific.**
Vilsoni Tausie. Suva: Institute of Pacific Studies, University of the South Pacific, in collaboration with the South Pacific Commission, 1980. 89p. map. bibliog.

With numerous references to Samoa, this work explores how traditional art forms and values might illuminate and inspire creative writing, the performing arts and even 'tourist art' in the islands. See also: 'Contemporary arts in Oceania: trying to stay alive in paradise as an artist' by Albert Wendt, in *Art and artists of Oceania*, edited by Sidney M. Mead, Bernie Kernot (Palmerston North, New Zealand: Dunmore Press; Mill Valley, California: Ethnographic Arts Publications, 1983, p. 198-209), a paper presented at the Second International Symposium on Arts of Oceania, held at the Victoria University, Wellington, in February 1978; and 'Southern presence: meetings with five Pacific artists' by Jane Griffin (*Art New Zealand*, no. 64 [Spring 1992], p. 85-89. bibliog.), in which Griffin interviews five Samoan artists working in Auckland, New Zealand: Fatu Feu'u, John Fule, Ioane Ioane, Lily Laita and Jim Vivieaere. All share an interest in techniques and subjects reflecting the artistic tradition of the South Pacific, myth and the interaction of cultures. There are nine illustrations, five of them in colour. Also of interest is 'The art of Fatu Feu'u' by Gwen Stacey (*Art New Zealand*, no. 45 [Summer 1987-88], p. 48-51), a brief discussion of Fatu Feu'u who includes Samoan motifs and images in his prints and paintings, many of which are in oil on hessian and reminiscent of the grid structure of traditional designs.

824 **The Seventh Pacific Festival of Arts (PFA), Western Samoa, 1996.**
Apia: Ministry of Youth, Sports and Cultural Affairs, 1995. 4 vols.

Represents advance publicity materials for the Seventh Pacific Festival of Arts. Volume one is entitled *Prospectus for the 7th Pacific Festival of Arts*; volume two *General background and information of the 7th PFA*; volume three *Map of Samoa showing venues*; and volume four *The great gathering of Polynesian double-hulled canoes*.

825 **The westernization of time and Samoan folk arts.**
John Enright. In: *Artistic heritage in a changing Pacific*. Edited by Philip J. C. Dark, Roger G. Rose. Honolulu: University of Hawai'i Press, 1993, p. 116-20. bibliog.

'Over the past quarter century the forces of modernization have enjoyed a far greater influence in American Samoa than they have in Western Samoa'. This assertion is examined through a comparison of current practices of traditional material art forms, particularly the arts of plaiting pandanus (*laufala*) and making and decorating mulberry barkcloth (*siapo*), all time-intensive activities. The accelerated erosion of vernacular craft practices in American Samoa is ascribed in large part to 'the increased Westernization of time in American Samoa as compared to Western Samoa'. Strategies devised to assist native artisans in dealing with 'stress introduced by the time bind' include a Samoan Master Apprenticeship programme (in which traditional experts are paid to pass on their craft skills to apprentices of their choice), practical assistance to artisans in the outer islands, and the introduction and cultivation of the paper mulberry plant on remote Swain's Island.

Folklore

Cosmogony and origin myths

826 **The Samoan story of creation (with original text).**
John Fraser. *Journal of the Polynesian Society*, vol. 1 (1892), p. 164-89.

An extensive discussion of Samoan cosmogony, based on the text of a well known myth. See also: *Die samoanische Schöpfungssage und Anschließendes aus der Südsee* (The Samoan myth of creation and related topics from the South Pacific) by Adolph Bastian (Berlin: Felber, 1894. 50p.); 'Die samoanische Schöpfungssage" (The Samoan myth of creation) by W. von Bülow (*Internationales Archiv für Ethnologie*, vol. 12 [1899], p. 58-78, 129-45); and 'Samoanische Schöpfungssage und Urgeschichte' (Samoan myth of creation and prehistory) by W. von Bülow (*Globus*, vol. 71 [1897], p. 375-79).

827 **Schöpfungs- und Urzeitmythen aus Samoa.** (Creation and primeval myths from Samoa.)
Dorothee Schneider-Christians. *Anthropos*, vol. 89 (1994), p. 125-35. bibliog.

Provides the German texts of seventeen myths. The enduring influence of such orally transmitted traditions is discussed in Dr Schneider-Christians' dissertation, *Die alte Religion und das Christentum Samoas* (The old religion and Samoan Christianity), Dr. phil., University of Bonn, 1992.

828 **Sina and her eel: the origin of the cocoanut [sic] in Samoa.**
Translated by Johannes C. Andersen. *Journal of the Polynesian Society*, vol. 34 (1925), p. 142-45.

The legend of Sina is known and loved throughout Polynesia, as a major 'origin' story – in this case of how the coconut came to the islands. Sina is the most common proper name for women in Samoa. Another version of this well known story is 'Sina and her eel in Samoa', in *Myths and legends of the Polynesians* by Johannes C. Andersen

(London; Bombay; Sydney: George G. Harrap, 1928, p. 250-53). See also 'L'origine du cocotier d'après une légende samoane' (The origin of the coconut tree according to a Samoan legend) by G. de Bigault (*Missions Catholiques* [Lyon], vol. 71 [1939], p. 495-98, 514-17).

Oral tradition, legends and mythology

829 **Dictionary of Polynesian mythology.**

Robert D. Craig. Westport, Connecticut: Greenwood Press, 1989. 409p. map. bibliog.

Samoan gods, demigods and mythological heroes are exhaustively listed and annotated in this well-indexed, alphabetically arranged dictionary, with its extensive bibliography of sources. Craig's scholarly introduction surveys the whole field of Polynesian mythology, orally transmitted up to only a century ago and so retaining much of its early, pristine character. Published sources relating to Samoan mythology include collections of ethnographic material (including myths and legends) made by George A. Turner (1818-91), Augustin Friedrich Krämer (1865-1941), T. A. Powell, John Fraser, John B. Stair, Otto Stuebel, Erich Schultz, C. Steubel, Brother Herman of Leone and Even Hovdhaugen. See also *Pacific mythology: an encyclopedia of myth and legend* by Jan Knappert, illustrated by Elizabeth Knappert (London: Aquarian Press/Thorsons, 1992. 336p. map. bibliog.).

830 ***Fāgogo*: fables from Samoa in Samoan and English.**

Richard Moyle. Auckland: Auckland University Press; Oxford: Oxford University Press, 1981. 314p. bibliog.

The seventeen *fāgogo* collected, arranged and translated by Moyle are transcripts from his original fieldtapes, collected in 1966-69 in Savai'i, 'Upolu and Ta'ū (Manu'a). They appear exactly as they were told, unlike those collected by Brother Herman (composites of several versions) and Krämer (from written sources). Most *fāgogo* contain one or more songs, which Moyle gives in Old Notation. The stories, told mostly at night, privately and inside individual homes, are thoroughly analysed in Moyle's extensive, scholarly introduction (p. 7-49). They represent a valuable source of description of and comment on Samoan society.

831 **From the land of Nāfanua: Samoan oral texts in transcription with translation, notes and vocabulary.**

Even Hovdhaugen. Oslo: Norwegian University Press, 1987. 224p. bibliog. (Institute for Comparative Research in Human Culture. Series B; vol. 72).

Professor Hovdhaugen of the University of Oslo collected these seven stories in 1982-83, in the village of Neiafu on Savai'i. The storytellers were Ali'imalemanu Falē (illustrated) and Moti Afatia. This is one of the most useful of recent books on Samoan language and legends, for its superb notes and its extensive vocabulary (p. 122-218). The bibliography (p. 219-24) includes most essential works on Samoan and on related Polynesian languages. There are parallel Samoan and English texts, with the Samoan lightly edited to the forms of the literary language (e.g. *t* for *k*).

832 ***Samoa ne'i galo*: oral traditions and legends of Samoa.**
Auckland, New Zealand: Polynesian (Pasifika) Press, 1994. 144p.

This collection was originally compiled by the Western Samoa Ministry for Youth, Sports and Cultural Affairs, to prevent valuable oral traditions from being lost. There are explanations of proverbial expressions, notes on legends, photographs of important sites, and line drawings illustrating the text. See also: *'O ou laufanua o tua'a lava ia/Your homelands are your forefathers* by Lafai Sauoaiga, artwork by Sekuini Fa'afia Esera ([Wanganui, New Zealand]: Vasa-i-Faletea, [1991]. 143p.); *Samoa: its customs and traditions* (Tutuila, American Samoa: Samoan Cultural Committee, 1958. 2nd ed. 43p.), an introduction to Samoan traditional society, prepared for use in the High School of American Samoa; 'Legends of Samoa' by O. F. Nelson (*Journal of the Polynesian Society*, vol. 34 [1925], p. 124-45); 'Jottings on the mythology and spirit-lore of old Samoa' by John B. Stair (*Journal of the Polynesian Society*, vol. 5 [1896], p. 32-57); and *Traditions des îles Samoa* (Traditions of the Samoan Islands) by Pierre-Adolphe Lesson (Paris: Leroux, 1876. 16p.), an interesting selection of early Samoan myths and legends, first published in *Revue d'Anthropologie* (vol. 5 [1876], p. 589-604).

833 **The story of Karongoa.**
Edited by H. E. Maude. Suva: Institute of Pacific Studies, University of the South Pacific, 1991. 107p. bibliog.

According to Gilbertese *mythistoire*, *Karongoa* was the first *bōti* (traditional seating place) to be founded, on Samoa itself and by the *utū* (clan) who lived around Kaintikuaba and whose *unim'āne* (elders) were later to lead the migration to Tungaru (Gilbert Islands). This pivotal story in Gilbertese history was narrated by an *unim'āne* of the *Bōti* of Karongoa in 1934, transcribed by Tione Baraka of Taboiaki on Berū, translated by the Rev. George H. Eastman of the London Missionary Society, and edited, annotated and revised by H. E. Maude, formerly Resident Commissioner of the Gilbert and Ellice Islands Colony. For other stories highlighting the links between Samoa and the Gilbert Islands, see: 'The legend of the coming of Nareau from Samoa to Tarawa, and his return to Samoa', edited by J. E. Newell (*Journal of the Polynesian Society*, vol. 4 [Dec. 1895], p. 231-35); *An anthology of Gilbertese oral tradition from the Grimble Papers and other collections; translated by A. F. Grimble and Reid Cowell*, edited by H. C. Maude, H. E. Maude (Suva: Institute of Pacific Studies, University of the South Pacific, 1994. 289p. bibliog.); and *In their own words: history and society in Gilbertese oral tradition* by Kambati K. Uriam (Canberra: *The Journal of Pacific History*, 1995. 207p. map. bibliog.).

834 ***Tala o le vavau*: the myths, legends and customs of old Samoa; adapted from the collections of C. Steubel and Bro. Herman.**
Illustrated by Iosua Toafa, cover design by Fatu Feu'u. Auckland, New Zealand: Polynesian (Pasifika) Press, 1987. revised ed. 190p.

This work was first published as *Myths and legends of Samoa: Tala o le vavau* (Wellington; Sydney; London: A. H. & A. W. Reed; Apia: Wesley Productions, 1976. 157p.). Part one contains the Samoan texts (wholly without glottal stops), and part two the English translations, in the same order. This is a valuable introduction to traditional beliefs, especially interesting with regard to such customs as ascertaining truth, wedding gifts, gifts of fine mats, and 'biting off the little finger'.

835 **The war between the gods of ‘Upolu and Savai‘i: a Samoan story from 1890.**
John Charlot. *Journal of Pacific History*, vol. 23, no. 1 (April 1988), p. 80-85. bibliog.

A commentary on and English translation of a story which explained terrifying signs and portents, at a time which seemed ominous to the Samoans, as being caused by war between the *aitu* of the two islands. The Samoan text and a German translation appear in *Samoanische Texte: under Beihülfe von Eingeborenen gesammelt und übersetzt* (Samoan texts: collected and translated with the assistance of natives) by Oskar Stübel, edited by F. W. K. Müller (Berlin: Dietrich Reimer, 1896. 196p. [Veröffentlichungen aus dem Kgl. Museum für Völkerkunde, no. 4]). The Samoan text alone is reprinted in *‘O tu ma tala fa‘aSamoa mai le tusi a Oskar Stuebel 1896*, edited by John Charlot (Pago Pago, 1973).

Proverbial expressions

836 **Proverbial expressions of the Samoans.**
Collected, translated and explained by Dr Erich Schultz, translated into English by Brother Herman. Wellington: Polynesian Society, 1953. 140p. (Memoir, no. 27). Revised reprint, 1965. (Polynesian Paperback, no. 1).

This superb collection of 560 annotated proverbs, in Samoan and English, was published serially in *Journal of the Polynesian Society*, vols. 58-59. It contains an index to all Samoan words. The German original is *Sprichwörtliche Redensarten der Samoaner, gesammelt, übersetzt und erklärt* (Proverbial expressions of the Samoans, collected, translated and explained) by Erich Schultz (Apia: Lübke, 1906. 274p.; Berlin: Süsserot, 1910). There is also a very literal translation, published in only five copies (one in the Alexander Turnbull Library, Wellington): *Proverbial sayings of the Samoans* by Erich Schultz, translated by Heinrich Neffgen (Apia: Lübke, 1916-17. 2 parts). A further 800 or more traditional sayings are assembled and analysed in *Problems of the structure of concepts in Samoa: an investigation of vernacular statement and meaning* by George Bertram Milner (London: London School of Economics and Political Science, 1968. 2 vols. bibliog. [PhD Thesis, University of London]).

837 **Proverbs, phrases and similes of the Samoans.**
Penisimani, George Brown. Papakura, New Zealand: [R. McMillan, 1984, 35p.]. Available from P. E. Chamberlain, P.O. Box 313, Papakura, South Auckland, New Zealand.

This culturally and linguistically important collection of 206 proverbs in Samoan, with English translations, was made by the Rev. George Brown with the help of Penisimani. It was originally published, in Brown’s name only, in *Australasian Association for the Advancement of Science, Reports* (Melbourne), vol. 14 (1914), p. 401-33. The selection of proverbs was made by Penisimani whom Brown describes as ‘one of the most intelligent of the Samoan peoples’.

838 **Samoan proverbial expressions: *alagā'upu fa'a-Samoa.***
Collected, translated and explained by Dr E. Schultz, translated into English by Brother Herman, cover design by Iosua Toafa. Auckland, New Zealand: Polynesian (Pasifika) Press; Suva: Institute of Pacific Studies, University of the South Pacific, 1980. 140p. Reprinted, 1985.

This reproduces the 560 Samoan proverbs, with English translations and notes, of the Polynesian Society's revised edition of 1965, but regrettably omits the important index of Samoan words. A Samoan-language edition was announced in 1980.

Sports and Recreation

Traditional

839 **An account of the game of *tāgāti'a*.**
Richard Moyle. *Journal of the Polynesian Society*, vol. 79, no. 2 (June 1970), p. 233-44. bibliog.

A detailed account of the traditional game of javelin throwing, formerly often played by as many as one hundred people at a time. There is a music transcription of one associated song, and a musical analysis of six others, all in the style of other children's songs.

840 **Das Kinderspiel in Western Samoa und Tonga: eine vergleichende Analyse zur autochthonen Bewegungskultur.** (Children's games in Western Samoa and Tonga: a comparative analysis of indigenous play.)
Rüdiger Schwartz. Münster, Germany: Lit, 1992. 589p. map. bibliog. (Bremer Asien-Pazifik Studien, no. 6).

An extensive comparison of Samoan and Tongan children's games of all kinds, and of the accompanying rituals and songs. Though the two groups share many West Polynesian games, there are also very many significant differences. See also 'Changing patterns of Samoan games' by M. Thomas (*South Pacific Bulletin*, vol. 26, no. 2 [1976], p. 18-23), an observant (and entertaining) study of the evolution of play in American Samoa, and of new elements, many of which have been adopted from foreign models seen on television.

841 ***Lafoga tupe*: an ethno-historical account of a Polynesian game.**
Martin Orans, Daniel Pouesi. *Anthropos*, vol. 82, no. 1/3 (1987), p. 35-45. bibliog.

A rare account of the origin and rules of a traditional Samoan game. *Lafoga* is played with a set of *tupe*, concave disks cut out of coconut shells and polished, which are tossed up in the air and caught in a container.

842 **String figures from Fiji and Western Polynesia.**
James Hornell. Honolulu: Bernice P. Bishop Museum, 1927. 88p. bibliog. (Bulletin, no. 39).

Hornell illustrates and discusses the intricate string figure game which he had identified in Western Polynesia (including Samoa) and in Fiji, suggesting that this leisure pastime was gradually dying out.

Modern

843 **Kirikiti.** (Cricket.)
Feaua'i Burgess, photographs by Barry Clothier. Wellington: Learning Media, Ministry of Education, 1991.

A study kit on cricket (in its classical form and *fa'a-Sāmoa*), comprising three booklets, a sound cassette and twelve study prints in a folder.

844 ***Manusamoa; tusi-ata Sekuini Esera.***
Fereni [Pepe] Ete, with photographs by Sekuini Esera. Wellington: Aoga Fa'afaiaoga o Aoga Amata, 1993. 13p.

Illustrated with splendid team and action photographs, this Samoan-language booklet, aimed at fans of school age, is a tribute to Western Samoa's successful national rugby football team, *Manu Samoa.*

845 **Sixth South Pacific Games handbook: a complete record of the South Pacific Games, 1963-1975.**
Edited by R. Yarrow in association with T. Isaacs. Suva: *Fiji Times*, 1979. 128p.

A comprehensive guide to the triennial South Pacific Games, including statistical records of the first five Games and records of South Pacific athletes in the Olympic Games and in other major sporting events.

Libraries, Museums and Archives

Libraries

846 Agricultural information: the role of the library at the USP School of Agriculture.

Barbara Bird, Mikki Valasi, Bob Yehl. *Fiji Library Association Journal*, no. 13 (June 1985), p. 57-64.

The library of the University of the South Pacific School of Agriculture (USP/SOA) at Alafua, Western Samoa, provides agricultural information services nationally and regionally. A brief historical background is followed by a description of current services. The assistance of the United States Agency for International Development (USAID) is acknowledged.

847 A directory of libraries and information sources in Hawaii and the Pacific islands.

Compiled by A. L. Luster, edited by Y. Bartko, M. Smith. Honolulu: Hawai'i Library Association, 1981. 6th ed. 125p.

A useful guide, updated at irregular intervals, to the holdings, special collections and services of 244 libraries. Several of the major institutions in Hawai'i, such as the Hamilton Library of the University of Hawai'i at Mānoa, the Bernice P. Bishop Museum and the Institute for Polynesian Studies at La'ie, have resources of outstanding importance for research on the Pacific islands generally.

848 The library at Vailima.

A. E. Day. *Library Review*, vol. 25, no. 3/4 (Autumn/Winter 1975/6), p. 107-10. bibliog.

A brief account of Robert Louis Stevenson's private library. With his death the books passed to his widow, then to his daughter. They were auctioned in November 1914 and January 1915. The catalogues show the breadth and depth of Stevenson's reading. See also 'The Fale'ula library' by William Churchill (*Bulletin of the American*

Geographical Society, vol. 41 [1909], p. 305-43), which describes the contents of the important private library of the American Consul in Samoa from 1896-99. William Churchill (1859-1920) was a linguist with a special interest in the languages of Polynesia. The library at Fale'ula (his villa in Brooklyn, New York) was particularly rich in works on Samoa and on linguistics. Churchill regarded this inventory of his library as a contribution to 'that Polynesian bibliography which becomes more and more needed'. Also of interest is 'The earliest Samoan prints' by William Churchill (*Journal of the Polynesian Society*, vol. 24 [1915], p. 65-68).

849 **Library services in Tonga and Samoa.**
Joe Hallein. *Australian Library Journal*, vol. 29, no. 1 (Feb. 1980), p. 29-32.

Hallein visited Tonga and Western Samoa in 1979, to assess their need for library and instructional resource programmes, to be funded by the Australian Development Assistance Bureau. Both countries have had some library services (including secondary school libraries), but development to full potential has been inhibited by inadequate financial resources, lack of trained staff and dearth of material written at an appropriate level. An earlier study is 'Library conditions in Western Samoa' by M. T. Te'o (*Libri*, vol. 18, no. 3-4 [1968], p. 216-22), a sober, well informed overview of Western Samoa's fragmentary and underdeveloped public library services and of the many problems of capital investment, staff training and stocking which have yet to be overcome.

Museums

850 **Rhetoric and reality: the frustrations of cultural conservation in American Samoa, a case history.**
John Enright. *Pacific Arts* (USA), no. 5 (Jan. 1992), p. 8-11.

In this paper presented to the 17th Pacific Science Congress, Enright notes the tensions inherent in the confrontation of two radically different cultures in Samoa, and discusses the confusion of Samoan culture and *fa'a-Sāmoa* (Samoan way). The only museum in Samoa is the underfunded Jean P. Haydon Museum in Fagatogo, Tutuila. Local interests are pitted against academic needs as road-building threatens archaeological sites. The author feels that it is essential that an institutional Samoan identity be established, with a museum, cultural centre and historic preservation programme. 'The role of the museum and cultural center in arts education' by Elizabeth Tatar (*Pacific Arts* [USA], no. 5 [Jan. 1992], p. 12-13) criticizes Enright's view. Tatar questions the traditional concept of a museum as an authoritative and authenticating form, and asks whether non-Western traditional cultures need museums in the Western sense.

Archives

851 **Archival sources in Britain for the study of mission history: an outline guide and select bibliography.**
Rosemary Seton. *International Bulletin of Mission Research*, vol. 18, no. 2 (1994), p. 66-70. bibliog.

The archivist of the University of London School of Oriental and African Studies (SOAS) surveys the abundant and outstandingly rich British archives relevant to mission history. These notably include the records and archives of the London Missionary Society, held at SOAS, which contain many important documents relating to Samoa, from John Williams' journals onwards.

852 **Calendar of the George Handy Bates Samoan papers at the University of Delaware.**
Prepared by William Ditto Lewis. Wilmington, Delaware: W. N. Cann, 1942. 41p.

George H. Bates was the American commissioner in the inconclusive investigation of Samoan affairs in 1886. The inability of Bates, Thurston (for Britain) and Travers (for Germany) to agree on how to resolve the situation brought about the Washington conference on 22 June 1887, adjourned until 29 April 1889 in Berlin.

853 **Directory of archives and manuscripts repositories in New Zealand, the Cook Islands, Fiji, Niue, Tokelau, Tonga and Western Samoa.**
Edited by Frank Rogers. Plimmerton, New Zealand: Archives Press, 1992. 73p. (Archives New Zealand, no. 4).

The indispensable guide to unpublished materials stored in libraries and archives which are not always as well known as they deserve to be. Each entry gives location, general information and a brief description of the material held.

854 **Family history sources in the Pacific islands.**
Robert D. Craig. [Salt Lake City, Utah]: Corporation of the President of the Church of Jesus Christ of Latter-day Saints, 1980. 12p. bibliog. (World Conference on Records: Preserving Our Heritage, August 12-15, 1980. Series 827).

This paper offers guidance to genealogists on archival and other sources for family history in the islands (including Samoa). Among the institutions discussed are: the Mitchell Library, Sydney, NSW; Pacific Manuscripts Bureau, Canberra, ACT; and Bernice P. Bishop Museum, Honolulu. The major source of genealogy of chiefs of Samoa is *Die Samoa-Inseln* by Augustin Krämer (q.v.), of which several English translations have been made (including an elusive one published by the Administration of Western Samoa in 1942).

855 **Pacific material in the archives of the British and Foreign Bible Society.**

Kathleen Cann, W. N. Gunson. *Journal of Pacific History*, vol. 23, no. 2 (Oct. 1988), p. 223-25.

The letterbooks of the BFBS (founded in 1804) contain considerable correspondence with missionaries in the Pacific islands, for the years 1804-56 and 1901-05. The Samoan correspondence is from William Day, Samuel Ella, Thomas Heath, William Mills, Archibald Wright Murray, James Povey Sunderland, George Turner, John C. Williams and John Williams.

856 **Preliminary inventory of the records of the Government of American Samoa (Record group 126).**

Compiled by Peggy Welco. Washington, DC: Government Printing Office, 1969. 17p. (Federal Records Center).

A first listing of records relating to the period between 1900 and 1966. The seven-page introduction provides a good, concise account of the political history of American involvement in Samoa.

857 **The Samoan archives: an annotated list of the archival material of the various governments of Western Samoa from the middle of the nineteenth century to the first quarter of the twentieth century.**

Ashby J. Fristoe. Honolulu: University of Hawai'i, at Mānoa, 1977. 117p. bibliog. (Pacific Islands Studies Program, Miscellaneous Work Papers 1977, no. 2).

Indigenous Samoan governments of the 19th century produced relatively few documents, and even fewer have survived in Samoa. This splendid survey is, then, essentially a list of the voluminous archival records relating to Samoa produced and subsequently preserved by the governments of Great Britain, Germany, USA and New Zealand (the military occupant and mandatory power from 1914 to 1962). Greater detail may be found in the calendars of documents published by the major depositories (specified by Fristoe).

858 **Western Samoa: establishment of a national archive.**

D. L. Thomas. Paris: UNESCO, 1986. 9p.

Records are constantly under threat of deterioration in tropical conditions. Thomas briefly surveys the range of extant records that should be preserved, the likely volume of future archives, and the parameters of suitable, climatically controlled storage ideally required. He recommends the establishment of a national archive service, with trained staff and spacious accommodation. See also 'Microfilming of the archives of German Samoa' (*Archifacts*, no. 4 [Dec. 1987], p. 17-18), an outline of work to be carried out on the archives of the German Colonial Administration of Samoa and of the German Consulate in Samoa. When sorted, repaired and filmed, the records will be available to libraries and archives worldwide, as microfilms. See also *The archives of the Diocese of Samoa and Tokelau*, compiled by Th. B. Cook (Apia: Diocesan Office Fetuolemoana, [1982]. 70p.), a detailed, indispensable guide to the archives and records of the Roman Catholic Diocese of Samoa and Tokelau.

Books and Publishing

General

859 **Book development in the Western Pacific.**
Canberra: Australian Government Publishing Service, 1981. 41p.

This report on the first Regional Seminar on Book Development in the Western Pacific, held in Sydney, New South Wales, in 1980, reviews the status and problems of publishing in island states, country by country, including Western Samoa.

860 **Books from the Pacific islands 1995/6.**
Suva: Institute of Pacific Studies, University of the South Pacific, 1995. 20p.

Since the Institute of Pacific Studies was established in 1976, over 2,000 Pacific islanders have had their work published in association with the IPS. The Institute also assists the South Pacific Creative Arts Society (*Mana* Publications) and the South Pacific Social Sciences Association with their publications. These are all included in this comprehensive, indispensable catalogue, issued annually, and arranged by subject, with a country index. A new section lists available video tapes.

861 **The University of the South Pacific: Publications.**
Suva: Pacific Information Centre, University of the South Pacific, 1981- . annual.

Each issue includes 'works written, published, authorised or sponsored by USP or individuals (officials, staff members, students) associated with USP'. Materials are divided into two main categories: monographs and periodicals, serially numbered. Within each category, items are grouped according to the section of USP responsible for publication. Theses are listed in the 'General' section. Full bibliographical references are not given. There is an alphabetical author/title index, referring to serial numbers. The issue for 1994 extends up to September 1994, and covers 652 publications, including 15 from the School of Agriculture at Alafua, Western Samoa. Publications of the South Pacific Regional Environment Programme (SPREP), centred in Apia, are included.

Samoa

862 **Samoan language publications in the Alexander Turnbull Library.**
Wellington: Alexander Turnbull Library, 1992. [86p.].

An unpaginated copy of the catalogue cards in the library's shelf-list of its Samoan-language collection, 'provided to facilitate further upgrading of the bibliographic information to enable greater research use of the collection'. Though the standard of cataloguing varies greatly and sometimes tantalizingly, this remains an indispensable introduction to printed works in Samoan.

863 ***'O tusi i le gagana Samoa*: the needs, problems and opportunities confronting the development of quality Samoan language books.**
Robert G. Holding. [Wellington; Winston Churchill Memorial Trust, 1992]. 31 leaves.

A research report on the vernacular literature needs of Samoa, focusing on the need for 'quality' reading for children, young people and adults. The likely sales of books in Samoan are small, thus making some degree of subsidy necessary and desirable.

Mass Media

General

864 **The contemporary Pacific islands press.**
Suzanna Layton. St. Lucia, Queensland: Department of Journalism, University of Queensland, 1992. 187p. bibliog.

The media in the Pacific islands are discussed in an exceptionally well informed 'Overview' (p. 7-38). In detailed directory format, the following sections cover island print media (p. 39-122), print media with a Pacific focus (p. 123-39), news services (p. 141-42), professional associations (p. 143-45) and regional broadcast media (p. 147-70). In each section, territories (including American Samoa and Western Samoa) are in alphabetical order. See also: *The Pacific islands press: a directory* by J. Richstad, M. McMillan, R. Barney (Honolulu: University Press of Hawai'i, 1973); and *Pacific eyes: media in the South Pacific* by the International Federation of Journalists (IFJ) (Port Moresby: IFJ/AJA, 1990).

865 **Mass communication and journalism in the Pacific islands: a bibliography.**
Jim Richstad, Michael McMillan, Jackie Bowen. Honolulu: University Press of Hawaii, for the East-West Communication Institute, East-West Center, 1978. 300p. (An East-West Center Book).

This excellent guide to the history of communication media of all kinds, from missionary newspapers to radio, television and the PEACESAT project, has sections on American Samoa (p. 28-42) and Western Samoa (p. 274-84). It is particularly useful for tracing the appearance and disappearance of local newspapers in the islands.

866 **Press, radio and tv guide: Australia, New Zealand and the Pacific islands.**
Sydney: Media Monitors NJP, 1914- . annual.

Issued with varying periodicity and publishers over the years, this is a directory of media and advertising agency addresses, contact individuals and publishing details. For details of radio and television stations, see *World Radio TV handbook* (WRTH) (Amsterdam; New York: Billboard Books, 1996. 608p. maps). The 1996 volume is the fiftieth anniversary edition of this indispensable annual publication.

Newspapers and periodicals

American Samoa

867 **Leo o Samoa.** (The Voice of Samoa.)
Pago Pago: Journalism Class, American Samoa Community College, 1980- . 6 pa (monthly during school year).

Relaunched in January 1990, this free newspaper, in both English and Samoan, focuses on campus news and education. It has a circulation of about 1,000 copies.

868 **Pacific Hotline.**
Pago Pago: Lavata'i Publications, 1990- . weekly.

A free general interest newsletter carrying display and classified advertising, entertainment listings, family features, crossword puzzles and recipes.

869 **Samoa Daily News.**
Pago Pago: *Samoa News* Inc., 1969- . 260 pa (Monday to Friday).

Formerly published weekly as *Samoa News*, this tabloid newspaper, covering local, regional and overseas news, in English and Samoan, has a circulation of about 2,500 copies.

870 **Samoa Journal.**
Pago Pago: *Samoa Journal*, 1984- . 104 pa.

This semi-weekly tabloid newspaper, in English and Samoan, combines local news with international features. It has a circulation of about 2,500 copies.

871 **Warriors in Action.**
Pago Pago: Journalism Class, Tafuna High School, 1984- . monthly.

An entertaining newspaper containing school news, editorials, letters, poems, cartoons, dedications, display and classified advertising. It has a circulation of about 300 copies.

Western Samoa

872 **Samoa Observer.**

Apia: Samoa Observer, 1979- . 156 pa.

This tri-weekly (Wednesday, Friday, Sunday) tabloid newspaper, in English and Samoan, has a circulation of about 5,000 copies. There is also a New Zealand edition, published in Auckland.

873 **Samoa Weekly.**

Apia: *Samoa Weekly*, 1977- . weekly.

This tabloid newspaper, in Samoan and English, contains national and international news, features and comment. It has a circulation of about 4,500 copies.

874 **Sāvali.** (The Messenger.)

Apia: Public Relations Division, Prime Minister's Department, 1904- . 104 pa.

Sāvali is the official journal of the Western Samoan government, with Samoan and English editions covering government news and national events. The Samoan edition also includes Land and Titles Court decisions. Appearing in tabloid format, it has a circulation of about 3,000 copies.

875 **Talamua.** (Latest News.)

Apia: *Talamua* Publications Ltd., 19?- . monthly.

A news magazine which covers national, regional and international events and issues of interest to Samoans.

New Zealand

876 **Le Manu Samoa International Weekly.** (Samoan Messenger.)

Tokoroa, Auckland, New Zealand: *Le Manu Samoa*, 1991- . weekly.

A free newspaper, in Samoan and English, covering entertainment (*tala fāgogo ma fa'afiafiaga*) and sports. There is also some coverage of local and Western Samoan news, with display advertising. It is distributed in New Zealand and Western Samoa, with a circulation of about 4,250 copies.

877 **Pacific Network Newspaper.**

Wellington: *Pacific Network Newspaper*, 1994- . monthly.

Provides news of current events and issues in New Zealand and Western Polynesia, published in Samoan, Maori, Cook Islands Maori, Tongan, Niuean and English.

878 **Samoa Observer – New Zealand Edition.**
Auckland, New Zealand: *Samoa Observer – New Zealand Edition*, 1990- . weekly.

This tabloid newspaper contains news and features of interest to Samoan communities in New Zealand, in English and Samoan.

879 **Samoa Sun.**
Papatoetoe, New Zealand: *Samoa Star*, 1991- . weekly.

This is the successor of the *Samoa Star*, which was published from 1989 to May 1991. Appearing in tabloid form, this carries general news of Samoans, and in particular of Samoans in New Zealand, especially in the Auckland area.

880 **Samoana.** (Things Samoan.)
Auckland, New Zealand: *Samoana*, 1979- . weekly.

This tabloid newspaper, in Samoan, contains news and features of interest to the Samoan community in Auckland.

881 **Taulogologo: le nusipepa a Samoa i Ueligitone.** (The Informer: the Samoan Newspaper in Wellington.)
Wellington: Crenel Company Limited, 1993-94. biweekly.

A Samoan-language, general interest newspaper for Samoan residents in the Wellington area. It commenced publication in November 1993, but ceased in November 1994.

Hawai'i

882 **Le Mau: Samoa Tonga International Newsmagazine.**
Honolulu: Taupou Productions, 1989- . 24 pa.

Formerly a monthly, this tabloid covers general news and features of interest to the Tongan and Samoan communities in Hawai'i, written in Samoan, Tongan or English. It has correspondents in American Samoa, Western Samoa and New Zealand, and uses reports from *Samoa Journal* and *Samoa Daily News*. It has a circulation of about 20,000.

883 **Samoa-Hawai'i Island News.**
Waimanalo, Hawai'i: 'Aiga Publications Inc., 1989- . weekly.

This tabloid newspaper, in Samoan, contains news of interest to the Samoans living in Hawai'i, California, Utah and other parts of the United States.

Professional Journals

Journals

884 **Asia Pacific Viewpoint.**
Oxford: Blackwell Publishers, 1996- . 3 pa.

From April 1996, this esteemed scholarly journal, formerly *Pacific Viewpoint*, is published from Oxford, but it continues to be edited by the Department of Geography, Victoria University of Wellington, New Zealand. Coverage focuses on the interaction of countries in the region (e.g. international investment, international trade and migration), on the concept of the Asia Pacific region as an economic and socio-political entity, and on the environmental preconditions and consequences of development initiatives. Papers based on solid fieldwork experience and on recent graduate research are featured.

885 **The Contemporary Pacific: a Journal of Island Affairs.**
Honolulu: Center for Pacific Island Studies and University of Hawai'i Press, 1989- . semiannual.

A prestigious journal devoted to current problems in the Pacific islands, as interpreted by a wide range of disciplines in the humanities and social sciences. Besides its authoritative articles and book reviews, *The Contemporary Pacific* is noted for its stimulating 'Dialogue' and 'Resources' sections, and for 'Political Reviews' of recent events in Melanesia, Micronesia and Polynesia (including American Samoa and Western Samoa).

886 **Forum News.**
Suva: Secretariat, South Pacific Forum, 1971?- . quarterly.

A newsletter covering all topics likely to be of interest to member states of the South Pacific Forum, together with SPF news and interviews. It is distributed free of charge, with a circulation of about 750 copies.

887 **The Journal of Pacific Studies.**
Suva: School of Social and Economic Development, University of the South Pacific, 1975- . annual.

Concerned with all aspects of economic and social development in the Pacific islands, this scholarly journal seeks to emphasize practical applications of theory, with soundly researched articles and relevant bibliographies.

888 **Journal of the Polynesian Society.**
Wellington: Polynesian Society, 1892- . quarterly.

Now published from the Department of Maori Studies at the University of Auckland, this esteemed journal promotes 'the scholarly study of past and present New Zealand Maori and other Pacific Island peoples and cultures', in articles, reviews, memoirs and monographs. The two available indexes are: *The Journal of the Polynesian Society: index volumes 1-75, 1892-1965* by C. R. H. Taylor (Wellington: Polynesian Society, 1969. 88p.); and *Journal of the Polynesian Society: centennial index 1892-1991*, compiled by Dorothy Brown (Auckland, New Zealand: Polynesian Society, 1993. 279p. [Memoir, no. 50]). Both indexes are in single alphabetical sequence of author, title and subject. Brown lists book, film and recording reviews in three additional alphabetical sequences. She also acknowledges by name 'the many Pacific Islanders co-workers whose recorded or translated oral traditions were originally published under the name of the collector'.

889 **Oceania.**
Sydney: University of Sydney, 1930- . quarterly.

Now published under the aegis of the Australian National Research Council, this scholarly journal is devoted to the study of the indigenous peoples of Australia, Papua New Guinea and the Pacific islands, including Samoa.

890 **The Outrigger.**
Haywards Heath, England: Pacific Islands Society of the United Kingdom and Ireland (PISUKI), 1983- . quarterly.

This lively and well informed magazine contains news of the Pacific islands and of islanders living in Great Britain and Ireland. It has a circulation of about 500 copies. Among PISUKI's affiliated kindred organizations are the Western Samoa (UK) Association and Friends of Polynesia, an Anglican association.

891 **Pacific Islands Monthly.**
Suva: *Pacific Islands Monthly*, 1930- . monthly.

This is undoubtedly the best known periodical covering Pacific regional news, sports and features, now in its sixty-sixth year of publication (volume 66, 1996), after a change of publisher. Appearing in tabloid format, it has a circulation of about 7,500. *Pacific Islands Yearbook* is now published annually by the same firm, the seventeenth edition having appeared in 1994 with the imprint of Fiji Times Ltd.

892 **Pacific Magazine.**
Honolulu: Pacific Magazine Corporation, 1982- . bimonthly.

Using a format similar to *Newsweek*, *PM* has correspondents in most Pacific territories and provides good coverage on all aspects of current island life and activities, with pictures, articles, news reports and book reviews. Territories closely associated with the USA, such as the states of Micronesia and American Samoa, often figure prominently in its pages.

893 **Pacific Studies: a Journal devoted to the Study of the Pacific – its Islands and adjacent Countries.**
Honolulu: Institute for Polynesian Studies, Brigham Young University-Hawai'i, 1977- . quarterly.

Initially issued twice and then thrice yearly, and now a quarterly published in association with the Polynesian Cultural Center, *Pacific Studies* ranges widely in anthropology, archaeology, art history, ethnomusicology, folklore, geography, history, sociolinguistics, political science and sociology. Its editorial board consists of twenty-five esteemed Oceanists. An index to vols. 1-9 appeared in vol. 10, no. 1 (Nov. 1986), p. 151-95, and subsequent indexes each cover two volumes. Major libraries collaborate in compiling 'Recent Pacific islands publications: selected acquisitions ...', listing books and reports but not articles in periodicals.

894 **South Sea Digest.**
Sydney: Nationwide News Ltd., 1980- . 25 pa.

A newsletter and information service covering events in the Pacific islands.

895 **UNSW Centre for South Pacific Studies Newsletter.**
Kensington, New South Wales: Centre for South Pacific Studies, University of New South Wales, 1987- . quarterly.

A supremely useful current awareness newsletter, covering all areas of the South Pacific, notably including Samoa. 'The Centre for South Pacific Studies collects, collates and distributes information from a diversity of disciplines in printed and electronic form about the peoples and places of the South Pacific'. It acts as a home for research in the Pacific region. Each issue contains the following sections: 'News from the Centre and UNSW'; 'Conferences and events'; 'Employment, courses & funding'; 'New publications'; 'Periodicals'; 'Film, video & audio'; 'Catalogues'; 'Internet & databases'; and 'Bulletin board'.

The Journal of Pacific History.
See item no. 164.

Pacific Journal of Theology: Journal of the South Pacific Association of Theological Schools.
See item no. 341.

Pacific Health Dialog: Journal of Community Health and Clinical Medicine for the Pacific.
See item no. 464.

Pacificland News.
See item no. 590.

Alafua Agricultural Bulletin.
See item no. 595.

Pacifica: Journal of the Pacific Islands Study Circle of Great Britain.
See item no. 628.

Directions: Journal of Educational Studies.
See item no. 681.

Education Innovations in the Pacific.
See item no. 682.

Pacific Science.
See item no. 701.

South Pacific Research Register.
See item no. 720.

***Mana*: a South Pacific Journal of Language and Literature.**
See item no. 723.

Span: Journal of the South Pacific Association for Commonwealth Literature and Language Studies.
See item no. 726.

Periodical indexes

896 **Cumulative Index to the *Pacific Islands Monthly*, Volumes 1 to 15.**
Compiled by M. Woodhouse, edited by R. Langdon. Sydney: Pacific Publications, 1968.

This index to *Pacific Islands Monthly* from August 1930 to July 1945 covers fifteen years of economic depression followed by war with Japan, when *PIM* was virtually the only readily accessible source of news of events and people in the islands. It is arranged in nine sections, on aircraft, authors, biographies, book reviews, companies, letters to the editor, poems and short stories, ships and territories (eighteen geographical headings).

897 **Index to the Pacific Island articles in the *Deutsche Kolonialzeitung*, 1886-1915.**
Hans Ballin, Patricia Lehua Tanaka. Honolulu: Bernice P. Bishop Museum, 1986. 30p.

Deutsche Kolonialzeitung was the official journal of the German Colonial Society, devoted to imperial expansion. This selective index covers articles on Pacific colonial history, politics and government from 1886 to 1915, when all Germany's Pacific colonies were finally lost. There are numerous references to Samoa.

898 **Indexing the islands: creating a Pacific periodical database.**
Karen M. Peacock. *The Contemporary Pacific*, vol. 5, no. 2 (Fall 1993), p. 432-35.

Karen Peacock is the librarian of the immense Pacific Collection, Hamilton Library, University of Hawai'i at Mānoa, Honolulu. Here she outlines the development since 1990 of the Hawai'i and Pacific databases, including the comprehensive Hawai'i Pacific Journal Index. The databases can be accessed, using such systems as Internet or Bitnet, through the joint University of Hawai'i-Colorado Association of Research Libraries (UHCARL) network at telnet uhcarl.lib.hawaii.edu or telnet 128.171.19.3.

899 **South Pacific periodicals index.**
Suva: Pacific Information Centre, University of the South Pacific Library, 1984- . irregular.

This retitled continuation of *Bibliography of periodical articles relating to the South Pacific* seeks to index retrospectively all articles of island relevance in over 500 periodicals held by the USP Library. Entries are arranged alphabetically by subject and within each subject alphabetically by author, with full bibliographical details.

Encyclopaedias and Directories

General

900 **The Far East and Australasia 1997.**
London: Europa Publications, 1996. 28th ed. 1,191p. 2 maps. bibliog.

An authoritative, summary guide to the political events and economic developments of 1996 accompanies basic directory information for each territory, including American Samoa (p. 830-33) and Western Samoa (p. 849-54).

901 **Pacific islands yearbook.**
Edited by Norman Douglas, Ngaire Douglas. Suva: Fiji Times, 1994. 17th ed. 767p. maps. bibliogs.

First published in 1932 and intended as an annual publication, this is the most useful reference work of first recourse for all of the Pacific island territories, summarizing essential facts. There are useful sections on American Samoa (p. 61-79) and Western Samoa (p. 731-55), each with a map and bibliography. The introductory sections comprise an islands summary and Pacific chronology and cover Pacific islands economies, decolonization and political change, Pacific islander migration and intergovernmental organizations. There is a map of the Pacific islands, published by Angus & Robertson in association with Nationwide News, in the back-cover pocket.

902 **Stewart's handbook of the Pacific islands.**
Percy S. Allen. Sydney: McCarron, Stewart, 1922. 10th ed. 566p. map. bibliog.

First published in 1907, this handbook is important for its lists of officials, principal expatriate residents and their occupations, chief business houses, missionaries, and, in the case of 'American Samoa' (p. 82-90), US Navy governors and officials. 'Western Samoa' (p. 47-81) includes an outline history, trade statistics, customs and taxation provisions, and 'Terms of the Mandate' (p. 79-81). The useful, unannotated 'Bibliography of works on the Pacific islands' (p. 519-66) lists 100 works on Samoa (p. 547-50).

903 **Who's who in the South Pacific.**
[Wellington: South Pacific Division, Ministry of Foreign Affairs and Trade], 1995. 19p.

Updated at irregular intervals, this lists with brief biographies the politicians, diplomats, officials, businessmen and professional people held to be of significance in each territory, including American Samoa and Western Samoa.

Samoa

904 **The cyclopedia of Samoa (illustrated).**
Apia: Commercial Printers, 1984. Fourth printing, 1988. 113p.

A facsimile edition of the Samoan section of *The cyclopedia of Samoa, Tonga, Tahiti and the Cook Islands* (Sydney: McCarron Stewart, 1907. variously paginated. maps). It provides an unmatched, lavishly illustrated description of German Samoa after seven years of occupation, with rare photographs and short biographies of officials, traders, missionaries and prominent citizens (mostly Europeans). The Samoans pictured are Tamasese, Tamasese's wife, Mata'afa, Pastor Alama, 'Princess' Fa'a-mu, Vao (*tāupou* of Āpia), and Fai ('Star of first Troupe'). This highly informative account of Samoa was edited jointly by Percy S. Allen and W. Farmer Whyte.

905 **The cyclopedia of Samoa, Tonga, Tahiti and the Cook Islands (illustrated).**
Papakura, New Zealand: R. McMillan, 1983. each section paged separately. maps.

A facsimile reprint of the work of the same name first published in Sydney in 1907 by McCarron Stewart. The Samoan section has been reprinted separately as *The cyclopedia of Samoa (illustrated)* (q.v.).

906 **Handbook of Western Samoa.**
Wellington: W. A. G. Skinner, Government Printer, 1925. 174p. 2 maps. bibliog.

Compiled and published by authority of the Administration of Western Samoa, this well illustrated and still useful handbook 'is designed to give in popular form concise and accurate information concerning the Territory, its people and affairs'. Section I comprises: history; physical features; fauna and flora; climate and meteorology; the Samoan people; and Christian missions in Samoa. Section II provides the text of the League of Nations mandate for German Samoa and also covers: government departments; products and fields for development; land tenure; labour; and tourist information. The ten appendices cover essential matters such as taxation; shipping and freights; postage rates and regulations; and a splendid bibliography, notable for its extensive lists of official documents of the American, British and New Zealand governments.

Bibliographies and Catalogues

Pacific

907 **Bibliographie de l'Océanie.** (Bibliography of Oceania.)
Paris: Société des Océanistes, Musée de l'Homme, 1946-76. irregular.

Initially compiled by subject (and later also subdivided by territory) by Édouard Reitman and Patrick O'Reilly, this selective bibliography of books and articles relating to Melanesia, Micronesia, Polynesia and, at first, Australia is an essential bibliographical resource for humanities and social sciences from 1939 to 1976. Its twenty-ninth and, sadly, final issue appeared as *Bibliographie de l'Océanie, 1972-1976*, compiled by Renée Heyum (Paris: Société des Océanistes, Musée de l'Homme, 1982. 480p.). See also *Océanie I à XXXIV (1930-1964)* by J. Guiart, F. Herry, R. Heyum, C. Panoff (Paris: Centre Documentaire pour l'Océanie, 1966. not paginated. [Bibliographies Analytiques, no. 1]), which lists 888 items, arranged geographically and annotated in French.

908 **A bibliography of bibliographies of the South Pacific.**
Ida Leeson. London; Melbourne; New York: Oxford University Press, 1954. 61p.

Published under the auspices of the South Pacific Commission, as its 'first bibliographical task', this is a completely revised edition of the draft version circulated by the Commission in 1951. It lists and annotates 376 existing bibliographies, including some in books and articles. 'General bibliographies' is followed by 'Bibliographies of particular areas' (with Western Samoa under 'New Zealand territories' and American Samoa under 'United States territories'), and by eleven subject bibliographies. Ida Leeson was the greatly respected Librarian of the Mitchell Library, Sydney, from 1932 to 1946.

909 **A bibliography of Pacific island theses and dissertations.**
W. G. Coppell, Susan Stratigos. Canberra: Research School of Pacific Studies, Australian National University; La'ie, Hawai'i: Institute for Polynesian Studies, Brigham Young University-Hawai'i, 1983. 520p. bibliog.

Updates the bibliography by Diane Dickson and Carol Dossor (q.v.) and also perpetuates its errors. The work is arranged alphabetically by author, with an analytical subject index. There is a guide to the abbreviations of degree titles, a directory of universities and colleges, and a bibliography of the sources used in compilation.

910 **Bibliotheca Polynesiana: a catalogue of some of the books in the Polynesiana collection formed by the late Bjarne Kroepelien and now in the Oslo University Library.**
Rolf Du Rietz. Oslo: privately published by the heirs of Bjarne Kroepelien, 1969. 455p.

This annotated reference catalogue of 1,368 works provides *inter alia* scholarly bibliographical descriptions, for book collectors, of the many editions of Pacific voyages of exploration, including those to Samoa by Jacob Roggeveen, Louis-Antoine de Bougainville, and the ill-fated Jean-François de Galaup de La Pérouse.

911 **Complete annotated catalogue: PMB manuscripts series, microfilms PMB 1-1030.**
Edited by Gillian Scott. Canberra: Pacific Manuscripts Bureau, Research School of Pacific Studies, Australian National University, 1991. 876p.

American Samoa and Western Samoa are well represented in this indispensable research guide. Manuscripts available include the papers of: Dr Wilhelm Heinrich Solf; R. P. Gilson; Brother Fred Henry; O. F. Nelson; William Blacklock; John Chauner Williams; Jan Kubary; and Samuel Swain. The German Administration of Samoa is represented by PMB 479, the Roman Catholic Church by PMB 184-90, and the London Missionary Society by PMB 95-97, 126-28, 130-32 and 141-44. See also *Short titles and index to microfilms PMB DOC 1-1000 (Manuscript series)* (Canberra: Pacific Manuscripts Bureau, Australian National University, 1980. 56p.), a brief, adequately indexed guide which is a convenient starting point for an initial search of the first one thousand microfilms. For specification of content the full catalogue is necessary.

912 **Complete annotated catalogue: PMB printed document series, microforms PMB Doc. 1-400.**
Edited by Bess Flores. Canberra: Pacific Manuscripts Bureau, Research School of Pacific Studies, Australian National University, 1991. 159p.

Microforms are listed in serial order, with titles and inclusive dates, and are indexed by names and subjects. Among the periodicals is *Pacific Islands Monthly*, 1930-70 (PMB Doc. 331-67). Of Samoan interest are John Quincy Adams (PMB Doc. 43); Henry Lawrence Bassett (PMB Doc. 45); *Les Missions Catholiques* (PMB Doc.

62-98); *Annales des Missions de la Société de Marie* (PMB Doc. 174-80, 194-98); *Lettres aux missionnaires* (PMB Doc. 207); and O. F. Nelson (PMB Doc. 213).

913 **Essai de bibliographie du Pacifique.** (Attempt at a bibliography of the Pacific.)
Léonce Jore. Paris: Éditions Duchartre, 1931. 235p.

Commissioned by the governor of the Établissements français de l'Océanie on the occasion of the Paris Exposition Internationale, this unannotated, patchy, amateurish bibliography is made up of: an interesting chronological discussion of books on the Pacific from 1520-1930; 'Ouvrages divers' (Various works) (p. 59-145); 'Articles de revues et bulletins de sociétés' (Articles in journals and society newsletters) (p. 147-94), particularly useful for eight French journals; and the geographically arranged 'Ouvrages et articles concernant diverses îles du Pacifique' (Works and articles relating to various Pacific islands) (p. 195-233). The specific section on Samoa (p. 223-26) mainly comprises well known works, with only a few references to useful articles in less accessible journals.

914 **Islands of the Pacific: a selected list of references.**
Compiled by Helen F. Conover. Washington, DC: Division of Bibliography, Library of Congress, 1943. 181p.

An unannotated bibliography 'designed to indicate modern and available sources for research', this supplements the *Subject Catalogue of the Royal Empire Society* (1931), by covering mainly the period from 1931 to 1943. Sections include 'American Samoa' (p. 57-63) and 'Western Samoa' (p. 121-23). The work is indexed by author and by subject.

915 **Pacific basin and Oceania.**
Compiled by Gerald W. Fry, Rufino Mauricio. Oxford; Santa Barbara; Denver, Colorado: Clio Press, 1987. 468p. map. (World Bibliographical Series, vol. 70).

This thoughtfully annotated bibliography covers the Pacific region generally, Melanesia, Micronesia and Polynesia. It is an excellent, well selected guide to 1,178 recent publications of significance. Indexed by authors, titles and subjects, it includes an up-to-date selection for Samoa (p. 307-22).

916 **A Pacific bibliography: printed matter relating to the native peoples of Polynesia, Melanesia and Micronesia.**
C. R. H. Taylor. Oxford: Clarendon Press, 1965. 2nd ed. 692p. map.

The first edition of this substantial, indispensable bibliography was published by the Polynesian Society (Wellington, 1951). This second edition is 'as complete as possible up to 1960, but only a handful of items since have been included'. The bibliography is arranged in four regional sections: Oceania, Polynesia, Melanesia and Micronesia. Within each region books and articles are classified first geographically and then by subject. There is thorough coverage of bibliography, general works, ethnographic subjects, language, folklore and material culture. 'Samoa (Navigator Islands)' is extensively covered (p. 267-87).

917 **Pacific island bibliography.**
Floyd M. Cammack, Shiro Saito. New York: Scarecrow Press, 1962. 421p.

Based on a selection of 1,727 works in the Pacific Collection at the University of Hawai'i's Gregg M. Sinclair Library, this is primarily concerned with the social sciences, including education and languages. Non-printed materials, including theses, are listed irrespective of date, but most entries for printed works are limited to titles published since the completion in 1948 of the first edition of C. R. H. Taylor's *A Pacific bibliography* (Wellington: Polynesian Society, 1951). Duplication of Taylor's entries has been avoided where possible. Arranged broadly under Oceania, Melanesia, Micronesia, Polynesia, and then territorially, it is indexed by author and title with entries for specific islands, languages, ships and persons. Locations are given for rare items. Section 4.9 (items 1537-635) relates specifically to Samoa.

918 **Pacific island studies: a survey of the literature.**
Edited by M. M. Jackson. New York: Greenwood Press, 1986. 244p. bibliog. (Bibliographies and Indexes in Sociology, no. 7).

A critical survey of economic, political, social and ethnographic studies, which provides full bibliographic details. A general overview is followed by a commentary on works relating to Polynesia (including Samoa), Micronesia, Melanesia and Australia.

919 **Pacific islands and trust territories: a select bibliography.**
United States Department of the Army. Washington, DC: Department of the Army, 1971. 171p. maps. bibliog. (DA pamphlets 550-10).

An annotated bibliography of unclassified publications, mainly covering the period 1965-70, compiled by the analysts of the Army Library, Washington, DC. It attempts 'to present a balanced picture of the problems and prospects in the Pacific Islands in general and in the Trust Territories of the Pacific in particular'. Publications specifically on Eastern (American) Samoa and Western Samoa (with a map of administrative divisions) are listed on p. 58-60. Appendix S (p. 149-53) reprints the US Department of State publication 8345 of November 1969, *The independent state of Western Samoa: background notes.*

920 **Pacific islands dissertations and theses from the University of Hawai'i, 1923-1990, with 1991-1993 supplement.**
Compiled by Lynette Furuhashi. Honolulu: Center for Pacific Islands Studies, University of Hawai'i at Mānoa, 1994. 130p. (Occasional Paper, no. 37).

The first thesis written and accepted at the University of Hawai'i was in 1914, and the first pertaining to the Pacific islands in 1923. This bibliography of 465 items is arranged geographically (Oceania, Melanesia, Micronesia, Polynesia and United States-administered islands), with each section then subdivided by territory. Theses solely on Hawai'i are excluded. Each item comprises author, title, date, pagination, degree, field of study, University of Hawai'i Library call number, and whether available from University Microfilms International. The work is indexed by author, degree, field of study, title and date of acceptance. American Samoa, Western Samoa and Samoans in California and Hawai'i are well represented.

921 **Le Pacifique Sud: bibliographie des thèses et mémoires récents/The South Pacific: a bibliography of the recent theses and dissertations.**
Frédéric Angleviel, Michel Charleux, William G. Coppell, edited by Jean-Pierre Doumenge. Bordeaux, France: Centre de Recherche sur les Espaces Tropicaux-CRET; Centre d'Études de Géographie Tropicale-CEGET-CNRS, 1990. 276p. map. bibliog. (Collection 'Îles et Archipels', no. 13).

This bilingual bibliography of theses and dissertations (at bachelor, master and doctoral levels) contains nearly 3,000 references. Arrangement is alphabetical by author, numbered serially. There are indexes by geographical area and by subject. Caution in use is advised, as there are many errors (e.g. in 2384, 2532, 2888, etc.).

922 **South Pacific bibliography 1992-1993.**
Suva: Pacific Information Centre, University of the South Pacific, 1994. 172p.

Based on new accessions to the USP Library, this is an exceptionally useful bibliography of books, periodicals, official and intergovernmental reports, and articles. It has particular value for its listing of elusive publications printed in the islands. See also *Recent Additions: Pacific* (Suva: Pacific Information Centre, University of the South Pacific, c. 1981- . monthly. [nos. 134-46 cover additions to the USP Library, October 1993-September 1994]).

923 **World catalogue of theses on the Pacific islands.**
Compiled by Diane Dickson, Carol Dossor. Canberra: Australian National University Press, 1970. 123p. (Pacific Monographs, no. 1).

Based on ANU microform holdings and taking the place of *Index of social science theses on the South Pacific* (Nouméa, New Caledonia: South Pacific Commission, 1957. [SPC Technical Paper, no. 102]), this geographically arranged bibliography of over 1,000 dissertations and theses is an essential guide to research (often unpublished) to about 1968.

A botanical bibliography of the islands of the Pacific.
See item no. 127.

Island bibliographies: Micronesian botany; Land environment and ecology of coral atolls; Vegetation of tropical Pacific islands.
See item no. 128.

Papuasia and Oceania.
See item no. 129.

Pacific history journal bibliography.
See item no. 165.

A select bibliography relating to Germany in the Pacific and Far East, 1870-1914.
See item no. 223.

Pacific Islander Americans: an annotated bibliography in the social sciences.
See item no. 273.

Austronesian and other languages of the Pacific and South-East Asia: an annotated catalogue of theses and dissertations.
See item no. 289.

Mormons in the Pacific: a bibliography.
See item no. 375.

Women in the South Pacific: a bibliography.
See item no. 461.

Medical and socio-medical studies in the Pacific islands: a catalogue of theses and dissertations.
See item no. 462.

SPEC bibliography.
See item no. 586.

Bibliography of soil fertility and soil management in Pacific Island countries.
See item no. 589.

Education in the Pacific islands: a selective bibliography.
See item no. 678.

A world catalogue of theses and dissertations concerning the education of the peoples of the Pacific islands (including the New Zealand Maori).
See item no. 679.

Preliminary bibliography on traditional science and technology in the Pacific islands: partly annotated.
See item no. 702.

South Pacific literature written in English: a selected bibliography.
See item no. 725.

The art of Oceania: a bibliography.
See item no. 797.

An annotated bibliography of Oceanic music and dance.
See item no. 810.

Mass communication and journalism in the Pacific islands: a bibliography.
See item no. 865.

Samoa

924 **Catalogue of theses and dissertations relating to the Samoan Islands.**

William G. Coppell. Suva: University of the South Pacific Library, 1978. 31p. (Selected Bibliography, no. 5).

Arranged alphabetically by author and with a subject index, this extensive (though not exhaustive) catalogue includes theses and dissertations from all parts of the world, at bachelor, master and doctoral levels. BD theses of the Pacific Theological College are included.

925 **A check list of selected material on Samoa.**

Compiled and edited by Janet Aileen Pereira. Malifa, Western Samoa: Samoan History Writing Project, Western Samoa Extension Centre, University of the South Pacific, 1983. 2 vols.

This bibliography (arranged by subject, then alphabetically by author) is part of the Samoan History Writing Project, financed by the United Nations Development Programme and assisted by the Government of Western Samoa. The project, visualized and co-ordinated by Albert Wendt, set out to rewrite the history of Samoa from a more 'Samoan' perspective. Volume one, *General bibliography* (437p.) and volume two, *Agriculture* (112p.), were both compiled with the co-operation of fifty-seven libraries and institutions worldwide. Volume one covers all of Samoa until partition in 1900, then concentrates on Western Samoa, with 'American Samoa: selected works' at p. 386-88. Volume two 'attempts to give the reader some idea of the extent of agricultural research in Western Samoa'. Despite its having only an author index, many incomplete references, and some typing errors, this is one of the most useful Samoan bibliographies available. It incorporates an earlier work, *Samoa History Writing Project: a source booklet 'fa'aafu fa'aufi'*, compiled by P. Meleisea and M. Meleisea (Apia: Western Samoa Extension Centre, University of the South Pacific, 1980).

926 **Pacific Basin Development Council reference system: literature related to American Samoa, Guam, and the Northern Mariana Islands.**

Carolyn K. Imamura. Honolulu: Pacific Basin Development Council, 1985. 848p.

This unannotated bibliography contains 3,854 alphabetically arranged author entries, with keywords indicating geographic areas. It includes books, monographs, government reports, theses and periodical articles. See also *A list of books (with references to periodicals) on Samoa and Guam* by the Library of Congress (A.P.C. Griffin, Division of Bibliography) (Washington, DC: Government Printing Office, 1901. 54p.), in which books on Samoa are listed alphabetically by author, government, and titles of serials (p. 3-29), with exceptionally useful, paginated analyses of content. Articles in periodicals (p. 30-41) are arranged chronologically from 1840 to 1901, as are articles in United States consular reports, 1881-1901 (p. 42-44). This bibliography is still of considerable value, for its coverage of elusive 19th-century publications. Also useful is *Bibliography on Fiji & Samoa* by Morgan A. Tuimaleali'ifano (1993- .

Electronic medium), a bibliography which is compiled from the SIIN network and stored at listserv. To access it send the command: listserv @ unb.ca: GET ISLANDS LEGEND SIIN-L[.]

927 **Samoan Islands bibliography.**

Lowell D. Holmes. Wichita, Kansas: Poly Concepts Publishing Co., 1984. 335p.

Arranged under forty-four subject headings and then alphabetically by author or title, this extensive bibliography is offset from computer printout and is often hard to read. It also uses uppercase type and so wholly lacks diacritics. In addition, it contains no index and no annotation, but many errors and many inexplicable omissions. For detailed criticism of this disappointing work, see the review by Richard M. Moyle in *Journal of the Polynesian Society* (vol. 95, no. 2 [June 1986], p. 268-71. bibliog.). See also *Bibliographic list of books, magazine articles, notes and some unpublished material* by Edward W. Johnson (Pago Pago: Edward W. Johnson, 1955. 648p.). A xerox copy of the typescript of this voluminous bibliography is located in the South Pacific Collection at the University of California, Santa Cruz (Z 4891.J6).

Rose Atoll: an annotated bibliography.
See item no. 23.

Bibliography of Swain's Island, American Samoa.
See item no. 25.

The Samoan 'imbroglio': a select bibliography.
See item no. 204.

Samoans in Hawai'i: a bibliography.
See item no. 280.

The Samoan language: a guide to the literature.
See item no. 290.

Bibliographie des publications de la Mission Mariste des Îles Samoa, 1862-1976.
See item no. 356.

The Samoa controversy: a select bibliography.
See item no. 454.

American Samoa resource management bibliography.
See item no. 602.

A selectively annotated bibliography of social, cultural and economic material relating to fishery development in Hawaii, American Samoa, and Micronesia.
See item no. 612.

Western Samoa fisheries bibliography.
See item no. 617.

A bibliography of energy literature for U.S. Micronesia and American Samoa.
See item no. 706.

Audio-visual Media

General

928 **Guidelines for audio and audiovisual recording in the South Pacific.**

Edgar Waters. Canberra: National Library of Australia, 1995. 22p.

Customary usages in relatively conservative islands of the South Pacific, such as Samoa, were well established long before the advent of video cameras and cassette recorders, and the uninvited use of such devices can give offence. Waters applies good sense to the recording of island life, and recommends approaches based on respect, courtesy and the recognition of mutual advantage.

Film catalogues

929 **Made in paradise: Hollywood's films of Hawai'i and the South Seas.**

Luis L. Reyes, with contributions by Ed Rampell. Honolulu: Mutual Publishing, 1995. 382p. bibliog.

With at least one film still to almost every glossy page, this is a visually outstanding guide to American films and TV series set in Pacific Island locations. Each entry provides director, scriptwriter, producer and principal cast members, and describes the production of the film. All names and titles are indexed. Films with Samoan backgrounds include: *The Hurricane* (1937); *South of Pago Pago* (1940); *Moana of the South Seas* (1926); *Return to Paradise* (1953), filmed in Lefaga; and Albert Wendt's *Sons for the Return Home* (1979). Samoan stars include Moira Walker and Felise Va'a.

930 **Moving images of the Pacific islands: a guide to films and videos.**
Compiled by Diane Aoki, Norman Douglas, edited by Diane Aoki. Honolulu: Center for Pacific Islands Studies, University of Hawai'i at Mānoa, 1994. 347p. bibliog.

The most comprehensive inventory of films and video tapes about the islands of the Pacific, from Robert J. Flaherty's *Moana*, to television documentaries. Full production and distribution details are provided in most cases, and the entries are thoroughly indexed by maker, title and subject. It updates *Moving images of the Pacific Islands: a catalogue of films and videos*, edited by M. C. Miller (Honolulu: Center for Pacific Islands Studies, School of Hawaiian, Asian and Pacific Studies, University of Hawai'i at Mānoa, 1989. 206p. bibliog. [Occasional Papers, no. 34]), which provides for each item: country/island; subject; holding library; duration; format; colour or monochrome; date; series; producer; distributor; and cost. Still useful is *A guide to films about the Pacific islands*, compiled by J. D. Hamnett (Honolulu: Pacific Islands Studies Program, University of Hawai'i, 1986. 148p.). Each entry specifies film title, length, type, colour or monochrome, date and subject, with producer and distributor (when known) and a brief abstract.

931 **Premier catalogue sélectif international de films ethnographiques sur la région du Pacifique.** (A first international selective catalogue of ethnographical films about the Pacific region.)
Paris: UNESCO, 1970. 342p.

This valuable reference work gives detailed content notes, year of production, film type, length, and distributor for over 341 films about islands in the Pacific, including (sparsely) Samoa. Australia and New Zealand account for thirty per cent of all productions, and the Federal Republic of Germany for twenty per cent.

Film histories

932 ***Moana* and the Pacific.**
Paul Rotha. In: *Robert J. Flaherty: a biography*. Paul Rotha, edited by Jay Ruby. Philadelphia: University of Pennsylvania Press, 1983, p. 51-94, 296, 333-36. bibliog. (p. 347-52).

A well informed account, by an authority on documentary films, of the making of Flaherty's *Moana* (1923-25) in Savai'i. Nine illustrations of scenes in the film follow p. 94. See also: *The innocent eye: the life of Robert J. Flaherty* by Arthur Calder-Marshall (London: W. H. Allen, 1963); *Robert J. Flaherty: photographer/filmmaker*, edited by Jo-Anne Birnie Danzker (Vancouver, Canada: Vancouver Art Gallery, 1979); *Robert Flaherty: a guide to references and resources* by William T. Murphy (Boston, Massachusetts: G. K. Hall, 1978); 'Flaherty's poetic *Moana*' by John Grierson (*New York Sun*, 8 February 1926); and Flaherty's own account, 'Picture making in the South Seas' in *Film Daily Yearbook 1924* (New York, p. 9-13).

933 **Sanderson on Samoa.**
P. Smith. *Onfilm: New Zealand Motion Picture Industry Magazine*, vol. 7, no. 3 (April-May 1990), p. 9-10.

An illustrated interview with the New Zealand actor and director Martyn Sanderson, who talks about his career to date, and discusses his movie *Flying fox in a freedom tree* (New Zealand/Western Samoa, Martyn Sanderson, 1989) based on the prizewinning novel of the same name by Albert Wendt.

934 **The South Seas: *Moana*; *Tabu*.**
Richard Griffith. In: *The world of Robert Flaherty*. Richard Griffith. London: Victor Gollancz, 1953, p. 45-79.

Largely based on the published accounts by Robert and Frances Flaherty, this is the story of Flaherty's two Pacific silent films. *Moana*, filmed in Sāfune, Savai'i, is compared with *Tabu*, filmed in Tahiti in 1929. There are fifteen striking stills from the two films, together with a photograph of Robert Flaherty and the German director F. W. Murnau. Murnau, formerly of the UFA studios at Neubabelsberg, collaborated with Flaherty in making *Tabu*.

Films and video recordings

935 ***Fa'a Samoa*: the Samoan way.**
Photography and narrative by Lowell D. Holmes. Aptos, California: Documentary Films, n.d. [1963?]. colour sound film. 17 mins.

Covers housebuilding, fishing, cooking and ceremonial life in the village of Fitiuta, Ta'ū, American Samoa, the subject of Holmes' *Samoan village* (1974). See also *American Samoa: paradise lost?* (WNET-TV. Film, 55 minutes, colour. Available from Indiana University Audio Visual Center, Bloomington, IN 47405, USA), an excellent, still relevant documentary film on the problems arising from culture change, made in the late 1960s in Tutuila and the Manu'a islands.

936 **JVC video anthology of world music and dance 30.**
Tokyo: JVC, 1993. videocassette.

Provides four tracks of Western Samoan music and dance recorded at the Fourth Festival of Pacific Arts, Tahiti, in 1985.

937 **Margaret Mead and Samoa.**
Frank Heimans. Cremorne, New South Wales: Cinetel Productions, 1988. colour film. 51 mins. Available from Cinetel Productions Ltd., 15 Fifth avenue, Cremorne 2090, NSW, Australia.

An award-winning documentary film debating the issues raised by Derek Freeman's refutation of Margaret Mead's theories (expressed in *Coming of age in Samoa* [q.v.]). Contemporary footage, including the Manu'a islands, is complemented by archive film.

938 **Matai Samoa.**

George Bertram Milner. London: Royal Anthropological Institute, 1989. videocassette. 65 mins. colour. (RA/VHS 179).

The archival footage (18 minutes of the total film) shot by Milner while engaged in linguistic fieldwork in Samoa in 1955 and 1959 focuses on the traditional Samoan way of life. This footage is then discussed and analysed by Christina Toren, a South Pacific specialist, and the Reverend Lalomilo Kamu, a Samoan scholar. 'The interview gives a rare opportunity to hear a scholar from the filmed group comment on and explain the symbolism behind the pictures'. See also *Chiefs* by John Mayer (Honolulu: Pachyderm Films, 1983. Videocassette. 28 mins. colour), an idealized depiction of public ceremonies in Āpia and village life from the *matai* point of view, filmed on the occasion of the twentieth anniversary in 1982 of Western Samoa's independence.

939 **Moana: a romance of the Golden Age.**

Production: Famous-Players-Lasky, USA, (1923-25). 7 reels (c. 90 min.). 6,055 feet.

The New York première of this classic silent film (starring Ta'avale, Fa'agase and Tu'ugaita) was on 7 February 1926, and the London première in late May 1926. The Museum of Modern Art Film Library, New York, and the National Film Archive, London, hold prints for non-theatrical distribution. The copyright is held by the original distributor, Paramount Pictures Corporation. The technical cast is as follows: script, direction and photography by Robert J. Flaherty and Frances Hubbard Flaherty; production assistant, David Flaherty; technical assistant, Lancelot H. Clark; and titles written by Robert J. Flaherty and Julian Johnson.

940 **Taking the opportunity: a programme about 3 Samoans in the workforce, produced by Gibson Group.**

[Wellington]: Vocational Guidance Service, Department of Labour, 1987. videocassette. 17 mins. sound. colour. ½ in.

A videorecording which traces the experiences at work of three Samoans resident in New Zealand. See also *'O le Maota ete malu ai* (A sound house), filmed and directed by To'oa Mata'afa, Val Asi, technical supervisor Athina Tsoulis (Auckland, New Zealand: Workers' Education Association [WEA], [1991]. Videocassette. c. 20 mins. sound. colour. ½ in.), a challenging videorecording of the housing problems of Samoans in New Zealand, produced by the WEA.

941 ***Teine Samoa*: a girl of Samoa.**

Gibson Film Productions, 1982. film. 22 mins. colour. Available from Journal Films, Inc., 930 Pitner Avenue, Evanston, IL 60202, USA.

An accurate portrayal of the life of a teenage girl in Matāuta village, Faleālili, southern 'Upolu.

942 **USP Samoa cultural programme 1991.**

Suva: Institute of Pacific Studies, University of the South Pacific, 1991. videocassette.

A thrilling compilation of Samoan traditional songs and dances expertly performed by Samoan students at the University of the South Pacific. It is available in PAL, NTSC and SECAM systems. See also *USP Samoa cultural programme 1992* (Suva: Institute of Pacific Studies, University of the South Pacific, 1992).

Sound recordings

943 **American Samoan spectacular.**
Viking Records, 1972. VP 360, LP.

Presents the choir of the American Samoan Arts Council as recorded at the South Pacific Festival of Arts, Suva, in 1972.

944 **Anthems and farewells of the Pacific.**
Wellington: A. H. & A. W. Reed, Hibiscus Records, 1974. HLS-54, stereo/mono 12" LP or cassette (TC-54).

A compilation of national anthems and songs of farewell of the Pacific islands, played by the band of the Royal Fiji Military Forces. See also *World of the South Pacific* (Wellington: A. H. & A. W. Reed, Hibiscus Records, 1974. HLS-47, stereo/mono 12" LP or cassette [TC-47]), a compilation of recordings made at the South Pacific Festival of Arts, Suva, in 1972. It includes one track performed by the choir of the Western Samoa Teachers' Training College (also found on Hibiscus HLS-24).

945 **Music from Western Samoa: from conch shell to disco.**
Washington, DC: Smithsonian Institution, Folkways Records, 1984. FE 4270, LP.

Comprises representative recordings made in 1982 and sleeve notes by Ad and Lucia Linkels. A compact disc version is also available: *Fa'a-Sāmoa: the Samoan way ... between conch shell and disco* (1995, Pan 2066; Anthology of Pacific Music, no. 6). See also *Sea music of many islands: the Pacific heritage* (Washington, DC: Smithsonian Institution, Folkways Records, 1981. FSS 38405, LP), a compilation of recordings made at the Festival of the Sea 1980, San Francisco, including one track of Samoan music performed by the group *Fetu o le Afiafi*. Of historical importance is *The demonstration collection of E. M. von Hornbostel and the Berlin Phonogramm-Archiv* (Washington, DC: Smithsonian Institution, Folkways Records, 1963. FE 4175, LP), a compilation including one track from Sawaii (i.e. Savai'i), German Samoa, originally recorded in 1911 on wax cylinder. A similar compilation of importance is *Samoan songs: a historical collection* (Institute for Musicology of the University of Basel, Switzerland. Musicaphon BM 30 SL 2705, LP).

946 **The music of Samoa: an authentic sound picture.**
Wellington: A. H. & A. W. Reed, Hibiscus Records, 1973. HLS-55, stereo/mono 12" LP or cassette (TC-55).

Contains recordings of a wide range of Samoan music collected between 1967 and 1969 by musicologist Richard M. Moyle, who wrote the sleeve notes.

947 ***Porineshia no ongaku*: music of Polynesia.**
Tokyo: JVC, 1994. 5 compact discs, with 5 pamphlets. (JVC World Sounds Special, VICG 5271-VICG 5275).

Comprises five digital, stereo 4¾in. sound discs, recorded on location in 1977-90, of Polynesian traditional music and songs. The discs cover: Tahiti, Society Islands; Tuamotu, Austral Islands; Easter Island, Marquesas Islands; Samoa, Tonga (V1CG 5274); and New Zealand, Cook Islands. See also: *South Pacific songs and rhythms* (Playasound Records, 1988. PS 65018, CD), a compilation including two tracks of music from Western Samoa recorded at the Fourth Festival of Pacific Arts, Tahiti, 1985; and *Spirit of Polynesia* (Saydisc Records, 1993. CDSDL 403, CD), a compilation including two tracks from Western Samoa recorded in 1979, with recordings and sleeve notes by David Fanshawe.

948 **Samoa i Sisifo.** (Western Samoa.)
Wellington: A. H. & A. W. Reed, Hibiscus Records. HLS-21, stereo/mono 12" LP or cassette (TC-21).

A choir of 200 from the Western Samoa Teachers' Training College in Āpia performs traditional dance songs in 'a record of remarkable richness that conveys the very great vitality and beauty of these islands'. See also: *From the heart of Polynesia* (Wellington: A. H. & A. W. Reed, Hibiscus Records. HLS-14, stereo/mono 12" LP or cassette [TC-14]), in which the renowned choir of Chanel College, Āpia, presents a broad selection of Samoan traditional songs; and *Tama Samoa sauni mai vi'iga* (Samoa's sons and daughters present songs of praise) (Wellington: Kiwi/Pacific Records, Hibiscus Records, 1989. TCHLS-130, audio cassette), a varied programme by the Grey Lynn Samoan Congregational Christian Church Choir.

949 **Samoan song and rhythm.**
Wellington: A. H. & A. W. Reed, Hibiscus Records. HLS-24, stereo/mono 12" LP or cassette (TC-24).

The 'wild spirit' of Samoa inspires these *fiafia* and *siva* dances and exuberant songs performed by the students of the Western Samoa Teachers' Training College in Āpia, in which 'Discipline is matched with spirit, authenticity and entertainment go hand-in-hand'. See also: *Samoa sings* (Wellington: A. H. & A. W. Reed, Hibiscus Records. HLS-6, stereo/mono 12" LP or cassette [TC-6]), presenting The Girls of Matautu, favourite performers at Aggie Grey's hotel in Āpia, who have their own special brand of island melody, dynamic and exciting; *The best of Samoa* (Wellington: A. H. & A. W. Reed, Hibiscus Records. HLS-11, stereo/mono 12" LP or cassette [TC-11]), in which The Talofa Village Entertainers perform traditional Samoan songs, dances and knife dancing, including a *tāupou* dance; and *Flight to paradise* by the Tusitala Band (Wellington: Hibiscus Records, 1986. sound disc. 39 mins. analog. 33⅓ rpm. stereo. 12 in.), a selection of Samoan songs and rhythms performed by the popular Tusitala Band.

950 **Samoan songs of worship.**
Wellington: A. H. & A. W. Reed, Hibiscus Records. HLS-26, stereo/mono 12" LP or cassette (TC-26).

Over 200 students of the Western Samoa Teachers' Training College, directed by Tiresa Malietoa and singing in four parts, provide beautifully balanced choral performances of the favourite hymns of all religious denominations in Samoa. See also *Aleluia amene* (Wellington: A. H. & A. W. Reed, Hibiscus Records, 1979. HLS-77, stereo/mono 12" LP or cassette [TC-77]), which offers hymns and religious songs performed by the Tālimatau Methodist Church Choir.

Indexes

There follow three separate indexes: authors (personal and corporate); titles; and subjects. Title entries are italicized and refer either to the main titles, or to many of the other works cited in the annotations. The numbers refer to bibliographical entry rather than page number. Individual index entries are arranged in alphabetical sequence.

Index of Authors

C

F

G

M

N

O

P

Q

R

S

T

X

Y

Z

Index of Titles

C

D

E

G

J

K

L

M

N

O

P

S

T

U

V

W

Y

Z

Index of Subjects

C

D

E

F

M

N

O

P

T

Map of Samoa

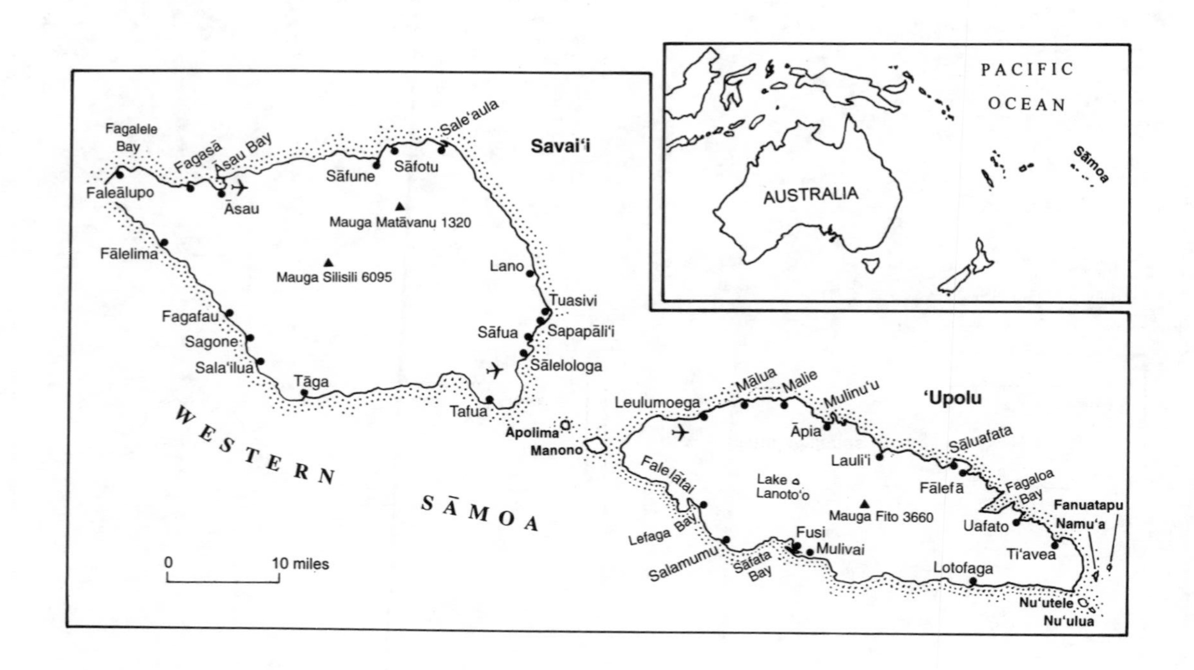
PACIFIC
OCEAN
AUSTRALIA
Sāmoa
Savai'i
Fagalele Bay
Fagasā
Āsau Bay
Faleālupo
Āsau
Sāfune
Sāfotu
Sale'aula
Mauga Matāvanu 1320
Mauga Silisili 6095
Fālelima
Fagafau
Sagone
Sala'ilua
Tāga
Lano
Tuasivi
Sāfua
Sapapāli'i
Sālelologa
Tafua
Apolima
Manono
WESTERN
SĀMOA
0
10 miles
'Upolu
Leulumoega
Mālua
Malie
Mulinu'u
Āpia
Lauli'i
Sāluafata
Falelātai
Lake Lanoto'o
Mauga Fito 3660
Fālefā
Fagaloa Bay
Fanuatapu
Namu'a
Uafato
Ti'avea
Lefaga Bay
Salamumu
Sāfata Bay
Fusi
Mulivai
Lotofaga
Nu'utele
Nu'ulua

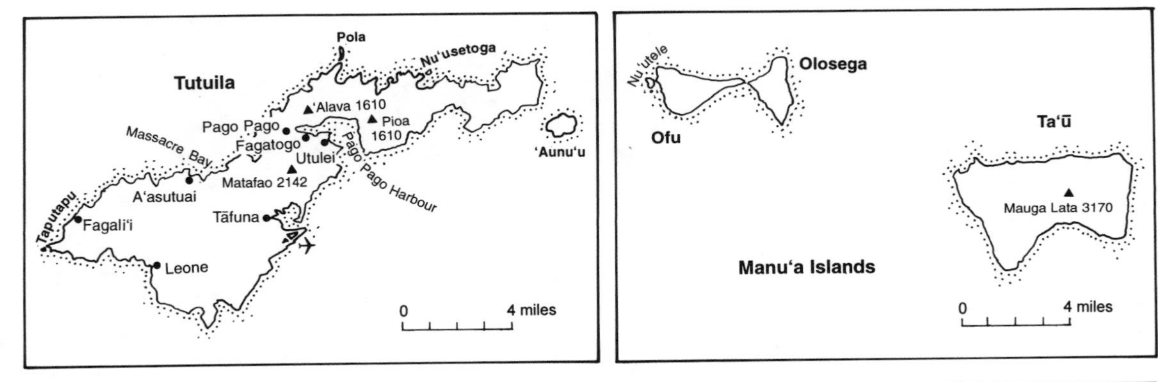

A M E R I C A N S Ā M O A

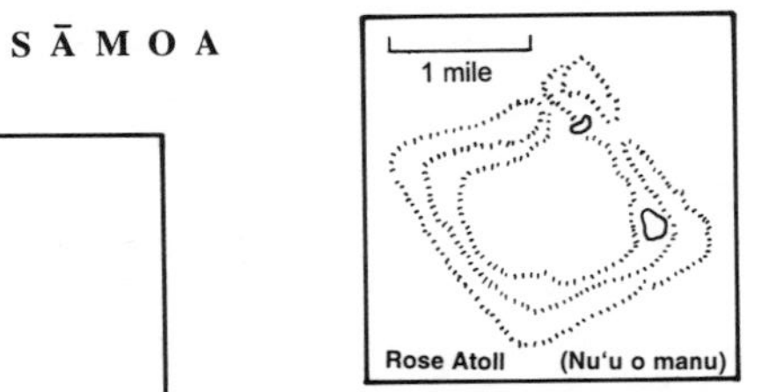

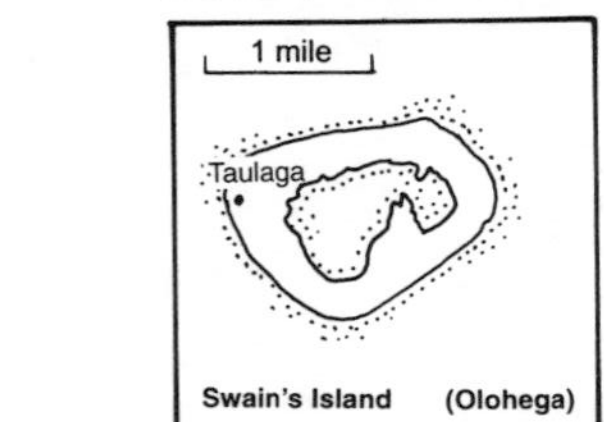

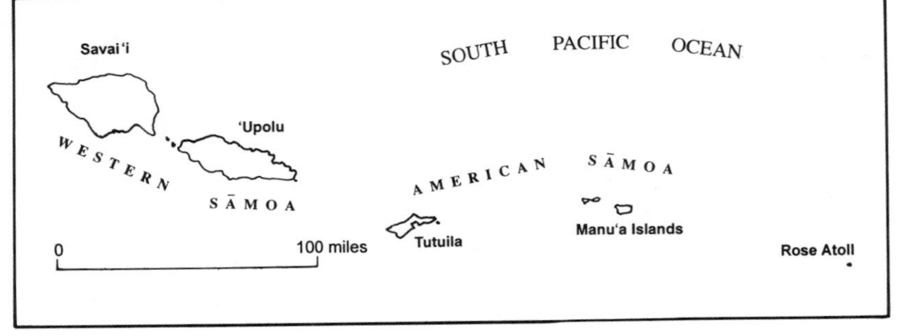

ALSO FROM CLIO PRESS

INTERNATIONAL ORGANIZATIONS SERIES

Each volume in the International Organizations Series is either devoted to one specific organization, or to a number of different organizations operating in a particular region, or engaged in a specific field of activity. The scope of the series is wide-ranging and includes intergovernmental organizations, international non-governmental organizations, and national bodies dealing with international issues. The series is aimed mainly at the English-speaker and each volume provides a selective, annotated, critical bibliography of the organization, or organizations, concerned. The bibliographies cover books, articles, pamphlets, directories, databases and theses and, wherever possible, attention is focused on material about the organizations rather than on the organizations' own publications. Notwithstanding this, the most important official publications, and guides to those publications, will be included. The views expressed in individual volumes, however, are not necessarily those of the publishers.

VOLUMES IN THE SERIES

1 *European Communities*, John Paxton
2 *Arab Regional Organizations*, Frank A. Clements
3 *Comecon: The Rise and Fall of an International Socialist Organization*, Jenny Brine
4 *International Monetary Fund*, Anne C. M. Salda
5 *The Commonwealth*, Patricia M. Larby and Harry Hannam
6 *The French Secret Services*, Martyn Cornick and Peter Morris
7 *Organization of African Unity*, Gordon Harris
8 *North Atlantic Treaty Organization*, Phil Williams
9 *World Bank*, Anne C. M. Salda
10 *United Nations System*, Joseph P Baratta
11 *Organization of American States*, David Sheinin
12 *The British Secret Services*, Philip H. J. Davies
13 *The Israeli Secret Services*, Frank A. Clements